The Cornwallis Papers

The Campaigns of 1780 and 1781

in

The Southern Theatre of the American Revolutionary War

Volume II

Arranged and edited by

Ian Saberton

The Naval & Military Press Ltd

Published by
The Naval & Military Press Ltd

Unit 10 Ridgewood Industrial Park,
Uckfield, East Sussex,
TN22 5QE England

Tel: +44 (0) 1825 749494
Fax: +44 (0) 1825 765701

www.naval-military-press.com
www.military-genealogy.com
www.militarymaproom.com

Documents hitherto unpublished © Crown copyright 2010

Documents previously published in which Crown copyright subsists
© Crown copyright

Introductory chapters, footnotes and other editorial matter © Ian Saberton 2010

The right of Ian Saberton to be identified as author of the introductory chapters, footnotes and other editorial matter in this work has been asserted in accordance with sections 77 and 78 of the UK Copyright, Designs and Patents Act 1988

ISBN	Volume I	9781845747923
ISBN	Volume II	9781845747916
ISBN	Volume III	9781845747909
ISBN	Volume IV	9781845747893
ISBN	Volume V	9781845747886
ISBN	Volume VI	9781845747879

Printed and bound in Great Britain by
CPI Antony Rowe, Chippenham and Eastbourne

CONTENTS

Editorial Method   v

PART FOUR
THE GLORIOUS SIXTEENTH AND THE ACTION AT FISHING CREEK
16th to 23rd August 1780

18.	Introduction to the rest of Part Four	3
19.	Letters from Cornwallis to Germain, Clinton, Arbuthnot, and others	
	1 – To Germain	7
	2 – To Clinton and Arbuthnot	15
	3 – To others	19

PART FIVE
THE AUTUMN CAMPAIGN
24th August to 31st October 1780

20.	Introduction to the rest of Part Five	25
21.	Letters to or from Germain, Clinton, Arbuthnot, or Leslie	
	1 – To Germain	36
	2 – To or from Clinton, Arbuthnot or Leslie	41
22.	Correspondence between Cornwallis, or Rawdon, and Balfour	62
23.	Correspondence between Cornwallis and Ferguson etc	140
24.	Correspondence between Cornwallis or Rawdon and Cruger or Innes	168
25.	Correspondence with Wemyss, De Peyster, Gray, and Hamilton	
	1 – With Wemyss, De Peyster and Gray	208
	2 – With Hamilton	226
26.	Letters to or from Camden or the Waxhaws etc	
	1 – To or from Turnbull	232
	2 – From Moncrief	266

iii

	3 – To or from England, Hill, or Macleod	268
	4 – To or from McArthur	280
	5 – To or concerning Tarleton	284
	6 – To or from commissaries	286
	7 – To or from physicians attending the enemy	289
27.	Letters to or from Savannah, St Augustine, and Pensacola	
	1 – To or from Savannah	292
	2 – From St Augustine	307
	3 – From Pensacola	314
28.	Miscellaneous papers	
	1 - Correspondence with Simpson	315
	2 – From or relating to Cruden	320
	3 – Correspondence with the Royal Militia	329
	4 – Correspondence with the enemy	336
	5 – From Carden	343
	6 – Intelligence	344
	7 – Intercepted papers	348
	8 – The Journal of Lieutenant John Money	356
Index		367

Editorial method

Subject to the following modifications, the editorial method remains the same as described in volume I.

Omitted papers

Though belonging to the period covered by this volume, the following papers in the series PRO 30/11/- are omitted on the ground that they do not relate to the southern campaigns or are too inconsequential: 3(31), (35), (38), (228), (243), (244), and (287); 64(50); 65(2) and (4); 91(1), (3), (7), and (15); 101(4) and (16); 104(1); 105(1); and 106(7) and (8).

Footnotes

As a general rule biographical footnotes on persons who are not the subject of such notes in this volume will be found in volume I.

Titles of works cited in abbreviated form in footnotes

Appletons'
   Appletons' Cyclopædia of American Biography (New York, 1888-)

Army Lists
   A list of the general and field officers... (London, 1754-77), together with *A list of all the officers of the army...* (London, 1778-)

Bailey and Cooper, *SC House of Representatives*
   Walter and N Louise Bailey, Elizabeth Ivey Cooper, et al, *Biographical Directory of the South Carolina House of Representatives* (University of South Carolina Press, 1977-81)

Boatner, *Encyclopedia*
   Mark Mayo Boatner III, *Encyclopedia of the American Revolution* (D McKay Co, 1966)

Cashin, *The King's Ranger*
   Edward J Cashin, *The King's Ranger: Thomas Brown and the American Revolution on the Southern Frontier* (Fordham University Press, 1999)

Cashin Jr and Robertson, *Augusta*
   Edward J Cashin Jr and Heard Robertson, *Augusta and the American Revolution: Events in the Georgia Back Country 1773-1783* (Richmond County Historical Society, 1975)

Clark, *Loyalists in the Southern Campaign*
   Murtie June Clark, *Loyalists in the Southern Campaign of the Revolutionary War*, volume I (Genealogical Publishing Co, 2003)

Clinton, *The American Rebellion*
> Sir Henry Clinton, *The American Rebellion,* edited by William B Willcox (Yale University Press, 1954)

The Clinton Papers
> The Papers of Sir Henry Clinton (William L Clements Library, University of Michigan)

Coldham, *Loyalist Claims*
> Peter Wilson Coldham, *American Loyalist Claims* (National Genealogical Society, 1980)

DAB
> *Dictionary of American Biography* (New York, 1928-1958)

Davie, *Revolutionary War Sketches*
> William R Davie, *The Revolutionary War Sketches of William R Davie,* edited by Blackwell P Robinson (NC Department of Cultural Resources, Division of Archives and History, 1976)

Davies ed, *Docs of the Am Rev*
> K G Davies ed, *Documents of the American Revolution 1770-1783,* volume XVIII (Irish Academic Press, 1978)

DGB
> *Dictionary of Georgia Biography,* edited by Kenneth Coleman and Charles Stephen Gurr (University of Georgia Press, 1983)

Draper, *King's Mountain*
> Lyman C Draper, *King's Mountain and its Heroes* (Cincinnati, 1881)

Ewald, *Diary*
> Johann Ewald, *Diary of the American War: A Hessian Journal,* translated and edited by Joseph P Tustin (Yale University Press, 1979)

Garden, *Anecdotes* (1st Series)
> Alexander Garden, *Anecdotes of the Revolutionary War* (Charleston, 1822)

Garden, *Anecdotes* (2nd series)
> Alexander Garden, *Anecdotes of the American Revolution, Second Series* (Charleston, 1828)

Gibbes, *Documentary History*
> Robert W Gibbes, *Documentary History of the American Revolution* (The Reprint Company, 1972)

The Greene Papers
> *The Papers of General Nathanael Greene,* volumes VI-IX, edited by Richard K Showman, Dennis M Conrad, Roger N Parks, et al (University of North Carolina Press, 1991-7)

Gregg, *The Old Cheraws*
    Alexander Gregg, *History of the Old Cheraws* (The Reprint Company, 1975)

Hanger, *An Address to the Army*
    George Hanger, *An Address to the Army in reply to Strictures of Roderick M'Kenzie (late Lieutenant in the 71st Regiment) on Tarleton's History of the Campaigns of 1780 and 1781* (London, 1789)

Hay ed, *Soldiers from NC*
    Gertrude Sloan Hay ed, *Roster of Soldiers from North Carolina in the American Revolution* (Reprint, Genealogical Publishing Co Inc, 1988)

Heitman, *Historical Register*
    Francis B Heitman, *Historical Register of the Officers of the Continental Army during the War of the Revolution* (Reprint, Clearfield Publishing Co Inc, 2000)

Hunter, *Sketches of Western NC*
    C L Hunter, *Sketches of Western North Carolina, Historical and Biographical* (Raleigh, 1877)

James, *Marion*
    William Dobein James, *A Sketch of the Life of Brig Gen Francis Marion* (Reprint, Continental Book Co, Marietta GA, 1948)

Johnson, *Greene*
    William Johnson, *Sketches of the Life and Correspondence of Nathanael Greene* (Charleston, 1822)

Johnston, *Commissioned Officers in the Medical Service*
    William Johnston, *Roll of Commissioned Officers in the Medical Service of the British Army: 20 June 1727 to 23 June 1898* (Reprint, The Wellcome Historical Medical Library, 1968)

Lambert, *SC Loyalists*
    Robert Stansbury Lambert, *South Carolina Loyalists in the American Revolution* (University of South Carolina Press, 1987)

Lee, *Memoirs*
    Henry Lee, *Memoirs of the War in the Southern Department of the United States* (Revised edition, New York, 1869)

Lossing, *Pictorial Field-Book*
    Benson J Lossing, *The Pictorial Field-Book of the Revolution* (New York, 1855)

Marshall, *Royal Naval Biography*
    John Marshall, *Royal Naval Biography* (London, 1823-35)

McCrady, *SC in the Rev 1775-1780*
    Edward McCrady, *The History of South Carolina in the Revolution 1775-1780* (The Macmillan Co, New York, 1901)

McCrady, *SC in the Rev 1780-1783*
    Edward McCrady, *The History of South Carolina in the Revolution 1780-1783* (The Macmillan Co, New York, 1902)

Moss, *SC Patriots*
    Bobby Gilmer Moss, *Roster of South Carolina Patriots in the American Revolution* (Genealogical Publishing Co Inc, 1983)

Moultrie, *Memoirs*
    William Moultrie, *Memoirs of the American Revolution* (New York, 1802)

ODNB
    Oxford Dictionary of National Biography (Oxford University Press, 2004)

Powell ed, *Dictionary of NC Biography*
    William Stevens Powell ed, *Dictionary of North Carolina Biography* (University of North Carolina Press, 1979-1996)

Ramsay, *Rev of SC*
    David Ramsay, *The History of the Revolution of South-Carolina from a British Province to an Independent State* (Trenton, 1785)

Rankin, *Marion*
    Hugh F Rankin, *Francis Marion: The Swamp Fox* (Thomas Y Crowell Company, 1973)

Raymond, 'British American Corps'
    W O Raymond, 'Roll of Officers of the British American or Loyalist Corps', *Collections of the New Brunswick Historical Society*, ii, 1899

Robinson, *Davie*
    Blackwell P Robinson, *William R Davie* (University of North Carolina Press, 1957)

Robinson, *NC Guide*
    Blackwell P Robinson ed, *The North Carolina Guide* (University of North Carolina Press, 1955)

Rogers Jr, *Georgetown County*
    George C Rogers Jr, *The History of Georgetown County, South Carolina* (University of South Carolina Press, 1970)

Ross ed, *Cornwallis Correspondence*
    Charles Ross ed, *Correspondence of Charles, First Marquis Cornwallis*, volume I (London, 1859)

Royal Regiment of Artillery
    List of Officers of the Royal Regiment of Artillery from the Year 1716 to the Year 1899 (London, 1900)

Sabine, *Biographical Sketches*
   Lorenzo Sabine, *Biographical Sketches of Loyalists of the American Revolution* (Boston, 1864)

Salley Jr, *Orangeburg County*
   A S Salley Jr, *The History of Orangeburg County, South Carolina, from its first Settlement to the close of the Revolutionary War* (Orangeburg, 1898)

SCHGM
   The South Carolina Historical and Genealogical Magazine (Charleston, 1900-)

State Records of NC
   Walter Clark ed, *The State Records of North Carolina* (Winston and Goldsboro NC, 1895-1907)

Stevens, *Clinton-Cornwallis Controversy*
   Benjamin Franklin Stevens, *The Campaign in Virginia 1781: the Clinton Cornwallis Controversy* (London, 1887-8)

Syrett and DiNardo ed, *The Commissioned Sea Officers*
   David Syrett and R L DiNardo ed, *The Commissioned Sea Officers of the Royal Navy 1660-1815* (Navy Records Society, 1994)

Tarleton, *Campaigns*
   Banastre Tarleton, *A History of the Campaigns of 1780 and 1781 in the Southern Provinces of North America* (London, 1787)

Uhlendorf ed, *The Siege of Charleston*
   Bernhard A Uhlendorf ed, *The Siege of Charleston* (University of Michigan Press, 1938)

Valentine, *The British Establishment*
   Alan Valentine, *The British Establishment, 1760-1784: An Eighteenth-Century Biographical Dictionary* (University of Oklahoma Press, 1970)

Wheeler, *Historical Sketches*
   John Hill Wheeler, *Historical Sketches of North Carolina from 1584 to 1851* (Reprint, Clearfield Company Inc, 2000)

Wheeler, *Reminiscences*
   John Hill Wheeler, *Reminiscences and Memoirs of North Carolina and Eminent North Carolinians* (Reprint, Genealogical Publishing Co, 1966)

Willcox, *Portrait of a General*
   William B Willcox, *Portrait of a General: Sir Henry Clinton in the War of Independence* (Alfred A Knopf, 1964)

The Cornwallis Papers

PART FOUR

The Glorious Sixteenth[1]

and

The Action at Fishing Creek

16th to 23rd August 1780

---

[1] The Glorious Sixteenth is an apt description of a momentous day in the annals of the British Army. First used in these Papers by Balfour, the expression began falling into disuse as considerations of political correctness sadly intruded. Yet militarily it remains from a British perspective as accurate as ever, and in this sense it is high time that we saw its revival.

CHAPTER 18

Introduction to the rest of Part Four

About two o'clock in the morning of the 16th, as Gates and Cornwallis advanced towards each other, their vans collided eight miles north of Camden.

Gates's army was not in the best of shape. On the march from Coxe's Mill his men had traversed a barren country abounding in sandy plains, intersected by swamps, very thinly inhabited, and largely destitute of provisions and forage. They had had to subsist on precarious supplies of corn meal and lean beef, of which they often did not receive a half ration. At times the crop of grain had been new and unfit for use, but out of necessity many had plucked the green ears, which, when boiled with beef and eaten with green peaches instead of bread, provided a seemingly palatable repast, but one found to have painful effects. On the 15th, as they were about to march from Rugeley's towards Camden, the men were issued with a full ration of corn meal and meat. There being no rum in camp — the customary heart warmer and stimulant for unusual exertion, Gates had the bright idea of issuing to each man one gill of molasses from the hospital store, brought down by Stevens from Virginia. It proved to be a medicine indeed, an untimely physic. As the night progressed, the men prepared hasty meals of quick-baked bread and meat with a dessert of mush or dumplings mixed with the molasses. It operated so cathartically that, in the words of Otho Williams, Gates's Deputy Adjutant General, 'very many of the men... were breaking the ranks all night and were certainly much debilitated before the action commenced in the morning'.

According to Williams, Gates had with him 3,052 rank and file fit for duty, of whom more than two thirds were militia.

Cornwallis had had to leave behind at Camden near 800 men who were sick and unfit for duty. If we compare his letter of the 21st[2] with Tarleton's *Campaigns* and Rawdon's troop

---

[2] See p 11.

return of the 13th[3], we may obtain a pretty accurate breakdown of the troops he brought to the field. Taking into account that only part of the Royal North Carolina Regiment, say 150 rank and file, were with him, allowing for a small corps of light infantry, say 120 rank and file, not mentioned in Rawdon's return[4], and subtracting the rank and file who would have fallen ill between the date of the return and the commencement of the march, say 30, we arrive at a total of 1,850 rank and file who accompanied Cornwallis. Of these only 170 (Bryan's loyalists) were militia.

Gates had of course committed a strategic blunder in marching into South Carolina. Far better if he had remained on the frontier, so reliant was he on militia. Forcing Cornwallis to remain compact, he would have facilitated inroads into the Back Country by revolutionary irregulars, perhaps supported by one or two small detachments of Continentals. Already much of the vast territory east of the Wateree and Santee had been overrun by irregulars in this way.

As adumbrated in his letter of the 21st, Cornwallis's reasons for attacking Gates were sound. There was much to gain by a victory, but it was most disingenuous of him to state that there was little to lose by a defeat. An army had been lost at Saratoga. If another had been lost at Camden, the political repercussions in Britain would have been so pronounced that, as with Yorktown, they would almost certainly have led to a termination of the war and a recognition of American independence.

Apart from omitting to point out that Bryan's loyalists formed the extremity of his left wing, Cornwallis provides from a British perspective a brief account of the ensuing battle and of the events leading up to it. It is unnecessary to elaborate here, except to disclose the formation of Gates's troops as the battle began, together with the turning point of the day.

On Gates's right wing lay Gist's 2nd brigade, composed of one Delaware and three Maryland regiments; in the centre, the artillery and Caswell's North Carolina militia; and on the left, Stevens' Virginia militia, flanked by Armand's corps. Two hundred yards in the rear Smallwood's 1st Maryland brigade was held in reserve. Kalb, who commanded the right wing, had taken his place in the line, whereas Gates and his staff occupied a position behind the 1st Maryland brigade.

Informed that Cornwallis's men had yet to deploy on their right, Gates ordered Stevens to attack. It was the last order he gave, but it was too late. By the time that Stevens received it, the British right had deployed. Cornwallis promptly ordered it to advance on perceiving a movement among Stevens' men, and it did so with such vigour, firing and huzzaing, that almost the entire militia forming Gates's left and centre were thrown into panic. Abandoning their loaded arms, they fled. Cornwallis's whole force now fell upon the grossly outnumbered Continentals forming the 1st and 2nd brigades, who, despite displaying the utmost bravery, were demolished within the hour. More than half were killed or captured and the rest fled after Gates to regroup in North Carolina. Kalb was mortally wounded and died three days

---

[3] See vol I, p 233.

[4] The light companies who had just arrived from Ninety Six.

later. Of Cornwallis's men, 68 were killed, 245 wounded, and 11 were missing — a price well worth paying for so great an advantage.

The victory was as much a testament to the prowess of British American troops as it was to that of the British. It was swiftly followed on the 18th by Tarleton's rout of Sumter at Fishing Creek. The crushing effect of these successes was unaffected by a setback at Musgrove's Mill on Enoree. While commanding there a mixed force of British American troops and militia, Alexander Innes was defeated on the 19th by Clark, Shelby and Williams, who, on hearing of the disaster at Camden, promptly retreated over the border.

Captured at Camden and Fishing Creek were a number of militiamen who had perfidiously sworn allegiance to the Crown, enrolled in the royal militia, and gone off to the enemy. Although all deserved the halter for their treachery, only 'some few of the most hardened... were actually executed', another instance of the lenity of Cornwallis. He did go on to order Cruger, Ferguson and Turnbull to execute persons of the same description, but mitigated his order by stating that, if there were many, only several of the ringleaders were to be hanged. Needless to say, revolutionary propaganda malevolently exaggerated the extent of the executions and it has percolated down to the present day.

Superficially, the way now appeared open for the autumn campaign.

§ - §

Principal papers and works consulted in the writing of this chapter

The Cornwallis Papers (UK National Archives, Kew)

Charles Stedman, *History of the Origin, Progress, and Termination of the American War* (London, 1792)

Banastre Tarleton, *A History of the Campaigns of 1780 and 1781 in the Southern Provinces of North America* (London, 1787)

Christopher Ward, *The War of the Revolution* (The Macmillan Company NY, 1952)

Otho Holland Williams, 'A Narrative of the Campaign of 1780', Appendix B to volume I of William Johnson, *Sketches of the Life and Correspondence of Nathanael Greene* (Charleston, 1822)

§ - §

CHAPTER 19

Letters from Cornwallis to Germain, Clinton, Arbuthnot, and others

1 - To Germain

Cornwallis to Germain, 20th August 1780[1]   76(1): C

Nº 1   Camden
August 20th 1780

Rt Hon Lord George Germain etc etc etc[2]

My Lord

Your Lordship will have been informed by Sir Henry Clinton of every thing that passed in the province of South Carolina from the reduction of Charlestown to the defeat of the corps under Colonel Buford by the great exertion and valour of Lt Colonel Tarleton.

Sir Henry soon afterwards embarked for New York and appointed me to the command of His Majesty's forces in the southern provinces. I was then at Camden, but the corps with me being totally destitute of military stores, cloathing, rum, salt and other articles necessary for troops in the operations of the field, and provisions of all kinds being deficient, almost

---

[1] Published in Stevens, *Clinton-Cornwallis Controvery*, i, 241. There are no material differences.

[2] The third son of the Duke of Dorset, Lord George Germain (1716-1785) had been Secretary of State for the Colonies since late 1775, an office he would hold until February 1782. His involvement in the war is intermittently dealt with in these Papers.

approaching to a famine in North Carolina, it was impossible for me to penetrate into that province before the harvest. I therefore employed myself in fixing posts of troops from the Pedee to the Savannah Rivers to awe the disaffected and encourage the loyal inhabitants, and I took every measure in my power to raise some Provincial corps and to establish a militia, as well for the defence as for the internal government of South Carolina. One Provincial corps to consist of five hundred men was put in commission to be raised between the Pedee and Wateree to be commanded by Mr Harrison with the rank of major, and another of the same number was ordered to be raised in the District of Ninety Six to be commanded by Mr Cunningham, to whom, on account of his active loyalty for several years past, I gave the rank of lt colonel; and there appeared to be great reason to expect that both these corps would be soon compleated, as well as the first South Carolina Regiment, which was composed of refugees who had now returned to their native country.

In the District of Ninety Six, by far the most populous and powerfull of the province, Lt Colonel Balfour by his great attention and diligence, and by the active assistance of Major Ferguson, who was appointed Inspector General of the Militia of this province by Sir Henry Clinton, had formed seven battalions of militia consisting of above four thousand men and entirely composed of persons well affected to the British Government, which were so regulated that they could with ease furnish fifteen hundred men at a short notice for the defence of the frontier or any other home service. But I must take this opportunity of observing that this militia can be of little use for distant military operations, as they will not stir without an horse, and on that account your Lordship will easily conceive the impossibility of keeping a number of them together without destroying the country. Many battalions were likewise formed by myself and other officers on the very extensive line from Broad River to Cheraws, but they were in general either weak or not much to be relied on for their fidelity.

In order to protect the raising of Harrison's corps and to awe a large tract of disaffected country between the Pedee and Black River, I posted Major McArthur with the 71st Regiment and a troop of dragoons at Cheraw Hill on the Pedee, where his detachment was plentifully supplied by the country with provisions of all kinds. Other small posts were likewise established in the front and on the left of Camden, where the people were known to be ill disposed, and the main body of the corps was posted at Camden, which, for this country, is reckoned a tolerably healthy place, and where the troops could most conveniently subsist and receive the necessary supplies of various kinds from Charlestown. I likewise had settled good channels of correspondence with our friends in North Carolina and had given them positive directions to attend to their harvests and to remain quiet untill I could march to their relief. In this business I was greatly assisted by Governor Martin, from whose abilities and zeal for the service I have on many occasions derived great advantages, and which I must beg that your Lordship will please to represent in the strongest terms to His Majesty.

Having made the above arrangements, and every thing wearing the face of tranquillity and submission, I set out on the 21st of June for Charlestown, leaving the command of the troops on the frontier to Lord Rawdon, who was, after Brigadier General Paterson, the Commandant of Charlestown, the next officer in rank to me in the province.

About this time I heard that two thousand of the Maryland and Delaware Continental troops were entering North Carolina under Major General Baron de Kalbe and that he meant to take his quarters at Hillsborough. There was then in that country a corps of three hundred

Virginia light infantry under Colonel Porterfield, some militia at Salisbury and Charlottetown under Generals Rutherford and Sumpter, and a large body of militia at Cross Creek under General Caswall. As all these corps were at a great distance from us, and as I knew it to be impossible to march any considerable body of men across the province of North Carolina before the harvest, I did not expect that our posts on the frontier would be much disturbed for two months, and by that time I hoped to be able to undertake offensive operations.

I had much business to do at Charlestown in regulating the civil and commercial affairs of the town and country, in endeavouring to form a militia in the lower districts, and in forwarding the preparations for taking the field at the time intended. The business of the country was particularly difficult, for many parts of the lower districts are extremely rebellious and this climate (except in Charlestown) is so bad within an hundred miles of the coast, from the end of June untill the middle of October, that troops could not be stationed among them during that period without a certainty of their being rendered useless for some time for military service, if not entirely lost; and our principal friends for the same reasons were extremely unwilling to remain in the country during that period to assist in forming the militia and establishing some kind of government. However, under all these difficulties the business was going on, when our tranquillity was first disturbed by the accounts of a premature rising of our friends in Tryon County, North Carolina, in the latter end of June, who, having assembled without concert, plan or proper leaders, were two days after surprised and totally routed by the son of General Rutherford. Many of them fled into this province, where their reports tended much to terrify our friends and encourage our enemies; and about the same time, notwithstanding my injunctions to the contrary, another body of loyalists rose at the forks of the Yadkin under Colonel Bryan (driven to it, as they said, by the most barbarous persecution) and after a long and difficult march joined Major McArthur at the Cheraws to the amount of upwards of 700 men.

Hostilities now commenced in different parts of the frontier. General Sumpter, an active and daring man, assembled at Catawba about a thousand men, chiefly refugees from South Carolina and Georgia, and was constantly menacing our small posts and putting us under the necessity of calling out the militia of Ninety Six. He was joined by many disaffected persons who had been enrolled in our militia, but as there was no serious alarm, I was very unwilling to put the troops in motion before our preparations were compleat and during the intense heat of the summer.

Baron de Kalbe moved early in July to Deep River, where he was joined first by General Caswall from Cross Creek, and about the 25th by General Gates, who took the command of the army; but as he was still above an hundred miles from Major McArthur, which was the nearest post to him, Lord Rawdon did not think it necessary to make any material alteration in the disposition of the troops. From this time untill the 20th of July many skirmishes happened on the frontiers of Ninety Six and towards Waxhaw, but none of any material consequence. The enemy had, however, in the mean time filled this province with their emissaries, and in all the eastern part of it were planning a general revolt, which our lenity had left but too much in their power. The Cheraw Hill was a post of great consequence and had the appearance of being healthy, but it proved so much the contrary, and sickness came on so rapidly, that in nine days at least two thirds of the 71st Regiment were taken ill of fevers and agues and rendered unfit for service. About this time the enemy were known to be in motion, but the rigour of their government (many of our principal friends in North

Carolina being confined in dungeons, loaded with irons, and several having been put to death) had so intimidated those on whose good will and ability to give the most accurate intelligence we had the greatest reason to depend that Lord Rawdon could obtain no certain accounts of them.

The salvation of the 71st Regiment as well as every other consideration determined his Lordship to withdraw the post at Cheraw Hill. This the active incendiaries of the enemy represented as an act of fear and so encouraged the disaffected and terrified the wavering that the whole country between Pedee and Black River openly avowed the principles of rebellion and, collecting in parties, commenced acts of hostility.

Our Cheraw militia, having seized and bound their field officers, attacked and took some boats on the Pedee in which Major McArthur was sending near one hundred of his sick to Georgetown. I was greatly alarmed for a small detachment which I had sent under Major Wemyss to reduce the people of Georgetown to some order, and for my water communication on the Santee, on which at that time a large quantity of rum, salt, arms and military stores were moving in boats up to Camden.

At this time General Sumpter, whose numbers were much augmented by the present prospect of affairs, attacked our post at Rocky Mount, but was repulsed by the steady and gallant defence of Lt Colonel Turnbull and the small corps under his command. It now appeared that General Gates was advancing with his whole force from North Carolina, and Lord Rawdon (whose capacity and zeal for the service I cannot too much commend) saw the necessity of contracting his posts and securing Camden, where we had all our stores and above 700 sick, but he could not immediately withdraw his whole force to that place without a certainty of losing his communication with Charlestown and exposing the posts dependent on the Ninety Six command to be surrounded and cut off. He therefore continued Lt Colonel Turnbull at Rocky Mount, reinforced his post at Hanging Rock, and placed himself with the principal force at Robertson's on the west branch of Linches Creek. The post at Hanging Rock was attacked by General Sumpter a few days after his repulse from Rocky Mount and very nearly carried; the bravery of Captain McCullough, since dead of his wounds, and of the infantry of the Legion preserved it. Lord Rawdon waited for Gates at Robertson's with the 23rd, 33rd, 71st and Volunteers of Ireland, who came up but did not think proper to attack him. In the mean time his Lordship performed the arduous task of removing the sick of the 71st Regiment to Camden. General Gates shewing no disposition to attack the corps at Robertson's, Lord Rawdon, wisely apprehending that his intention might be either to reinforce Sumpter and make a more vigorous attack on the posts at Rocky Mount or Hanging Rock or, by getting round his right, destroy his stores and take his sick at Camden, retired from Robertson's to that place, where he was joined by the corps which had been before moved from Hanging Rock to Rugeley's Mill, and directed Lt Colonel Turnbull to quit Rocky Mount and either come down the west side of the Wateree to Camden or fall back on the militia posts commanded by Major Ferguson on Broad River.

All these incidents and movements on both sides were regularly reported to me while at Charlestown by Lord Rawdon, and I shall have the honour of informing your Lordship of the consequences in my next dispatch, which will be written tomorrow.

I have the honour to be with great respect
Your Lordship's most obedient and most humble servant

[CORNWALLIS]

[*Annotated:*]

Original per Captain Ross, who sailed in the *Providence* frigate from Charles Town September 3rd 1780.

Cornwallis to Germain, 21st August 1780[3]   76(9): C

N° 2

Camden
August 21st 1780

Rt Hon Lord George Germain etc etc etc

My Lord

It is with great pleasure that I communicate to your Lordship an account of a compleat victory obtained on the 16th instant by His Majesty's troops under my command over the rebel southern army commanded by General Gates.

In my dispatch N° 1 I had the honour to inform your Lordship that while at Charlestown I was regularly acquainted by Lord Rawdon with every material incident or movement made by the enemy or by the troops under his Lordship's command. On the 9th two expresses arrived with an account that General Gates was advancing towards Lynches Creek with his whole army, supposed to amount to 6,000 men exclusive of a detachment of 1,000 men under General Sumpter, who, after having in vain attempted to force the posts at Rocky Mount and Hanging Rock, was believed to be at that time trying to get round the left of our position to cut off our communication with the Congarees and Charlestown; that the disaffected country between Pedee and Black River had actually revolted; and that Lord Rawdon was contracting his posts and preparing to assemble his force at Camden.

In consequence of this information, after finishing some important points of business at Charlestown, I set out on the evening of the 10th and arrived at Camden on the night between the 13th and 14th and there found Lord Rawdon with our whole force, except Lt Colonel Turnbull's small detachment, which fell back from Rocky Mount to Major Ferguson's posts of the militia of Ninety Six on Little River.

I had now my option to make, either to retire or attack the enemy, for the position at Camden was a bad one to be attacked in, and by General Sumpter's advancing down the Wateree my supplies must have failed me in a few days.

---

[3] Published in Stevens, op cit, i, 249. There are no material differences.

I saw no difficulty in making good my retreat to Charlestown with the troops that were able to march, but in taking that resolution I must have not only left near 800 sick and a great quantity of stores at this place but I clearly saw the loss of the whole province except Charlestown, and of all Georgia except Savannah, as immediate consequences, besides forfeiting all pretensions to future confidence from our friends in this part of America.

On the other hand, there was no doubt of the rebel army being well appointed and of its number being upwards of five thousand men exclusive of General Sumpter's detachment and of a corps of Virginia militia of 12 or 1500 men either actually joined or expected to join the main body every hour; and my own corps, which never was numerous, was now reduced by sickness and other casualties to about 1,400 fighting men of regulars and Provincials with 4 or 500 militia and North Carolina refugees. However, the greatest part of the troops that I had being perfectly good, and having left Charlestown sufficiently garrisoned and provided for a siege, and seeing little to lose by a defeat and much to gain by a victory, I resolved to take the first good opportunity to attack the rebel army. Accordingly I took great pains to procure good information of their movements and position, and I learned that they had encamped, after marching from Hanging Rock, at Colonel Rugeley's about 12 miles from hence on the afternoon of the 14th. After consulting some intelligent people well acquainted with the ground, I determined to march at ten o'clock on the night of the 15th and to attack at day break, pointing my principal force against their Continentals, who from good intelligence I knew to be badly posted close to Colonel Rugeley's house. Late in the evening I received information that the Virginians had joined that day. However, that having been expected, I did not alter my plan but marched at the hour appointed, leaving the defence of Camden to some Provincials[4], militia and convalescents and a detachment of the 63rd Regiment, which, by being mounted on horses which they had pressed on the road, it was hoped would arrive in the course of the night.

I had proceeded nine miles, when about half an hour past two in the morning my advanced guard fell in with the enemy. By the weight of the fire I was convinced they were in considerable force and was soon assured by some deserters and prisoners that it was the whole rebel army on its march to attack us at Camden. I immediately halted and formed, and, the enemy doing the same, the firing soon ceas'd. Confiding in the disciplined courage of His Majesty's troops and well apprized by several intelligent inhabitants that the ground on which both armies stood, being narrowed by swamps on the right and left, was extremely favourable for my numbers, I did not chuse to hazard the great stake for which I was going to fight to the uncertainty and confusion to which an action in the dark is so particularly liable; but, having taken measures that the enemy should not have it in their power to avoid an engagement on that ground, I resolved to defer the attack 'till day. At the dawn I made my last disposition and formed the troops in the following order: the division of the right consisting of a small corps of light infantry, the 23rd and 33rd Regiments under the command of Lt Colonel Webster; the division of the left consisting of the Volunteers of Ireland, infantry of the Legion and part of Lt Colonel Hamilton's North Carolina Regiment under the command of Lord Rawdon, with two six and two three pounders which were commanded by Lieutenant McCloud. The 71st Regiment with two six pounders was formed as a reserve, one

---

[4] *some Provincials*: part of the Royal North Carolina Regiment and the remnants of the Prince of Wales's American Regiment.

battalion in the rear of the division of the right, the other of that of the left, and the cavalry of the Legion in the rear and (the country being woody) close to the 71st Regiment with orders to seize any opportunity that might offer to break the enemy's line and to be ready to protect our own in case any corps should meet with a check.

This disposition was just made when I perceived that the enemy, having persisted in their resolution to fight, were form'd in two lines opposite and near to us, and observing a movement on their left, which I supposed to be with an intention to make some alteration in their order, I directed Lt Colonel Webster to begin the attack, which was done with great vigour, and in a few minutes the action was general along the whole front. It was at this time a dead calm with a little haziness in the air, which, preventing the smoke from rising, occasioned so thick a darkness that it was difficult to see the effect of a very heavy and well supported fire on both sides. Our line continued to advance in good order and with the cool intrepidity of experienced British soldiers, keeping up a constant fire or making use of bayonets as opportunities offered, and, after an obstinate resistance for three quarters of an hour, threw the enemy into total confusion and forced them to give way in all quarters. At this instant I ordered the cavalry to compleat the route, which was performed with their usual promptitude and gallantry, and after doing great execution on the field of battle, they continued the pursuit to Hanging Rock, 22 miles from the place where the action happened, during which many of the enemy were slain, a number of prisoners, near 150 waggons (in one of which was a brass cannon, the carriage of which had been damaged in the skirmish of the night), a considerable quantity of military stores, and all the baggage and camp equipage of the rebel army fell into our hands.

The loss of the enemy was very considerable: a number of colours and seven pieces of brass cannon (being all their artillery that were in the action) with all their ammunition waggons were taken; between eight and nine hundred were killed, among that number Brigadier General Gregory[5]; and about one thousand prisoners, many of them wounded, of which number were Major General Baron de Kalbe, since dead, and Brigadier General Rutherford.

I have the honour to inclose a return of killed and wounded on our side[6]. The loss of so many brave men is much to be lamented, but the number is moderate in proportion to so great

---

[5] Isaac Gregory was a native of Pasquotank County, North Carolina, and had been involved politically and militarily in revolutionary affairs since 1775. In autumn of that year he was appointed to the Committee of Safety for Edenton District, and in the following April was commissioned Colonel of the 2nd Regiment of the Pasquotank revolutionary militia. Seven months later he represented his county in the Provincial Congress which in December adopted a revolutionary constitution for North Carolina. When Camden County was separated out from Pasquotank, he was elected its first Senator in 1778 and would continue to serve intermittently in the legislature until 1796. By 1780 a brigadier general in the North Carolina revolutionary militia, he and a small part of his brigade – the rest having fled the field – fought bravely in the Battle of Camden, during which he was bayoneted twice and captured. Contrary to Cornwallis's assertion, he did not die. Exchanged in June 1781 under the cartel with Greene, he would immediately assume command of North Carolina revolutionary militia holding a position south of Portsmouth, Virginia, at the edge of the Dismal Swamp. His home, Fairfield, is still standing. A mansion built in the mid 1700s, it lies some two and a half miles from the village of Camden, North Carolina. (Wheeler, *Historical Sketches*, i, 73, 81, 86; Wheeler, *Reminiscences*, 99; McCrady, *SC in the Rev 1775-1780*, 677-8; *The Greene Papers*, viii and ix, *passim*; Robinson, *NC Guide*, 303)

[6] *a return..*: no extant copy. It is printed in Tarleton, *Campaigns*, 137-9.

an advantage.

The behaviour of His Majesty's troops in general was beyond all praise; it did honour to themselves and to their country. I was particularly indebted to Colonel Lord Rawdon and to Lt Colonel Webster for the distinguished courage and ability with which they conducted their respective divisions; and the capacity and vigour of Lt Colonel Tarleton at the head of the cavalry deserve my highest commendations. Lieutenant McCloud exerted himself greatly in the conduct of our artillery. My aid-de-camp, Captain Ross, and Lieutenant Haldane[7] of the Engineers, who acted in that capacity, rendered me most essential service; and the publick officers, Major of Brigade England, who acted as Deputy Adjutant General, and the Majors of Brigade Manley and Doyle, shewed the most active and zealous attention to their duty. Governour Martin became again a military man and behaved with the spirit of a young volunteer.

The fatigue of the troops rendered them incapable of further exertion on the day of the action; but as I saw the importance of destroying or dispersing, if possible, the corps under General Sumpter, as it might prove a foundation for assembling the routed army, on the morning of the 17th I detached Lt Colonel Tarleton with the Legion cavalry and infantry and the corps of light infantry, making in all about 350 men, with orders to attack him wherever he could find him, and at the same time I sent orders to Lt Colonel Turnbull and Major Ferguson, at that time on Little River, to put their corps in motion immediately and on their side to pursue and endeavour to attack General Sumpter. Lt Colonel Tarleton executed this service with his usual activity and military address. He procured good information of Sumpter's movements and by forced and concealed marches came up with and surprized him in the middle of the day on the 18th near the Catawba Fords. He totally destroyed or dispersed his detachment consisting then of 700 men, killing 150 on the spot and taking two pieces of brass cannon and 300 prisoners and 44 waggons. He likewise retook 100 of our men who had fallen into their hands, partly at the action at Hanging Rock and partly in escorting some waggons from Congarees to Camden, and he released 150 of our militia men or friendly country people who had been seized by the rebels. Captain Campbell, who commanded the light infantry, a very promising officer, was unfortunately killed in this affair. Our loss otherways was trifling. This action is too brilliant to need any comment of mine and will, I have no doubt, highly recommend Lt Colonel Tarleton to His Majesty's favour.

The rebel forces being at present dispersed, the internal commotions and insurrections in the province will now subside, but I shall give directions to inflict exemplary punishment on some of the most guilty in hopes to deter others in future from sporting with allegiance, with oaths, and with the lenity and generosity of the British Government.

---

[7] Educated at Woolwich, Henry Haldane (1750-1825) had been commissioned an ensign in the Corps of Engineers on 1st April 1771 and was promoted to lieutenant some six years later. In 1776 he embarked for North America and by 1778 was acting as aide-de-camp to the Commandant at New York. Coming south in 1780, he reverted to his profession of engineer during the siege of Charlestown. Afterwards he would act as one of Cornwallis's aides-de-camp throughout the southern campaigns while continuing at times to serve as an engineer. He would be among the troops who capitulated at Yorktown. After the war he accompanied Cornwallis to India, again serving as his aide-de-camp, and was appointed Quartermaster General there. Returning to England in 1794, he was promoted to lt colonel one year later. (*Army Lists*; Stevens, *Clinton-Cornwallis Controversy*, ii, 435)

On the morning of the 17th I dispatched proper people into North Carolina with directions to our friends there to take arms and assemble immediately and to seize the most violent people and all military stores and magazines belonging to the rebels and to intercept all straglers from the routed army; and I have promised to march without loss of time to their support. Some necessary supplies for the army are now on their way from Charlestown and I hope that their arrival will enable me to move in a few days.

My aid-de-camp, Captain Ross, will have the honour of delivering this dispatch to your Lordship and will be able to give you the fullest account of the state of the army and country. He is a very deserving officer and I take the liberty of recommending him to your Lordship's favour and patronage.

I have the honour to be with great respect
Your Lordship's most obedient and most humble servant

[CORNWALLIS]

[*Annotated*:]

Original per Captain Ross, who sailed in the *Providence* frigate from Charles Town September 4th 1780.

§ - §

2 - To Clinton and Arbuthnot

***Cornwallis to Clinton, 23rd August 1780*[8]**   72(42): C

Camden
August 23rd 1780

Sir

Your Excellency will have in all probability received my letters of the 6th and 10th[9] by Captain Lutwidge. The opportunity was so safe, and I am at present so hurried with business, with every body belonging to me sick, that I shall omit sending the duplicates until another opportunity.

I left Charlestown on the evening of the 10th and arrived here in the night of the 13th,

---

[8] Published in Stevens, op cit, i, 257. There are no material differences.

[9] *letters of the 6th and 10th*: see vol I, pp 175 and 179.

having suffered the most anxious suspense on the road, where I met frequently the most alarming reports and had the greatest reason to apprehend that if our affairs did not speedily take a more favorable turn, the greatest part of the inhabitants between Camden and Charlestown would appear in arms against us.

As I thought it of the greatest consequence to His Majesty's Service that the account of the important event of the 16th should be communicated with all possible expedition to the Secretary of State, and as your Excellency told me in a conversation at Williams's house that if I fought a battle and took cannon I should write directly to England, I have on this occasion dispatched my aid de camp, Captain Ross, with the letters to Lord George Germain of which I have the honor to enclose to you the copies.

I must beg leave to recommend in the strongest manner to you the brave troops who fought with me on that day. Their behaviour was indeed above all praise and deserves every encouragement. Poor Major Mecan died a few days before the action. As I cannot possibly dispense with Lt Colonel Balfour's remaining at Charlestown, where he is of infinite use, I must particularly request that you will please to appoint some active good officer to the majority of the 23rd Regiment.

I have not yet heard any accounts from North Carolina, but I hope that our friends will immediately take arms as I have directed them to do. The diversion in the Chesapeak will be of the utmost importance. The troops here have gained reputation but they have lost numbers, and there can be no doubt that the enemy will use every effort to repel an attack, which, if successfull, must end in their losing all the southern colonies.

I have likewise to observe that, if a general exchange should take place, the enemy's prisoners should in my opinion be delivered at the same place as ours are sent to. The rebels now confined at Charlestown are almost all Continentals and of the old country and would, if released from hence, soon form a corps on the frontiers of Virginia far superior in number to the troops under my command; and I do not think, if the prisoners were all removed, that I could draw any considerable reinforcement from the garrison of Charlestown, considering the great distance we shall be removed from thence.

It is difficult to form a plan of operations, which must depend so much on circumstances; but it at present appears to me that I should endeavor to get as soon as possible to Hillsborough and there assemble, and try to arrange, the friends who are inclined to arm in our favour and endeavor to form a very large magazine for the winter of flour and meal from the country and of rum, salt etc from Cross Creek, which I understand to be about eighty miles' carriage. But all this will depend on the operations your Excellency may think proper to pursue in the Chesapeak, which appears to me, next to the security of New York, to be one of the most important objects of the war. I can only repeat what I have often had the honor of saying to you: that wherever you may think my presence may be most conducive to His Majesty's Service, thither I am at all times ready and willing to go.

When I found that General Gates was advancing towards Camden, I sent orders to the commanding officer at Ninety Six to push parties of militia supported by Provincials in the rear of his right and endeavor to harrass his convoys and be ready to take advantage of any success that we might have against him. I have since a report that Lt Colonel Innes, in attempting this service, fell in on the 19th with a party of rebels[10], when he was deserted by the militia, and himself wounded in the neck, and about fifty officers and men of his Provincials killed, wounded or taken. The rebels who were pursuing him heard of our successes against Gates and Sumpter and went off with great precipitation. Major Wemys performed his march from George Town without loss or difficulty and is now in the neighbourhood of this place.

I am sorry to say that I fear Major Harrison will totally fail in his attempt to raise a corps.

Our sickness is great and truly alarming. The officers are particularly affected. Doctor Hayes and almost all the hospital surgeons are laid up. Every person of my family and every public officer[11] of the army is now incapable of doing his duty.

I have the honor to be, sir,
Your most obedient and most humble servant

[CORNWALLIS]

Cornwallis to Clinton, 23rd August 1780   72(45): ADf

Camden
August 23rd 1780

Sir

You will see by the returns that poor Captain Malcolm of the 33rd is killed. I beg leave to recommend Captain Lieutenant Gore to succeed to the company, eldest Lieutenant Nichols, who has been long in the service and was wounded very severely at Brandywine, to the captain lieutenantcy, and eldest Ensign Collington, who was dangerously wounded on the 16th, to the lieutenantcy. As Captain Ingram, who was promoted from my regiment to the 70th, was particularly patronized by me, I should be much pleased to have him return, if he chuses it, to the 33rd and let Lieutenant Nichols go to his place in the 70th. If, however, your Excellency sees any impropriety in it, I beg to wave it and adhere to my recommendation of Lieutenant Nichols.

I believe there is a lieutenantcy in the 33rd vacant by the promotion of Lieutenant St Leger at home. If any notification of it should be come to you, I should recommend the second ensign, Fenwick, to succeed to it, and the two vacant ensigncys will give you an opportunity of fullfilling your obliging intentions to Webster, whose wounds, 'tho' painfull, are not dangerous.

---

[10] The action at Musgrove's Mill.

[11] *every public officer*: majors of brigade and officers such as those in the Quartermaster General's Department.

I have the honor to be, sir,
Your most obedient and most humble servant

[CORNWALLIS]

Cornwallis to Arbuthnot, 23rd August 1780   79(33): ADfS

Camden
August 23rd 1780

His Excellency Vice Admiral Arbuthnot etc etc etc

Dear Sir

By the letter[12] which Captain Lutwidge will have delivered to you from me, you will have seen that things did not bear a very peaceable or a very pleasing aspect. By the copies of my letters to the Secretary of State, which I have the honour of inclosing to you, you will find that the prospect is much brightened. The General told me before he left Charlestown that, in case of any event of importance such as gaining a battle and taking canon, I should send directly to England. I hope you will agree with me in thinking that the affair of the 16th was of importance enough to require its being transmitted to the Secretary of State by the speediest and safest conveyance. I have therefore dispatched Ross and desired Henry either to carry him in his own ship or, if that was impossible, to send him home in any of the King's ships which he should think proper for the occasion. I, however, prefer'd the *Providence* and have reason to think it will end in his going in her. If that should be the case, I trust to your forgiving me for sending away your ship, and that you will not forget *Charlestown harbour*.

Altho' our victory was as compleat as possible, still much remains to be done. It is absolutely necessary, in order to reap any benefit whatever from our success, or indeed to keep this province, for me to march into the extremity of North Carolina, which march of upwards of 200 miles I must undertake with an army as much enfeebled by sickness as you ever saw one in the West Indies, without magazines or a proper supply of horses for the purpose. I have urged in the strongest manner to the General the necessity of a diversion in the Chesapeak and I must earnestly beg your assistance in it. I am not very well, hurried to death with business, and have not one person of my family well enough to give me the smallest assistance. Every body assures us that if we get a little farther into the country, we shall be much healthier. Excuse my writing any more and believe me to be

Your very faithfull servant

CORNWALLIS

§ - §

---

[12] *the letter*: Cornwallis to Arbuthnot, 10th August, vol I, p 180.

3 - To others

Cornwallis to Cruger, 18th August 1780[13]

Camden
August 18th 1780

Lt Colonel Cruger

Sir

I have the pleasure to inform you that on the morning of the 16th I attacked and totally defeated General Gates's army. Above 1,000 were killed and wounded and about 800 taken prisoners. We are in possession of eight pieces of brass cannon — all they had in the field —, all their ammunition waggons, a great number of arms, and 130 baggage waggons. In short, there never was a more complete victory. I have written to Lt Colonel Turnbull, who is with Major Ferguson on Little River, to push on to Waxhaw after General Sumpter, whose detachment is at present the only collected force of the rebels in all this country. Lt Colonel Tarleton is in pursuit of Sumpter on this side. I have given orders that all the inhabitants of this province who had *submitted* and who have taken part in this revolt should be punished with the greatest rigour, that they should be imprisoned, and their whole property taken from them or destroyed. I have likewise directed that compensation should be made out of their effects to the persons who have been *plundered* and oppressed by them. I have ordered in the most positive manner that every militia man who had borne arms with us and had afterwards joined the enemy should be immediately hanged. I have now, Sir, only to desire that you will take the most *vigorous* measures to *extinguish the rebellion* in the district in which you command and that you will obey in the strictest manner the directions I have given in this letter relative to the treatment of the country. I intend sending a frigate directly to England. Any letters which you may send immediately to Charlestown will be in time for it.

I am etc

CORNWALLIS

[*Subscribed*:]

Our loss is about 300 killed and wounded, chiefly of the 33rd Regiment and Volunteers of Ireland.

---

[13] Published in Ross ed, *Cornwallis Correspondence*, i, 56-7.

Haldane to Turnbull or Ferguson, 20th August 1780   79(27): ACS

Head Quarters, Camden
20th August 1780

Lt Colonel Turnbull or Major Ferguson

Dear Sir

Lord Cornwallis has directed me to give you this early information of the successfull attack made by Lt Colonel Tarleton on the evening of the 18th on the party of the enemy commanded by Sumpter, having killed 150, taken 300 prisoners with two pieces of cannon and redeemed our friends from captivity. His Lordship desires that you will most rigidly put in execution his orders relative to the treatment of the persons concerned in this last general revolt, but if there should be many of the description ordered to be hanged, you will be pleased to execute several of the ringleaders and detain the others in prison untill Lord Cornwallis's pleasure is known.

I have the honour to be, dear sir, etc

HH

[*Endorsed*:]

The same to Lt Colonel Cruger, and that 'You will be pleased to order Captain Frazer[14], who has lately obtained a warrant to raise a company, to come immediately to Head Quarters.'[15]

---

[14] Thomas Fraser. See vol I, p 243, note 11.

[15] In a letter of the same date to Balfour (79(25)) Haldane informs him of Tarleton's success and of Cornwallis's directions to Turnbull and Cruger on the treatment of prisoners guilty of treachery.

Cornwallis to Amherst, 21st August 1780

79(29): C

Camden
21st August 1780

Rt Hon Lord Amherst[16] etc etc etc

My Lord

I have the pleasure to inform your Lordship that the troops under my command gained a most compleat victory over the rebel southern army, commanded by General Gates, on the 16th of this month.

I must beg leave to refer your Lordship, for the particulars of the action and the transactions in this province since I have had the honour to command, to my letters to the Secretary of State and to Captain Ross, my aide de camp, who is a most intelligent officer and whom I take the liberty of recommending to your Lordship in the strongest manner.

I must beg your favour and patronage for the brave troops who fought that day under my orders and whose behaviour surpassed any thing I have ever seen before. Lord Rawdon and Lt Colonel Webster deserve my highest encomiums, and I trust that your Lordship will lose no opportunity of reminding His Majesty of their very distinguished merit.

Your Lordship will see the account of the brilliant action of Lt Colonel Tarleton. I think it my duty to declare that he is one of the most promising officers I ever knew. I have no private connexion with him nor any motive for recommending him but the desire of seeing extraordinary merit rewarded and of placing him in such a rank as may enable him to render the most essential services to his King and country.

From the repeated instances which I have observed of His Majesty's kind disposition towards me, and from Captain Ross's great merit and long services, I can have no doubt of his receiving some distinguished mark of favour. I shall, however, be infinitely obliged to your Lordship if you will allow him to return to me, as it would be very inconvenient to me to be deprived of his assistance.

I have the honour to be etc

[CORNWALLIS]

---

[16] Jeffrey, Lord Amherst (1717-1797) had been Commander-in-Chief of the British Army since early 1778, a post something like a modern chief of staff that also included command of home forces and a seat in the cabinet. Uncomfortable in the presence of politicians, he was a taciturn cabinet colleague and exerted relatively little influence on the overall direction of the war in America, though, with the serious prospect by 1779 of a Franco-Spanish invasion, he became opposed to sending more troops overseas. In a long career his greatest achievement was the conquest of Canada during the Seven Years' War. A low point was his approach at that time, and during the Pontiac War, toward native Americans, whom he detested. (*ODNB*)

Cornwallis to Henry, 21st August 1780 *79(31): C*

Camden
21st August 1780

Captain Henry or officer commanding His Majesty's ships
  in Charlestown harbour

Sir

As it is of the utmost importance that the news of the victory of the 16th should be known as soon as possible in England, I must desire that you will if practicable carry my aide de camp, Captain Ross, in your own ship immediately to England. If that cannot be, I am to request that you will send him in a King's ship which shall appear to you to be tolerably safe and likely to make an expeditious passage. If you find that likewise impossible, the *Hero* armed merchant ship must be taken for that service. You will therefore, in that case, be so kind as to hire her at a fair price, with or without consent, and man her properly for the voyage. I am, however, very solicitous that Captain Ross with my dispatches should go in a man of war. I shall likewise have occasion to send dispatches of great consequence in a few days to New York and beg you will be pleased to prepare the most convenient vessel for that purpose. I am very sorry to be so troublesome to you, but must plead the exigency of the service for my excuse. As, from the present appearance of things, there is great reason to suppose that we shall have occasion for a naval co-operation in Cape Fear River, I have to desire, in case you should go home yourself with the dispatches, that you will inform the officer left in the command of His Majesty's ships at Charlestown that Lt Colonel Balfour, Commandant of Charlestown, will be employed by me in forwarding such supplies and reinforcements as I may have occasion for, and that I beg that any application or requisition coming from him may be considered as proceeding immediately from me.

I am, sir, etc

[CORNWALLIS]

§ - §

PART FIVE

The Autumn Campaign

24th August to 31st October 1780

CHAPTER 20

Introduction to the rest of Part Five

As events would prove, the autumn campaign was a very risky venture indeed, yet despite the operational difficulties attending it Cornwallis saw no option but to go on to the offensive. As he had explained to Clinton, 'It may be doubted by some whether the invasion of North Carolina may be a prudent measure, but I am convinced it is a necessary one and that, if we do not attack that province, we must give up both South Carolina and Georgia and retire within the walls of Charlestown.'

Throughout the campaign a pressing concern would be the sickliness of the troops, whether they were those who marched with Cornwallis or those who were intended to join him later from Camden.

An immediate problem, which delayed the march, was the formation of supply trains. Waggons there were aplenty, what with those taken in the recent engagements and others pressed from Orangeburg and Ninety Six, but, for reasons set out later in these Papers, horses, gear, conductors and drivers were wanting.

Another cause of delay was the severe lack of provision at Camden, exacerbated by additional mouths to feed after the Battle. On 31st August Cornwallis remarked to Balfour, 'Hitherto, so far from being able to get a few days' [*provision*] beforehand, which is absolutely necessary for our march, we are this day without either flour or meal and Tarleton's horses have had no forage since the action.'

Against all the odds Cornwallis managed to assemble a proviant train of thirty-eight waggons by 7th September, twenty of which were loaded with a puncheon of rum in each and the rest with flour and salt. At daybreak, accompanied by two 3-pounders, he marched towards Charlotte with the 23rd, 33rd and Volunteers of Ireland, leaving behind material numbers of their dead, sick and wounded. Two days later he reached the border settlement at the Waxhaws and was joined by Bryan's militia. The troops soon set up camp on Waxhaw Creek, living on wheat collected and ground from the plantations in the neighbourhood, most of which were owned by Scotch-Irish revolutionaries who had fled.

On 8th September Tarleton crossed the Wateree at Camden Ferry and advanced with the British Legion and a detachment of the 71st's light troops towards White's Mill on Fishing Creek. While there on the 17th, he fell ill of a violent attack of yellow fever. His entire command was now needed to protect him and it was not until the 23rd that he became well enough to be moved to Blair's Mill on the Catawba. Crossing on the same day at the ford there, which was six hundred yards wide and three and a half feet deep, the Legion joined Cornwallis. All in all, Tarleton's illness was one of the main reasons for setting back the entry into Charlotte. It took place on the 26th.

By then Cornwallis had been reinforced by the 71st, but both battalions were much depleted, not only by their dead and wounded in the Battle, but also by their sick who had fallen down earlier at Cheraw Hill. Many, who were recovering, had relapsed before their march and returned to the hospital at Camden. Accompanied by a detachment of artillery with two 6-pounders, a few pioneers, the convalescents of the 33rd, and two supply trains, one of rum and salt, and the other of artillery stores, arms and ammunition, the remains of the 71st arrived at the Waxhaws on the 21st, but they too were in poor shape, adding considerably to the sick of the other regiments there, who by that date amounted to above 120 and were daily increasing. When Cornwallis advanced to Charlotte, the debris of the 71st was left at Waxhaw Creek to form a staging post.

Meanwhile Wemyss had been engaged on his expedition to the Pee Dee, designed to pacify the vast expanse of territory east of Camden no longer under British control. He had been ordered by Cornwallis to endeavour to form a militia in the Cheraw District, to disarm the untrustworthy, to make prisoners of those who had at first submitted — or lived quietly at home – and then revolted, to destroy or confiscate their property, and to hang those who had voluntarily enrolled in the royal militia and then gone over traitorously to the enemy. Wemyss set out from the High Hills of Santee on 6th September with 80 to 100 men of the 63rd and was joined at Kingstree Bridge by a detachment of the Royal North Carolina Regiment (100), Harrison's corps (50), and Bryan's militia (50). All were mounted. He burnt and laid waste about fifty houses and plantations mostly belonging to those who had taken up arms in breach of their paroles or oaths of allegiance, but only some twenty prisoners were taken and only one man, 'a notorious villain', having been convicted by court martial, was executed. Nothing could be done with forming a militia, the disaffection was so rife. Wemyss and his party arrived back at Camden on 4th October.

As Wemyss prepared to march, Moncrief with the 7th (Royal Fusiliers) quit Charlestown on 4th September to be joined two days later by Ball's and Wigfall's militia at Lenud's Ferry. He proceeded to repossess Georgetown, where he assembled Cassells' militia, and went on to scour the lower parts of the district, destroying the property of those who had revolted, dispatching their slaves for the works at Charlestown, and appropriating some 150 horses for use to the north. After posting Ball and Wigfall at three ferries on Black River and leaving Cassells to patrol between there and the Pee Dee, he marched on the 21st for Camden, where he arrived one week later with the 7th (all mounted). The militia that he left behind performed as badly as usual. Shortly before midnight on the 28th Ball was routed by Marion at Black Mingo, Wigfall appears to have fled, and Cassells, fearing attack, evacuated Georgetown on the 29th or 30th, despite being protected by an offshore galley. The town was reoccupied three weeks later by a detachment sent by Balfour under the command of Lieutenant Blucke of the 23rd.

Although Wemyss and Moncrief did not overstep the rules of warfare of their day, writers down the years have criticised them for severity, turning a blind eye to that practised by revolutionary irregulars east of the Wateree and Santee ever since McArthur quit Cheraw Hill in mid July. Yes, they were severe, but were their actions proportionate and defensible? That is the question. Cornwallis answered it in part when writing to Rawdon on 4th August: 'It is absolutely necessary to inflict some exemplary punishment on the militia and inhabitants of that part of the country. On the moment we advance, we shall find an enemy in our rear... some force must be sent to reduce and intimidate that country or the communication between the upper army and Charlestown will be impracticable.' In sanctioning the measures to be taken by Wemyss and Moncrief, Cornwallis came the closest he ever did to adopting in South Carolina the policy of deterrence favoured by Tarleton[1]. The measures were in fact the only option available to him east of the Wateree and Santee, where the vast majority of the inhabitants were so virulently disaffected that lenity and conciliation stood no chance. They had to be tried, and indeed the devastation wrought by Wemyss and Moncrief may have prevented or deterred quite a few there from presenting a threat in the shorter term, but in the longer term the territory would remain a running sore while ever the British remained outside Charlestown. In other respects the expeditions failed. So short was Cornwallis of regular or British American troops to garrison the territory (those who took part in the expeditions being intended to reinforce him at Charlotte) that reliance had to be placed on militia to take their place. Yet, as we have seen, none could be formed by Wemyss, whilst those left by Moncrief were not up to the job. It has been argued — unconvincingly, it may be said — that the expeditions served only to turn many against the Crown, but the inhabitants there were already so preponderantly and actively opposed that this proposition is unfounded.

Like Wemyss and Moncrief, Ferguson had been busy too. In compliance with Cornwallis's instructions he left Sugar Creek for Camden on 23rd August to discuss the part to be played by his corps and the Back Country militia in forthcoming operations. He rejoined his corps on 1st September near Fair Forest Creek, having obtained Cornwallis's approval to his making a rather hazardous advance into Tryon County, North Carolina, the purpose of which was to secure the left of Cornwallis's march. He was then to join the troops at Charlotte so that his corps and the militia might accompany the onward advance. Having crossed the frontier on the 7th, he proceeded to pass some time in and around Gilbertown, defeating McDowell at Cane Creek on the 12th. He then attempted to settle the county by disarming the disaffected and putting their arms into the hands of loyalists who came in. On the 14th he had some 650 militia with him, but they were old and infirm and part neither armed nor trained. By the 28th, when he was seeking to intercept Clark, his militia had increased to under 800, but of what quality he does not say. In the meantime he had mustered 500 loyalists within 25 miles of Gilbertown, 'half of whom are of the first class and arm'd', while another body nearly as numerous had been formed on the Catawba from its head forty miles downwards. Aware by now of the revolutionary parties gathering to oppose him, he was confident that, centrical as he was, he would prevent a general junction and remain master of the field. How wrong he was we shall relate later in this chapter.

---

[1] See vol I, pp 155-6.

As Cornwallis lingered at the Waxhaws, Elijah Clark, who had returned with about 200 men to the Ceded Lands in Georgia, incited some 500 more to join him and on 14th September made a surprise attack on Brown's post at Augusta. It was a close-run thing. Brown held out courageously but was saved only by the spirited and active conduct of Cruger, who came promptly to his relief. Clark with many of his party fled across the Savannah River and crossed some two weeks later into North Carolina, going off at the head of Saluda at a gap beyond Ferguson's reach. After the attack severe measures were taken to pacify the Ceded Lands.

Of the 2nd division intended to reinforce Cornwallis at Charlotte, only the 7th came up, much depleted by 106 sick left behind at Camden. Accompanying it were 150 convalescents - some for the 23rd, some for the 33rd, and the rest for the 71st – and a supply train of ten puncheons of rum and fifty-six bushels of salt. On 5th October they all arrived at the Waxhaws, and two days later the 7th, but not the convalescents, advanced to Charlotte. The rest of the 2nd division consisting of the 63rd and the Royal North Carolina Regiment never came up. Of the 71st, which had been posted at the Waxhaws, the 2nd Battalion was ordered forward on the 1st, whereas the 1st Battalion, which had initially been intended to meet Ferguson at Armour's Ford[2], was given its marching orders on the 8th. Together, they would have brought to Charlotte the numerous sick and convalescents left behind with them.

On 7th October Cornwallis explained his plan of campaign to Wemyss: 'The object of marching into North Carolina is only to raise men, which, from every account I have received of the number of our friends, there is great reason to hope may be done to a very considerable amount. For this purpose I shall move in about ten or twelve days to Salisbury and from thence invite all loyalists of the neighbouring countys to repair to our standard to be formed into Provincial corps and armed, clothed and appointed as soon as we can do it. From thence I mean to move my whole force down to Cross Creek [*to raise the Highlanders*]. As it will then be about the middle of November, I hope the lower country will be healthy. I shall then be in full communication with our shipping and shall receive all the arms and clothing that Charlestown can afford.' Wemyss, who had been intended to command an intermediate post at Charlotte, now to be abandoned due to the inveteracy of the locality, was instructed to operate again east of Camden before joining Cornwallis at Cross Creek, but his orders were almost immediately countermanded.

For Cornwallis, overstretched as he was, it was now that the chickens came home to roost.

Of the risks he was running, some would have been apparent to him at the start of the campaign, aware as he was that it might be an imprudent measure. Among the greatest risks was that of losing control of much of South Carolina and Georgia, so few were the troops that he left behind. Charlestown and Savannah were safe, but what about the rest of the country? If we leave aside the relative backwater of Georgetown, there were only two principal posts in South Carolina outside Charlestown – at Camden and the village of Ninety Six. Left to garrison Camden were the New York Volunteers and the South Carolina Royalist Regiment under the overall command of Lt Colonel George Turnbull, who, in the words of Cornwallis, 'tho'... not a great genius,... is a plain rightheaded man'. According to Turnbull, the South

---

[2] The ford lay near the mouth of the south fork of the Catawba. It was deep and crossing was at times dangerous.

Carolina Royalists, who did not arrive until 17th September, made a very sorry appearance and on the 22nd did duty for no more than 160 rank and file. By 2nd October only 91 of them were fit for duty, as some had fallen down with the small pox and others presumably with the other illnesses prevalent there. Two days later those fit for duty in both corps came to a total of 247. Admittedly, part of Hamilton's Royal North Carolina Regiment was also at Camden in September, as was the debris of the 63rd, and both were augmented by the arrival of Wemyss' party at the beginning of October. Yet neither corps formed part of the garrison, for both were awaiting orders (which never came) to reinforce Cornwallis. On 20th October, as Wemyss and the remains of the 63rd were about to depart next day for Ninety Six, the three British American regiments afforded no more than 300 men fit for duty. All in all, given the need to maintain the post of Camden itself, the garrison had precious few troops for exerting control over the vast expanse of territory dependent on it or for supporting the royal militia to this end. Alone, the royal militia were in Turnbull's eyes a busted flush. As he would soon observe, '... our officers of militia in general are not near so active as the rebels, and great numbers of their privates are ready to turn against us when an opportunity offers... Depend on it, militia will never do any good without regular troops.' With so few troops in the garrison to support them, the militia were, if attacked, an edifice waiting to crumble, far beyond the reach of Cornwallis to sustain them if he had penetrated deeper into North Carolina, taking Ferguson and Hamilton with him. That was the risk. Nor would it have been markedly lessened if an intermediate post under Wemyss had been established at Charlotte, so composed would it have been of convalescents. The risk was in fact low for only so long as Cornwallis remained within reach, Wemyss and Hamilton were not brought up to reinforce him, and Ferguson continued to protect the northern border against incursions. Even so, control of the area east of Camden had long been lost, and despite the deterrent effect of Wemyss' expedition, nothing could be done to reassert it. Cornwallis desperately sought to scrape the barrel at Camden for a further foray there, but it was all to no avail. Nothing really effective could be done but to advance Tynes' militia to the forks of Black River, where they were promptly routed by Marion, and to await Tarleton's punitive but brief incursion in November.

The situation at Ninety Six was pretty parlous too. Garrisoning the village were the 1st Battalion, De Lancey's Brigade, and the 3rd Battalion, New Jersey Volunteers, under the overall command of Lt Colonel John Harris Cruger. He had with him near 300 men fit for duty. As with Camden, the problem was not so much the post itself as the vast hinterland. Split as it was into tracts of loyalists and revolutionaries, the most worrying parts were the Long Cane settlement and the tract contiguous to it, being the catchment areas of King's and Kirkland's regiments. There the inhabitants were preponderantly disaffected and the bulk of the two regiments was not to be relied on. Of almost equal concern was a rebellious tract of 50 miles about the Tyger and Enoree, where the inhabitants had mostly fled and were waiting for Cornwallis and Ferguson to move on before they returned and commenced hostilities. In general the royal militia left behind by Ferguson were reluctant to turn out, and in any event Cruger was exceedingly short of men to support them. With Ferguson on the northern border and on his march to join Cornwallis, Cruger was of opinion that, if a tenuous hold on the district was to be maintained, a body of regular or British American troops was essential to occupy the area between the Broad and Saluda Rivers vacated by Ferguson. Unfortunately, none was available, and so there was a high risk that the district would be overrun. An intermediate post, if established at Charlotte, would have been too remote to have any effect. As matters turned out, Ferguson's defeat so dispirited the loyalists, and indeed the majority of them were so wearied by the long continuance of the war, that to a man they became unwilling to turn out and were ready to submit as soon as the enemy entered the territory. By then fearful of the threat to his post, Cruger was reduced to a bare defensive, controlling no more than the ground on which the post stood and an area five miles around. The situation was relieved only by the abandonment of the autumn campaign.

Despite the defeat of Clark, the British hold on the back parts of Georgia remained precarious. We have no record of the casualties sustained at Augusta, but at the time of Clark's attack Brown's garrison consisted of 199 men of the King's Rangers fit for duty, 35 members of the Indian Department, 100 convalescents of the King's Rangers and New Jersey Volunteers, and 500 native Americans who happened to be visiting the village. After the attack Cruger left upwards of 200 militia to complete the work of scouring the Ceded Lands. With so remarkably few troops and militia to maintain control of Augusta and the hinterland, the door remained open to enemy incursions, particularly after Ferguson's defeat, when Cruger was no longer in a position to come to Brown's aid. Here again, the situation was relieved only by Cornwallis's withdrawal to Winnsborough.

When asked by a journalist what would throw his administration off course, the British Prime Minister Harold Macmillan replied, 'Events, my dear boy, events.' It was now at Charlotte that unforeseen events conspired to terminate the autumn campaign.

The first of these was the entirely unexpected ferocity with which the inhabitants of the locality continued resolutely to oppose the occupation of Charlotte itself.[3] On 3rd October Cornwallis commented to Balfour, 'This County of Mecklenburg is the most rebellious and inveterate that I have met with in this country, not excepting any part of the Jerseys.' It soon became apparent that the village was completely unsuitable for a small intermediate post, so effectually would it have been blockaded and so high would have been the risk of its being taken out in detail. Preoccupied with defending itself, the post would have exerted no control over the surrounding territory and afforded no protection to messengers coming to and from Cornwallis as he pursued his onward march. Extraordinarily difficult as it already was to communicate with South Carolina (almost all of the messengers being waylaid), Cornwallis faced the prospect of totally losing the communication if he proceeded farther. He nevertheless contemplated advancing as late as the 11th, but as Rawdon explained to Balfour, the lack of communication with South Carolina brought about by the inveteracy of the Mecklenburg inhabitants, the uncertainty of cooperation with a diversionary force intended for the Chesapeake, and the possible consequences of a second event of calamitous proportions convinced him that he had to turn back. He quit Charlotte at sunset on the 14th.

The second event was the defeat of Ferguson. Why, as he became increasingly aware of the formidable force gathering to oppose him, he did not press ahead to join Cornwallis has long remained a puzzle. The answer may at first have lain partly in his having ideas beyond his station, that is to say, in his reluctance to forego a separate command, which he had previously exercised on more than one occasion, and partly, as evinced by these Papers, in his belief that he could take on and defeat his opponents himself. If initially the answer, it was eventually overtaken by another as Ferguson began to realise that his hopes of success

---

[3] See, for example, Tarleton, *Campaigns*, 159-161, and Hanger, *An Address to the Army*, 66-70.

were doubtful. Taking post on the 6th at King's Mountain, 'where I do not think that I can be forced by a stronger enemy than that against us', he called for 2 or 300 of Floyd's militia to join him the following evening unless they were destined for another service. With such a reinforcement 'we do not think ourselves inferior to the enemy if you are pleas'd to order us forward; but help so near at hand, it appear'd to me improper of myself to commit any thing to hasard.' It soon became clear that he was egregiously mistaken in believing that the risks of advancing outweighed for the time being those of remaining where he was. The terrain at King's Mountain proved ideal for an onslaught by revolutionary irregulars and he was totally defeated in the afternoon of the 7th. Ferguson was killed and his entire party consisting of the American Volunteers and some 800 militia was captured or killed.

Cornwallis for his part was not free of blame for the disaster. The war had shown that detachments such as Ferguson's were ever attended with danger and had thrown up various instances of their fatal and ruinous effects. While, admittedly, having sound reasons for not reinforcing Ferguson offensively, Cornwallis appears to have taken no account — at least in the short term — of the need to support him for defence.

Nothing is so certain as the unexpected, and it was the unexpected, magnifying the risks of losing territory to the south, that ultimately put paid to the northward invasion.

On 8th or 9th October Cornwallis had fallen ill with a feverish cold and the command had now devolved on Rawdon. His mettle was soon tested during the harrowing withdrawal from Charlotte. The troops began by taking the road leading to the Old Nation Ford on the Catawba and were guided by William McCafferty, a Scotch-Irish merchant in Charlotte who had remained behind in an endeavour to save his property. According to Joseph Graham, a revolutionary officer in the locality, 'McCafferty led them the road to the right about two miles below Charlotte, which goes to Park's Mill. When they got near that place, he suggested that they were on the wrong road and that he must ride a little out of the way to the left to find the right one. When he got a short distance from them, he wheeled about, as he well knew the country, and left them. The scene of confusion and disorder which succeeded among them is not easily described. They were two miles to the right of the road they intended to go, the night was dark, and being near Cedar Creek, they were intercepted by high hills and deep ravines. They attempted at different places to file to their left along byways in order to reach the main road; but finally most of them got into the woods, were separated into parties, and kept halooing to find which way their comrades had gone. By midnight they were three or four miles apart and appeared to be panic-struck lest the Americans should come upon them in that situation. They did not concentrate until noon the next day about seven miles from Charlotte. Owing to the difficult passes they took, the darkness of the night, and the scare upon them they left behind them forty wagons and considerable booty which was found dispersed for the most part near Park's Mill.' Completing the picture are the remarks of Charles Stedman, a British commissary who was present: 'In this retreat the King's troops suffered much, encountered the greatest difficulties; the soldiers had no tents; it rained for several days without intermission; the roads were over their shoes in water and mud. At night, when the army took up its ground, it encamped in the woods in a most unhealthy climate, for many days without rum. Sometimes the army had beef and no bread; at other times bread and no beef. For five days it was supported upon indian corn, which was collected as it stood in the field, five ears of which were the allowance for two soldiers for twenty-four hours... The water that the army drank was frequently as thick as puddle. Few armies ever encountered greater difficulties and hardships; the soldiers bore them with great patience and without a murmur. Their attachment to their commander supported them in the day of adversity, knowing, as they did, that their officers' and even Lords Cornwallis and Rawdon's fare was not better than their own. Yet, with all their resolution and patience, they could not have proceeded but for the personal exertions of the militia, who, with a zeal that did them infinite honour, rendered the most important services [*in obtaining provisions*].' It was only on the 21st, when the Catawba was passed at Lands Ford, that matters began to take a turn for the better.

The troops arrived at Winnsborough on the 29th, less the 7th Regiment and the sick, who had been sent to Camden. The village presented certain important advantages for an encampment. According to Tarleton, 'Its spacious plantations yielded a tolerable post; its centrical situation between the Broad River and the Wateree afforded protection to Ninety Six and Camden; and its vicinity to the Dutch Forks, and a rich country in the rear, promised abundant supplies of flour, forage, and cattle.'

It is easy to be wise after the event when we look back on the autumn campaign, but the question is not so much why the campaign was delayed – to which this chapter provides the answers – as why it ever took place. The plan was devised when South Carolina was in a quiescent state. As long as it remained so, it seemed reasonable to assume that public order could be maintained by leaving relatively few troops in support of the royal militia. Yet by the time that the campaign began the situation had markedly worsened. The territory east of the Wateree and Santee was in open revolt, the Back Country had been the scene of various actions and might be so again, and much of the royal militia was not to be relied on. Whether, in the light of the changed circumstances, it was right to throw caution to the winds and proceed with the original plan is debatable. On the one hand, much was to be gained if by entering North Carolina the many loyalists there would take up arms, but worryingly, when summoned to do so after the Battle of Camden, none had complied. On the other, much was to be lost if success or failure in North Carolina was vitiated or attended by losing control of much of the territory to the south. Overall, as belatedly recognised by Cornwallis when he brought Leslie to join him, it would have been better to call for a reinforcement before the campaign began so that South Carolina might have been left with a much larger number of troops to defend it. If such a call had been made and complied with, Cornwallis would have closed the door on the high risks set out earlier in this chapter.

Propelling Cornwallis to precipitate action was the political imperative of making progress swiftly. Unfortunately for him, he struck the wrong balance between political and military considerations, acted prematurely, and the collapse of the campaign almost inevitably ensued. '*Festina lente!*'[4] would have been a better maxim for success.

The autumn campaign is not the only occasion in these Papers when we shall question Cornwallis's strategic judgement. Part and parcel of it was his assessment, as stated at the beginning of this chapter, that it was necessary to retire within the walls of Charlestown unless the invasion of North Carolina was attempted. Such an apocalyptic view was at variance with Clinton's instructions of 1st June, which more or less implied that offensive

---

[4] 'Make haste slowly!' (Suetonius, *Augustus*, 25)

action had to be consistent with the security of Charlestown and its dependencies. Maintaining control of South Carolina — and incidentally Georgia — was thus the primary object, there were sufficient troops for this purpose, and the invasion of North Carolina was contingent on this requirement continuing to be met.

During the autumn campaign the war in the back parts of the Carolinas plumbed new depths of savagery. Unusually for a period in which writers out of delicacy omitted the details of barbarities, Ferguson on 1st October gave Cornwallis a graphic account of a particularly shocking case which he also mentioned in a call to arms published in unexpurgated form by Samuel Cole Williams: 'Two old men have been brought in here to day most barbarously maim'd by a party of Cleveland's men, who, after drinking with them in disguise for some time, fell upon them, altho unarm'd, and after butchering two young men, one of whom a son to one of the old, left them for dead and I fear past recovery.' They had lopped off the father's arms. Ferguson went on to observe, 'It appears from various accounts that Cleveland gives orders for such cowardly acts of cruelty,' a valid point also made elsewhere in these Papers.

Another low was reached at the close of the Battle of King's Mountain and in the ensuing days. Taking part in the Battle on the revolutionary side were 440 overmountain men, 310 North Carolinians, and 160 men from South Carolina. Courageous, hardy, but often uncultivated in mind or manners, they were expert marksmen ideally suited to take on Ferguson. Momentous as their victory was, it was tarnished by maltreatment of their prisoners, beginning at the surrender. Despite the white flags and kerchiefs raised by the loyalists, many revolutionaries continued firing until they were weary of the slaughter. In consequence 157 loyalists, but only 28 revolutionaries, were killed, and the numbers of wounded on either side were quite disproportionate too. The night was spent on the battlefield, but the cries of the wounded loyalists were little heeded and next day they were left to perish, having been stripped of their clothes and blankets. During the march of the rest into captivity 'there seems to have been individual cases of savage severity, even to murder, exercised towards the prisoners', so much so that Colonel William Campbell felt it necessary in his general orders of the 11th to 'request the officers of all ranks in the army to endeavor to restrain the disorderly manner of slaughtering and disturbing the prisoners'. Anthony Allaire, one of Ferguson's officers, gave an example of the sort of maltreatment that went on: 'Several of the militia that were worn out with fatigue, not being able to keep up, were cut down and trodden to death in the mire.' Perhaps the worst example, because it was 'officially' sanctioned, was the holding of a mock trial at Bickerstaff's Old Fields on the 14th, when some thirty of the loyalists were condemned to death and nine summarily hanged. As to Ferguson, the hatred of the revolutionaries was so intense that, not content with stripping his body naked, they urinated on it.

Maltreatment of loyalists east of Camden was also taking a downward turn. Although relatively few, they were being plundered and either dispersed or murdered in cold blood. By mid September Richard England at Camden was reporting to Cornwallis, 'There are hourly people coming in from Peedee giving dreadful accounts of the depredations committing there by the rebels. They bring in with them all their family, Negroes etc.'

Cornwallis for his part was also culpable. Despite implying to Germain on 23rd September that native Americans were to remain quietly at home, presumably on account of their indiscriminate form of warfare, he four days later agreed to Balfour's proposal to employ the Cherokees against the overmountain settlers, 'altho' it is positively contrary to my instructions'. 'Great nations,' observed George Hanger, 'have many individuals amongst them who as individuals are men of the greatest honour and probity, but great nations (speaking politically of them) are great rogues in their transactions with their natural enemy. So are great ministers and great generals, although in their private characters *they are all honourable men.*' By late October Brown at Augusta was busily arranging matters, and shortly afterwards the Cherokee attacks began. The upshot was that the overmountain settlers became too preoccupied with defending themselves to present a further threat to South Carolina and Georgia. The Cherokees would pay a high price for going on the warpath, many of their towns being razed to the ground in December and March.

The pressing need for more cavalry or mounted men becomes ever more apparent in this Part, given that the enemy were mostly mounted militia who could not be overtaken by infantry. 'Horse is the thing to cover this country,' commented Cruger, who was supported by Turnbull's following observation: 'Dragoons or mounted men must be got to check these rebells which lays waste the country and murders the well affected in cold blood.' For this reason Cornwallis approved the raising of a number of dragoons: two, possibly three, troops of 40 men each for Ninety Six, one of 60 for Camden, and possibly another of 60 for Georgetown. 'Altho' these corps may be expensive,' he remarked, 'I am convinced there can be no other means of securing the vast tract of country that it is necessary to guard.'

As ever, the British were losing the propaganda war. According to Cornwallis, 'Favorable accounts for us circulate very slowly, whilst the most improbable lies fly like lightning through the province.' The pernicious effect on the territory between Camden and the Pee Dee was described by Wemyss in a letter from Cheraw Hill: 'I have offered pardon to all people now in arms who have not broke their paroles or oath of allegiance that will surrender themselves, but without any effect. They are deluded in a most extraordinary manner by reports of a large army coming from the northward, the arrival of a French fleet and army etc etc,' none of which was presently true as far as the war in the south was concerned.

Now that King's Mountain had effectively demolished the royal militia as a force to be reckoned with in the Back Country, it had become incumbent on Cornwallis to plug the gap with regular and British American troops. Before again attempting an invasion of North Carolina, he had come to recognise that a reinforcement of such troops was essential, not only to secure the territory behind him, but also to supplement his force for the onward advance.

Having recovered from his illness, Cornwallis formally resumed his command on 1st November.

§ - §

Principal papers and works consulted in the writing of this chapter

The Cornwallis Papers (UK National Archives, Kew)

Lyman C Draper, *King's Mountain and its Heroes* (Cincinnati, 1881)

Marianne McLeod Gilchrist, *Patrick Ferguson, 'A Man of Some Genius'* (NMS Publishing, 2003)

Joseph Graham, 'Narrative', in William Henry Hoyt ed, *The Papers of Archibald D Murphey* (Publications of the North Carolina Historical Commission, Raleigh, 1914)

George Hanger, *An Address to the Army* (London, 1789)

George Hanger, *Anticipation of the Freedom of Brabant* (London, 1792)

David Schenck, *North Carolina 1780-81* (Raleigh, 1889)

Charles Stedman, *History of the Origin, Progress, and Termination of the American War* (London, 1792)

Banastre Tarleton, *A History of the Campaigns of 1780 and 1781 in the Southern Provinces of North America* (London, 1787)

Samuel Cole Williams, *Tennessee during the Revolutionary War* (University of Tennessee Press, 1974)

§ - §

CHAPTER 21

Letters to or from Germain, Clinton, Arbuthnot or Leslie

1 - To Germain

Cornwallis to Germain, 19th September 1780[1]   76(17): C

Nº 3

Camp at Waxhaw
September 19th 1780

Rt Hon Lord George Germain etc etc etc

My Lord

I had the honor to inform your Lordship in my letter of the 21st of August[2] that I had dispatched proper people into North Carolina to exhort our friends in that province to take arms, to seize military stores and magazines of the enemy, and to intercept all stragglers of the routed army.

Some parties of our friends who had embodied themselves near the Pedee disarmed several of the enemy's stragglers, but the leading persons of the loyalists were so undecided in their councils that they lost the critical time of availing themselves of our success and even suffered General Gates to pass to Hillsborough with a guard of six men only. They continue, however,

---

[1] Published in Stevens, *Clinton-Cornwallis Controversy*, i, 264. There are no differences.

[2] *my letter..*: see p 11.

to give me the strongest assurances of support when His Majesty's troops shall have penetrated into the interior parts of the province. The patience and fortitude with which they endure the most cruel torments and suffer the most violent oppressions that a country ever laboured under convince me that they are sincere, at least as far as their affection to the cause of Great Britain.

The number of prisoners taken in the actions of the 16th and 18th of last month occasioned great inconvenience to us in the small village of Camden, which was so crouded, and so sickly, I was afraid that the close place in which we were obliged to confine them might produce some pestilential fever during the excessive hot weather. I therefore sent them off to Charlestown as early as possible by divisions of one hundred and fifty each under the escort of thirty eight men, about two thirds of which were composed of the 63rd and Prince of Wales's Regiments and the rest militia. In order to cover their march, although I did not apprehend much danger, I posted Major Wemys with about one hundred men of the 63rd Regiment on the High Hills of Santee, and I sent Lt Colonel Tarleton with a detachment of the Legion and Lt Colonel Hamilton's corps and some militia to Ratcliffe's Bridge on Linches Creek, which I thought would effectually awe all the lower country. The disaffection, however, in the country east of Santee is so great that the account of our victory could not penetrate into it, any person daring to speak of it being threatened with instant death; and so great was the ignorance in which these people were kept that on the night of the 23rd of August a party of about two hundred of the inhabitants in the neighbourhood of Black River under the command of Colonel Marion went to Murray's Ferry, where they passed some men in canoes, drove away our militia guard, who fled at the first shot, and destroyed the ferry boats to prevent our making our escape from General Gates over the Santee. On the 24th they were proceeding to do the same at Nelson's Ferry when they heard of the march of the 1st division of prisoners and that they were to halt that night at Sumpter's house about six miles east of the ferry. The ensign of the militia of the escort contrived to get over to the enemy and conducted them to the attack of Sumpter's house, the consequence of which was that our escort was taken and the prisoners released. By this time some patroles of Lt Colonel Tarleton's to Kingstree Bridge on Black River had spread the alarm in that country; and the enemy, being perfectly convinced by the prisoners of General Gates's total defeat, retired with great precipitation to Georgetown. Great part of the escort escaped from them, and above eighty of the prisoners, all Continentals either English or Irish, declared their determination to proceed to Charlestown.

I am sorry to inform your Lordship that the troops under my command, as well officers as men, have continued very sickly ever since the action. In hopes that the change of air might be usefull I moved from Camden on the 7th of this month with the 23rd, 33rd and Volunteers of Ireland and encamped on Waxhaw Creek. Lt Colonel Tarleton marched the next day with the light troops up the west side of the Catawba River. The 71st Regiment, who are beginning a little to recover, are to join me in a few days. Major Wemyss is gone with part of the 63rd Regiment and of Lt Colonel Hamilton's corps to endeavour to form a militia in the District of Cheraws on whose fidelity we may place some dependance, and to punish those traitors who, after voluntarily engaging in our militia, deserted to the enemy. Detachments are likewise gone for the same purpose to Georgetown.

I must assure your Lordship that His Majesty's Service has derived the greatest advantages from the ability and great exertion of Lt Colonel Balfour in the very important post of

Commandant of Charlestown, where he has put every thing into such perfect order, and has formed so respectable a militia, that with the concurrence of Major Moncrief, the chief engineer, he is enabled to spare another battalion for the field notwithstanding the increase of prisoners, in consequence of which the 7th Regiment is now on its march to join me.

By the capitulation of Charlestown the town militia were allowed to remain on parole and their property in town was to be secured to them. About twenty or thirty of them who had been the ringleaders of rebellion in this province held constant meetings from which they carried on a correspondence with the enemy and with all the disaffected parts of the province, and received, in order to propagate it throughout the town and country adjacent, General Gates's proclamation[3]. They advanced in the most publick and insolent manner the grossest falsehoods tending to encourage the disaffected and to terrify the well disposed inhabitants and seemed to imagine that their parole was intended only to protect them without laying them under any restraint whatever. It was impossible, with safety to the town full of rebel prisoners, to suffer them to persevere in these dangerous practices. I therefore ordered them to be seized and transported with their baggage to St Augustine, where they will remain on parole without a possibility of hurting the interests of Great Britain. I am aware that this proceeding may raise a clamour amongst the enemies of my country, but I am fully convinced that it was as just as it was absolutely necessary.[4]

I transmit to your Lordship a copy of a proclamation[5] which I thought myself under the necessity of issuing relative to the sequestration of rebel property. The severe mortification which it must occasion to His Majesty's loyal subjects on this continent to see their estates confiscated and themselves and their families reduced to beggary, whilst their inhuman persecutors, who have brought ruin and destruction on them, are suffered to persist openly in the avowal of rebellion and to continue to enjoy by permission of the British Government the full possession of their property, renders this measure in my opinion absolutely indispensable, and as it can affect no future plan and only appropriates those funds to the present use of Government which would otherwise be employed against it, I flatter myself that it will meet with His Majesty's approbation.

The great sickness of the army, the intense heat, and the necessity of totally subduing the rebel country between the Santee and Pedee have detained me longer than I could have wished on the frontiers of this province. I am likewise anxious to hear from New York, from whence I have no accounts since the 15th of July. I hope, however, that nothing can prevent my entering North Carolina before the end of this month.

---

[3] *Gates's proclamation*: dated 4th August, it appears in Tarleton, *Campaigns*, 140-2. Offering pardon to those South Carolinians who had been induced to acquiesce in British rule, it invited them, when called upon, to rise in opposition to it. Exempted from the offer were those who had 'exercised acts of barbarity and depredations on the persons of their fellow citizens' and those who would continue to side with the British.

[4] Among many others, a tendentious account of this event appears in McCrady, *SC in the Rev 1775-1780*, 716-726.

[5] *a proclamation*: see pp 323-4.

I have the honour to be
Your Lordship's most obedient and most humble servant

[CORNWALLIS]

Cornwallis to Germain, 21st September 1780[6]

76(21): C

Nº 4

Waxhaw
September 21st 1780

Rt Hon Lord George Germain etc etc etc

My Lord

I have received accounts from Lt Colonel Cruger commanding at Ninety Six that a rebel Colonel Clarke, who had retired to the mountains, had returned to the Ceded Lands in Georgia, where the inhabitants are universally disaffected and where he had reason to apprehend a very serious insurrection. Reports have come through several channels that Lt Colonel Brown of the Florida Rangers, who is stationed with his corps at Augusta, was actually attacked at that place, but I have no certain information of it.

Lt Colonel Cruger has marched with about 200 Provincials and what militia he could collect into the Long Cane settlement, which lies to the westward of Ninety Six towards the Savannah River, and which is much inclined to rebellion. He will endeavour to establish tranquillity there and then proceed if necessary into the Ceded Lands. I sincerely hope that Lt Colonel Cruger will be able to suppress this insurrection without requiring any assistance from me, which might occasion some delay in our operations. Major Ferguson with about eighty Provincials and five or six hundred militia has made an incursion into the mountainous parts of Tryon County, where he has gained some advantages over the rebel militia and dispersed some parties who were said to be marching to join the insurgents on the Ceded Lands.

I omitted mentioning to your Lordship that Major Harrison had failed in his attempt to raise a Provincial corps, and that I was obliged to put a stop to Lt Colonel Cunningham, who was more likely to succeed, on finding that all the principal officers of Ninety Six were entering into it, by which means I should have been totally deprived of the use of that militia for the present, and that it would have been several months before any service could be expected from his corps.

By the arrival of the packet at Charlestown, which brought me His Majesty's Speech and the Addresses of the Houses of Parliament transmitted by your Lordship, together with the Acts of the last session relative to America[7], I learn that the Post Office has established that

---

[6] Published in Davies ed, *Docs of the Am Rev*, xviii, 172-3. There is only one difference: as published in Davies, the third paragraph inserts the words 'of the militia' after 'all the principal officers'.

[7] The papers received by Cornwallis are not extant.

regular channel of intercourse, which will be very convenient and give the greatest satisfaction to this province.

I have the honor to be
Your Lordship's most obedient and most humble servant

[CORNWALLIS]

Cornwallis to Germain, 23rd September 1780 — 76(22): ADfS

Nº 5

Camp at Waxhaw
September 23rd 1780

Rt Hon Lord George Germain etc etc etc

My Lord

In my dispatch Nº 4 I informed your Lordship that I had some reason to apprehend that Lt Colonel Brown, who was stationed with the Florida Rangers at Augusta and who was holding a talk with the Indians, had been attacked by a body of rebels from the Ceded Lands.

I received a letter from Lt Colonel Cruger[8] informing me that 700 rebels under Colonel Clarke had surprized the Indian camp and killed several of them and taken the stores intended for them, that they afterwards attacked Lt Colonel Brown, who retired to a small work, which he defended for above two days without water and was during the whole time canonaded by two guns which the enemy had taken from him.

Lt Colonel Cruger, whose zeal, spirit and activity on this occasion cannot be too much commended, arrived just in time to save him and the remains of his corps. The enemy fled with the utmost precipitation, leaving the guns and great part of the stores. The Indians pursued and scalped several of them.

It may be proper to observe to your Lordship that the Indians were on a peaceable and friendly visit to Lt Colonel Brown, who had directions to give them presents and to exhort them to remain quietly at home and take no part in the present troubles in this country.

Lt Colonel Cruger commends very much the gallant defence made by Lt Colonel Brown and the garrison of Augusta.

I have the honour to be
Your Lordship's most obedient and most humble servant

CORNWALLIS

---

[8] *a letter...*: of 19th September. See p 190.

2 - To or from Clinton, Arbuthnot or Leslie

Cornwallis to Clinton, 29th August 1780 [9]   *72(47): ADf*

Camden
August 29th 1780

Sir

I send duplicates of my letters of the 23rd and of those of the 6th and 10th of this month[10]. Nothing very material has occurred since the 23rd. We receive the strongest professions of friendship from North Carolina. Our friends, however, do not seem inclined to rise untill they see our army in motion. The severity of the rebel government has so terrified and totally subdued the minds of the people that it is very difficult to rouse them to any exertions. The taking that violent and cruel incendiary, General Rutherford, has been a lucky circumstance, but the indefatigable Sumpter is again in the field and is beating up for recruits with the greatest assiduity. Major Wemys is going with a detachment of the 63rd Regiment mounted, some refugees, Provincials and militia to disarm in the most rigid manner the country between Santee and Pedee and to punish severely all those who submitted or pretended to live peaceably under His Majesty's Government since the reduction of Charlestown and have joined in this second revolt; and I ordered him to hang up all those militia men who were concerned in seizing their officers and capturing the sick of the 71st Regiment. I have myself ordered several militia men to be executed who had voluntarily enrolled themselves and borne arms with us and afterwards revolted to the enemy.

The number of prisoners was a great inconvenience to us here in a small village so crowded and sickly. I was afraid that the close place in which we were obliged to confine them might produce some pestilential fever during the excessive hot weather. I therefore sent them off as early as possible by divisions of 150 each under the escort of 38 men, about two thirds of which were composed of the 63rd and Prince of Wales's Regiments, the rest militia. In order to cover their march, altho' I did not apprehend much danger, I posted Major Wemys with a part of the 63rd at the High Hills of Santee, and I sent Lt Colonel Tarleton with a detachment of the Legion and Lt Colonel Hamilton's corps and some militia to Ratcliffe's Bridge on Linches Creek, which I thought would effectually awe all the lower country. The disaffection, however, in the country east of Santee is so great that the account of our victory could not penetrate into it, any person daring to speak of it being threatned with instant death; and so great was the ignorance in which these people were kept that on the night of the 23rd a party of about 200 mounted militia under a Colonel Marion went to Murray's Ferry, where they passed some men in canoes, drove away our militia guard, and destroyed the ferry boats to prevent our making our escape from General Gates over the Santee. On the 24th they were proceeding to do the same at Nelson's Ferry when they heard of the march of the 1st division

---

[9] Published in Stevens, op cit, i, 261. There are no material differences.

[10] See pp 15-18 and vol I, pp 175 and 179.

of prisoners and that they were to halt that night at Sumpter's house, which halting place was not very well chosen by the Quarter Master General. The ensign of the militia of the escort contrived to get over to the enemy and conducted them to the attack, the consequence of which was that our escort was taken and the prisoners released. By this time some patroles of Lt Colonel Tarleton's to Kingstree Bridge on Black River had spread the alarm in their rear, and being perfectly convinced by the prisoners of General Gates's total defeat, they retired with great precipitation to Georgetown. Great part of the escort escaped from them, and above eighty of the prisoners, all Continentals either English or Irish, declared their determination to proceed to Charlestown. I am assured that not more than 12 of the escort and 40 of the prisoners were carried off by the enemy. I believe that Captain Roberts of the 63rd, who commanded the escort, did his duty perfectly well and was not to blame in any respect.[11]

I hope to be able to move my first division in eight or nine days into North Carolina by Charlottetown and Salisbury. The second will follow in about ten days after with convalescents and stores. I shall leave the New York Volunteers and Innes's corps to take care of this place untill the sick and stores can be removed. Our sickness at present is rather at a stand, the recovery's nearly keeping place with the falling down. I dread the convalescents not being able to march, but it is very tempting to try it, as a move of forty or fifty miles would put us into a much better climate. Ferguson is to move into Tryon County with some militia whom he says he is sure he can depend on for doing their duty and fighting well, but I am sorry to say that his own experience as well as that of every other officer is totally against him. I am very anxious to hear again from the northward, as our accounts of the French fleet were very imperfect. I most sincerely hope that nothing can happen to prevent your Excellency's intended diversion in the Chesapeak. If unfortunately any unforeseen cause should make it impossible, I should hope that you will see the absolute necessity of adding some force to the Carolinas.

[I have the honour to be
Your most obedient and most humble servant

CORNWALLIS]

---

[11] Cornwallis's exculpation of Captain Lieutenant Jonathan Roberts was premature, as five days later Wemyss was to write to Cornwallis, strongly implying negligence. Roberts had spent his entire career in the 63rd Regiment, entering as an ensign on 25th July 1771 and rising to lieutenant in June 1775 and to captain lieutenant three years later. Now on parole, he would perhaps be exchanged in October. (*The Cornwallis Papers*; *Army Lists*)

Cornwallis to Clinton, 3rd September 1780   *72(51): ADf*

Camden
September 3rd 1780

Sir Henry Clinton KB etc etc etc

Sir

As it is very uncertain whether I shall be able to procure a tolerably safe conveyance for my dispatches to New York, it being impossible to spare either the *Loyalist* or *Sandwich* without interfering with the convoy of provisions and galleys to Cape Fear River or leaving this port totally unguarded, I shall desire Lt Colonel Balfour to send triplicates and quadruplicates by the best opportunities he can find, appointing a trusty person to go in each vessel on whom he can depend for sinking the dispatches in case of imminent danger.

Ever since the reduction of Charlestown a number of the principal and most violent inhabitants have held constant meetings in town and carried on correspondence with the country to keep up the flame of rebellion and impose on the ignorant by spreading false reports throughout the whole province to encourage the disaffected and intimidate the others. I was so convinced of the necessity of putting a stop to their proceedings that I had thoughts of seizing the heads of the cabal before I left Charlestown, but coming from thence in an hurry and apprehending that, in the critical situation in which affairs then stood, it might be considered rather as an act of fear than of justice, I resolved to defer it untill something decisive happened between the two armies. After the action I directed Lt Colonel Balfour, in case their cabals still continued, to apprehend those whom Mr Simpson thought the most dangerous amongst them, in consequence of which order the persons whose names I have the honour of inclosing to you[12] were on the morning of the 27th put on board of the *Sandwich* and were informed that they were to proceed with their baggage to St Augustine, where they would be allowed to remain on their parole. Perhaps it may be found necessary to add a few more to the inclosed list. Mr Simpson is clearly of opinion that the changing their place of residence on parole from Charlestown to St Augustine is no breach of the capitulation, but as I have intelligence of their corresponding with the enemy, of their propagating false reports, and receiving General Gates's proclamation, there cannot in my opinion remain a doubt that the measure will appear as just as it was expedient. Lt Colonel Balfour, whose indefatigable attention to his very important charge I cannot enough commend, feels himself so secured by this last event that, by putting the prisoners taken in the late actions on board of prison ships, he is enabled to send the 7th Regiment to join the army. This regiment, altho' it does not consist of more than 220 men doing duty, is still a very valuable acquisition to me and, added to the sanguine hopes that your Excellency will be able soon to carry into execution your intentions of a diversion in the Chesapeak, will make me undertake my arduous march with some confidence.

The great fatigue which the cavalry underwent during the violent heat of the summer, their great exertions in the action and pursuit of the 16th and the two subsequent days untill the

---

[12] *the persons..*: see pp 77-8.

defeat of Sumpter, and the scarcity of forage have reduced the horses to the most wretched condition. My only hopes are in the abilities of Tarleton, which supply every deficiency.

I have the honour to be
Your most obedient and most humble servant

[CORNWALLIS]

Cornwallis to Clinton, 22nd and 23rd September 1780[13]   72(53): ADfS

Camp at Waxhaw
September 22nd 1780

His Excellency Sir Henry Clinton KB etc etc etc

Sir

A few days ago the *Granville* packet arrived from England and I find that a monthly packet is established by the Post Office between Falmouth and Charlestown. In consequence of this settled communication and the state of the southern provinces, which are not likely to be soon so quiet as to leave no anxiety upon the Minister's mind about them, I really thought that it would be considered as a criminal neglect by Government if the commanding officer suffered any good opportunity to pass without communicating the situation of affairs in this part of the world. I inclose to your Excellency duplicates of my dispatches N° 3 and 4 to Lord George Germain[14].

Our anxiety is very great to hear from New York. Various reports relative to affairs to the northward come in from the country. Amongst others it is said that your Excellency has gained a very great advantage over General Washington and taken West Point. I most sincerely wish it may be true.

Our sickness has been increasing all this month, but as the weather is now growing cooler, I have great hopes we shall find a favourable change.

I marched from Camden on the 7th with the 23rd, 33rd and Volunteers of Ireland, meaning to take post here and live on the flour of this rebellious settlement untill the 71st should be in a condition to join me, as a great number of their men who had missed the fever for some time were still too weak to march.

Tarleton passed the Wateree on the eighth and marched between it and Broad River, where he found plenty of forage. On the 16th he left his corps on Fishing Creek and came over to me to receive directions for his future operations. I ordered him to advance on the 18th, to

---

[13] An extract from paragraph 6 appears in Stevens, op cit, i, 269.

[14] *my dispatches..*: see pp 36 and 39.

push on if he could with safety as far as Charlottetown, and endeavour to strike some blow at one of the bodies of militia which were assembled in that neighbourhood under Generals Sumpter and Davidson[15] or a corps of cavalry under Major Davie[16], which consisted of about 100 and were esteemed rather better than militia. On the 19th I had the infinite mortification to hear that Lt Colonel Tarleton, instead of having marched, was very dangerously ill, and for two days I have been under the greatest anxiety for him. His fever has now intermitted and the surgeons think him out of danger. I wish much to remove him, as his corps is twenty miles from me and I do not approve of a corps consisting chiefly of cavalry remaining long together at a fixed post and twenty miles from any support. I cannot go to him without abandoning this country to the enemy and leaving some of my sick, which are so numerous that I have not waggons sufficient to remove them. I have sent Lieutenant Money[17] of the 63rd, who acts as my aid de camp and who is a very intelligent good officer, to get Tarleton put into a covered waggon as soon as it can be done with safety, and in the mean time to keep the corps alert. Hanger is here in a very weak state and every captain of the Legion, and indeed every officer but one of the cavalry, is left sick at Camden.

---

[15] Born in Lancaster County, Pennsylvania, William Lee Davidson (1746-1781) was soon brought by his parents to Rowan County, North Carolina. By 1780, as a field officer in the North Carolina Continental line, he had seen distinguished service in the northern theatre of operations and was now a brigadier general in the North Carolina revolutionary militia commanding the Salisbury District. He would be killed at Cowan's Ford, North Carolina, on 1st February 1781 when opposing Cornwallis's passage of the Catawba. Davidson College and Davidson Counties in North Carolina and Tennessee are named after him. (Chalmers Gaston Davidson, *The Life and Times of Brigadier-General William Lee Davidson* (Davidson College NC, 1951), *passim*.

[16] Born in England, William Richardson Davie (1756-1820) was brought to Waxhaw, South Carolina, in 1763 and educated at Queen's Museum College, Charlotte, and at Princeton. From there he went on to study law at Salisbury, North Carolina, and was licensed to practise in 1780. Having helped to raise a troop of cavalry, he took part in the action at Stono Ferry in June 1779 and was seriously wounded. Now recovered, he had raised and equipped at his own expense another troop of cavalry and two troops of mounted infantry and participated in the action at Hanging Rock on 6th August 1780. For the rest of the year he operated in the Waxhaws and was notably involved in the action at Wahab's plantation and in an encounter with the van of Cornwallis's force on its entry into Charlotte. When Greene arrived in December, Davie was pressed into accepting the post of Commissary General and played an indispensable part in feeding the southern revolutionary forces. After the war he became a successful lawyer, an influential member of the North Carolina legislature, and Governor, besides being appointed Peace Commissioner to France. He was also responsible for the establishment and endowment of the University of North Carolina. He retired from politics in 1805 and spent his remaining years at 'Tivoli', his plantation in Lancaster County, South Carolina. There have been two biographies of Davie, the first by Fordyce M Hubbard in Jared Sparks ed, *The Library of American Biography*, second series, xv (Boston, 1848), and the second by Blackwell P Robinson (the University of North Carolina Press, 1957), the nature of which may be deduced from the writer's prefatory remark that 'a careful check of all available sources has failed to reveal any blemish in Davie's private or public career', a remark which, if nothing else, is at variance with Davie's owning and dealing in slaves (see, for example, p 348). The latter biography was sponsored by the North Carolina Society of the Cincinnati. Davie's own revolutionary war sketches, edited by Robinson, were published by the North Carolina Department of Cultural Resources in 1976.

[17] From East Bergholt in Suffolk, John Money (*c*. 1755-1780) had been commissioned an ensign in the 63rd on 12th July 1773 and was promoted to lieutenant in the regiment on 23rd November 1775. With the absence of Alexander Ross, who had been dispatched to England with news of the Battle of Camden, Money joined Cornwallis's suite as an aide-de-camp at the end of August. He has left an interesting journal, which appears at the end of this volume, in which he describes events in September leading to the occupation of Charlotte. After the disablement and paroling of Wemyss at Fish Dam Ford, Money would assume command of the 63rd and take part in the action at Blackstocks. He was mortally wounded and died at Brierly's Ferry on 1st December. According to Cornwallis, he was 'a most promising officer'; according to an adversary, he was remembered with 'grateful respect'. (*Army Lists*; *The Cornwallis Papers*; Garden, *Anecdotes* (2nd series), 103)

A very serious and to me a very unexpected insurrection has happened on the Ceded Lands in Georgia. The object of it I believe to be chiefly the presents and stores collected there by Colonel Brown for the Indians. Your Excellency will see by his letter[18] that he was in great danger. I hope, however, Colonel Cruger will arrive in time to save him and that it will not occasion any material retardment in our operations. I do not know what field pieces Colonel Brown had with him, and which he mentions to have fallen into the enemy's hands, but I hope and trust they were not brass. If nothing material happens to obstruct my plan of operations, I mean, as soon as Lt Colonel Tarleton can be removed, to proceed with the 23rd, 33rd, Volunteers of Ireland and Legion to Charlottetown and leave the 71st here untill the sick can be brought on to us. I then mean to make some redoubts and establish a fixed post at that place and give the command of it to Major Wemys, whose regiment is so totally demolished by sickness that it will not be fit for actual service for some months. To that place I shall bring up all the sick from Camden who have any chance of being serviceable before Christmas, and trust to opportunities for their joining the army. The post at Charlottetown will be a great security to all this frontier of South Carolina, which, even if we were possessed of the greatest part of North Carolina, would be liable to be infested by parties who have retired with their effects over the mountains and mean to take every opportunity of carrying on a predatory war; and it will, I hope, prevent insurrections in this country, which is very disaffected. I then think of moving on my principal force to Salisbury, which will open the country sufficiently for us to see what assistance we may really expect from our friends in North Carolina and will give us a free communication with the Highlanders, on whom my greatest dependence is placed. If from the state of affairs to the northward your Excellency should think it probable that our operations may proceed in North Carolina, I shall be in want of arms. Great numbers of those taken in the late actions were broke in the first rage of the soldiers, and as I have found the militia to fail so totally when put to the trial in this province, I am determined to try Provincial corps alone in the next, who must all be armed with a firelock and bayonet.

I inclose to your Excellency a proclamation which I thought it absolutely necessary to issue in regard to the sequestration of rebel property. I have given my reasons for it in my letter to the Secretary of State[19]. It will give me great satisfaction to receive your approbation of it.

September 23rd

I did not finish my letter in hopes of hearing from Lt Colonel Cruger and have now the satisfaction of inclosing his letter of the 19th[20], which has made me pretty easy about that business.

I have the satisfaction of informing you that Lt Colonel Tarleton was well enough this morning to be moved in a litter and he is now close to the ford. I am not sure whether they

---

[18] *his letter*: of 15th September. See p 189.

[19] *my letter..*: see p 36.

[20] *his letter..*: see p 190.

will be able to get the litter over the ford, but at any rate he is much safer.

I have the honour to be, sir,
Your most obedient and most humble servant

CORNWALLIS

Cornwallis to Arbuthnot, 23rd September 1780   80(37): C

Camp at Waxhaw
September 23rd 1780

His Excellency Vice Admiral Arbuthnot etc etc etc

Dear Sir

It is very long since we have had any news from the northward and you may easily imagine that we are exceeding anxious. The enemy informs us that the French fleet and army under Messrs Ternay[21] and Rochambeau[22] arrived at Rhode Island on the 9th of July. They talk of a second division being arrived at Boston, but as none of them speak with certainty about it, I take the liberty of doubting that part of the story. I have done myself the honor of sending you four copies of the history of our proceedings, some of which I hope you have received. A dangerous insurrection happened lately on the Ceded Lands, which are on the Savanah River above Augusta. Seven hundred rebels surprised Lt Colonel Brown with his garrison of three hundred men and about the same number of Indians, to whom he was giving presents and entertainments, took his cannon and several of his men. However, he retired to a little work, where he defended himself two days without water, when Lt Colonel Cruger came to his assistance, drove off the rebels, who retired with the greatest precipitation, and retook the canon. You see we have not quite a life of peace and quiet. I am sure I need not remind you of our naval weakness at Charlestown. The *Sandwich* must absolutely go with

---

[21] Charles Louis d'Arsac, Chevalier de Ternay (1722-1780), was of an old Breton family with a naval tradition. Re-entering the French naval service as an admiral in 1779, he had recently escorted Rochambeau's expeditionary force to North America, arriving off Newport, Rhode Island, on 10th July with eight ships of the line, two frigates, and two bomb-galliots. He would die of a fever in Newport on 15th December. 'He was,' wrote Lafayette, 'a very rough and obstinate man, but firm and clear in all his views, and, taking all things into consideration, we have sustained a great loss.' (Boatner, *Encyclopedia*, 1093-4)

[22] Jean Baptiste Donatien de Vimeur, Comte de Rochambeau (1725-1807) was a lt general commanding the French expeditionary force. Consisting of 5,500 men, it had arrived in thirty transports escorted by Admiral Ternay (see above). At a meeting with Washington on 21st September Rochambeau had resisted Washington's inclination to launch an assault on New York without command of the sea. Soon he would place his troops in winter quarters at Rhode Island. With the coming of the summer he would be involved with Washington in a strategic diversion against New York in the hope of drawing British troops from the south. When in August he learned of the imminent arrival of de Grasse, he would support the march to Virginia and take part in the Yorktown campaign. It fell to him to sign the articles of capitulation on behalf of the land forces of France. The event was the high point of a military career distinguished by personal bravery, fine strategic and tactical awareness, and administrative skill. Although a disciplinarian, he displayed an unusual solicitude for the welfare of his men. (Boatner, op cit, 938-940; *DAB*)

the galleys into Cape Fear River if we make any progress in North Carolina. I have entire confidence in your care for the good of the service and your regard for your friends to the southward and shall not presume to dictate to you.

I hear that Captain Fortescue[23], Lady Lothian's brother, is coming out to this station in a sloop. Any favour you can shew him I shall consider as the greatest personal obligation conferred on myself.

Governor Martin desires me to present his best respects.

I am, dear sir,
Most faithfully yours

CORNWALLIS

[*Postscript in Cornwallis's hand*:]

I have sent you a 6th proclamation[24], of which I hope you will approve.

Clinton to Cornwallis, 20th September 1780   *3(54): LS*

New York
September 20th 1780

The Earl Cornwallis

My Lord

I was honored with your Lordship's dispatches by the *Triton* on the 24th ultimo[25], and I had the pleasure of receiving early yesterday morning your letters of the 23rd of that month[26], by a small schooner from Charles Town, informing me of the compleat victory obtained by your Lordship on the 16th over the rebel southern army commanded by General Gates, upon which event I most heartily congratulate your Lordship. And I am also to thank you for the early opportunity you took of communicating this very important success to the Minister.

---

[23] The Hon Matthew Fortescue (1754-1842) was the second son of Matthew, second Earl Fortescue. Commissioned a lieutenant in the Royal Navy on 3rd September 1775, he was coming out to the North American station in command of the *Daphne*, a 20-gun sloop. He would be promoted to commander on 22nd June 1781 and to post-captain on 24th May 1782. (Marshall, *Royal Naval Biography*; Syrett and DiNardo ed, *The Commissioned Sea Officers*)

[24] *6th proclamation*: the one relating to sequestration issued on 16th September. See pp 323-4.

[25] *your Lordship's dispatches..*: see vol I, pp 175-180.

[26] *your letters..*: see pp 15-18.

At the same time, my Lord, permit me to convey thro' your Lordship to the troops who acted under your orders the very high sense I entertain of their spirited conduct on that glorious occasion. My most grateful acknowledgements are sincerely offered to your Lordship, to Colonel Lord Rawdon, the Lieutenant Colonels Webster and Tarleton and the other officers and men of your army. And I have no doubt you will soon receive from His Majesty the fullest approbation and praise which such signal services deserve.

I have always thought operation in Chesapeak of the greatest importance and have often represented to Admiral Arbuthnot the necessity of making a diversion in your Lordship's favor in that quarter but have not been able 'till now to obtain a convoy for this purpose. I have communicated to Sir George Rodney my wishes to send an expedition thither and he has most chearfully consented to grant every necessary naval assistance. In the course, therefore, of a very few days it will be dispatched, every thing having been in great forwardness before Sir George's arrival in consequence of Admiral Arbuthnot's having sent me all the ships he could spare for that service.

Your Lordship will receive inclosed a sketch of the instructions I intend to give Major General Leslie, who will command the expedition, which will give a general idea of the design of that move, but if your Lordship should wish any particular cooperation from that armament, General Leslie will of course consider himself under your Lordship's orders and pay every obedience thereto.

I have ever had an eye to what your Lordship mentions relative to the delivery of the enemy's prisoners, and General Phillips, who is now at Elizabeth Town conferring with General Lincoln upon the subject of a general exchange, has received his instructions accordingly.

In consequence of your Lordship's desire I have directed the Deputy Paymaster at Charles Town to receive the Commandant's warrants for the subsistence of the troops in garrison in your Lordship's absence, and a deputy paymaster will be sent with the expedition to attend the army in the field.

I have much pleasure in confirming your Lordship's appointment of Major Hanger to the Legion as well as in approving of your having allowed pay and forage money to Lt Colonels Webster and Clarke as brigadiers and of your intention of offering the same to Lord Rawdon; and I am also willing to extend the like allowance to Lt Colonel Balfour as Commandant of Charlestown for the reasons your Lordship mentions.

I shall be happy to pay every attention to your Lordship's recommendation relative to the succession in your own regiment as well as what you request respecting the appointment of a major to the 23rd in the room of Major Mecan.

I have the honor to inclose the copy of a letter I wrote to Lord George Germain and of his Lordship's answer respecting the option Lord Rawdon had made in favor of his Provincial rank, and I am happy in having it in my power to communicate to his Lordship the King's pleasure that he should still retain his rank of lt colonel in the line, which I beg leave to take this opportunity of doing thro' your Lordship.

I have the honor to be
Your Lordship's most obedient and most humble servant

H CLINTON

PS

I have the honor to inclose to your Lordship an extract of the Minister's letter to me upon the reduction of Charles Town.

Enclosure (1)
Sketch of instructions to Leslie   3(62): Df
for the expedition to the Chesapeake[27]

Major General Leslie

Sir

You will be pleased to proceed with the troops[28] embarked under your command to Chesapeak Bay, and upon your arrival at that place you will pursue such measures as you shall judge most likely to answer the purpose of this expedition, the principal object of which is to make a diversion in favor of Lt General Earl Cornwallis, who, by the time you arrive there, will probably be acting in the back parts of North Carolina.

The information you shall procure on the spot after your arrival at your destined port will point out to you the properest method of accomplishing this, but by that which I have received here I should judge it best to proceed up James River as high as possible in order to seize or destroy any magazines the enemy may have at Petersburg, Richmond or any of the places adjacent and finally to establish a post on Elizabeth River; but this, as well as the direction of every other operation, is submitted to Earl Cornwallis, with whom you are as soon as possible to communicate and afterwards to follow all such orders and directions as you shall from time to time receive from his Lordship.

HC

---

[27] The instructions when issued were dated 10th October and appear in Stevens, op cit, i, 270. They omit the marginal insertion mentioned in the next note.

[28] *the troops*: the words 'about three thousand' are inserted in the margin.

Enclosure (2)
Clinton to Germain, 3rd June 1780[29]   *3(45): C*

N° 92

Head Quarters
Charlestown
South Carolina
June 3rd 1780

Rt Hon Lord George Germain

My Lord

Lord Rawdon, in consequence of His Majesty's order signified to me by your Lordship, has resigned his commission of lt colonel in the army and made choice of that of colonel of Provincials.

In justice to his Lordship as well as to the King's Service I must observe that the expences Lord Rawdon has been at and the distinguished zeal he has shewn in forming the corps under his command render him worthy much commendation and make the alternative put to him a very mortifying one, whilst, on the other hand, the Volunteers of Ireland, bereft of a chief of his Lordship's rank in life and attention to the service, would probably have lost much in their strength and discipline.

Perhaps His Majesty may be graciously pleased to consider his Lordship in the light of an officer who, for the good of His Service and the preservation of a very serviceable corps, to which he felt a kind of parental attachment, has offered to relinquish rank essential to his future hopes as a soldier, and may in consequence restore to him his brevet of lt colonel in the army.

I have the honor to be with the greatest respect
Your Lordship's most obedient and most humble servant

H CLINTON

---

[29] Published in Stevens, op cit, i, 218. There are no differences.

Enclosure (3)
The order to which enclosure (2) refers 99(1): C

Extract from Barrington[30] to Howe, War Office, 18th May 1778

The Colonel of the 6th Regiment of Foot[31] having represented that one of his officers is appointed to a commission in some of the Provincial corps serving under your command, you will be pleased to direct Lieutenant Pettener to make his option between the two commissions; and if there are any other officers holding at the same time a commission in the regulars and in the Provincials, I conceive it will be right to give the like directions to them, agreeable to what was done with respect to Colonel McLean's and Colonel Goreham's corps.

Extract from Clinton to Barrington, New York, 12th August 1778

I perfectly agree in opinion with your Lordship that officers holding commissions in the regulars and Provincials at the same time should make their option, which they are to abide by, and will give directions accordingly as soon as the service can possibly admit of it.

Enclosure (4)
Extract from Germain to Clinton, Whitehall, 5th July 1780[32] 3(47): C

You will find by my separate letter of yesterday that it is not His Majesty's intention to confine you to so strict an observance of the general rule of no officers being permitted to hold commissions in a regular and Provincial corps at the same time as to prevent you from deviating from it in extraordinary cases, and that your having done so in favor of Majors Simcoe and Tarleton was approved by His Majesty. I also informed you that the general rule was not meant to affect the brevet rank of officers. It is therefore a great concern to me to find Lord Rawdon had resigned his rank of lt colonel in the army when he made his option of colonel of Provincials. The King is fully sensible of his Lordship's merit and of the great advantage which the corps under his command has derived from his Lordship's attention to it, and is well pleased his Lordship has chosen to continue at the head of it; but His Majesty commands me signify to you His royal pleasure that you do immediately acquaint his Lordship that he still retains his rank of lt colonel in the army.

---

[30] William Wildman Barrington (1717-1793), 2nd Viscount Barrington in the Irish peerage, had become Secretary at War in 1755, a post he was to hold, in two spells, for nineteen years until December 1778. More a capable administrator than a politician, he was a hardliner on America, firm in his view that the King's subjects everywhere owed obedience to Parliament. When, however, the revolutionary war began, he personally favoured the withdrawal of the army and the use of the navy to reduce America to submission. (*ODNB*)

[31] *6th Regiment of Foot*: a footnote adds 'not under Sir William Howe's command'.

[32] The complete letter appears in Stevens, op cit, i, 229. This extract contains no differences.

Enclosure (5)
Extract from Germain to Clinton (N° 63), 3(64) : C
Whitehall, 4th July 1780[33]

On the 15th of last month I had the very great pleasure to receive from the Earl of Lincoln[34] your dispatches numbered from 85 to 91 inclusive and immediately laid them before the King.

The glorious and important event of the reduction of Charles Town and the destruction or capture of the whole rebel land and naval force that defended it, related in N° 88, gave His Majesty the highest satisfaction, especially as it was atchieved with so inconsiderable a loss of his brave troops, a circumstance which in His Majesty's judgement at all times greatly inhances the value of a victory and reflects particular honor on the General; and His Majesty commanded me to express to you His entire approbation of your conduct and to assure you it had fully answered the very high expectations he had entertained of your great military abilities and zealous exertion of them in His Service. The honorable testimony you give of the distinguished merit of the officers who executed your orders, and of the fortitude and alacrity of the troops that served under them, was particularly pleasing to the King, and it is His Majesty's royal pleasure that you do acquaint both officers and soldiers, British, foreign and Provincial, that their intrepid and gallant behaviour is highly approved by His Majesty; but although in this general praise every officer and soldier is included, His Majesty commands me to desire you will express to Lieutenant General Earl Cornwallis, Majors General Leslie, Huyn[35] and Kosborth[36], Brigadier General Paterson, Lt Colonel Webster, Lt Colonel Tarleton, Major Ferguson and Major Moncrief His Majesty's particular satisfaction in their conduct. The merit of the latter officer was highly distinguished in the defence and preservation of Savannah; it has now been equally conspicuous in the attack and reduction of Charles Town.

It is a further pleasure to me, upon this joyful occasion, to be able to inform you that His Majesty has been graciously pleased, in consequence of your recommendation, to confer the

---

[33] Received by the *Roebuck* packet, 1st September.

[34] Thomas Pelham Clinton (1752-1795), Earl of Lincoln, was the second son of Henry, Duke of Newcastle, and a cousin of Sir Henry Clinton, to whom he had served as an aide-de-camp. Educated at Eton and Angers, he was a captain in the 1st Regiment of Foot Guards (the Grenadier Guards), a rank which carried with it a lt colonelcy. He succeeded to the dukedom in 1794. (Valentine, *The British Establishment*, i, 183-4; *Army Lists*)

[35] Born at Niederbeisheim, Hesse-Cassel, Johann Christoph von Huyn (1720-1780) was a major general in the Hessian service and commander of the Garrison Regiment von Huyn. On the Charlestown expedition he had been in command of a brigade made up of his own and the British 63rd and 64th Regiments. After the capitulation, though his regiment remained at Charlestown, he returned to New York, suffering from consumption, and died there on 25th July. (Uhlendorf ed, *The Siege of Charleston*, 12; Ewald, *Diary*, 411n)

[36] Heinrich Julius von Kospoth was a major general in the Hessian service. He had commanded four Hessian grenadier battalions during the siege of Charlestown and returned with them to New York. (Uhlendorf ed, op cit, *passim*)

rank of major in the army upon Lt Colonels Simcoe and Tarleton and Captain Robertson[37]. Major Ferguson would likewise have been promoted to the same rank had not your attention to his services anticipated the King's purpose; and care will be taken, in making out Major Tarleton's commission, to give him seniority to the major of the Liverpool Regiment. His Majesty likewise approves of your appointment of Colonels Stirling[38] and Patterson[39] and Lt Colonel Leland[40] to be brigadiers, and of having given that rank also to Colonel Dalrymple[41].

The events in West Florida, which Major General Campbell's correspondence has given you a detail of, are very unfortunate, and unless Sir Peter Parker[42] has sent a considerable naval force to the relief of Pensacola, which at the time of its attack I have reason to believe he was in a condition to spare, I am very apprehensive that it will fall into the hands of the Spaniards, though I was glad to find by letters from the officers in the Indian Department that a large body of the Creeks were gone down to join General Campbell, and should they arrive before the town is invested, they may enable him to keep the enemy at a distance on the land side and give time for succour to arrive from Jamaica. You were certainly sufficiently early in apprizing the commanders of His Majesty's ships on that station of the weakness of the garrison and the danger to which it was exposed, and I have repeatedly signified to the Governor of Jamaica His Majesty's commands to pay attention to the safety of West Florida, and also to the commanders of the King's ships through the Lords of the Admiralty. The indifference therefore about its preservation, which appears in Sir Peter Parker's answers to you and Major General Campbell, is altogether unaccountable.

---

[37] Of the Robertsons holding the rank of captain, Germain is probably referring to Archibald Robertson, Deputy Quartermaster General. (Clinton, *The American Rebellion*, 488)

[38] The second son of Sir Henry Stirling Bt, Thomas Stirling (1733-1808) was commissioned into the Dutch Scots Brigade in 1747 and served in it for ten years. Transferring to the British Army, he was commissioned a captain in the 42nd Highlanders (The Black Watch) on 24th March 1757 and saw service in Canada and Martinique in 1759 and at Havana in 1762. Promoted to major in 1770, he became Lt Colonel of the 42nd on 7th September 1771 and went on to lead it throughout the revolutionary war, notably in the capture of New York and Fort Washington. Promoted to colonel in the army on 19th August 1779, he had not taken part in the Charlestown expedition but had been seriously wounded in June while leading a brigade at Springfield, New Jersey. He would succeed to the baronetcy in 1799 and become a full general two years later. (Valentine, op cit, ii, 828-9; *ODNB*; *Appletons'*; *Army Lists*)

[39] *Patterson*: spelt "Paterson" in 3(76) and 99(9), which are other copies of this extract.

[40] John Leland had been promoted to lt colonel in the army on 25th May 1772 after having seen service in the 98th Regiment. Some two years later he was appointed to the equal rank of captain in the 1st Regiment of Foot Guards (the Grenadier Guards). (*Army Lists*)

[41] William Dalrymple (?-1807) had been promoted to colonel in the army on 29th August 1777 after having served as Lt Colonel of the 14th Regiment. He was now Quartermaster General in America, a post to which he had been appointed by Clinton after arriving at Charlestown on 10th May with dispatches from Germain. At the end of August Clinton had sent him back to England with an oral request to Germain that either he (Clinton) or the uncooperative Arbuthnot be replaced. (*Army Lists*; Clinton, op cit, 171n, 205; Willcox, *Portrait of a General*, 355)

[42] Sir Peter Parker (1721-1811) was a vice admiral commanding at Jamaica. Relations between him and the Governor, John Dalling, had broken down, and despite repeated solicitations Parker would fail to provide naval support for the reinforcement of Pensacola, which fell in May 1781. (Boatner, *Encyclopedia*, 831-2)

Rawdon to Leslie, 24th October 1780[43]   *3(267): C*

                                              Camp near the Indian Lands, west of the Catawba River
                                                                           South Carolina
                                                                               October 24th 1780

Hon Major General Leslie commanding on an expedition

Sir

Lord Cornwallis not being sufficiently recovered from a severe fever which lately attacked him to be able to write to you, his Lordship has desired that I should have the honor of communicating with you upon the subject of the present service.

The Commander in Chief has transmitted to Lord Cornwallis a copy of the instructions under which you are to act. At the time when Petersburg was suggested as an adviseable point for a diversion which might cooperate with our intended efforts for the reduction of North Carolina, it was imagined that the tranquillity of South Carolina was assured, and the repeated assertions which were sent to us by the loyalists in North Carolina gave us reason to hope that their number and their zeal would not only facilitate the restoration of His Majesty's Government in that province but might also supply a force for more extensive operations. Events unfortunately have not answered to those flattering promises.

The approach of General Gates's army unveiled to us a fund of disaffection in this province of which we could have formed no idea, and even the dispersion of that force did not extinguish the ferment which the hope of its support had raised. To this hour the majority of the inhabitants of that tract between the Pedee and the Santee are in arms against us, and when we last heard from Charlestown, they were in possession of George Town, from which they had dislodg'd our militia. It was hoped that the rising which was expected of our friends in North Carolina might awe that district into quiet. Therefore, after giving them a little chastisement by making the 7th Regiment take that route on its way to the army, Lord Cornwallis advanced to Charlotteburg. Major Ferguson, with about eight hundred militia collected from the neighbourhood of Ninety Six, had previously marched into Tryon County to protect our friends who were supposed to be numerous there, and it was intended that he should cross the Catawba River and endeavour to preserve tranquillity in the rear of the army. A numerous enemy now appeared on the frontiers, drawn from Nolachucki and other settlements beyond the mountains, whose very names had been unknown to us. A body of these, joined by the inhabitants of the Ceded Lands in Georgia, made a sudden and violent attack upon Augusta. The post was gallantly defended by Lt Colonel Browne till he was relieved by the activity of Lt Colonel Cruger; but Major Ferguson, by endeavouring to intercept the enemy in their retreat, unfortunately gave time for fresh bodys of them to pass the mountains and to unite into a corps far superior to that which he commanded. They came up with him and after a sharp action entirely defeated him. Ferguson was killed and all his party either slain or taken. By the enemy's having secured all the passes on the Catawba,

---

[43] Published in Stevens, op cit, i, 271. There are several, mostly inconsequential differences. Writing on 29th October (p 137), Balfour hoped Rawdon's letter would sail with the *Iris* that day.

Lord Cornwallis (who was waiting at Charlotteburg for a convoy of stores) received but confused accounts of the affair for some time. At length the truth reached him; and the delay, equally with the precautions which the enemy had taken to keep their victory from his knowledge, gave his Lordship great reason to fear for the safety of Ninety Six. To save that district was indispensible for the security of the rest of the province, and Lord Cornwallis saw no means of effecting it but by passing the Catawba River with his army, for it was so weakened by sickness that it would not bear detachment. After much fatigue on the march occasioned by violent rains, we passed the river three days ago. We then received the first intelligence respecting our different posts in this province which had reached us for near three weeks, every express from Camden having been waylaid, and some of them murdered by the inhabitants. Ninety Six is safe, the corps which defeated Ferguson having (in consequence of our movement) crossed the Catawba and joined Smallwood[44] on the Yadkin. In our present position we have received the first intimation of the expedition under your command. At present we fear that we are too far asunder to render your cooperation very effectual. No force has presented itself to us whose opposition would have been thought serious against this army; but then we have little hopes of bringing the affair to the issue of an action. The enemy are mostly mounted militia, not to be overtaken by our infantry nor to be safely pursued in this strong country by our cavalry. Our fear is that instead of meeting us they would slip by us into this province, were we to proceed far from it, and might again stimulate the disaffected to serious insurrection. This apprehension, you will judge, sir, must greatly circumscribe our efforts. Indeed Lord Cornwallis cannot hope that he shall be able to undertake any thing upon such a scale as either to aid you or much to benefit from you in your present situation. The Commander in Chief has signified to Lord Cornwallis that his Lordship is at liberty to give you any direction for further cooperation which may appear to him expedient, but his Excellency has complied so fully and completely with Lord Cornwallis's request by sending so powerfull a force to make a diversion in the Chesapeak that his Lordship fears he should require too much were he to draw you into the more immediate service of this district. His Lordship is likewise delicate in this point because he does not know how far, by drawing you from the Chesapeak, he might interfere with any other purposes to which the Commander in Chief may have destined your troops. Under these circumstances Lord Cornwallis thinks himself obliged to leave you at liberty to pursue whatsoever measures may appear to your judgement best for His Majesty's Service and most consonant to the views of the Commander in Chief. No time is specified to Lord Cornwallis as the limitation of your stay to the southward. Should your knowledge of Sir Henry Clinton's desires prompt you to make a trial upon North Carolina, Cape Fear River appears to us to be the only part where your efforts are at present likely to be effectual. A descent

---

[44] William Smallwood (1732-1792) had recently superseded Richard Caswell in command of the North Carolina revolutionary militia while remaining a divisional commander under Gates. A native of Maryland, he had taken his seat in the provincial assembly there in 1761 and served as a delegate to the provincial convention in 1775. Commissioned as colonel of a Maryland revolutionary regiment in January 1776, he marched north to join Washington and was wounded at White Plains in October, the same month in which he was promoted to brigadier general in the Continental line. Going south in 1780, he was separated from his brigade in the Battle of Camden and swept to the rear by the flood of fugitives. Despite doing nothing in the battle, he was promoted in September to major general and received in October the thanks of Congress. When Greene superseded Gates in December, Smallwood would refuse to become subordinate to Steuben, who was Greene's second in command, and return to Maryland, partly to forward recruits and supplies, but mainly in a vain attempt to persuade Congress to antedate his commission by two years. After the war he would serve as Governor of Maryland for three consecutive one-year terms. (*DAB*; Heitman, *Historical Register*, 500-1; *Appletons'*; *The Greene Papers*, vi, *passim*, vii, 11)

there would be the surest means of joining and arming the friends of Government as well as of cooperating with this army. This, therefore, would naturally be the point to which Lord Cornwallis would bring you did he conceive himself at liberty so absolutely to dispose of you. It must be remarked, however, that there are two difficultys in this plan. The first is that the country from Cape Fear to Cross Creek (the Highland settlement) produces so little that it would be requisite in penetrating thro' it to carry your provisions with you. The second is that no vessel larger than a frigate can pass the bar of Cape Fear harbour. Whatsoever you decide, Lord Cornwallis desires earnestly to hear from you as soon as possible. It is uncertain yet what steps this army, if left to itself, must pursue, but it will be ready at least to act vigorously in aid to any plan which you may undertake. Lord Cornwallis begs that you may inform the Commander in Chief of our circumstances and that you will have the goodness to mention how highly sensible his Lordship is to the very effectual manner in which his Excellency has endeavoured to ease the operations of this army. The measure must have been attended with the most favorable consequences had not accidents which no foresight could expect so greatly altered the complexion of affairs in this province. Lord Cornwallis desires me to add how much satisfaction he should feel in having your assistance upon this service did it promise more favorably for you; but should the intentions of the Commander in Chief have left you at liberty to make the attempt at Cape Fear, the success which would probably attend that essential service would be doubly pleasing to Lord Cornwallis from the opportunity it would most likely give him of congratulating you in person.

Allow me to add my hopes that the course of the service will put it in my power to assure you personally how much I have the honor to be, sir,

Your most obedient and very faithful servant

RAWDON

Rawdon to Clinton, 28th October 1780[45]   3(297): ADfS

Camp between Broad River and the Catawba
South Carolina
October 28th 1780

His Excellency Sir Henry Clinton KB
Commander in Chief etc

Sir

Lord Cornwallis having been so reduced by a severe fever as to be still unable to write, he has desired that I should have the honor of addressing your Excellency in regard to our present situation. But few days have passed since Lord Cornwallis received your Excellency's dispatch of the [20th] of September. In consequence of it his Lordship directed that I should immediately send a letter to meet General Lesslie in the Chesapeak giving him the fullest

---

[45] Published in Stevens, op cit, i, 277. The letter as sent was dated the 29th. There is no other material difference.

information respecting our prospects and the present temper of the country. I have the honor to enclose a copy of that letter. Something remains to be said in addition to it of a nature which Lord Cornwallis judged inexpedient to unveil excepting to your Excellency. For some time after the arrival of His Majesty's troops at Camden repeated messages were sent to Head Quarters by the friends of Government in North Carolina expressing their impatience to rise and join the King's standard. The impossibility of subsisting that additional force at Camden and the accounts which they themselves gave of the distressing scarcity of provisions in North Carolina obliged Lord Cornwallis to entreat that they would remain quiet till the new crop might enable us to join them. In the mean time General Gates's army advanced. We were greatly surprized, and no less grieved, that no information whatsoever of its movements was conveyed to us by persons so deeply interested in the event as the North Carolina loyalists. Upon the 16th of August that army was so entirely dispersed that it was clear no number of them could for a considerable time be collected. Orders were therefore dispatched to our friends stating that the hour which they had so strongly pressed was now arrived and exhorting them to stand forth and prevent the junction of the scattered enemy. Immediate support was promised to them. In the fullest confidence that this event was to take place, Lord Cornwallis ventured to press your Excellency for co-operation in the Chesapeak, hoping that the assistance of the North Carolinians might furnish a force for yet further efforts. Not a single man, however, attempted to improve the favorable moment or obeyed that summons for which they had before been so impatient. It was hoped that our approach might get the better of their timidity, yet during the considerable period whilst we were waiting at Charlotteburg for our stores they did not even furnish us with the smallest information respecting the force collecting against us. In short, sir, we may have a powerful body of friends in North Carolina, and indeed we have cause to be convinced that many of the inhabitants wish well to His Majesty's arms, but they have not given evidence enough either of their numbers or of their activity to justify the stake of this province for the uncertain advantages that might attend immediate junction with our North Carolinian adherents. There is too much reason to conceive that such must have been the risque. Whilst this army lay at Charlotteburg, Georgetown was taken from our militia by the rebels, and the whole country to the east of Santee gave such proofs of general defection that even the militia of the High Hills could not be prevailed upon to join a party of troops who were sent to protect our boats upon the river. The defeat of Major Ferguson had so dispirited this part of the country, and indeed the majority of the loyal subjects were so wearied by the long continuance of the campaign, that Lt Colonel Cruger commanding at Ninety Six sent information to Lord Cornwallis that the whole country had determined to submit as soon as the rebels should enter it. From these circumstances, from the consideration that delay does not extinguish our hopes in North Carolina, and from the long fatigue of the troops, which made it seriously requisite to give some refreshment to the army, Lord Cornwallis has resolved upon retiring to a position which may secure the frontiers without separating his force. In this situation we shall always be ready for movement whensoever opportunity shall recommend it or circumstances require it, but the first care must be to put Camden and Ninety Six in a better state of defence and to furnish them with ample stores of salt provision. Lord Cornwallis foresees all the difficulties of a defensive war, yet his Lordship thinks they cannot be weighed against the dangers which must have attended an obstinate adherence to his former plan.

I am instructed by Lord Cornwallis to express in the strongest terms his Lordship's feelings with regard to the very effectual measures which your Excellency had taken to forward his operations. His Lordship hopes that his fears of abusing your Excellency's goodness in that particular may not have led him to neglect making use of a force intended by your Excellency to be employed by him, but as his Lordship knew not how far your Excellency might aim at other purposes in the Chesapeak (to which point his Lordship's entreaty for co-operation was originally confined), he could not think of assuming the power to order Major General Lesslie to the Cape Fear River, tho' he pointed out the utility of the measure in case it should be conceived within the extent of your Excellency's purposes.

Lord Cornwallis further desires me to say that he feels infinitely obliged by the very flattering testimonies of approbation with which your Excellency has been pleased to honor his success on the 16th of August. He has signified your Excellency's thanks to the officers and men, who receive them with grateful acknowledgement.

I have the honor to be, sir, with the highest respect
Your Excellency's etc

RAWDON

Rawdon to Leslie, 31st October 1780[46] 3(335): C

Camp between Broad River and the Catawba
South Carolina
October 31st 1780

Hon Major General Leslie commanding an expedition

Sir

I had the honor to write to you on the 24th instant by direction of Lord Cornwallis, transmitting to you his Lordship's sentiments relative to your expedition as far as it might be designed to affect his operations.

In that letter I stated the events which had frustrated our hopes of penetrating into the heart of North Carolina and arming the loyalists in our cause, and I marked the little prospect of our deriving any assistance from you or of our rendering you any service whilst your efforts were exerted in so distant a quarter as the Chesapeak. I added Lord Cornwallis's opinion that you could in no manner cooperate effectually with this army unless by landing in the Cape Fear River and penetrating to the Highland settlement near Cross Creek, but I subjoined that his Lordship would not venture to order the descent at Cape Fear lest he should counteract some purpose to which the Commander in Chief might have destined the troops under your command.

Upon further considerations Lord Cornwallis fears that he may not have expressed himself strongly enough with regard to the expediency of the above movement. The difficulty which

---

[46] Published in Ross ed, *Cornwallis Correspondence*, i, 64-5. Writing on 10th November, Balfour indicated that the letter would sail with a fast sloop the following day.

must attend a defensive war on this frontier, and the fear that he may neglect means which the Commander in Chief perhaps expects him to employ, induce Lord Cornwallis to request that you will undertake the descent and operations recommended upon the Cape Fear River; but the request is made upon this sole and express condition: that you think yourself fully authorised by your knowledge of the Commander in Chief's intentions to take this step, and that you do not apprehend any view of his Excellency's will be thwarted by this mode of employing your force.

Lord Cornwallis hopes for the most speedy communication of your resolutions on this point. A movement upon our part without the assurance of your cooperation (which I am to repeat can only be effectual in Cape Fear River) promises but little and hazards much; but this army will be held in constant readiness to act with the utmost vigor in your support.

I have the honor to be, sir, with great respect and esteem
Your most obedient and very faithfull servant

RAWDON

Rawdon to Clinton, 31st October 1780[47]   3(330): C

Camp between Broad River and the Catawba
October 31st 1780

His Excellency Sir Henry Clinton KB etc etc etc

Sir

By Lord Cornwallis's directions I had the honor of writing to your Excellency on the 29th instant, detailing to your Excellency the circumstances which had obliged Lord Cornwallis to relinquish the attempt of penetrating to Hillsborough, and enclosing the copy of a letter which his Lordship made me write to Major General Leslie upon that occasion.

On further consideration his Lordship, reflecting upon the difficultys of a defensive war and the hopes which your Excellency would probably build of our success in this quarter, has thought it adviseable not only to recommend more strongly to Major General Leslie a plan which may enable us to take an active part, but even to make it his request, in case it should not be incompatible with your Excellency's further arrangements.

Lord Cornwallis is particularly induced to invite Major General Leslie to cooperation in Cape Fear River by the supposition that your Excellency may not want those troops during the winter, and they may join your Excellency in the spring scarcely later than should they, on the approach of that season, sail from any part of the Chesapeak Bay.

A further motive proceeds from the little prospect that the expedition on its original plan

---

[47] Published in Stevens, op cit, i, 284. There are no material differences.

should compass any service adequate to its force and to your Excellency's expectations. However, as views might subsist which were not explained to Lord Cornwallis, his Lordship has not ventured absolutely to order the descent in Cape Fear River, and the enclosed copy of the second letter written to Major General Leslie will satisfy your Excellency upon what terms the measure has been pressed.

I have the honor to be, sir, with the highest respect
Your Excellency's most obedient servant

RAWDON

CHAPTER 22

Correspondence between Cornwallis, or Rawdon, and Balfour

Cornwallis to Balfour, 24th August 1780 79(35): C

Camden
24th August 1780

Lt Colonel Balfour

Dear Balfour

I yesterday received your letter to Ross[1]. You find I have anticipated your wishes about the naval business. Colonel Mills is not yet arrived. Your plan of employing the militia on the east of Santee is in general very right. I must, however, from circumstances make some alterations, and some regulars must go with an intelligent officer, I think Wemyss, to punish the Cheraws. I send you a copy of an order which I have given to the respective colonels of militia hereabouts and at 96[2]. I have heard nothing of Innes. I cannot learn that any party of the enemy are any where collected. The largest body I heard of going off together was 50 men with General Stevens[3]. I will send you my letters for New York tomorrow or next day.

---

[1] *your letter to Ross*: not extant.

[2] *an order..*: no extant copy. See p 332, note 21.

[3] Born in Culpeper County, Virginia, Edward Stevens (1745-1820) had commanded a battalion of revolutionary militia in the action at the Great Bridge in December 1775. Eleven months later he was commissioned Colonel of the 10th Virginia Continental Regiment but resigned at the end of January 1778. Having become in the following year a brigadier general in the Virginia revolutionary militia, he joined Gates on 14th August 1780 near Camden, bringing with him 800 men, but in the ensuing battle two days later they, like most of the militia, generally threw down their loaded guns and fled. Sometime later he and the remains of his men would rejoin the

I should be happy to see you at the head of the Fuzileers, but I am well convinced that you must be sensible how necessary your presence is at Charlestown and how impossible it is to spare you from thence. England writes to Ross. Pray assure him of my best wishes and that I shall expect to see him before Xmas. I don't think it would be right for me to meddle in the business of the majority of the *Welsh*. Ross must receive some mark of favour at home, and he would not wish to have great obligations to [*blank*][4]. I have given to the militia colonels in this neighbourhood 100 dollars each for their own use and another 100 to be distributed in gratuities by them amongst their officers and men. I am much hurried in writing my New York letters and can only return you my sincere thanks for your kind feelings for my success.

Yours most faithfully

[CORNWALLIS]

[*Subscribed*:]

Hurry off Ross.

We have got up some rum.

Send down a number of hand bills with a summary account of our success that I may disperse them in North Carolina, as our cause suffers so much by the falsehoods and misrepresentations of the rebels. Ross will speak to you about a press.

The orders to the militia colonels about property will only be given to those on the frontier and relate only to those concerned in the 2nd revolt, so that it will not materially interfere with my proclamation relative to property, which I shall now issue without loss of time.

You will oblige me by dating your letters on the day of the month instead of the week.

Cornwallis to Balfour, 29th August 1780   79(45): C

Cambden
29th August 1780

Dear Balfour

I inclose to you the duplicates for New York and shall send triplicates in a very few days. You must be sensible how important it is that they should hear from us. In regard to the

---

southern army at Hillsborough and take part in the Battle of Guilford, where they fought well. Severely wounded in the battle, he would retire to Virginia but recover in time to join Lafayette with a brigade of militia and participate in the Yorktown campaign. From 1782 to 1790 he sat in the Virginia Senate. (*Appletons*'; Heitman, *Historical Register*, 519; Boatner, *Encyclopedia*, 167, 1058-9)

[4] The original no doubt contained a reference to Clinton, which was omitted here from delicacy.

rebel officers, my idea is that the field officers should remain at Orangeburgh and the others be paroled to any island you please. I thought perhaps that the field officers might be better at a distance from Charlestown. However, I beg you will alter this as you please; it is entirely left to you. If they remain at Orangeburgh, they must be allowed to draw rations for their servants, and a militia guard at the court house must be allowed a little salt and rum. General Rutherford, that cruel and infamous persecutor, and Lt Colonel Isaacs[5] I should wish to send on parole to St Augustine, where they will be out of the way of doing mischief. I forgot to desire you to notify our success to their Excellencys Governors Sir James Wright and Tonyn and say that I was too busy to write myself. Wemyss will inform you when he will begin his march for the low country. You will please at the same time to order Ball and Wigfall[6] to George Town. I think of moving with the 1st division in eight or nine days. The second, consisting of the 63rd and, if nothing can come from Charlestown, of a poor battalion of the 71st, and all the convalescents able to march, to follow in about ten days, and Trumbull's[7] and Innis's will take care of Camden untill the sick and stores can be moved. The Orangeburgh militia must have all sorts of douceurs, and I think of employing them in guarding the country and the road between this place and Nelson's Ferry to protect every thing that goes down by water to Cooke's Landing, which must be the conveyance of most of our sick and wounded and all the stores. We are still exceedingly ill supplied with draft horses. You will hardly believe that after all our successes the Quarter Master General can furnish only 26 teams, which he calls fit for service, except those attach'd to the regiments. Poor England, who was to have put all this to rights, is exceedingly ill. I have set Money to work. Haldane is recovering but Hayes is still very bad. I hope Ross is gone. If not, repeat to him my kindest and most sincere good wishes. I have not thought it necessary to write to England about the release of the prisoners but have explained it fully to Sir Henry Clinton. I remember Ross mention'd to you the endeavouring to get some waggons from Colleton County to bring up rum and stores. Ferguson is going to advance with some militia and his

---

[5] Elijah Isaacks was probably born not long after 1725, the year – or thereabouts – when his father Samuel migrated from Scotland or Wales to Frederick County, Virginia. Sometime after 1754 Elijah moved on to South Carolina, and from there to Wilkes County, North Carolina, becoming a colonel in the Salisbury District of the North Carolina revolutionary militia. Taken prisoner at the Battle of Camden, he was now to be transported to St Augustine, presumably because he was an active revolutionary with a reputation for severity, a charge levelled against him after the war by the loyalist David Fanning. In June 1781 he would be exchanged under the cartel with Greene and afterwards be promoted to brigadier general of militia. During the early 1780s he served as a Senator for Wilkes County in the North Carolina Assembly. (S J Isaacks, *The Isaacks Clan in America and Texas* (El Paso, 1935, revised 1995); *State Records of NC*, xv, 292, xxii, 211-3; Hay ed, *Soldiers from NC*, 392-3)

[6] Of John Wigfall little is known. Upon the adoption of a temporary revolutionary constitution for South Carolina in March 1776 he was commissioned a Justice of the Peace for Charlestown District. Now, more than four years later, he had accepted a commission of colonel in the royal militia and would be mainly involved in securing the ferries on the lower Santee, though his operations would at times be extended to Georgetown and the ferries on Black River. When in the spring of 1781 the tide in South Carolina turned in favour of the revolutionaries, he would resign his commission but would nevertheless fail to save himself from being included in the Banishment and Confiscation Act passed in January 1782 by the revolutionary assembly at Jacksonborough. After the war he would petition the assembly for relief and be supported by a parade of witnesses who testified to their humane treatment at his hands. Little though we know of him, it is sufficient to suggest that he may have been a fair-weather friend to whichever side was in the ascendancy. (A S Salley Jr, *Journal of the General Assembly of South Carolina, March 26, 1776 -April 11, 1776* (Historical Commission of South Carolina, 1906); *The Cornwallis Papers*; Sabine, *Biographical Sketches*, ii, 595-6; Lambert, *SC Loyalists*, 287, 292-3)

[7] *Trumbull's*: a miscopying of 'Turnbull's'.

own miserable naked corps to Gilbertown and Tryon County. I think it rather hazardous, but he says he cannot positively get them to stay longer where they are; and to be sure, this is a favorable time for advancing, and if ever those people will fight, it is when they attack and not when they are attacked. I hope you correspond constantly with Ninety Six and are perfectly assured of General W[8]. When we are a good way off, it will be well to be sure of that quarter. It is the greatest comfort to me to leave the province in your hands.

I am etc

[CORNWALLIS]

Cornwallis to Balfour, 31st August 1780   79(47): C

Camden
August 31st 1780

Lt Colonel Balfour

Dear Balfour

I received last night by Mr Cruden Ross's letter of the 27th[9], by which I am glad to find that he is immediately going in the *Providence* and that you have cleared Charlestown of that set of villains who would never have allowed us to retain the peaceable possession of this province. General Rutherford and Colonel Isaacs will follow them. You will be kind enough to write to Tonyn and say any thing you please in my name, as I do not apprehend the guests will be very agreeable to him. I inclose to you my instructions to Wemyss[10] and I think that business had better go on in the manner that I before mentioned to you. The situation of this province requires the most serious attention. The insolence and perfidy of our enemys and the timidity and supiness of our friends is hardly to be credited. The former make severity absolutely necessary. I think Wemyss may be trusted. I have not yet got my answer about the *Charlestown battalion*, but a paragraph in Ross's letter gives me some hopes. He says, 'Balfour can spare the 64th for three weeks.' By that time some convalescents who will not be equal to the fatigue of our march may be on their way to Charlestown by taking the advantage of the water to Cooke's and from Monk's Corner. I shall say no more, convinced most fully as I am of your zeal for the service and affection for me. Ross carried the *dictionary*[11] to town with him. I must beg you will send another. From what I saw of the

---

[8] *W*: Williamson.

[9] *Ross's letter..*: not extant.

[10] *my instructions to Wemyss*: of 28th August, p 208.

[11] *the dictionary*: it was for use as an enciphering tool, with identical copies being kept by the sender and recipient. Each word was enciphered by three numbers: the first referred to the page number, the second to the column on the page, and the third to the position of the word in the column. For example, '281-1-25' meant the 25th word in the first column on page 281. To indicate use of the cipher, Cornwallis and Balfour placed 'B' before the first

other edition, I think it will do. You will likewise be so kind as to cut the maps of Virginia and Maryland out of my American atlas and put them on canvas and send them to me, and at the same time some very thin writing paper, the use of which you well know. I have sent duplicates to you to be forwarded to New York and shall send triplicates in two or three days. I wish you to take every possible method of getting them convey'd. I will send several more copys, and every good sailing vessel may take one. There must, however, be a carefull, trusty man on board each vessel whose care it must be to see the pacquets properly loaded and slung and to engage to cut them away in case of danger. It is of infinite consequence that my letters should get soon to New York. I am not without hopes of some arrivals, as the wind was north east on Monday and, I believe, Tuesday. We have plenty of waggons but the situation of the horses and gear is wretched beyond description. It occupies me almost entirely to provide remedys for it and to get some provision. Hitherto, so far from being able to get a few days' beforehand, which is absolutely necessary for our march, we are this day without either flour or meal and Tarleton's horses have had no forage since the action. The Quarter Master General and Commissary General accuse each other, but that neither fattens the soldier or the horse. I have placed Money in that department untill England's recovery, who is still very ill. Haldane is much better and Hayes mends slowly. I shall be in want of more money, and, as after a victory a man may venture to draw more freely, I wish you would speak to Gordon to send me a thousand pounds on the same footing as the other, putting Major Money's name instead of Ross's[12], and send it to me either by the *battalion* or by any safe conveyance. I will not suppose it possible that Ross can be with you.

Yours sincerely

CORNWALLIS

Summary of Cornwallis to Balfour, 31st August 1780   79(49): D

Camden
31st August 1780
Nine at night

Lord Cornwallis wrote to Colonel Balfour to acknowledge the receipt of Captain Ross's letter[13] informing him of the movement of the 7th Regiment and the militia battalions under the command of Colonels Ball and Wigfall, the whole commanded by Major Moncrief – that his Lordship approved of the plan and that it would not effect the general one.[14]

---

enciphered letter. A cipher more commonly used by the British was Ferguson's or a form of it. See p 82, note 42.

[12] Money had been put in charge of the military chest on 27th August 1780 when he assumed his post of aide-de-camp. See Money's Journal, p 356.

[13] *Captain Ross's letter*: not extant.

[14] The movement is described in greater detail in Balfour's letter of 31st August, which follows. See the second paragraph.

Balfour to Cornwallis, 31st August 1780 63(87): *ALS*

Charles Town
31st August 1780

Earl Cornwallis etc etc etc
Camden

My Lord

I was extremly glad to receive yours to'day of the 27th and cannot let an opportunity escape of saying that Ross is at Five Fathom Hole, having embarked last night in hopes of getting away today, but the wind has been contrary and prevented his sailing. I want him off much. He has wrote your Lordship so fully of the businesses on hand that I need not repeat them.

This morning I received a certain acount of the prisoners being safe (the last division) at Martin's, and that the 64th Regiment will be here on Sunday morning, in which case the 7th will move on Munday morning, cross at Bonneau's Ferry, and get to Laneu's Ferry on Wednesday, where boats are collecting to cross them over the Santee under the care of Ball and Wigfall, whose regiments are assembled on the different ferrys and will unite at Laneu's on Tuesday. Moncrief, the General, will have copys of your Lordship's orders to the militia commanding officers and proceed to George Town and follow the plan mentioned by Ross.

The forming a regiment at George Town I conceive to be absolutely necessary at present and it can be done under the eye of Wigfall, who should remain untill there is no further occasion for him. The lt colonel and major lately appointed to Cassells's regiment are very excellent men and will, I believe, exert themselves much to get their corps formed as fast as possible, having both propertys there and being well attached. Moncrieff seems to be as willing to carry your plans into execution as any one I ever saw; and I hope in a short time to be able to assure you that you need not look behind you for one shott. To this point, be assured, my principal attention shall be paid. I find Westerhaguern the most manigable, decent German I ever knew. We go on well, and am sure must continue to do so.

The moving the ringleaders and abetters of this business has had the best effects. Their number was a little ugmented yesterday, and I hope to see them all fairly off in two days. They are equal at present to the moving the 7th Regiment. The rout of the 63rd may, if your Lordship pleases, be effected[15] by the 7th's march, or they may communicate together, so as to leave no part unvisited or unpunished; and as your march will be in two divisions, I suppose you mean them to compose the last, in which case I shall be able to get up thirty puncheons of rum to you in time for them. As the waggons are in good order, I mean them to go all the way by land and trust nothing to accident. In two days I shall be able to say when you may expect them, but at all events you may depend upon them for the 2nd division.

---

[15] *effected*: affected.

Two hundred camp kettles and some hatchetts I hope to be able to get ready before you go. If not, at least one half, but I dare not promise too far.

McLeod comes tomorow evening, when I shall write of Rosses sailing, I hope. In the mean time you may depend upon the disposition of the George Town business going on as mentioned, if I get no counter orders. The galley will sail tomorow for George Town and carry some arms, rum and salt. I cannot think there will be any danger of keeping George Town with a regiment of militia, and if you choose it, I will relieve Wigfall with Balingall's, and his soon after by the Orangeburgh, and so on.

I mean to establish posts regularly to carry news papers to the magistrates and field officers of militia through the whole country, not to leave a suspicious man in the country of any consequence, and not a firelock but with a real friend. This, I hope with their present chastisement, will not fail to keep them at least quiet.

Moncrieff is not to be trusted away far. I must most seriously beg that he may return immediately. In short, your Lordship knows I *cannot* go on without him, situated as I am, and if you permit him to stay, I must also come along.

I ever am
Your most grateful

N BALFOUR

[*Subscribed*:]

For God sake do not get sick.

Balfour to Cornwallis, 1st September 1780   64(1): ALS

1st September

My Lord

I received the dispatches and duplicats today with yours of the 29th instant[16]. A small schooner with only six guns, but a remarkable quick sailer, is the only thing I can get to send to New York, and for the duplicates have sent out to look for the *Keppel* brigg, but if we can't get her, shall send something of force, the first that comes in or the *Loyalist*, but one of the two opportunitys shall be by a vessel of force, and as soon after one another as possible. Unlucky Ross is still at Five Fathom Hole, tumbling with an easterly wind these two days. I have just received a note from him mentioning the proclamation, which I shall attempt to take care shall be produced as you wish. He is in good spirits and says his ship

---

[16] *instant*: ultimo.

is well manned and a stout one. Hay[17] is gone with him; but the absolute necessity of having a man of activity and good sense to watch the affair of the prisoners' movements etc, and to whom I could entrust the execution of any order, has oblidged me to appoint Doctor Fraser as asistant untill your pleasure is known. Ten shillings a day is as little as I could offer such a man, and although I hope you will not here after complain of my numerous appointments, yet I shall not fail to make such as I think necessary to support and carry through the publick service; and as I have in this, as well as in every other point, unbounded confidence in your Lordship's support, I with pleasure undertake the business, hoping, when you shall find more use for me any where else, that you will send for me. My only stipulation is that you do not leave me *to another* command.

The printing affairs will go up tomorow to Monk's Corner and be with you in time.

The thirty puncheons of rum I mentioned yesterday setts out also tomorow night and will be at Camden in nine days at further from tomorow. The first division of prisoners came in this evening. The rest will be here tomorow; and by day break on Munday the 7th crosses to Bonneau's Ferry with Moncrieff and, by the best calculation I can make, will get to Camden about the 21st if nothing extraordinary happens — which I conceive will nearly answer your plan for the 2nd division. The 63rd having also scoured the higher parts of the country, I hope no part will be left unpunished that deserve it. Moncrieff will return, of course. I have already beged so hard about him that I shall only add a wish that you may leave an order for him in case he comes to Camden. The main point I mean to turn my attention to is the keeping every thing quiet behind you, and leave not a foe betwixt us.

I paid this day forty five guineas to those prisoners who were rescued, all of whom, and many more, are enlisted in the Legion and Volunteers of Ireland. I hope you mean to leave allways some people at Camden, however *few*, for I own it appears to me absolutely necessary. I shall cox the militia of Orangeburgh throughly and have no doubt of their keeping up the communication you mention, but a post at Camden of something Provincial with a prudent officer will keep all right in that higher quarter of the province, and communicate with *96*, of which I shall not be unmindful also.

The district of much consequence to you has been unfortunately managed — I mean the Congres. Captain Maxwell and Major Graeme, both prudent and disspassionate, agree in the cause of the revolt of so many in that quarter, viz, the bad management of Cary, who, although a very good man himself, is credulous and imposed upon by the worst people in the district, especialy by his major, a ruffian of the name of Bradley[18], who, Maxwell says, to

---

[17] Hay has not been positively identified, as his name was common in the services and elsewhere. He may have been Major George Hay, one of three commissaries of captures at Charlestown. (McCrady, *SC in the Rev 1775-1780*, 544)

[18] Of Bradley little is known. According to Cornwallis, he was a captain in Cary's regiment and had been very active at the head of his company at Camden whilst Gates was in the neighbourhood. This information suggests that he was the brother of Lieutenant Samuel Bradley, a fellow militiaman, who would be captured a few months later by a party of revolutionaries and hanged on Hobkirk's Hill, ostensibly because his brother had captured a man who was later hanged for deserting to Gates after holding a commission in the royal militia. (*The Cornwallis Papers*; Lambert, *SC Loyalists*, 202)

his knowledge has robbed and pillaged the plantions [*sic*], as he chose to call them dissafected, and drove off a great many to the enemy. In particular, Cary *never* has been in the district himself to arrange his regiment, which to me is a bad sign of his activity etc. At present every thing is in confusion there, and I realy do not know how to put it to rights unless you will send to Cary and Ancrum and regulate their differences, or send them to me and I will answer to put it to rights at least better than it is now, for I fear its breaking out when you are gone.

Arthur Middleton[19], the most violent and traiterous of the rebell tribe, is near you and has overstay'd his pass a month upon false pretences. I beg you'l send him here. I am assured that every intelligence he can procure is sent to Ruttlidge by him, and it is not all unlikely he has purposely chose his ground near you with that intent.

I own I wish you to move soon on acount of health as well as other reasons. Do not be affraid of your rear. I shall take care of that, if the whole garrison moves.

Wigfall and Ball will be at Lanew's Ferry on Tuesday and Moncrieff on Wednesday.

I think I have mentioned every thing for this day. Adieu. I beg you'l keep off the fever and ague.

Ever most sincerly and gratefully yours

N BALFOUR

---

[19] The son of Henry Middleton (see vol I, p 76, note 9), Arthur Middleton (1742-1787) was educated partly in South Carolina and partly in England, from where he returned to serve several terms in the Commons House of the South Carolina colonial legislature. As the revolution approached, he became an active member of the Provincial Congress and in 1775 sat on its General Committee, Secret Committee, and Council of Safety. A leading radical, he advocated not only the ostracism of all who refused to subscribe to the Continental Association subversive of the Crown but also the attachment of the estates of those who fled the colony. He also looked without disfavour on such activities as the tarring and feathering of loyalists. In February 1776 he was appointed to a committee of eleven to draw up a temporary revolutionary constitution for South Carolina. A few days later he was elected to the Continental Congress but did not repair there until the work of the committee was completed and a constitution adopted. He arrived in Philadelphia in time to sign the Declaration of Independence. Now, in 1780, he had been taken prisoner at Charlestown and would soon be transported to St Augustine for activities incompatible with his status. Exchanged in July 1781 under the cartel with Greene, he would resume his seat in the Continental Congress and be elected to the Jacksonborough assembly. He died at Goose Creek. (*DAB*; *The Cornwallis Papers*)

Enclosure
Return of captured prisoners sent to Charlestown 3(28): DS

Return of Rebel Prisoners of War sent to Charlestown by General Earl Cornwallis and lodged on board the Two Sisters and Concord Transports, 2nd September 1780

Number of Continentals	Number of Militia	Total
260	192	452

JAMES FRASER[20]

Cornwallis to Balfour, 3rd and 6th September 1780   80(1): C

Camden
September 3rd 1780

Dear Balfour

I this morning received Ross's letter of the 30th[21]. As much as I wished him gone, I cannot help hoping that he was not over the bar on Friday night as it blew a hurricane with us. I received the inclosed letter from Cruger[22]. I leave it to your discretion, as I think you are more capable of judging of the justice of the demand than myself. Cruger talks of Williamson as desirous of observing neutrallity. I hope, however, that he goes much beyond that.

I propose moving about the 6th or 7th to Waxhaw with the 23rd, 33rd, Volunteers of Ireland and Legion, where I shall remain ten days, by which time I hope the 71st will be able to join me. I shall then decide whether it will be better for me to wait there or at Charlottetown until the 2nd division consisting of 63rd, 7th and Hamilton's corps will be ready to begin their march from this place.

I hope by getting rid of every body belonging to the Quarter Master General's Department, and by paying conductors, drivers etc their wages instead of putting them into our own pockets, to procure a sufficient provision train to enable us to subsist. As things have been managed, unless I had kept a number of waggons pressed from Orangeburgh and Ninety Six, contrary to possitive promise, but with assurance of handsome pay, I could neither have gone forward nor have remained here, where we have been perpetually within a few hours of starving.

---

[20] Currently a commissary of prisoners, James Fraser would soon transfer as a commissary to the Department of Captures in Charlestown, administering it jointly with two others. (McCrady, op cit, 544)

[21] *Ross's letter..*: not extant.

[22] *the inclosed letter..*: of 1st September, p 175.

September 6th

I waited to finish my letter for the arrival of McLeod, who came yesterday. I move tomorrow to Waxhaw and perhaps to Charlottetown with the troops I mentioned. The 71st will follow very soon, and the 2nd division, the existance of which I owe to your exertions and management, will follow as soon as it conveniently can. I will leave the most possitive orders about Moncrief. I shall send up about 100 more prisoners under the escort of some convalescents of the Prince of Wales's Regiment and some invalids of the 16th making in all above 40. As they are to go all the way to Charlestown, we need only trouble you for boats to meet them at Monk's Corner, and even that is not necessary if any inconvenience attends the sending them. Eleven captured guns will go down by water to Nelson's Ferry. McLeod says he spoke to Trail[23] about having horses ready for them. I likewise mean to embark about eighty of our wounded whom the surgeons think proper to move to Charlestown, but they shall not leave this place until you notify to the commanding officer here that carriages will be ready at Nelson's Ferry to convey them to Monk's Corner.

I intend to leave Turnbull here with his own corps, joined by his light company and Innes's, and to make three or four small redoubts. I do not, however, think it impossible that some months hence either Waxhaw or even Charlottetown may be found a more convenient station for him and that it may answer better for preserving the peace of this province. However, I shall not remove him from hence without weighing the matter very maturely and consulting with you upon it, being fully convinced that one enemy in the rear is worse than five in the front. Cruger says that the attempting to raise Cunningham's corps will totally ruin the militia of 96, and he adds that Cunningham himself is convinced of it, on which account I told him I thought he had better give it up. Indeed, the raising corps does not succeed in this province. Harrison has totally failed and I don't see that Innes has 200 men fit for service. The Congarees is now the part of the province the most neglected as to militia and very disaffected. Mr Ancrum is a smooth tongued gentleman, but I very much suspect his loyalty. His overseers were constantly going backward and forward to Sumpter, and every one he recommends is inclined to rebellion. Mr Lord is certainly a rebel, but do not trust Mr Ancrum. I will answer with my life for Carey, but he has had infinite difficulties to struggle with and is a modest, diffident man. Five out of six of his whole district are rebels and he has been constantly called out with part of his regiment on actual service during the whole summer. He opposed Sumpter in arms until he was deserted by his people, and afterwards contrived to make his escape before Tarleton's action. So far from being desirous of command, it was with the utmost difficulty I could prevail on him to take it, and I am very sure that nothing but his determined zeal for the cause could make him continue in it. There is a Captain Bradley of his regiment who was very active at the head of his company at this place whilst Gates was in the neighbourhood. I can easily conceive him guilty of plundering, as the sole object of the militia is to *break up*, as they call it, their neighbours of the opposite party. After all I have said of Carey, he will be glad to give up the Congarees to any person who can make any thing of them. I have told you my opinions of the men from the best

---

[23] Peter Trail(e) (*c.* 1740-1795) was a major in the Royal Regiment of Artillery. He had entered the regiment as a cadet in 1755 before being commissioned as a 1st lieutenant on 1st January 1759. Twelve years later he rose to the rank of captain, but the date of his promotion to major is unknown. Now, in 1780, he was the senior artillery officer in the Southern Department and had commanded the artillery during the siege of Charlestown. He died at Leith. (*Royal Regiment of Artillery*, 7, 7A)

intelligence I have been able to procure and shall be vastly obliged to you if you can put it in some way that can succeed. Colonel Cassils and Lt Colonel Grey of Mills's regiment have both made their escape. I have sent them to Wemys and directed Cassils afterwards to go to Moncrief.

I promised to recommend it to you that Mrs Doyle should have a quarter in Charlestown. I inclose a letter to Colonel Clarke[24]. I told him that you would assist him with any supplies in your power. Moncrief will have mentioned to you what stores were wanting at Augustine. You must likewise desire Captain Ardesoif or the commanding officer of the navy to write to Lieutenant Mowbray[25], who commands the gallies and gun boats at Augustine, to desire him not to destroy any gun boats that Lt Colonel Clarke may think useful for the defence of the place.

Cunningham was with me this morning. He very handsomely acquiesed in giving up the corps, altho' he said he was sure he could have raised it. Cruger thinks he is distressed and that some allowance should be made to him. He says himself that he has distributed near £100 amongst his recruiting officers which he cannot recall. What he really has expended should in my opinion be repaid to him, and 100 dollars be given to him every quarter until his affairs get into a better state. This business you will be kind enough to settle with Cruger.

We shall have no occasion for the clothing at Monk's Corner except what may be wanting for Lt Colonel Hamilton's North Carolina corps. The rest had better be returned to Charles Town, and such part of it sent to Cape Fear River as you and the Inspector General shall think will be useful for the season. The only serviceable regiment I expect to raise in North Carolina will be the Highlanders under Governor Martin. I intend to purchase for them some plaids of the 71st which they do not want and which, McArthur tells me, are ordered from Savannah to Charles Town.

It is not possible that we should be able to open any communication with the Cape Fear River before the 2nd week of October, and not probably so soon. However, it may be right to have the vessels in the mouth of the river by that time.

If you are rich in salt provisions at Charles Town, it may be useful to send some pork as well as rum and salt, for the cattle in all the lower part of the country are very bad, and if it should be necessary, when the climate improves, to send any detachments towards the coast, the salt meat would be of great advantage to them. If De Rosset wishes to go with the vessels to Cape Fear River, I have no objection. You have done very properly in appointing Doctor Fraser, and I beg you will accept the fullest authority for appointments and secret service money.

I cannot express how much I am obliged to you. Without your assistance I could not have carried on the King's Service. I inclose the triplicates for New York and duplicates for

---

[24] *a letter..*: of 5th September, p 302.

[25] John Mowbray had been commissioned a lieutenant in the Royal Navy on 28th March 1780. He would not progress further in the service. (Syrett and DiNardo ed, *The Commissioned Sea Officers*)

England.

I am etc etc etc

[CORNWALLIS]

Balfour to Cornwallis, 4th September 1780 — 64(13): ALS

Munday, 4th September
2 o'clock noon

My Lord

Ross is sailed. He went about eight o'clock on Sunday morning with a delightful wind. I give him twenty five days only.

The New York packet, with your dispatches, I have now in my hand to deliver. It is carried by a very remarkable sailing schooner, who volontiers the business. Your dispatches are entrusted to a young ensign of the 46th Regiment you may remember here. A very fine lad, and I have no doubt he will take care that they do not fall into the enemy's hands.

In two days hence the *Keppell* brigg will carry the duplicates. She is just come in and is ordred to be got ready immediately. As soon as the triplicates arrive, they shall be sent in the very best manner I can.

The Fusiliers crossed the Cooper to Bonneau's Ferry early this morning, and expect they will cross the Santee on Thursday. Moncrieff is fully instructed, and am certain he will do us great service in the business, but I must beg that you will be so good as to take care of ordering him back, for I am a little affraid. Inclosed is a list of arrivals today and a sort of journal of the captain of the packet from Jamaica. The sick men of the 63rd are come in one of the vessels from Savanah.

All the recruits of the Legion, with fifty ship cuttlasses, sett out yesterday for Camden, also those of the Volunteers of Ireland, amounting to upwards of fifty men. Also I mean to send many men that are able to march belonging to different corps with your army.

A sloop with the 71st cloathing and arms is come from Savanah, but have no idea of their being wanted now.

Inclosed is a list of waggons etc etc that you may be certain of[26], with the times of their leaving this place, that your Lordship may know what to depend upon from this.

---

[26] *a list..*: not extant.

Colliton County can produce no waggons, as I am informed by Ballingall[27]. I have directed every thing that can move to carry up Provincial stores, those most wanted first from Monk's Corner, and desired McKinnon that, as soon as he has seen all the affairs of the harness etc clear, to sett out for Camden to forward and asist that unfortunate department. Allow me to mention one Oldfield[28], a lieutenant of marines who is here now and comes tomorow to Camden, as a very active, bustling lad that would be of use to England. I had him with me at Ninety Six.

I beg your Lordship will excuse this hasty scrawl and believe me

Ever most gratefully yours

N BALFOUR

PS

The money comes by different officers as soon as possible. The St Augustine gentry sail to night.

Enclosure (1)
List of arrivals in Charlestown harbour, 4th September 1780 64(17): DS

Superintendent's Office
4th September 1780

Entered Inwards

Schooner *Two Friends*, Robert Farquhar Master, from St Augustine with 257 barrels turpentine.

---

[27] Robert Ballingall was a Scottish immigrant who had become a substantial planter in South Carolina. In the summer of 1780 he had been commissioned Colonel of the Colleton County Regiment of the royal militia, a regiment whose catchment area lay south-west of Charlestown in the coastal parishes bounded by Charlestown, Orangeburg District and the Salkehatchie River. In the coming months he and his regiment would be principally deployed in Georgetown District, but as the year advanced, Cornwallis and Balfour began to suspect that the men were disaffected and that no great reliance could be placed on them. In mid November Balfour reported that they were so totally disaffected that 'very few assembled and *those* very soon deserted'. During the winter of 1781 Ballingall would be appointed one of the Commissioners of Claims for Slave Property, and in January 1782 he would see his estates confiscated by act of the revolutionary assembly at Jacksonborough. (Lambert, *SC Loyalists*, 120, 241; *The Cornwallis Papers*; The SC Banishment and Confiscation Act 1782)

[28] A descendant of Sir Anthony Oldfield Bt, John Nicholls Oldfield (?-1793) was a lieutenant in the Royal Marines who would serve with disinction during the coming months on the staff of the Quartermaster General's Department at Camden. He would resign his commission in 1789 and die on his small estate at Westbourne, Sussex. His only son John (1789-1863) would have a distinguished career in the Royal Engineers, rising to Colonel-Commandant with the rank of general, and being knighted for his services at Waterloo and in the occupation of Paris. (*ODNB*)

Arrived in the Harbour

His Majesty's Ship The *Hydra*

The *Diligence* packet from Pensacola

A brigantine from Glasgow

A ditto from Georgia also

Sundry small craft.

ROB^T McCULLOH[29]
Deputy Superintendent

Enclosure (2)
Report from the captain of the Jamaica packet   64(16): DS

Charlestown
4th September 1780

On my departure from Jamaica the 2nd July last, accounts was received of seventeen sail of Spanish line of battle ships and a number of transports having been seen of Dominica beating up for Martinique, supposed intended to form a junction with the French fleet. Orders were immediately given out that a number of Negroes were to be raised for the publick works, and the forts on the island put into the best state of defence possible. It was pub[l]ish'd in the papers there that the fleet for Great Britain were to be in readyness to sail on the first of August and that several vessels intended for this and Georgia were to take the benifit of the convoy. Nothing hapn'd on my passage to Pensacola worthy of remark. On my arrival there I found His Majesty's Ship of War *Mentor* of 24 guns, the *Hound* and *Port Royal* sloops, *Earl Bathurst* store ship, 2 transports and 5 merchant ships, all which were detained by an embargoe. The fort on Gage Hill was nearly finish'd and the troops in general healthy there, but a number of them had deserted to the Spanish on account of the reward offer'd by Don Galvez to British deserters.

JOHN FARGIE
Commanding the *Diligence* packett boat

---

[29] There is reason to suspect that McCulloh belonged to a British mercantile family of that name, of which the key member was Henry. It had been involved in the affairs of North Carolina and made a practice of soliciting appointments to port offices. (T W Lipscomb to the editor, 22nd August 2006; John Cannon, 'Henry McCulloch and Henry McCulloh', *William and Mary Quarterly*, 3rd ser, xv (1958), 71-3; Charles G Sellars Jr, 'Private Profits and British Colonial Policy: The Speculations of Henry McCulloh', *William and Mary Quarterly,* 3rd ser, viii (1951), 535-551)

Enclosure (3)
Persons transported to St Augustine 3(33): D

*List of the Names of the Disaffected Inhabitants of Charlestown
who have been sent to Augustine, 3rd September 1780*[30]

Names	Address	Comments
Christopher Gadsden	N° 1 Bay Street continued	
John Edwards	57 Meeting Street	
Thomas Fergusson	1 Freind Street	
Thomas Savage	49 Church Street	
Doctor Ramsay	Broad Street between Mrs Ellis and the Tin Man for the Barrack Master	
Reverend Robert Smith	95 Church Street	Sick in bed
Edward Rutledge	10 Bay Street continued	
Hugh Rutledge	Ditto	
Alexander Moultrie	31 Broad Street	
Jacob Read	28 ditto	
Thomas Heyward (judge)	78 Church Street	
Peter Timothy	91 Meeting Street	
Doctor Fayseaux	90 ditto	
John Ernest Poyas	83 ditto	
~~Hugh Swinton~~	118 ditto	In the country
Edward McReddy	23 Bay Street	
~~Peter Bocquet~~	40 ditto	In the country on parole
Edward North	56 ditto	
Edward Blake	1 Legare Street	
Richard Hudson	Oposite N° 6 Legare Street	
John Budd	73 Church Street	
Josiah Smith Jun°	N° 53 Meeting Street	

---

[30] In the left margin there is a cross against each name, except that of the Reverend Robert Smith, which is ticked, and the two which are struck through. These three persons, and Dr Fayssoux as belonging to the Continental hospital, were not transported.

John Loveday	25 ditto	
Anthony Toomer	3 Legare Street	
Isaac Holmes	8 ditto	
Richard Lushington	3 Hazell Street	
Thomas Singleton	45 Broad Street	
George Flagg	23 King Street	
John Sanson		
William Hazell Gibbes		
John Todd		
[John] Parker		

Balfour to Cornwallis, 5th September 1780 64(24): ALS

Charles Town
5th September

My Lord

I did myself the honor of writing you yesterday and only now trouble you with this to say that the galley for George Town, the schooner with dispatches for New York, and the transport with the *rebellious* are sailed, and that the *Keppell* brig will sail tomorow evening with the duplicates or sooner if possible. I am sorry to tell you that the bottom of the *Sandwich* is so bad as to be obliged to be hove down, and wish she may be in time for the necessary services I hope that she will be wanted for. However, I shall take every possible care to get the galleys in order etc etc and shall asist her repair with all possible expedition. General Moultrie has wrote a violent letter, as I expected, concerning the arrested citizens. However, as he boldly talks of *this state* and is otherwise very exceptionable in his expressions, I have been extremly laconick in my answer[31].

As the *Hydra* is arrived, Captain Gardner[32] has taken the command and will sail with his convoy in about a fortnight. Do you mean all the invalids to go home with him?

I am extremly uneasy at that total want of activity in your departments. I fear much it will entangle your movements. I sent you a state of all we could do and McKinnon comes to asist. He will be in time to the second division arrangement, if the first can only get away

---

[31] For the exchange of letters and Balfour's further comments, see pp 111-3.

[32] Alan Gardner (1742-1808/9) was a post-captain who was dispatched from Jamaica to England in 1780 while in charge of a convoy, but it is doubtful whether he called in at Charlestown. Balfour, who had a habit of misspelling surnames, may be referring to Edward Garner (?-1781) or William Garner (?-1787), both of whom were post-captains. (*ODNB*; Syrett and DiNardo ed, *The Commissioned Sea Officers*)

tolerably. The idea of entring a barren country is horrid, but I suppose it must be. I beg to know when you think the cooperation may be necessary — I mean the shipping part of it - that I may take care to have it ready and every thing else that I can move.

If we are fortunate enough to do that in proper time and compleatly secure your rear, I would hope the way will be made some little smoother.

Inclosed is the acounts from Jamaica[33]. This day a vessel from Antigua in twelve days brings the movements of the fleets, viz:

On the 12th of July the enemy's fleet sailed from Guadalupe and seperated soon after with the Spanish squadron, which bore away for the Havanah. Where the French are, God knows - supposed gone to the Cape[34]. Sir George Rodney gone to St Lucia for the hurricane season.

The Antigua merchant who brought me this also says that he spoke a packet from England in twenty five days, who told him positively of our fleet of observation having captured the homeward bound Santo Domingo fleet consisting of thirty sail. So much for publick news, but nothing from New York.

I am with every wish for your happiness and success
Yours most sincerly

N BALFOUR

PS

I send £900 by Lieutenant McKenzie[35]. The rest in dollars come by another hand.

Cornwallis to Balfour, 12th September 1780   80(17): C

Camp at Crawford's on Waxhaw Creek
September 12th 1780

Lt Colonel Balfour
Commandant of Charlestown

Dear Balfour

I last night received yours of the 5th. Hitherto we have gone on very well, but few relapses, and this settlement well stocked with forage and provisions. I shall probably *remain here* 10 *days* at *least*. The 63rd Regiment arrived at Camden in a very sickly state. I have

---

[33] *the acounts..*: not extant.

[34] *the Cape*: Cape François on the north coast of Haiti.

[35] Perhaps Charles or John Mackenzie, both of whom had been commissioned lieutenants in the 2nd Battalion, 71st (Highland) Regiment, in December 1775. (*Army Lists*)

great hopes of their recovering there, for the troops never suffer'd much at that place, and I hear the 71st are getting up very fast. I received a letter from Cruger with the inclosed papers[36]. The obliging the prisoners on parole to take an oath of allegiance is too absurd to bear a moment's arguing upon. I must beg of you to take this business into your hands, as it would be impossible for me to carry on the voluminous correspondence with which it may be attended, considering the business on which I am going. You will likewise be able to judge better than I can do of the propriety of removing those officers whom Lt Colonel Brown mentions. I beg in all matters that you will, whenever you think proper, make use of the words: 'I am particularly directed by Lord Cornwallis'. I send you a copy of a letter I received from Cruger with my answer to it[37]. I have no certain accounts of the enemy. I rather think that Gates is gone on to Virginia and perhaps to Congress to exculpate himself and press for reinforcements, but this is only surmise from what dropp'd from the surgeon. You may depend on hearing from me frequently. It is wonderfull that we have no accounts from the northward.

I am, my dear Balfour, with great truth
Most faithfully yours

CORNWALLIS

Balfour to Cornwallis, 8th September 1780   64(34): ALS

Charles Town
8th September 1780

I have but little to say since my letter by McKenzie of the light infantry, who I hope arrives safe with the cash, the proclamation etc. I feared the want of any other safe opportunity and rather trusted too much to one person.

It seems the *Keppel* brig has been wishing to take some part actively and landed about a fortnight ago a party of twenty men in Cape Fear harbour, marched to a place they call Fort Johnston near the harbour (and intended for the defence of it), spiked the 12 pounder that was there, demolished the work intended for some more guns, took eight prisoners, and wounded three or four of the others, who attempted to escape.

I wish much to have some idea of your movements that I may *try* to get the sea business in train — I mean, to know nerely when they may be expected by you; also, how the communication is to be kept up, and if you wish any militia to be put upon the road betwixt you and Camden.

---

[36] For the extant enclosures, see pp 183-4

[37] For Cruger's letter of 7th September and Cornwallis's reply of the 12th, see pp 182 and 185.

The gentleman[38] sent for in a hurry by Tarleton is come and setts out tomorow for the army, as I was quite in the dark what to send him about.

The convoy[39] of the *Hydra* is to sail on the 26th instant. Don't you send duplicates?[40] No arrivals from New York to my astonishment.

I shall send the letters the moment they come from thence, and mean to place Captain Maxwell of Brown's corps, an intelligent officer, to command the militia upon the communication betwixt Camden and this. His post will be at Nielson's Ferry.

I find the 63rd are marched. Moncrieff will be at George Town to'day. I hope they will communicate. Every happiness and success attend you. I long to hear of you now every day. I have stopped every floating navy thing till I know what you want.

I ever am
Your Lordship's much obliged and most faithful servant

N BALFOUR

[*Subscribed*:]

I want much the Town Major of the Welsh Fuzileers that I mentioned to Money.

No paper can be got such as you want.

Cornwallis to Balfour, 13th September 1780

80(20): C

Camp at Crawford's on Waxhaw Creek
September 13th 1780

Lt Colonel Balfour
Commandant of Charlestown

Dear Balfour

I have just received yours of the 8th. You will have received information on several points that you mention soon after you wrote to me.

---

[38] *The gentleman*: almost certainly Captain de Treville, a French officer in the revolutionary service, who was to act as a British spy.

[39] *the convoy*: to England.

[40] Duplicates for England had been enclosed with Cornwallis's letter to Balfour of 3rd and 6th September. See p 71.

The *Keppel* brig has done vastly well. Those preparations at Fort Johnson meant no good to our provisions. Some galleys of the lightest draft of the water will be necessary. I am informed that they can go up very near to Cross Creek. You will see by the map that Black River, which I am told is not fordable any where between the height of Cross Creek and its fork, will be a great security to our navigation. I hear there is plenty of wheat about Charlottesburg and Salisbury, and in about three weeks the indian corn will be fit to grind, so that I hope we shall be in no danger of starving, but we must positively get healthier or there is no doing any thing. I find the ague and fever all over this country full as much as at Camden. They say go 40 or 50 miles farther and you will be healthy. It was the same language before we left Camden. There is no trusting such dangerous experiments. I will write very fully to you about posts in this country before we move. The militia of 96 must certainly have a constant one about the Ennoree or Tyger Rivers as Cruger proposes. Here is a tract of 50 miles in length, all rebellious and almost entirely deserted. There can be no doubt but the inhabitants will return on the army's moving on and commence hostilitys in their way. I therefore at present think it will be absolutely necessary to establish a post with redoubts at Charlottesburg. The 63rd Regiment is totally *hors de combat* and unfit for any active service. It appears to me that the debris of that regiment with a detachment from Innes's corps under the major[41] will be equal to this service and, by keeping eighty or one hundred horses to make occasional expeditions, will perfectly awe this rebellious tract. Detachments of militia of Rugely's, Turner's, Phillips's and Carey's regiments must endeavour to keep the country clear between Charlotte and Camden, which latter post, though weaken'd in numbers, will be greatly strengthened by the other. An old Colonel Mills of Tryon County, who was the first man that rose this summer in North Carolina, has offered to raise a corps and give the command of it to Captain Dunlap of the Queen's Rangers, who is serving with Ferguson. Dunlap is an active, spirited officer and, if he could get only two hundred men, would be very usefull in that country. These are my present undigested ideas and resources. I hope to put them into some form before we move, which cannot be very soon. The route by which I send this letter I think perfectly safe. I yesterday put a few words in cypher, but I think Ferguson has a better style of cypher than ours, much easier and quicker[42]. I will make out one on his principle and send it to you, and we may use which we find to answer best. Your Town Major of the Fuzileers is very ill at Camden. My impatience to hear from New York increases every hour. Write your sentiments to me freely.

I am, dear Balfour,
Very sincerely yours

CORNWALLIS

---

[41] *the Major*: Wemyss.

[42] *Ferguson has a better style of cypher..*: the enciphering device had two concentric rings, the outer of which consisted of the letters of the alphabet, and the inner a series of numbers. To form a cipher the numbers in the inner ring were aligned with the letters in the outer, and the key to the cipher was the number aligned with the letter 'A', which always appeared first in an enciphered document. It was therefore a simple matter for the recipient to make the same alignment, and so decipher the document. Numbers not part of the cipher were sometimes inserted to confuse an unauthorised recipient. Occasionally other numbers were added to those that were part of the cipher. For example, if 'A' were '6', it may sometimes be encoded as '56'. One number was used for both 'I' and 'J', and one for 'U' and 'V'.

Balfour to Cornwallis, 9th September 1780   64(38): ALS

Charles Town
9th September

A few hours ago a packet from England arrived who sailed *only* the 12th of July, and, of course, not much news. I have no letters but one from Broderick referring me to Ross for all things. He says he is much better, as is Fitzroy[43]. I have seen no papers or letters yet further, wishing to get your packet dispatched to catch you as soon as possible.

Your letter of the 6th is just arrived. Every thing shall be done that can be done about the shipping getting in time to Cape Fear River. *That*, and having nothing to make you cast a look behind, shall be my study, you may rest assured. Colonel Cassells' coming is lucky, as I am told he is a sensible man. The galleys, I know, will be all ready, and I hope to send you four, but the *Sandwich* is the great point, and she most unfortunately is in the most crazy case. However, I shall sett every carpenter in Charles Town to work upon her, and think from the great willingness in the navy that she will be in time. Salt pork shall be sent etc etc etc.

The *Hydra* sails on the 28th or 29th if you have any answer to the letters now sent. Being in haste to catch Captain King[44], who is sett out, I have only time to return you my most grateful thanks for your approbation of my conduct, which, be assured, shall be chiefly and sóly directed to follow your wishes and directions.

I ever am
Yours most sincely

N BALFOUR

PS

I mean to send a quarter cask of Madeira, mentioned by England, up in time for the 2nd division, but it can't be for the first, I know. I shall attend to every point in your letter but have not time to answer them now.

---

[43] Perhaps George Fitzroy, who was about the same age as Brodrick and a lieutenant in the 3rd (The King's Own) Regiment of Dragoons. In October his father, Charles, who was colonel of the regiment, would be created Baron Southampton, a title inherited by George in 1797. (*ODNB*; *Army Lists*)

[44] Having served for three years as an ensign in the 57th Regiment, James King had transferred to the Provincial establishment, becoming a lieutenant in Simcoe's Queen's Rangers and then a captain in Rawdon's Volunteers of Ireland. He would still be with the regiment when it was taken on to the British establishment in 1782. On its disbandment at the close of the war, he was placed on the British half-pay list. (*Army Lists*; The Clinton Papers, vol 44(8))

Cornwallis to Balfour, 15th September 1780 80(23): C

Camp at Waxhaw
September 15th 1780

Lt Colonel Balfour
Commandant of Charlestown

Dear Balfour

I inclose two letters[45] that came by a flag and have permitted Mr Drayton[46] to proceed to Charlestown as the case seem'd compassionate. If he does not behave properly, you will of course soon dismiss him. Nothing material has happen'd in this part of the country. I am sorry that we do not yet find it grow healthy. I am much obliged to you for forwarding so quick my letters from England. The mobs have entirely subsided[47] and I hope every body will be averse to the raising them again. I recollect that I did not answer your query about the invalids going home with the *Hydra*'s convoy. I fancy most of those that are passed by the Board for Discharges are unfit for any other service. You may detain any that you may think usefull untill another opportunity.

We have a pleasant camp, hilly and pretty open, dry ground, excellent water and plenty of provisions. If all that will not keep us from falling sick, I shall despair.

I am, dear Balfour,
Your[s] most sincerely

CORNWALLIS

[*Subscribed*:]

Mr T[48] told me that several men of Colonel Lechmere's battalion of Beaufort militia declared to him that they would join the rebels whenever it was in their power.

---

[45] *two letters*: no extant copies, but Gates's is summarised in Money's Journal for the 15th, p 363.

[46] Cornwallis may be referring to William Drayton (1732-1790), a sometime Chief Justice of East Florida, who had been suspended from office for being 'the head of a faction against administration'. Known to have been in South Carolina in 1780, Drayton was the great-grandson of Thomas Drayton, who came to South Carolina from Barbados in 1679, and the first cousin of William Henry Drayton, the deceased revolutionary. (*DAB*)

[47] *The mobs..*: a reference to the Gordon riots of 2nd to 9th June.

[48] *Mr T*: de Treville.

Balfour to Cornwallis, 14th September 1780   64(55): ALS

Charles Town
14th September

This moment I am favoured with your Lordship's letter of the 8th and waited every day with an easterly wind for acounts from New York, but in vain.

I fear there are too good reasons to acount for the stoppage of vessels, viz, the privateers of force who are off this harbour, who have taken every thing that has sailed lately. Your dispatches, I hope, are excepted in the list. However, for fear that they should not, I have ordred the packet that came from England, who has sixteen guns, and a good sailer, to carry the triplicates to New York, although she had no orders from home, but was at the direction of the commanding officer here. I conceived she could perform no service more essential than this, and she could be better spared as the *Hydra* will answer to carry the mail to England. I have made a requisition to Captain Gardner for a convoy, and the *Loyalist* sees her[49] clear off this coast, and I have desired also that she may go as far as the Chesapeak with her. They sail the moment the wind is fair.

I have not heared from Moncrieff since he marched, but expect it every hour.

I hope soon to put this place in some state of defence, for the works were very near being perfectly useless; and as I conceived it rather dangerous to trust to the new works proposed by Moncrieff, especialy in his absence, I have determined to repair the old ones as quickly as possible and have seriously sett about it by employing a good many rebell prisoners and ordering a hundred Negroes from the country from the rebellious.

McKinnon, being at Camden, will be able to arrange all transportation for the wounded etc, after which I mean to order down all Provincial stores etc etc here to be ready for embarkation.

The *Sandwich* and galleys will be all ready by the 1st week of October, but by what I can learn, the rebell privateers are in Cape Fear harbour and they carry their prizes there. Will it not be necessary to send some additional naval force if we can get it by that time? However, I shall wait for your instructions etc etc and keep all things in getting ready that I think you may want.

I have directed more fresh meat to be killed and contracted for than hitherto used in the garrison, as I know it is an amazing saving and I think you would wish me never to have this place without three or four months' provision actualy in *the town*.

As to Cary's regiment, I by all means agree with your Lordship about the whole business, but conceive that Cary is not active enough for so very critical a district as he has.

---

[49] *her*: Balfour means the packet, as evinced by his letter of the 20th, p 90.

I have beged him in a letter to come here, when I think I will be able to settle with him and try to get a lt colonel he approves of etc. In short, in that and every other district on the frontiers, I shall exert myself to put in proper order as far as possibly I can. If Monsieur de Ternay or any of his friends come this way, you will soon hear of it. In the mean time I mean to put things in that situation that we may not be *quite* at his mercy. If he will give me three or four weeks, *law*[50], it will not hurt us!

The wine, tea and sugar is gone for Camden with the best horses we could get, and also a hundred pounds in silver.

I am sorry to tell you that the *Ceres* transport is lost by neglect and ignorance of the pilot on her voyage to Beaufort to take the stores from the *Vigilant*.

I ever am
Your Lordship's most obliged servant

N BALFOUR

Cornwallis to Balfour, 18th September 1780   80(25): C

Camp at Waxhaw
September 18th 1780

Lt Colonel Balfour
Commandant of Charlestown

Dear Balfour

Notwithstanding the situation of our camp, which promises health, that our men live well, have excellent huts and plenty of straw, still the sickness rather gains ground; and indeed, in spite of all the doctors may say, we have been full as healthy at Camden as at any other place. The 71st Regiment march from that place to day and will be here about the 23rd or 24th. Whether I shall then immediately proceed to Charlottesburg or remain some days longer here will depend on what I may hear of the state of the provisions forward and on the health of my troops. I cannot possibly, with any degree of prudence, proceed farther than Charlotte untill the 2nd division is ready to move (as this part of the country is so rebellious that I should instantly lose my communication) unless some very material object should present itself. I have sent Tarleton forward to frighten and scarify the militia. I am more convinced every day of the necessity of establishing a post where I mentioned in my letter of the 13th instant, and by every thing I hear of the country I should hope there would be no difficulty in having it supplied. I inclose to you a letter I received this morning from Cruger[51]. I think he seems to be rather more alarmed than is necessary. However, he is certainly right

---

[50] *law*: an exclamation.

[51] *a letter..*: of 13th September, p 186.

to take this opportunity of marching into that country as no material attack can at present be made on Ninety Six. I think it would be right for you to send some rum and salt as soon as you conveniently can to Camden, as my 2nd division will probably drain that place very compleatly when they leave it... As regular packets are now established to Charlestown, I think the commanding officer of this province would be highly criminal towards Government if he did not write to the Minister, for, as he will have found out by Ross's arrival that affairs here were not quite in so peaceable a situation as they were represented by the dispatches carried home by that distinguish'd officer Colonel Bruce[52], he must be rather anxious to hear from time to time a true state of things. I shall write to Lord George Germain by the *Hydra* and send duplicates by the packet. I will continue to correspond as long as I can with safety and must then transfer that agreeable office to you. As I shall be always able to send to you in cypher, you will be furnished from the army with authentick materials, and you may mention that you was directed by me to take the opportunity of the packet's sailing to inform his Lordship etc.

You will settle the time of the pacquet's sailing as shall best suit the convenience of the town, reserving one always for extraordinary occasions.

I have been busy in finally settling my proclamation[53] and commission to Cruden[54], both which are now accomplish'd, and I hope in the best manner. I have been obliged to make some alterations in Simpson's, which I hope, as my name is to stand at the bottom of it, he will forgive. Any unclaimed Negroes belonging to those estates in the present custody of the Commissioners, or in the possession of persons not authorized to keep them, I dare say you will think it right to order to be given up to Mr Cruden. Those who are *usefull* in the publick departments will remain where they are. I shall refer Mr Cruden to you on all decisions. His employment will create him many enemies, but whilst he executes his very difficult task with propriety and deserves your countenance, I am sure he will have it.

I am, dear Balfour, with great regard
Very sincerely yours

CORNWALLIS

[*Subscribed*:]

I shall send my letters for the *Hydra* in two or three days.

---

[52] Andrew Bruce was Lt Colonel of the 54th Regiment and an aide-de-camp to Clinton. In June he had sailed from Charlestown, charged with Clinton's dispatches for Germain. After a very long and tedious passage from Cork he would arrive back at Charlestown towards the end of February 1781 in the frigate *Assurance*. After staying there for some time, he went on to New York to advise Clinton of an imminent reinforcement of six British regiments from Europe. (*Army Lists*; *The Cornwallis Papers*, including the endorsement on 99(5); Willcox, *Portrait of a General*, 357, 360)

[53] *proclamation*: on sequestration. See pp 323-4.

[54] *commission to Cruden*: as Commissioner for Sequestered Estates. See p 320.

Cornwallis to Balfour, 21st September 1780

80(35): C

Waxhaw
September 21st 1780

Lt Colonel Balfour
Commandant of Charlestown

Dear Balfour

I informed you in my last letter that Tarleton was gone forward towards Charlotte, but I soon after heard that, instead of having marched, he was very dangerously ill. I have been very uneasy about him untill this morning. His fever has now intermitted and I hope he is safe.

I inclose letters from Cruger and Brown[55]. That business will, I fear, be troublesome. I suppose the guns he mentions were those taken by Brown's capitulation from the enemy, as I do not recollect that he took any up with him. I shall wait untill I hear again from Cruger before I decide what steps it may be necessary to take. Two or three volunteer companys of our militia, who had made some successfull scouts, contrived this morning to be totally surprized and routed by a Major Davy, who is a celebrated partizan in the Waxhaws[56].

Tarleton's illness is of the greatest inconvenience to me at present, as I not only lose his services but the whole corps must remain quite useless in order to protect him. I do not think I can move to Charlotte without the greatest difficulty unless the Legion can advance to clear the country of all the parties who would certainly infest our rear. Sumpter is with 3 or 400 militia on Allison's Creek at the head of the Indian settlement. Ferguson has made an incursion into Tryon County, by his account rather successfull, but Captain Dunlap of the Queen's Rangers, who was with him, is very badly wounded, which is particularly distressing as he was to have commanded a corps which old Mills of that county had engaged to raise for him and which with Dunlap's assistance might be very usefull.

You see that your naval force for Cape Fear will be in very good time, but I most earnestly hope that, before it goes, the Admiral will send us a serviceable reinforcement. If the harbour of Charlestown is to remain blocked up, our conquest will not be very profitable to Britain.

The unavoidable delays that have attended us will reduce our stock of rum. If it was possible to get up twenty puncheons, time enough for the 2nd division, it would be a great object; and I hardly think that division can leave Camden untill the 2nd week in October. I know you will do your utmost and shall say no more.

---

[55] *letters..*: see pp 187-190.

[56] A reference to the action at Wahab's plantation, mistakenly asserted by Davie to have involved part of the British Legion. (Davie, *Revolutionary War Sketches*, 22) Cornwallis's letter and Davidson's of the 21st (p 355) coincide in the date of the action, which has hitherto been uncertain.

I directed England, who is still at Camden, to inform himself very particularly on the state of our medicines and, if he apprehended a deficiency, to send an express immediately to you to save time. I shall send you copies of my letters to the Secretary of State that you may see where to take up the correspondence when I am obliged to drop it.

I am, dear Balfour, with great regard
Most sincerely

CORNWALLIS

Cornwallis to Balfour, 23rd September 1780   80(39): C

Waxhaw
September 23rd 1780

Lt Colonel Balfour
Commandant of Charlestown

Dear Balfour

I send letters to go to New York[57] by the first opportunity and an additional letter to Lord George Germain[58] with the account of the success of Cruger's expedition and the relief of Augusta. You will receive a copy of it and the duplicates of my letters to Lord George Germain, which you will get copied, and forward those I send you by the first opportunity after the sailing of the *Hydra*. Tarleton is vastly better. I got him conveyed this day to Blair's Mill on the east side of Catawba, and his corps will pass this evening. His illness has been truly unfortunate. It has prevented our demolishing the militia whilst they were assembling and has given time to the enemy to drive away cattle and carry off provisions. However, we are fortunate to save him and get the use of his corps, which could not leave Fishing Creek until he was well enough to be removed, and for which I was very uneasy as there was no officer with them capable of commanding them. Kinloch arrived this evening, but he is still very ill, and I am sure he will be laid up in three days. I will trouble you to inclose a copy of my sixth and last proclamation[59] to the Admiral, and one to the General and him when you send off my duplicates. A rebel officer, who came in yesterday with necessaries for the prisoners, and Monsieur [de Treville] agreed that no action had happened to the northward, nor any thing at all material except an unsuccessful attack on Paulus Hook by General Wayne.

I shall probably march to Charlottetown tomorrow evening or the next day in the morning. I flatter myself our communication will still be pretty safe. I shall, however, put every material paragraph into cypher. I will send you a copy of Ferguson's, which is easier to

---

[57] *letters to go to New York*: see pp 44 and 47.

[58] *an additional letter..*: see p 40.

[59] *proclamation*: on sequestration.

write, but I believe easier to make out. Both may be made use of in one letter, putting *B* in the front of yours and *F* of his. It will probably be a fortnight before I shall be able to leave Charlottetown. I have heard nothing of either Wemys or Moncrief and I dread hearing of their sickness. I wish I could say that we found any material amendment[60]. The 71st will remain here until the 2nd division are ready to march, unless I should have any particular reason for wanting them forward. I apprehend it will be necessary for me to send something to 96 and to erect some better works there and at Augusta. Innes's corps has only 160 duty men. From the gross misbehaviour of the militia of this province I intend in North Carolina to try raising corps only. I wish I had tryed it more at first here. I should wish all the serviceable arms that could possibly be spared to be sent in the *Sandwich*, as that article will be the most difficult to transport by land and will be much wanted, as our friends are every where rigidly disarmed in North Carolina. I have inclosed a copy of my proclamation to Lord George Germain, but I must beg you will send a printed one with my duplicates. Our sickness continues much the same. Very few die.

I am, dear Balfour,
Yours most sincerely

[CORNWALLIS]

Balfour to Cornwallis, 20th September 1780   64(83): ALS

Charles Town
20th September 1780

Your Lordship's letters of the 12th, 13th and 15th are just received. I wait impatiently every tide for a packet from New York but am now certain that the enemy's privateers, consisting of two twenty gun ships, a brig and a sloop, have been off this coast for a month past. I tremble for the *Keppell* brig, but the schooner I have no fears about. She was well commanded and sailed like the wind. The contrary winds has prevented the packet[61] sailing as I mentioned with the triplicates, and as the *Hydra*'s convoy now sails on the 25th, Captain Gardner has apply'd that they may all sail in company, as he conceives that they are not strong enough, either the *Loyalist* and the packet or the *Hydra* with the convoy, separately. In consequence of this application, I found I could not refuse, and indeed yesterday the officer at Fort Arbuthnot reported an action having been seen from the fort betwixt two ships, and the rebell ship was said to be beat off. However, the English ship has not yet made her appearance. In short, the harbour has been and is compleatly blocked up, and nothing but a frigate *can* bring us news from New York. Where can the *Triton* be! I fear nothing concerning South Carolina is thought of by land or water.

As it is a province so compleatly subdued, there can be no occasion.

---

[60] *amendment*: improvement.

[61] *the packet*: to New York.

The *Sandwich* and the galleys of smallest draft of water shall be in readiness, and the articles mentioned by Ross got also ready, but we must have something to asist against the privateers besides the *Sandwich*, I hope before they are wanted. We must have a frigate, which will be sufficient.

I have been a little allarmed with an acount of an attack upon Augusta by a Clark from the debris of Sumpter's corps, joined by the banditti of the Back Country, amounting to about two hundred or more, who passed the River Savannah and, coming into the Ceded Lands, were supposed to be joined by a larger number. The express came two days ago, and as it is not confirmed, I have every reason to believe it is not true as to the attack upon Augusta; but by a letter of the 14th from Crugar there is no doubt of Clark's having got into the Ceded Lands with the number mentioned.

Crugar has marched into the Long Cane settlement, and has ordred the militia to join him, which he thinks was necessary in order to prevent their joining Clark.

I have no doubt of its being totally a plundering party and that, the moment they find the country will not rise for them, that they will retire behind the mountains with what they can carry off. In my opinion the movements of your corps will perfectly settle every serious attempt in this country, but still, the keeping up the business is bad and ought if possible to be avoided. I own the best mode of at once stopping all these kind of expeditions appears to me to be the employing the Indians to clear certain districts where these people retreat to and resort.

Williamson's secretary has been with me to'day. He says that W is gone into the Long Cane settlement and means with Pickens to get the country to rise and asist Crugar in getting at Clark. If they do, and succeed, the business will soon be at an end; but if not, he says W is clearly of opinion to employ the Indians upon certain boundarys which could easily be assertained and would certainly effect the purpose, which is of consequence to attend to before it gains head and becomes perhaps too powerful for any of our posts when you are at a distance. By Crugar's letters he is very suspicious and uneasy about the country, great part of which I attribute to his finding himself at a distance from support and unacustomed to act for himself.

If I could get W to join with Cuningham and make an expedition against these trans mountain gentry, it would be by much the best mode of settling the business, but that I despair of, although I am certain that with good management he will do a great deal unless he is charged[62]. I have sent for him to come here when Clark's affair is over. I have wrote Crugar concerning the posts upon the Ennoree which I happen to know. And upon the whole, that Back Country will take a strict and an active officer; but with one, I cannot help thinking that, while your movements continue or untill *another* rebell force from the north makes its appearance, that the present corps will be sufficient. Any cooperation of the Indians would certainly secure it and keep it so, and prevent the only consequential danger: that of the enemy's getting, by a surprise or a small success, a large corps to endanger the communication and the internal parts of the province. I should wish to know your ideas upon

---

[62] *charged*: pressed aggressively.

this subject fuly. As to Georgia, Brown, Crugar etc etc, if you will be so good as to give me the out lines of what you wish, I can put an easy stop to your further trouble with them or the place in question.

I think you cannot find a proprer person than Dunlapp to command betwixt you and Charlottebergh, wherever you may be, while that communication lasts. He is active, knowing in the country and the maners of the country people, and very spirited. Whilst with me, he behaved very well, rather too forward in his patroles, by which he got into scrapes, but it is a fault that soon mends.

If Mills's regiment upon the Cheraws turns out tolerably, it will be a security. If not, thirty men from Turnbull would be a great matter, with an officer, to asist Mills in overawing that country. I like Balingall much. I have seen him and Lechmere[63] and ordred both their regiments, *when* properly arranged, to assemble on the 18th of October, and meant them to move towards the Cheraws, and act according to circumstances probably, to support Camden, Charlottebergh, Cheraws or George Town, and if necessary to be joined by Captain Maxwell, who commands on the Santee, with two hundred picked Orangeburghers and his own company of grenadiers, a *kind* of second line ready to move up when Turnbull calls for them. Ball's and Wigfall's I mean for Murray's, Lanew's and Santee Ferrys, ready to support Cassells or Tyne[64]. A galley and part of Brown's corps, with a good officer (if he's to be got), I wish to post at George Town. By this means I would bring the internal militia to support the external, and allways to have a sucession and some force formed. It will require coxing, which will require money, but while we are as we are, I humbly conceive that must

---

[63] Nicholas Lechmere (?-1782) had been Collector of Customs at Beaufort before the war and had married into the prominent Deveaux family of that place. In the summer of 1780 he had been commissioned Colonel of the Granville County Regiment of the royal militia, a regiment whose catchment area lay in part of Beaufort District. Besides acting there, his regiment would also see service in Georgetown District, but the same charge of disaffection levelled at Ballingall's regiment (see p 75, note 27) applied equally to his. In April 1781, while separated from his command, he would be captured at Pocotaligo by William Harden. Presumably paroled, he was by 1782 residing as a paid refugee in Charlestown, but sometime between 1st March and 31st May he died. (Lambert, *SC Loyalists*, 120, 175; *The Cornwallis Papers*; McCrady, *SC in the Rev 1780-1783*, 135; Clark, *Loyalists in the Southern Campaign*, 491-2)

[64] Of Samuel Tynes little is known except that militarily he and his men were an accident waiting to happen. A man of some prominence on the High Hills of Santee, he had enlisted in autumn 1775 in the troop of revolutionary light horse commanded by Matthew Singleton (see p 211, note 5), but perhaps being a covert loyalist, he has otherwise left no record of revolutionary military service. Although he was, according to Cornwallis, 'a weak, well intentioned man', he had on 14th June 1780 been commissioned major of the royal militia on the High Hills, but when part of his regiment was inspected on 4th September by Frederick De Peyster of Ferguson's corps, not a third of his men had arms, the rest having been disarmed on Cornwallis's march to Camden. Nevertheless, according to their officers, those assembled were to be trusted, and indeed they did subscribe to the resolutions agreed to by other militia regiments at Brandon's and Mobley's settlements. Now promoted to colonel, Tynes was soon to be involved in the accident that awaited him. Encamped at Tarcote in the fork of Black River, he took no precautions against attack, was surprised by Marion on 26th October, and was totally routed, losing all his arms. He himself was captured, a few of his men were slain, and many were taken prisoner. Of those that fled, a considerable number soon joined Marion, who in the action had lost not a single man. Some three weeks later Tynes would escape and be placed in command at his fortified house, but when all but twenty of the garrison deserted, he resigned his commission on 8th December. By 1782 he would have fled to Charlestown, where he received pay as a refugee major of militia until its evacuation. (Lambert, *SC Loyalists*, 117; *SCHGM*, i (1901), 184, 262; Clark, *Loyalists in the Southern Campaign*, i, 151, 493 et seq; *The Cornwallis Papers*; William Gilmore Simms, *The Life of Francis Marion* (Kessinger Publishing Company, 2004), ch 9)

not be considred. This place will soon be in some state of defence, and I mean it to be put into a real one with provisions for three months allways.

As to the communication business, the prisoners are arrived safe; the guns are at Monk's Corner; the wounded are to be at Neilson's on the 25th, where McKinnon with waggons meet them, send them to Monk's Corner, and keep the boats for Tarleton's *baggage* as per return, which has been expedited as much as possible, knowing the use they will be of. All the recruits and convalescents go up with this last conveyance. Colonel Hamilton's being already gone, and Turnbull's being ready, I think nothing remains but to prepare the water business etc etc. I have only received a few lines from Moncrief since he left me, which was to say that all went extremly well and that he was about to send off the Fusileers, but when, as he does not date his letter, I can't exactly say, but imagine they will be at Camden about the 28th with a good many fine horses, which I hope will do for the cavalry and is meant for them. This moment the transport that carried the rebellious to Augustine is arrived, and you have a letter from the Governor[65]. She saw the engagement last night off the bar and thinks the English ship is safe. Tarleton's accoutrements will be at Camden about the 1st of October certainly, if not a day or two sooner.

General Woodford having procured certificates that his life would be endangred by staying in this country from Doctors Hayes and Garden, I could not refuse him liberty of going to New York in the packet, taking his parole in case of the vessel's being taken etc. I most ardently hope that your invalids will get up, and I should humbly think no time will be lost if a week or two is spent near where you are and untill you hear from New York. Good pilots, I hope, will be found. We have two, and I do not wish to make much enquiry till necessary for more, but I understand the galleys can get near Cross Creek, and by every acount there is nothing to oppose the *Sandwich* in the river. I observe the situation of Black River with pleasure.

The moment any thing comes from New York I shall send it by express to be carefully convey'd. I am sure this is a sad bore, therefore shall only add that

I ever am with the most sincere attachment
Your Lordship's faithful humble servant

N BALFOUR

---

[65] *a letter..*: of 8th September, pp 312-3.

Balfour to Cornwallis, 20th and 22nd September 1780[66]   64(96): ALS

Charles Town
22nd September

By an opportunity just setting out for Camden I send you inclosed two letters[67] received a few hours ago, although of different dates. Sir James seems *now* to believe what was so strongly pressed upon him before and in his fears gives the directions that he ought to have done long ago. However, that he may not draw back I have inclosed his letter to Crugar to put in execution immediately. By the express that came with Crugar's letter I find the rebels have retired from the town and that the communication is opned betwixt Brown and him, so that there is no danger of the post. It will now be whether Clark will wait to fight them, which I cannot conceive likely as he has missed his booty. He will retreat, I dare say, with all expedition to that cursed nest beyond the mountains. Brown and Sir James has brought this business upon themselves but I hope it will have a good effect in future. Crugar's quick and judicious movement shews him to be the person you wanted in that command. I also inclose Moncrief's letter, arrived only this day. I dare say he has done the business, but in spite of his *outside* I believe he has not been so severe as Weemys or exactly calculated for that expedition. His horses will be an excellent supply, and I hope the supply that corps[68] has all together received lately will make them of consequence to your operations. Their accoutrements sett off to'night for Monk's Corner, and twenty more men with Captain Millar[69].

Captain Coffin[70] of Turnbull's corps has asked me permission to go express to you in order to obtain leave for his going to New York in the packet that he may try to succeed

---

[66] Although dated the 22nd, the letter is annotated: '20th and 22nd September 1780'. The reference to the address in the fourth paragraph suggests that the letter was mostly or entirely written on the 20th.

[67] *two letters..*: the one from Cruger is not extant.

[68] *that corps*: the British Legion.

[69] Thomas Millar (1753-1792) was a Scot with two years' service in the Provincial line. Promoted to captain in the British Legion infantry on 25th October 1779, he would presumably be captured with them at the Battle of Cowpens. At the close of the war he returned to Scotland and was placed on the Provincial half-pay list. He died at Leith. (WO 65/164(39) and WO 65/165(3) (National Archives, Kew); Sabine, *Biographical Sketches*, ii, 80)

[70] A Massachusetts loyalist, John Coffin (1751-1838) was now a captain commanding the light company of the New York Volunteers. An active, enterprising officer, he would soon be promoted by Cornwallis to the nominal rank of major, although Cornwallis had no power to do so, and be given command of two troops of dragoons to be raised for the Camden District. Perhaps the high point of his distinguished career in the south was his involvement in the defeat of Greene at the Battle of Hobkirk's Hill, which led to a mention in dispatches. On 28th August 1782 his rank was regularised when he became major in the King's American Regiment, a Provincial corps which was shortly to be taken on to the British establishment. With its disbandment at the close of the war he was placed on the British half-pay list and settled in St John, New Brunswick. For many years he served as a Member for King's County in the House of Assembly and as a Member of HM Council. He also raised and commanded a regiment in the War of 1812, eventually rising to the rank of major general. He died at Nerepis. (Lambert, *SC Loyalists*, 218; W O Raymond, 'Provincial Regiments', *The Dispatch* (New Brunswick); *The Cornwallis Papers*; WO 65/164(34) (National Archives, Kew))

Pattison in Brown's corps.

He was with me at Ninety Six and from every acount he will be a great acquisition to that corps and, if he can be spared at present, certainly deserves indulgence.

Every thing is preparing for the water business. The fleet sails certainly on the 26th, but of all this I wrote you a long acount two days ago.

Not a word from New York. I wish much to know, if any event worth mentioning happens at Augusta and arrives in time here for the *Hydra*, whether you would wish me to inform Lord George Germain of it if you have not time to receive the acounts and write - also whether the enclosed address[71], which this moment is put rough into my hand and am told is to be presented tomorow by all the principal leading loyalists and *newly* converted subjects, should be also sent home.

Every thing was mentioned in my last I could think of respecting the communication, and McKinnon this day sett off for Nielson's Ferry to take care of the wounded's transportation.

Twelve Negroes taken in arms on the glorious 16th (my absence from which can never be made up) are now prisoners of war and here. Will it not be worth while — to convince *black* that he must not fight against us — to sell them and buy shoes for your corps to be sent by the *shipps*?

I ever am
Most faithfully yours

N BALFOUR

Enclosure (1)
Wright to Balfour, 18th September 1780 64(73): LS

Savannah
18th September 1780

Lt Colonel Balfour etc etc

Sir

I am extremely concerned to acquaint you that I have recieved advice that most of the inhabitants of the Ceded Lands and some others from Carolina have armed themselves and attacked Colonel Brown's post at Augusta. No dispatches or accounts have been sent by him, but from the information received it appears beyond a doubt that the rebels have defeated him and the Indians with him and obliged him to retire into a kind of fort, and I am afraid that

---

[71] The enclosure is not extant. The address was published in the *Royal South-Carolina Gazette* on 21st September and is summarised in McCrady, *SC in the Rev 1775-1780*, 728-9.

he will be obliged to surrender and that they will possess themselves of all the Indian presents etc. I presume that the attack came so suddenly on Colonel Brown that he had not time to write or send a messenger express. I cannot with certainty say what number of rebels there was, as the people who are come to town differ in that respect. Some say 400, others say 700, and some even more than that. This is a most unfortunate affair. I conceive the principal object was the Indian presents to the amount of, I am well informed, £4,000 at prime cost, too great a temptation to have been risked at so weak a post; but when they have secured their plunder it is difficult to say whether they make off with it or what they may not attempt to do, especially if reinforced from South Carolina, which is not improbable. And this province is now intirely open from Augusta to Savannah without a single post or soldier, and here we have no works but one fort I think capable of recieving only about 400 men, and no other protection, for the old works are at too great a distance and wholly out of repair, washed, trodden and beat down, and I believe the whole military force here, *well and fit for service*, does not exceed 300 and not 150 of the militia, who it cannot be expected, and have it not in their power, to do duty without pay and subsistance, so that if they shou'd bend their course this way, you see what a situation we shall be in, especially when there is not a ship in the harbour, either man of war or merchant man, to give us any assistance.

Your letter to me on the subject of the people on the Ceded Lands, dated at Ninety Six the 27th of July[72], I did not recieve till the 16th of August, when I had the Council summoned and laid it before them, the result of which was my answer to you on 19th of August[73], which I presume you recieved and in which I mentioned Captain Manson's[74] report; and as he was going to Charles Town, I directed him to wait on Lord Cornwallis if there, and if gone, then to wait on you and acquaint you with his transactions there, from which and also from what Colonel Brown had wrote me relative to those people, which I mentioned in that letter, we concluded all was quiet there. However, recieving some private intelligence which seemed to contradict Manson's account, I determined to send a messenger

---

[72] *Your letter to me..*: no copy among *The Cornwallis Papers*.

[73] *my answer to you..*: for a manuscript copy, see The Colonial Records of Georgia (Georgia Department of Archives and History, Atlanta), vol 38, pt 2, 421.

[74] William Manson was an Orcadian who had been master of one of the ships owned by Thomas Brown's father, Jonas, a fact which accounts for Wright's calling him 'Captain'. A Quaker, he arrived at Savannah in December 1775, accompanied by a contingent of servants with whom he settled on the Ceded Lands near the Quaker township of Wrightsborough. Until Thomas Brown's arrival at Augusta in June 1780 Manson had been almost continually in trouble with the revolutionaries there for his royalist sympathies. Now, he had received the submission of John Dooly's regiment of revolutionary militia, sent 210 stand of arms to Augusta, and carried news of the pacification of the Ceded Lands to Wright. He then went on to convey the same message to Cornwallis or Balfour at Charlestown. For his loyalty he would be banished by the Georgia revolutionary assembly in May 1782 and see his property confiscated. Returning to Kirkwall in the Orkney Isles, he eventually purchased a handsome house on the principal street and became the Comptroller of Customs. (Cashin, *The King's Ranger, passim*; The Georgia Banishment and Confiscation Act 1782) For a more detailed account of his stay in Georgia, see Robert S Davis Jr, 'The Last Colonial Enthusiast: Captain William Manson in Revolutionary Georgia', *Atlanta Historical Journal*, xxviii (spring 1984), 23-38.

express with a letter to a Mr Waters[75], a gentleman of property and character who has been settled some years on the Ceded Lands, in order to know the real truth of the matter and to determine what was most proper to be done, and when I was hourly expecting his answer (which did not come), I reciev'd the above intelligence, which puts an intire end to what was in view. This province is now open to depredations as formerly, with this difference, that instead of having at least 1200 troops in and about Savannah we have only a few; and on consulting the gentlemen of the Council this day on the present immediate state of the province, we are all of opinion that the most effectual and best method of crushing the rebellion in the back parts of this province is for an army to march without loss of time into the Ceded Lands and to lay waste and destroy the whole territory, Mr Waters's and some very few which he may mention excepted. For these people the men have by their late conduct forfeited every claim to any favour or protection, and if in the execution of this measure any women or children shou'd be left destitute, we shall be ready to subscribe towards their support. We are further of opinion that, if some steps are not forthwith taken, the rebels, if they stay there, will increase, and no man can say what the consequences may not be with respect not only to this province but to South Carolina and the King's cause in general. I cannot presume to say what number of troops may be sufficient for the purpose of laying waste that settlement, and as they have all horses, it may be necessary that some horse go against them — but it only lyes with me to state or represent matters as clearly as in my power, and which I have now done.

I have the honor to be with perfect esteem, sir,
Your most obedient servant

JA WRIGHT

PS

I am informed that the rebels have two or three stockade forts in different parts of the Ceded Lands, which they built to defend themselves against the Indians.

---

[75] A wealthy inhabitant of the Ceded Lands, Thomas Waters was a committed loyalist who in 1775, while commanding Fort Dartmouth some sixty miles above Augusta, had nevertheless surrendered it to the revolutionaries without firing a shot. Some four years later his loyalism had led him to fall foul of the Grand Jury of Wilkes County (created by the revolutionaries out of the Ceded Lands), which recommended that he be prosecuted for aiding 'the British troops and the avowed enemies of the United States of America'. Now, in 1780, he would soon be commissioned colonel of 255 loyal militia on the Ceded Lands and in June 1781 would be among the garrison besieged at Augusta. Presumably captured and exchanged, he next surfaced in 1782 as Thomas Brown's deputy in the Indian Department, going on to lead the Cherokees against the Ceded Lands. The Cherokees were soon beaten, losing all their land south of the Savannah and east of the Chattahoochee, and Waters had to flee to St Augustine. For his sins he was banished from Georgia, and his property confiscated, by act of the revolutionary assembly, but later he was pardoned. (Cashin, *The King's Ranger*, 44, 122, 133, 155, 164, 191; Cashin Jr and Robertson, *Augusta*, 13, 61, 74; Grace Davidson, *The Early Records of Georgia: The Earliest Records of Wilkes County* (Southern Historical Press, 1967), ii, 10, 11; The Georgia Banishment and Confiscation Act 1782)

Enclosure (2)
Moncrief to Balfour, 20th September 1780   64(89): ALS

George Town
20th September 1780

Lt Colonel Balfour
Commandant etc

Dear Sir

I have now done all I can to punish the people in the lower parts of this county. Inclosed is a list of prisoners sent to Charlestown, John's Island etc[76]. I shall send you all the Negroes for the works at Charlestown and the horses to my friend Tarleton, which I flatter myself will be a very acceptable present. There are about 150 good ones.

The posts I think most proper for the militia to occupy are George Town 100 men, Ragg's Ferry 50, Black River Ferry 150, Potatoe Ferry 50, and Kings Tree Bridge 300, so that, should the enemy attempt to come forward to Black River, their rear will be exposed to the corps at Kingstree.

The disposition of the people does not require so strict a guard, but at all events we cannot be too guarded at present — have therfore weeded out the violent spirits.

Colonel Cassels's regiment is going to Britain's Neck, which is a very good post, but if he should hear of any superior force, he is to fall back to Black River. If he finds in the course of ten days that there is no force in his front, he will move up the corps left at Black River, Potatoe Ferry and Ragg's Ferry to cover the Pedee.

The Fuzileers (all mounted) are to march early tomorrow. I hope in four days they will reach Camden.

I am with much esteem, dear sir,
Your most obedient and most humble servant

JAMES MONCRIEF
Major of Engineers

---

[76] *a list of prisoners..*: if forwarded to Cornwallis, it is not extant.

Cornwallis to Balfour, 27th September 1780   *80(48A): ADfS*

Charlottetown
September 27th 1780

Lt Colonel Balfour

Dear Balfour

I yesterday received your letters of the 20th and 22nd but, as I was fatigued last night, postponed answering them untill morning. Colonel Davie staid for us here with some mounted riflemen and fired at the Legion from the houses, trusting to the strength of the country behind them and to their knowledge of it. However, we *cut up* about 14 of them and had only one man wounded and one horse killed. Hanger and Captain Macdonald[77] had slight contusions, and Captain Campbell[78] of the 71st light infantry was wounded but we hope not dangerously. Perhaps we might have followed up the blow farther, but I did not care to trust the corps too far or risk them much[79].

You will see your queries answered relative to Lord George Germain by the letters and dispatches sent to you on the 21st and 23rd. In regard to the address I submit it [to] you to send it or not as you think best. Great care should be taken by all officers who sincerely wish well to their country not to make Ministers too sanguine, and you know they are apt to lay too much stress on these kind of professions. The Negroes taken in arms should be sold and the money disposed of as you think proper.

I inclose to you a letter from Wemys with my answer[80]. I am much disappointed in that business and have taken the only steps in my power to endeavour still to make something of that district, which has been throughout so troublesome and fatal to us. Harrison most certainly will never be able to raise a corps. I think, if he has not lost all weight and influence in that country, he must be able to collect some people to defend their own country and property.

---

[77] Charles MacDonald was the first son of Allen and Flora MacDonald. He is believed to have arrived at Halifax, Nova Scotia, in the spring of 1776, and on 18th May he was almost immediately commissioned a lieutenant in the 2nd Battalion, Royal Highland Emigrants. Some three years later he transferred to Tarleton's British Legion as a captain of horse. Resigning his commission in 1782, he returned to Britain and was not placed on the half-pay list. At his death Lord MacDonald remarked, as he saw the remains lowered into the grave, 'There lies the most finished gentleman of my family and name.' (Robert Archibald Logan, 'Flora and Allen MacDonald in America', *Clan Donald Magazine*, No 4 (1968); *Army List 1779*; Sabine, *Biographical Sketches*, ii, 58)

[78] Campbell was a common name among captains in the 71st (Highland) Regiment. Charles (now dead) and Colin were captains in the 1st Battalion, whereas Patrick and Lawrence Robert were captains in the 2nd. According to Hanger, the Campbell who was wounded was the senior captain, an assertion which points to Patrick as the officer involved. He had been commissioned a captain in the 2nd Battalion on 25th November 1775. (*Army Lists*; Hanger, *An Address to the Army*, 57-8)

[79] *them much*: the following words are deleted, 'until Tarleton's arrival, whom I am in hopes of seeing in a day or two'.

[80] For the letters, see pp 214-6.

All accounts from the country talk of a second division of French, that the troops were landed at Boston, and the ships, said to be six or eight of the line, had joined Ternay at Rhode Island. They say our fleet is gone into Sandy Hook. All this is rebel intelligence. Nothing could give it the least weight with me if I was not so astonished at not hearing from New York. You are quite right to have every thing ready for our *naval cooperation*. I must, however, *receive* some *satisfactory account before* I can *venture* to *penetrate far* enough to make *use* of it. You will open all my public letters and all from the Commander in Chief and send me copies, putting the material passages into cypher. You know the sort of *account* I mean, and if you think it likely that I may *advance*, you will *order* the *naval force* to the place appointed.

I was very uneasy about the Augusta business and am very glad that by Cruger's spirited and decided conduct it has been so happily concluded. That Back Country certainly requires our very serious attention. Much will depend on the success of Cruger's expedition into the Ceded Lands. I see the necessity of making *use* of *the Indians* altho' it is positively contrary to my instructions. I therefore would have it done under the restrictions you mention, and desire you will give orders about it. I have the greatest hopes that Cruger will be equal to keeping that country without more assistance. If not, I must find out some mode of reinforcing him. I should wish at all events to employ *Williamson* and to give him every encouragement to take the most hearty part with us; there is nothing in reason that I would not do. I therefore beg you try to come to a thorough understanding with him. In regard to *Pickens*, I have great doubts. I have been told that there is a correspondence between him and *Sumter*, and that the former is to have 500 men ready, and that when I advance they are to form a junction. You may perhaps get to the bottom of this business. If any means can be fallen upon to secure the neutrality, if not the friendship, of the former, I shall think it very good economy. As to Sir James Wright's letter and distresses, he certainly may thank himself and Colonel Brown. His scheme of fixing posts at Ebenezer and other places on the Savanna River is the weakest in the world. Half of the men would die in three months and the remainder would be an easy prey to any enemy who could possibly attempt to enter the province.

The posts of Augusta and 96 are certainly the security of Georgia. If they are not sufficient, they must be strengthened.

On my advancing from Waxhaw, Generals Somner[81] and Davidson with about 11 or 1200

---

[81] Jethro Sumner (*c.* 1733-1785) was currently in command of those North Carolina revolutionary militia opposing Cornwallis. Born in Virginia, he had served as a lieutenant of militia in the Seven Years War before moving to Bute County, North Carolina, and establishing himself as a tavern owner and planter. With a fair education, military experience, business acumen, handsome physique, native ability, and attractive personality, he rose to prominence as a Justice of the Peace in 1768 and as Sheriff from 1772 to 1777. Elected to the North Carolina Provincial Congress in 1775, he was in April 1776 commissioned Colonel of the 3rd North Carolina Continental Regiment and saw considerable service in both the north and south, being promoted to brigadier general in January 1779. Because he was raising Continental recruits in North Carolina, he was not captured in the capitulation of Charlestown, nor was he involved in the Battle of Camden. Appointed shortly afterwards to his present command, he would soon retire to his home, piqued at the decision of the Assembly in North Carolina to appoint a Marylander, William Smallwood, to the overall command of the revolutionary militia there. In July 1781 he would reinforce Greene with a small brigade of raw Continentals, and some two months later they would perform well in the Battle of Eutaw Springs. For the rest of the war he was in command of revolutionary forces in North Carolina. At his death he owned some 20,000 acres and 34 slaves. (*DAB*; *The Greene Papers*, vi, 506n)

very bad militia retired from McAlpine's Creek on the Salisbury road. I have already given you an account of Davie. Sumter, who was at Bigger's Ferry on Catawba River, passed the river immediately. I was told that as his men were all mounted he intended getting into our rear, but I rather believe he is gone up the Catawba by the Dutch Forks and means to join Somner etc. Whilst we have such a force at Waxhaw and Camden and such a body of cavalry forward, the going into our rear would be a dangerous experiment. I believe I have mentioned every thing to you but I will soon write again.

Yours very sincerely

CORNWALLIS

[*Subscribed*:]

I promised Ferguson that the militia who went on the expedition with him into Tryon County should have a handsome gratuity. You will therefore please to answer any demand he may make on you.

Balfour to Cornwallis, 25th September 1780   64(108): ALS

Charles Town
25th September 1780

I am just now favoured with yours of the 18th and have much the same complaint to make of the effects of the climate here, for we do not get up at all — rather otherwise. Poor Westerhaugen is very ill and very much affraid of this country. However, it is surely near over and we may expect some healthy months to come.

Inclosed is Crugar's letter, by which you will see the business has turned out as we expected. I hope Brown and him will immediately proceed to the Ceded Lands and make examples and then obey the Governor's orders. I have wrote very fully upon this subject before, so shall not trouble you with a repetition. Brown was not willing to give up the presents but has by all acounts behaved with spirit and steadiness. Cruger's first movement (very judiciously made) certainly saved him. Could it be possible to spare him a small party of an officer and twenty of the Legion for that country, it might save much trouble, but you will want them so much that I cannot think of saying more, although Moncrieff and I think we have some title to take libertys with the Legion if our supplys get safe to the regiment. I am happy to think that corps will be so considerably augmented at present.

I much fear the Fusileers will fall far short in the numbers you expected. They have sent eighteen sick here from Georgetown, and that regiment has got the horrid idea in their head of the impossibility of escaping sickness in this country and that they will all die. By the shipping I shall be able, I doubt not, to send a very strong reinforcement of convalescents. Will you be so good, before you go further, to mention what transports you wish to come and in general some plan of the cooperation — I mean as to their proceeding up the river etc etc.

The necessity of an intermediate post, with works for defence, betwixt you and Camden appears every day more and more obvious, for, what from plundering partys and rebellious ones, the whole country will be in disturbance and liable to be wrought upon to rise in arms whenever they think they can do it with impunity. It is a most uphill business. However, it is impossible either to stand still long or look back. I must keep a certain force of militia allways embody'd to overawe the country and march frequently through the worst districts upon the frontiers. It is the only use they ever will be of. One grievance concerning them I must lay before you: the demands for provision money furnished for them in the country, added to the expence of our own posts, are so heavy that it will be impossible to answer them, beside the very bad policy of allowing the guineas to go into the country never more to be heared of.

Every part of your directions concerning packetts and other matters mentioned in your letters shall be punctualy attended to. I shall only trouble you in speaking to those points that are necessary to be mentioned.

Not a word from New York. You may rely upon it every thing is gone to the French fleet and they think no more of your situation than they do of those in India. Besides, the privateers swarm in our sight and are of too much force to allow any thing but a man of war to come here. However, I think they *dare* not leave us much longer in the dark and that, *before* you quit Charlotte, we will know something further from them — at least I ardently hope so.

The packet goes, as I mentioned, to New York and sails with the *Hydra* and the fleet as soon as your letters arrive. The *Loyalist* goes a short way to see them off the coast and returns. The *Hydra* answers the purpose of a packet at present and another will be here for your duplicates, but it was impossible to get another opportunity for your triplicates, which I fear will be wanted, to New York.

The very great inconvenience attending the delay of the packet I am extremly sorry for, but Captain Gardner and the sea people insisted so much upon the danger of sending her out that I could not interfere. Inclosed is the address[82] I mentioned in my last, and a letter just received from Williamson, to whom I shall talk very seriously when he comes here.

I ever am
Most faithfuly yours

N BALFOUR

---

[82] *address*: presumably the printed version, the enclosure is not extant. See also p 95, note 71.

Enclosure (1)
Cruger to Balfour, 19th September 1780　　　　　　　　　　　　　　64(75): LS

Augusta
September 19th 1780

Colonel Balfour

Sir

I did myself the honor yesterday morning to advise you of my being opposite to this place for the relief of Colonel Brown, who was attack'd on the 14th instant by a body of about 700 rebels under the command of Clark, who were so precipitate in their flight that we had only a few chance shot at them on the wing. We took a few prisoners, retook a field piece, and one iron gun — a 4 or 6 pounder, the rest of the iron ordnance, some amunition, five or six waggons and carts and 4 puncheons of rum, sav'd the town from being burnt, and, I flatter myself, stopt a most dangerous and daring insurrection that wou'd have been general in this part of the world had Mr Clark succeeded. The people of the country on both sides of the river, being yet amazingly disaffected, would have been in arms and like a torrent bore down the friends to Government. Nothing but a prudent timidity restrain'd their joining immediately.

A return of Colonel Brown's killed and wounded I expect immediately from him. The number of the rebels kill'd I can't ascertain. They left only about a dozen on the field unburied. Colonel Allen's surgeon, who was taken prisoner, tells me he dress'd above fifty of their wounded on the first day of the attack. I am now sending out parties of horse to pick up the traiterous rebels of this neighbourhood, who will be roughly handled, some very probably suspended for their good deeds.

Colonel Brown took possession and entrenched himself at a house where he had his Indian goods, many of which, and such King's stores as were in town at his barracks about two miles distance, fell into the hands of the rebels. I am told Clark and about a hundred of his men cross'd Little River last night. As soon as I get matters properly settled and arranged here, I shall return to Ninety Six and from thence most probably pay a visit to the Ceded Lands.

Brown had with him about 300 Indians. His little garrison acquired great honor by making a very gallant defence, being wholly without water for two days out of four, and little else to eat than raw pumkins.

Believe me with the greatest regard and respect, sir,
Your obedient and very humble servant

J H CRUGER
Lt Colonel

Enclosure (2)
Williamson to Balfour, 21st September 1780　　　　　　　　　　　　　64(95): LS

White Hall
21st September 1780

Sir

Before this Mr Brown[83] will have inform'd you of the reason of my not having waited on you in Charlestown agreeable to your request. I make no doubt, before this reaches you, Colonel Cruger will have acquainted you with what has happened in Georgia, but if not, Mr Brown can inform you of what has come to my knowledge of that affair. When I learnt that Clark and his party were in the country I went with Colonel Purves[84] and Captain Tutt[85] to Colonel Pickens's and sent for others of the principal inhabitants to meet me there, where I learn'd that only six of the people in that settlement had gone of, three of them sons of one Wm Lucky[86] who, having rescued their father from a party of militia who had made him prisoner on some suspicion, were then afraid to stay. I have since heard of three or four rash young fellows having join'd Clark while at Augusta, but can assure you that every thing has and will be done by the principal people to keep the country quiet, which have no dowbt can be effected as the people seem in general determined to adhere strictly to the capitulation, though it is impossible to be answerable for a very few distracted individuals. I shall meet the principal people in two or three days again and you may be assured every thing in our power will be done for the quiet of this part of the country.

---

[83] Malcom Brown was a shadowy figure who served as Andrew Williamson's secretary for most of the war. Perhaps a covert loyalist, he would be subjected to banishment and confiscation by act of the revolutionary assembly at Jacksonborough in early 1782. Nine years later he would petition the lower house of the legislature that he be removed from the act and be permitted to return. (Lilla M Hawes comp, 'The Papers of James Jackson 1781-1793', *Collections of the Georgia Historical Society* (Savannah, 1955), xi; The SC Banishment and Confiscation Act 1782; Petitions to the SC General Assembly 1789-1791, SC Archives; Will Graves and Robert Davis to the editor, 21st July and 5th August 2006)

[84] Born in Scotland, John Purvis (*c*. 1746-?) was in June 1775 commissioned a captain in the regiment of rangers raised by the South Carolina Provincial Congress. He was posted to Fort Charlotte. By June 1778 a major, he took part in Robert Howe's ill-fated invasion of East Florida. Now a lt colonel in the South Carolina revolutionary militia, he would by May 1781 have broken his parole and joined up with Andrew Pickens. (Moss, *SC Patriots*, 792 and 806 (John Reed); McCrady, *SC in the Rev 1775-1780*, 14, and *1780-1783*, 229; Heitman, *Historical Register*, 455)

[85] Benjamin Tutt, who may have been born in Virginia, had been a captain in the South Carolina revolutionary militia since 1775 and had commanded at Fort Rutledge. Like John Purvis (see above), he would have broken his parole by May 1781 and gone off to the enemy. His brothers Gabriel and Richard were also in the revolutionary service. (Will of Richard Tutt, *Virginia County Records: Spotsylvania County 1721-1800* (New York, 1905), Wills, 283; Moss, op cit, 806 (John Reed), 944; Revolutionary war pension application of John Reed (Pension No W.193))

[86] According to Moss, op cit, 586, a William Luckie Sr served in the revolutionary militia, as did five others with his surname.

I have the honour to be, sir,
Your most obedient humble servant

A W.MSON

Cornwallis to Balfour, 1st October 1780   81(1): ACS

Charlottetown
October 1st 1780

Lt Colonel Balfour
Commandant of Charlestown

Dear Balfour

I last night received your letter of the 25th and at the same time one from Cruger of the 23rd[87], of which I conclude you have a copy. By this time I hope every thing is quiet in those parts. When all opposition is over, I think Cruger should issue a proclamation similar to that I inclose to you[88], inviting those who have fled, perhaps with a few exceptions, to return to their habitations on condition of their bringing in their arms and giving their parole. In regard to cavalry, a detachment of the Legion would hardly answer; they have no officers to command distant detachments, having lost either by the sword or sickness all those of experience, and indeed the whole of them are very different when Tarleton is present or absent. I would rather try to raise two troops of dragoons, one to be stationed at 96, the other at Camden, of 60 men each, the former to be commanded by Cunningham, who may still keep the title of lt colonel as his warrant to raise a regiment of foot is only pos[t]poned, not totally laid aside. The Camden troop had better be commanded by some active young man from Charlestown or from the Provincial corps; there is nobody in that neighbourhood that would do at all. If you think this plan can be put into execution, I wish you would give the necessary orders for it as soon as possible. When I mentioned Cunningham's rank, it was from apprehension that, being possess'd of a warrant making him lt colonel, he might object to serve in a lower rank. Now I give you full liberty to appoint whom you please, and to make any alterations and additions, and even to add a troop for Georgetown if you think proper. Altho' these corps may be expensive, I am convinced there can be no other means of securing the vast tract of country that it is necessary to guard. The grievance you mention concerning the great demands of provision money for the militia is certainly very unpleasant. I hope the fund that Cruden's appointment will bring in may partly answer it, and as there will be several estates sequester'd which will be too near the frontier to put them under peaceable culture, the Negroes and stock on some of those may answer the payments you mention and save the guineas. I throw out this merely as a thing to be considered, being not at all certain that it would be either possible or expedient to do it. I wrote very fully to you on the 27th about the _naval cooperation_. Perhaps you may think I have put too much to your

---

[87] *one from Cruger..*: see p 192.

[88] *that I enclose to you*: see p 331, note 20.

discretion in a business of such importance. I do not, however, insist on your deciding unless it is very clear. If the *Chief promises* a *diversion* or wishes or *expects* me to *penetrate*, then your *part is clear*.

Sumpter has had a dispute with one Williams about command and is gone to refer it to Gates. In the mean time his people are plundering Tryon County. A flag of truce that I sent saw Williams at Kerrell's Ford[89]. He said he was going against Ferguson. He had only 150 men, many of whom with their arms I hope my proclamation will bring in. I shall hear soon what you have been able to do about the 20 puncheons of rum. I shall leave Hamilton's corps to bring them up from Camden. You may depend on hearing constantly from me.

I am with very sincere regard
Most faithfully yours

CORNWALLIS

Cornwallis to Balfour, 3rd October 1780　　　　81(10): C

Charlottetown
October 3rd 1780

Lt Colonel Balfour
Commandant of Charlestown

Dear Balfour

I inclose to you a letter I received yesterday from Major Wemyss[90], in consequence of which I sent an order last night to Turnbull[91] to add thirty men of the New York Volunteers to the fifty of Innes's and to keep in lieu of them thirty of our convalescents. I cannot think of any other means of remedying the evil at present. I directed Turnbull to send off Frazer's detachment immediately for fear of any misfortune happening to our militia in the lower districts. Colonel Grey will shew you a letter from me[92]. He seems a very sensible, spirited man and I hope may render us essential service.

We have nothing new here. The militia under Somner are on the Yadkin and there is no force of consequence in our front. This County of Mecklenburg is the most rebellious and inveterate that I have met with in this country, not excepting any part of the Jerseys.

---

[89] *Kerrell's Ford*: a corruption of 'Sherrald's Ford', which lay on the Catawba some 33 miles north-north-west of Charlotte. For corroboration, see Cornwallis's following letter, second paragraph.

[90] *a letter..*: of 30th September, p 216.

[91] *an order..*: see p 244.

[92] *a letter from me*: of 2nd October, p 219.

Sumpter's corps now under the command of Williams are at Sherrel's Ford above Oliphant's Mill. One of the colonels, who had drank too much grog, entrusted a friend with their scheme of returning to South Carolina as soon as our troops advanced. I shall take every measure in my power to guard against it. I am exceedingly anxious to raise a corps in Tryon County, but have not heard lately from Ferguson, nor do I know in what state Dunlap is. I am anxious to know the event of Cruger's march, but above all to hear from New York.

As I cannot think my letters will travel in perfect safety through so disaffected a country, I shall send all my publick letters to Ministers, Commander in Chief and Admiral (as long as I correspond with them, which perhaps may not happen again) open to you, and shall beg of you to send duplicates or triplicates as you may think proper. I must desire you to transmit my answer to the address of the loyal inhabitants of Charlestown.

I am, dear Balfour,
Most sincerely yours

[CORNWALLIS]

Enclosure
Reply to the loyal address, 3rd October 1780   *81(12): A(in part) Df*

Charlottetown
North Carolina
October 3rd 1780

To the Loyal Inhabitants of Charlestown, South Carolina

Gentlemen

It gives me great pleasure to be assured by you that my conduct has merited the approbation of the loyal inhabitants of Charlestown. I shall always endeavour to the utmost of my abilities to contribute to the honour and prosperity of my King and country and to the release of His Majesty's loyal subjects in America from the cruel and oppressive tyranny under which they have so long and so severely suffered.

I have the honor to be, gentlemen,
Your most obliged and most obedient humble servant

[CORNWALLIS]

Balfour to Cornwallis, 28th September 1780 — 64(114): ALS

Charles Town
28th September

Since I wrote yesterday[93], a vessel is arrived from Providence who says that by every acount from New York the French fleet is blocked up by ours at Rhode Island; that by a cartel ship from the Cape[94] the French squadron that had sailed as was supposed for France is returned there after convoying their homeward bound trade.

A snow has likewise escaped and got in from the privateers — from London the 25th of July. She brings the letters accompanying this[95], which are sent off immediately. I believe they are private, but supposed you would wish to see them as soon as possible.

The only news she brings is the capture of twenty sail of the Santo Domingo fleet and seeing a very large fleet a week ago within fifty leagues of this coast, which she supposes to be the Jamaica fleet for England. *I hope so.*

I send up about forty convalescents, all well enough to march, in order to get them clear of the rum here and to join their corps with your army. They will be in time for your 2nd division.

I forgot to mention Frazer that is now major to Innis' corps, it seems, as an officer you may depend upon, and very clever. To place him in a situation of consequence upon the communication will be necessary if your arrangements are not fixed. He is so very active that he may be of much service at present.

I ever am
Yours most faithfuly

N BALFOUR

---

[93] *Since I wrote yesterday*: the letter is not extant.

[94] *the Cape*: Cape François on the north coast of Haiti.

[95] The only extant letter is a private one from Lord Shelburne recommending a friend of his, a Doctor Trumbull, for appointment to the army as a physician (2(335)).

Cornwallis to Balfour, 5th October 1780 81(16): ACS

Charlottetown
October 5th 1780

Lt Colonel Balfour
Commandant of Charlestown

Dear Balfour

I received yours of the 28th, but the letter of the 27th is not yet arrived. I hope it was entrusted to Knecht, the commissary, who left Camden before the last express and who I suppose is delayed by the bad weather. Cruger's account is a good one. He has succeeded to my most sanguine expectations. Ferguson assures me that a large body of rebels are coming over the mountain[s] under Shelby[96] and McDowal[97], 1,500 or 2,000[98]. The corps lately commanded by Sumpter is gone up the Catawba to meet them. I have ordered McArthur with the 1st Battalion of the 71st to *take post at Armer's Ford*[99]. *Ferguson will meet him there.*

---

[96] Of Welsh parentage, Isaac Shelby (1750-1826) was born near the North Mountain in Frederick County, Maryland. Having acquired a plain English education and the principles of surveying, he moved with his father over the mountains to the Holston region in 1773 or 1774. Intermittently between then and mid 1780 he was involved in fighting native Americans and in acting as a commissary and surveyor. By the close of 1779 he had become a major in the Virginia revolutionary militia and a Member for Washington County in the Virginia revolutionary legislature, but when the boundary line between Virginia and North Carolina was run, he found himself residing south of the line and resigned his offices. Almost immediately he was commissioned colonel of the revolutionary militia in what was now Sullivan County, North Carolina. On hearing of the capitulation of Charlestown, he at once organised a force and in July joined Charles McDowell (see below) at the Cherokee Ford, South Carolina. He went on to take part in the capture of Thicketty Fort on 30th July, the action near Cedar Spring on 8th August, and the defeat of Alexander Innes at Musgrove's Mill eleven days later. Having then retreated beyond the mountains, he had played an instrumental part in initiating the expedition against Ferguson and would soon lead his men courageously in the Battle of King's Mountain. Of a sturdy and well-proportioned frame, slightly above medium height, with strongly marked features and a florid complexion, he would go on to play at times a prominent role in public affairs, serving *inter alia* as Governor of Kentucky for two terms. Habitually dignified and impressive in bearing, he is nevertheless described as having an affable and winning personality. He would die of apoplexy, having suffered a stroke six years earlier which left him physically but not mentally impaired. (*DAB*; Draper, *King's Mountain, passim*; *Appletons'*)

[97] Of Scotch-Irish descent, Charles McDowell (c. 1743-1815) was born in Winchester, Virginia, and brought to North Carolina sometime before 1758, when his father settled in Pleasant Garden, a beautiful tract of the Catawba valley. A senator in 1778, Charles had also become Colonel of the Burke County revolutionary militia. Recently, on 15th July, he had taken part in the action at Earle's Ford on North Pacolet and then retreated before Ferguson on the latter's advance into North Carolina. Now his men formed part of the band proposing to attack Ferguson, but he did not. As commanding officer in the locality, he would have expected to assume overall command, but the other colonels, having reservations about his lack of tact and efficiency, had chosen William Campbell of Virginia at a meeting on 2nd October. With their agreement McDowell had departed to request of Gates the appointment of a general officer, but his mission was to be overtaken by the Battle of King's Mountain five days later. Promoted to brigadier general of militia in 1782, he would again sit in the North Carolina Senate for the next four years. (Draper, *King's Mountain*, 80-1, 186-190, 471; *DAB*)

[98] See Ferguson to Cornwallis, 30th September, p 160.

[99] See Cornwallis to McArthur, 5th October, p 282.

This business must delay us. I must probably be obliged *to strike some blow that way*. My *present plan is, when I have cleared our flanks, to advance to Salisbury, stay there* long enough to *give our friends time* to *join, and then march to Cross Creek, raise the Highlanders, communicate with shipping*.

I have written to you so fully about every thing to the eastward that I have nothing to add. Your answer about the 20 puncheons of rum is not arrived. We begin to grow short.

You will send by *the ships as much arms, clothing* etc etc *as possible*. Take notice of the difference of the cypher. I have got a new one from Ferguson, which I will send you if a safe conveyance should offer.

I am, dear Balfour,
Most faithfully yours

CORNWALLIS

[*Subscribed*:]

I understood from Wemys that Colonel Mills had given up all hopes of forming his militia and wished to remove his family to some rebel plantation on the Savannah River, in consequence of which I desired you to give a colonel's commission to Lt Colonel Grey. I have since heard from Turnbull that Mills has been at Camden, asking for arms and amunition[100]. You will be kind enough to inquire about it and rectify any mistake.

Balfour to Cornwallis, 27th September 1780 64(112): ALS

Charles Town
27th September

I have this day received yours[101], and as to the rum and medicines they are ordred and will sett out tomorow morning early for Monk's Corner, and you may depend upon their arriving in time for the 2nd division if they march only on the 2nd week of October. Some salt shall also be sent and as good care taken of the post at Camden as possible. I rejoice to hear Tarleton is safe. The addition to his cavalry will soon recover him, I hope.

The Augusta business is over. I would suppose it was by no means any plan to stop your operations but merely a plundering party increased in hopes of the booty, and of course, if properly punished, will fall to the ground. I hope Crugar will visit and obey the Governor's directions as to the Ceded Lands.

---

[100] See Turnbull to Cornwallis, 2nd October, p 247.

[101] *yours*: of 21st and 23rd September, pp 88-90.

I am sorry to inform you that, by an express just now received, the transport sent round to bring the *Vigilant*'s stores here and her men is taken just off the bar by two twenty gun ships. This is the fate of allmost every vessel bound here, but at present it is particularly distressing as the men were wanted for the *Sandwich*. However, it is not for me to add to your perplexing circumstances. God knows they are fully sufficient in themselves, and I own I do not see the day light one could wish if you move further than Charlotte before we have something from New York. If a cooperation is necessary, I own I think it ought to be known something about before you are committed. If it is not, the sooner the movement is made the better, to follow up the astonishing success.

Pardon this liberty, dictated by a most ardent and hearty anxiety for your success.

I have been obliged to speak a little of my opinion to the navy about the enemy's privateers insulting us, and, as it would be leaving this port totally unprotected, have proposed that they should go out – viz, the *Hydra* and *Loyalist* – and at least shew themselves to these gentry before the fleet sails, which are now all ready. Captain Gouldsbrough[102] is taken in this ship. How he could risk the men of the *Vigilant* I cannot understand, as they could as well have come the inland navigation.

The *Hydra* and *Loyalist* sail this evening for a few days, when they come in for their convoy, and I am in hopes that, as this ship (a transport) was only taken yesterday, that they may be able to see them. If not, it is only a few days lost. The privateers were close in at the bar.

I have never sent you Moultrie's correspondence and mine upon the rebells sent to St Augustine. They are inclosed, and as you will see, every future observation of his upon that business is at an end. He has been amazingly civil ever since, and I understand Colonel Pinkney[103], his constant counsellor, framed the letter. His calling this province a *state* and his *believing* these worthy members of it uncapable of a breach of their paroles I thought by no means admissible even at the *worst* of times. Inclosed is a return of goods and produce shipt in the fleet[104]. I thought you might wish to see.

---

[102] Thomas Goldesborough (?-1828) had been promoted to commander in the Royal Navy on 25th January 1780, a rank which carried with it the courtesy title of captain. Pursuing an undistinguished career in the service, he would rise to post-captain on 1st December 1787 and be superannuated twenty years later. (Syrett and DiNardo ed, *The Commissioned Sea Officers*; Marshall, *Royal Naval Biography*)

[103] Educated in England and admitted to the Middle Temple there, Charles Cotesworth Pinckney (1746-1825) was now Colonel of the 1st South Carolina Continental Regiment and had been made prisoner in the capitulation of Charlestown. Not only had he been involved militarily in the revolutionary cause, first by taking leave from his regiment to serve for a time as an aide-de-camp to Washington, and then by participating in the ill-fated attempts on East Florida and Savannah, but he had also played a prominent role politically, being elected to the Provincial Congress in 1775 and to the lower house of the South Carolina revolutionary legislature some three years later. Exchanged under the cartel with Greene in June 1781, he would be elected to the Jacksonborough assembly and after the war continue to play a prominent role in public affairs. He was a cousin of Charles Pinckney (Vol I, p 311, note 8) and a brother of Thomas (p 238, note 9). (*DAB*; McCrady, *SC in the Rev 1775-1780* and *1780-1783, passim*; Heitman, *Historical Register*, 442)

[104] *a return..*: not extant.

Cruden is arrived, but of the proclamation and his affairs shall say nothing further, not having looked at it yet. You may depend upon my firmest support of him and forwarding your wishes upon that and every other occasion.

I ever am
Yours most truly

N BALFOUR

Enclosure (1)
Moultrie to Balfour, 1st September 1780[105] 64(7): C

Christ Church Parish
September 1st 1780

To Lt Colonel Nisbet Balfour etc

Sir

On perusing the paper of the 29th August of Robertson, McDonald and Cameron publish'd by authority, to my astonishment I find a paragraph to this effect: 'The following is a correct list of the persons sent on board the *Sandwich* yesterday morning,' and underneath the names of a number of the most respectable gentlemen inhabitants of this State, most of whose characters I am so well acquainted with that I cannot believe they would have been guilty of any breach of their parole or any article of the capitulation or done any thing to justify so rigorous a proceeding against them. I therefore think it my duty as senior Continental officer under the capitulation to demand a release of those gentlemen, particularly such as are entitled to the benefit of that act. This harsh proceeding demands my particular attention and I do therefore in behalf of the United States of America require that they be immediately admitted to return to their parole, as their being thus hurried on board a prison ship, and I fear without being heard, is a violation of the 9th article of the capitulation. If this demand cannot be comply'd with, I am to request that I may have leave to send an officer to Congress to represent this grievance that they may interpose in behalf of those gentlemen in the manner they shall think proper.

Doctor Fraser in a letter of the 28th of last month mentions that he was desir'd by you to assure me that it never was your intention to prevent Doctor Oliphant[106] attending the

---

[105] The first paragraph and Benson's following reply were published by Moultrie in his *Memoirs*, ii, 138-9. There are no material differences.

[106] Born in Perth, Scotland, David Oliphant (1720-1805) had become a physician before migrating in the late 1740s to South Carolina, where he took up residence at Dorchester, opened a medical practice, and became a planter and private tutor. A member of the Provincial Congress which reconvened in June 1775, he was appointed to its General Committee and five months later to its Council of Safety. When a temporary revolutionary constitution for South Carolina was adopted in March 1776, he was elected to the Legislative Council but resigned his seat in July 1776 when he was appointed Director General of Continental Hospitals in the Southern Department. Taken

American hospital. Notwithstanding this assurance Dr Oliphant informs me that he was on Wednesday last taken into custody of the Provost by a warrant from the Board of Police.

I am, sir,
Your most obedient and very humble servant

WILL MOULTRIE
Brigadier General

Enclosure (2)
Benson to Moultrie, undated   64(7): C

Sir

The Commandant will not return any answer to a letter wrote in such exceptionable and unwarrantable terms as that to him from General Moultrie dated the 1st instant, nor will he receive any further applications from him upon the subject of it.

By order of the Commandant

G BENSON
Major of Brigade

Balfour to Cornwallis, 1st October 1780   3(158): ALS

Charles Town
1st October 1780

I am distressed to inform you that yesterday I received a letter from Colonel Cassells to say that Marrion with a party had surprised his post at Black Mingo and that he found it necessary to evacuate George Town, where the enemy were last night. This kind of behaviour is too bad, but it is no more than I expected from these militia. I hope the galley will not come away, and if she does not, I must send Brown's corps consisting of forty men with the convalescents (about thirty) to retake it. The galley has twelve of the 63rd with her, which will join and all together make about ninety men, which with the rascaly militia I conceive will do the business of driving off Mr Marion, when some work must be thrown up and Brown's corps left to defend it, covred by a galley, and to be joined by Ballingall and

---

prisoner in the capitulation of Charlestown, he had been swiftly exchanged but had then been detained because of 'a civil suit, he being considerably indebted here'. He would be released in June 1781, but not before Surgeon General John Weir of the Convention army had been detained in retaliation by the Continental Board of War. Oliphant would go on to serve under Greene and represent St George's Parish, Dorchester, in the revolutionary assembly at Jacksonborough. He later moved to Rhode Island, where he married Nancy (Ann) Vernon, the daughter of Samuel Vernon, a prominent Newport merchant. (Moss, *SC Patriots*, 741; Henry A M Smith, 'The Town of Dorchester in South Carolina', *SCHGM*, vi (1905), 62; McCrady, *SC in the Rev 1775-1780*, 83, 115, and *1780-1783*, 557; *The Greene Papers*, vi, 481n, vii, 170-1, viii, 195, 383; *The Cornwallis Papers*)

Lechmer's regiments, who are ordred. This is the only mode I can think of to repossess George Town, where it is not possible to allow them to remain for obvious consequences. My great difficulty was to get an officer to command, and fortunately this morning I recolected a Major De Lancey[107] who was of Ferguson's corps, a lieutenant of the 18th Regiment who has seen a good deal of service and I know to be very active.

He is here in his way to New York in order to resign his majority in the Provincials and return home to his regiment. I have, however, stopt him for this service, which he has very handsomely agreed to take. Had he refused, it was impracticable for me to get another fitt for it. The unhealthiness of the place I fear most, but I am informed by the physicians that about the middle of this month there will be little danger. Indeed there is no alternative.

I have wrote to Turnbull and desired him to put Mills and Tyne upon their guards.

Our men of war are returned, having chased the rebells off the coast, but unable to come up with them. The fleet will sail tomorow. What we are then to do in the sea way I cannot tell. However, I think the *Loyalist* and *Sandwich* a perfect safe convoy to the place[108] you may want. I mean to send a flag of truce *there*[109] with the Draytons and an officer[110] in the room of Captains Roberts[111] and Goldsbury[112] of the navy, who has got a navy man of the rebells to be exchanged for him.

As to spare arms, four hundred and fifty or five hundred will, I fear, be the uttmost we can send you.

The total destruction of the horses makes me fear they will scarcely get the rum up. I find the acounts of them worse and worse. The medicines are sent off, and all, I still flatter myself, will get against the 12th or 14th of October. If they do not, believe me it is not in my power to do more.

---

[107] John Peter De Lancey (1753-1828) was a younger son of James, sometime Chief Justice and Lt Governor of the Province of New York. Educated in England, he entered the British Army as an ensign in 1771 and was now a captain lieutenant in the 18th (or Royal Irish) Regiment. By special dispensation he concurrently held a commission of major in the Pennsylvania Loyalists, a commission which he would relinquish before the close of the war. As Balfour remarks, he had seen a good deal of service, which included taking part in the Battles of Brandywine and Germantown. After the war he continued with the 18th Regiment until 1789, serving in Jersey and Gibraltar. He then returned to the United States to take up residence in Mamaroneck, New York, until his death. (*Appletons'*; *Army Lists*; Raymond, 'British American Corps'; Treasury 64/23(14) (National Archives, Kew))

[108] *the place*: Wilmington.

[109] *to send a flag of truce there*: in reality to gather intelligence, as indicated later in this letter and in Balfour's of 5th October, p 117.

[110] *an officer*: one in the revolutionary service to be exchanged for Roberts.

[111] *Roberts*: of the 63rd Regiment, he had been captured and paroled by Marion. See pp 41-2 and 213.

[112] *Goldsbury*: Goldesborough, the captain of a transport captured off Charlestown bar. It had been sent round to bring the *Vigilant*'s men and stores from Beaufort. See Balfour to Cornwallis, 27th September, p 110.

I send you a copy of the proclamation[113]. Cruden writes you upon it[114] and we shall proceed directly.

There is a Colonel Paulk of the North Carolina militia. I am desired to assure you [he] is to be got easily and that he wishes to come in. He is represented as a man of great influence and living near Charlotte.[115]

I am a little hurry'd with the fleet going and shall say nothing but that I shall hurry the flag of truce and *report all to you I can.*

Likewise, the George Town business shall be carried through as quickly as possible. I take so much upon myself in every way that I have not even time to report what I do from myself; but be assured the intention is to convince you how sincerly

I am
Yours

N BALFOUR

---

[113] *copy of the proclamation*: not extant. It would have been the printed version concerning sequestration.

[114] See Cruden to Cornwallis, 29th September, p 324.

[115] Balfour had in mind Colonel Thomas Polk (*c.* 1732-1794), to whom he may also have been referring when, in his letter to Cornwallis of 12th July (vol I, pp 248-50), he talked of the provision of intelligence by 'a man of considerable consequence'. That there was some foundation for Balfour's various comments is to a degree borne out by the following document among the Gates' Papers in the New-York Historical Society:

> 'From a number of suspicious circumstances respecting the conduct and behavior of Colonel Thomas Polk, Commissary General of Provisions for the State of North Carolina, and Commissary of Purchases for the Continental troops, it is our opinion that the said Colonel Polk should be directly ordered to Salisbury to answer for his conduct...
>
> 'Given unanimously as our opinion, this twelfth day of November 1780
>
> HORATIO GATES
ISAAC HUGER
ALLEN JONES
JOHN BUTLER'

Of Scotch-Irish descent, Polk was born in Cumberland County, Pennsylvania, and migrated in 1753 to the western part of North Carolina, where he quickly became a leader in his community by virtue of his personal qualities and comparatively superior education. He went on to represent Mecklenburg County for several years in the Commons House of the Provincial Assembly, served as a captain in the royal militia, aided Governor Tryon in his conflict with the Regulators, and acted as a surveyor in running the boundary line between the Carolinas. With the onset of the revolution he was commissioned Colonel of the 4th North Carolina Continental Regiment in April 1776 and went on to participate in the Battle of Brandywine and serve at Valley Forge. He resigned his commision in June 1778 when he lost his command on consolidation of the North Carolina regiments and failed to succeed Francis Nash as brigadier general. Some two years later he accepted two difficult appointments, first as Commissary General of Provisions for North Carolina, and second as Commissary of Purchases for the southern army under Gates, but would resign shortly after Greene assumed command. James Knox Polk, eleventh President of the United States, was the grandson of Thomas's elder brother, Ezekiel. (Lossing, *Pictorial Field-Book*, ii, 418; *DAB*; Wheeler, *Historical Sketches*, i, 79; *The Greene Papers*, vi, 560-1; Hunter, *Sketches of Western NC*, 56)

[*Subscribed*:]

We are sickly.

Cornwallis to Balfour, 7th October 1780   81(25): ACS

Charlottetown
October 7th 1780

Lt Colonel Balfour
Commandant of Charlestown

Dear Balfour

I yesterday received yours of the 27th and 1st. The contents of the latter are unpleasant. I have ordered Wemys <u>to mount</u> his <u>whole regiment and guard the country east of Santee and join me at Cross Creek</u>. He will send you a copy of my letter[116].

I can only beg that you will send all <u>the arms you can procure</u>, a great quantity of <u>woollens</u> and <u>cloth for Provincials of any colour</u>.

I am <u>uneasy about Ferguson</u> and <u>fear I must detach the Legion into Tryon County</u>.

I fear his getting into a scrape and have ordered him to <u>pass the Catawba</u>.

Sure, all this north east wind must produce something from New York or from England.

I must leave it to your discretion in great measure to direct the execution of the last proclamation[117], but I would have it begin immediately with all fugitives and Continental officers unless you see particular causes against it. In any instances where that is the case you may depend on my approving your reasons.

I am, dear Balfour,
Most sincerely yours

CORNWALLIS

[*Subscribed*:]

As I am much out of conceit with militia, I have written to Cruger that Cunningham's corps may go on. I would still have cavalry, either a part of it or separate, as you and Cruger think most likely to succeed. Cunningham's time for compleating his corps must be prolonged.

---

[116] *my letter*: of 7th October, p 222.

[117] *the last proclamation*: on sequestration.

Money to Balfour, 10th October 1780   *81(34): ACS*

Charlottetown
10th October 80

Lt Colonel Balfour

Sir

Lord Cornwallis desires me to acquaint you that his having a feverish cold upon him prevents his writing to you by this express. *As the communication is become now quite unsafe, his Lordship begs you will send copies* and *duplicates of any dispatches that may arrive for him in your own cypher, and that you* will *not send any of his private letters either from York or England.*

There is a *report of Ferguson having been routed* and *some say killed*. If his Lordship *hears nothing from him during the night, he means to detach Tarleton with the Legion to morrow at daybreak towards Ninety Six*.

I am, sir, etc

JM

Balfour to Cornwallis, 5th October 1780   *3(193): A(in part) LS*

Charles Town
October 5th 1780

My Lord

At last we have had an arrival from New York, the *Thames* frigate convoying an artillery store ship with three or four merchantmen. I likewise understand that a frigate sail'd some days before this fleet for this place with dispatches, but no officer from the *Thames* has yet been here to give me any information whatever. You will see the dispatches[118] are duplicates. The *Sandwich* will be *ready about the twelfth but not before*. *The galleys* will also be in readiness *with vessels of the smallest draft of water* I can procure. I mean them to *carry salt pork, rum and salt, five hundred spare arms, flints, musquet cartridges, ammunition for six and three pounders, Provincial clothing* etc, with any refreshments for the officers I can possibly procure by encouraging adventurers.

If I receive no directions from you respecting the mode of their proceeding, and the exact place of their destination, which was not ascertain'd to me by Captain Ross, I should wish to receive your Lordship's answer to this before *they sail*, and I apprehend they will then be in

---

[118] *the dispatches*: see pp 48-54.

sufficient time for what you mention of *the march of the second division*. *The flag of truce* will be back in time to inform of any *force or obstructions at the entrance of the harbour*.

The George Town business turns out greatly better than I expected. The party of militia posted at Black Mingo behaved with a good deal of spirit, had two men kill'd and eight wounded. The enemy's loss as reported to me was equal, with the addition of a captain kill'd. Marian's party has not increased and has not cross'd Black River.

As soon as the wind is fair, Major Delancey with *about 70 men* made up *from Brown's corps* and *some of the* recover'd men of your army will proceed to *George Town*.

I am assured the great danger of sickliness is over, but I have desir'd they may not yet for some time remain on the same spot.

I am well aware of the dangerous tendency of raising sanguine expectations *at home*. You may depend upon it they shall never spring from my authority.

I find now that the last cargo of rum will arrive in full time for the second division. I am confident the information respecting *Pickins* is not true – at least I heard the testimony of all the principal people in that country for thinking so. I shall send *for him* immediately and do as you desire. Cruger is certainly *weak for the two posts*, especially as he must detach to the *Ennoree*.

I shall obey your directions concerning the *Indians*.

I open'd a letter for you from Mr Weir[119], supposing it to be on the subject of provisions. In it he points out the *distresses* of the *army at* New York in the strongest terms, that they could *only hold out* till the *first* of *November*, that the *Thames* frigate is sent express to bring back a convoy in which he hopes to receive *6,000* barrels of rice and flour from us; but the half of this quantity is all we shall be able to muster up at present, keeping *four months* for the garrison. Weir desires to know what he is to do with the two pipes of Madeira wine of yours which he has. I have a large packet for you mark'd *Private* from General Phillips[120] which I am afraid to trust to the present conveyance.

By letters from New York I find that St George[121] was sent home with the rebel account of your victory over Mr Gates but did not sail till the 20th of September. Dalrymple is also gone home on what errand I don't know[122]. I am *sorry to find* the *disagreement between the Admiral and General is come to an open rupture* in a mutual accusation concerning an

---

[119] From February 1777 to September 1781 Daniel Weir was the Commissary General at New York in overall charge of the department. (Edward E Curtis, *The Organisation of the British Army in the American Revolution* (Oxford University Press, 1926), ch 4 and appendices thereto)

[120] *a large packet..*: the contents are not extant.

[121] *St George*: alternative transcription is 'Sr George'.

[122] *on what errand I don't know*: see p 54, note 41.

attack *on Rhode Island*. Lords Winchelsea[123] and Chewton[124] are arriv'd with Sir George Rodney, their regiment doing duty on board his fleet as marines. This is the principal news from New York. *The corps to embark with General Leslie are the Guards, 80th and 76th*. I suppose the *Daphne*, which sail'd before this fleet, is sent to remain here.

Being just lifting my head from a severe fever, I could not manage to write these dispatches myself, but Benson (whose prudence is perfectly safe) has.[125]

Lessly in a letter regretts your want of confidence in him and fears, by what he hears, that his removal from this province was owing to your recquisition for Patterson. The falsity of this I know, but some one has attempted to make him believe it, and I thought it right you should know of it, although the author *must* not be *NB*.

Balfour to Cornwallis, 10th October 1780   *3(205): ALS*

10th October

My recovery has been but slow and allmost retarded by hearing that the dispatches from New York were kept upon the road by an officer of the York Volunteers who was pitched upon to carry them from his being very well mounted and who had the strictest instructions to convey them quickly, instead of which, to my utter astonishment, I learnt that he was five days betwixt this and Monk's Corner. I have sent an express to take them from him and ordred him to be put in arrest.

Colonel Doyle[126], I hope, will bring your private letters safe, but this is the last

---

[123] George Finch (1752-1826), 9th Earl of Winchilsea and 4th Earl of Nottingham, had succeeded his uncle, Daniel, in 1769. Educated at Eton and Oxford, he served as a volunteer in America from 1776 and was commissioned major in Chewton's regiment (see below) in October 1779. Since January 1780 he had held the rank of lt colonel in the army. (Valentine, *The British Establishment*, i, 317; *Army Lists*)

[124] George Waldegrave (1751-1789), Viscount Chewton, was the eldest son of John, 3rd Earl Waldegrave, whom he succeeded in 1784. Educated at Eton, he entered the 3rd Regiment of Foot Guards (the Scots Guards) as an ensign in 1768 and rose to become a captain there in August 1773, a rank which carried with it a lt colonelcy. Having served as an aide-de-camp to Cornwallis in 1776 and 1777, he was appointed in the following year a lt colonel in the army and assumed command of the 87th Regiment in October 1779. On 4th May 1781 he would sail from New York in the *Richmond*, charged with Clinton's dispatches for Cornwallis, but would not reach him in Virginia until mid June, having called vainly at Charlestown and Wilmington. At the end of the year he would accompany Cornwallis in the *Greyhound* to England. (Valentine, op cit, ii, 896; *Army Lists*; *The Cornwallis Papers*)

[125] Unlike the rest of the letter, this and the following paragraph are in Balfour's hand.

[126] Born in Ireland, Wellbore Ellis Doyle (*c*. 1752-1798) had been commissioned an ensign in the 54th Regiment on 12th December 1770. Promoted to captain lieutenant in the regiment on 5th November 1777, he transferred to the Provincial establishment nine months later when he became lt colonel in Rawdon's newly raised Volunteers of Ireland. Placed on the British half-pay list at the close of the war, he apparently spent some time as a military envoy to Poland before receiving the lt colonelcy of the 14th Regiment in 1789 and seeing action in Flanders. Following his promotion to major general in 1795, he was given command of the expedition to the Isle d'Yeu off Brittany. A year later he was appointed Commander-in-Chief and acting Governor of Ceylon, where he died. An elder brother was John Doyle. (*Army Lists*; Raymond, 'British American Corps'; *ODNB*)

conveyance for letters of that kind I shall trust.

Doyle will tell you of every thing about New York much better than I can. I have but one letter from General Lessly — in high spirits.

By several acounts from New York I find Paterson is recovred and talks to every one of his coming here immediately. Should this be the case, how am I to manage with him?

I anxiously wait for your orders relative to the sea business, as I do not like to send them off before I hear, and am also affraid of being too late. The *Sandwich* will not be ready till the end of the week.

The George Town affair has been stopt by my illness but will now take place with Lieutenant Bluck[127] of the 23rd to command. The season is now so far advanced that I think there will not be much danger. Marrion talks big but keeps on the other side of Black River. I own I begin to doubt much of our keeping the Pedee quite clear. However, no operations will take place upon it that can effect *your operations*. It will only be the inroads of small partys, and which I hope your movements will in time entirely stopp.

We are busy with the supply for New York. Moncrieff is ill, as are most officers of the garrison.

I hope in God you keep out[128]. A short time now and the danger is over. I am not well able to say more than that

I ever am
Yours

NB

Balfour to Cornwallis, 13th October 1780   *3(222): ALS*

Charles Town
13th October 1780

My fears for the dispatches are so much increased by the recept of yours of the 5th just received that I send duplicates now. The officer of the New York Volunteers who took them

---

[127] Having entered the 23rd Regiment (Royal Welch Fusiliers) as a 2nd lieutenant on 20th January 1774, John Blucke had been promoted to 1st lieutenant in the regiment some two years later. News of his promotion to captain lieutenant in the regiment, effective from 9th August 1780, had not yet reached Charlestown. At the end of March 1781 he would serve as Deputy Judge Advocate at the General Court Martial which tried and acquitted Lieutenant Anthony Allaire of the Loyal American Regiment for the wilful murder of Ensign Robert Keating of the Prince of Wales's American Regiment. (*Army Lists*; WO 71/93(287) (National Archives, Kew))

[128] *keep out*: Balfour appears to be be hoping that Cornwallis keeps out of the way of sickness. He had not yet received Money's letter of the 10th (p 117).

from this deserves to be hanged, as he has kept them nine days and has been attending his cart instead of going express as he engaged. I have not sent duplicates of the Secretary of State's letter or General Phillipps's[129] as the contents are not absolutely necessary to be communicated, but them, and every other, shall come by the *ships*, which, now that I am clear about what you want and the exact *destination*, shall be hurried with every exertion. I think *they* will *sail* about the *26th* if I receive no orders to the contrary.

The *movement* of the *63rd* will, I doubt not, have every effect you intend. I mean Brown's corps to remain at *George Town* and am assured by Cassells they will be sufficient.

The cavalry business I shall forward directly. Officers to command them will be chiefly wanted. We have been amazingly sickly here, in so much that, to ease the duty and for several other reasons, I have put the *prisoners* on *board ship*.

Nothing from England. Duplicates by the *Iris*, who with the *Thames* is here. The *Galatea* at Savanah.

I shall attempt to get some faithful *messenger* to *send* to the *army* of *cooperation*. It may be easier here than with you.

The rum, I hope, is in time. By my last acounts of it, it must be.

I shall not write again before the *ships sail* unless something extraordinary happens worth mentioning.

I ever am
Yours most faithfuly

NB

Balfour to Cornwallis, 13th October 1780   3(224): ALS

Charles Town
13th October 1780

Inclosed is a letter just received by a Captain Bain and other two officers of the 60th Regiment, directed for the commanding officer here. They are all three prisoners, being all taken just off this harbour by the privateers, who are in full posession of this coast at present.

I beg to know your directions concerning the exchange of these gentlemen and how far you choose I should allow the plan of General Dalling to be put in execution here.

---

[129] If conveyed later to Cornwallis, the letters have not survived.

I am with sincere attachment
Yours

N BALFOUR

Enclosure
Dalling to the Commanding Officer at Charlestown   *3(226): LS*

Jamaica
July the 14th 1780

The Commanding Officer at Charles Town
South Carolina

Sir

As His Majesty has been graciously pleased to entrust to my command the forces now and to be employed in annoying the enemy on the Spanish Main, I think it will be found requisite, not only to ensure the conquests already made but likewise to promote the future success of His Majesty's arms in that quarter, to raise certain corps of volunteers in the different parts of His Majesty's American Dominions.

I should be apt to imagine that among the many deserters from the rebel army and even among the rebel prisoners now in Carolina many might be procured for the intended service. By thus removing such disaffected persons from your government, two good effects must naturally result, viz, of lessening the rebel force on the continent and of augmenting His Majesty's army on the Spanish Main.

I have therefore to that intent dispatched Captain Bain of the Royal Americans to Georgia and Carolina to endeavour to raise such corps of troops as I have judged requisite for the intended service. The captain is an approved and good officer. Give me leave therefore to recommend him to your protection, being confident that your patronage will be of the most signal service to him in effecting the purpose for which he is dispatched. I must also request that your Excellency will give orders to the Paymaster to make the necessary disbursements when the men he may raise are inspected by any officer your Excellency may think proper to appoint for that purpose. Captain Bain is also on the recruiting service for the First Battalion of the 60th Regiment.

I have the honor to be with the greatest respect, sir,
Your most obedient and most humble servant

JOHN DALLING[130]

---

[130] John Dalling (*c.* 1731-1798) had been Governor of Jamaica since September 1777 and was a major general in the regular army. At the time of writing he was pursuing what would prove to be an abortive attempt to maintain the occupancy of Fort St Juan, which guarded the entrance to Lake Nicaragua, and to establish a series of forts across

PS

For the intended service a number of batteaux and men to work them under proper officers will be wanting, the appointment of whom, as likewise the appointment of officers to the intended new rais'd corps from your province, I leave entirely at your disposal.

JD

Bain to Cornwallis, 18th October 1780   3(239): ALS

Charles Town
18th October 1780

My Lord

I have the honor of reporting to your Lordship my arrival at this place with two subalterns upon that duty explained by General Dalling in the enclosed papers.

I must also inform your Lordship that the ship in which we had taken our passage was unfortunately captured by the *Junius Brutus* rebel privateer off this bar, and some days after, on a parole, set ashore on one of the sea islands near Beaufort, from whence we immediately repair'd here, and should have proceeded to have personally made my report to your Lordship was I not prevented by my indisposition, the consequence of our severe and disagreeable situation after being set on shore on an uninhabited island.

May I be permitted humbly to request that your Lordship will permit Colonel Balfour to exchange us for rebel prisoners of equal rank at this place and that I may obtain leave to follow General Dalling's instructions, or only to recruit such men for the 1st Battalion of the 60th Regiment as I can pick up, within such restrictions as shall be enjoined me. Let me farther add a prayer that your Lordship will grant me an exchange individually if it is not admissible for the other officers, having a family in Jamaica and the honor of being intended for the service to be carried on against the Spanish Main.

I have the honor to be with the greatest respect, my Lord,
Your Lordship's most obedient and most humble servant

JAMES BAIN[131], Captain, 1st Battalion, 60th Regiment, station'd in Jamaica

---

the isthmus of Central America. In November he would give the order to withdraw the remaining troops. Military failure and a renewed threat of invasion were then compounded by a series of natural disasters, a financial crisis caused by a lack of specie, a deterioration in Dalling's relations with the legislature and Vice Admiral Sir Peter Parker, and high-handedness in office. Growing doubts over his conduct as Governor were heightened by the fall of Pensacola in May 1781, even though the failure to reinforce the post was not so much due to Dalling's unwillingness as to the navy's refusal to provide an escort. He was recalled and left office in November 1781. Shortly afterwards he was made a baronet. (*ODNB*; Boatner, *Encyclopedia*, 314)

[131] Having seen service as an ensign in the 77th (Highland) Regiment during the Seven Years' War, James Bain became a lieutenant in the army in 1761 and entered the 1st Battalion, 60th (or Royal American) Regiment eleven years later. On 14th May 1778 he was promoted to captain in the battalion. At the end of March 1781 he would serve as a member of the General Court Martial which tried and acquitted Lieutenant Anthony Allaire of the Loyal

[*Subscribed*:]

I beg leave to observe that the letter addressed to Sir Henry Clinton was intended for the perusal of the general commanding in this district, on which account I have the honor to inclose it.

JB

Enclosure (1)
Dalling to Bain, 29th July 1780　　　　　　　　　　　　　　　　　　　　　2(385): C

Jamaica
July 29th 1780

Captain Bain
60th Regiment of Foot

Sir

You are hereby directed to use your endeavours to procure a number of recruits for the service intended against the enemies of Great Britain.

You are in the choice of them to observe that they are neither too old nor too young, but active, strong and healthy.

*Whatever you shall see fit to promise them as a bounty they shall be intitled to receive on their arrival at this island. They are not, however, to expect above five pounds sterling, and out of it their necessary cloathing for the intended service shall be paid.

The copy of the circular letter wrote to the Governors and Commanders in Chief in the several colonies to which you may resort in the course of the recruiting service will be a guidance to you in the mode of having proper persons appointed to act as officers to those men. Some of them being sailors, and to act as batteau men on the lakes and rivers, may prove of great service.

I repose too much confidence in your prudence to think it necessary to add any thing further than that whatever expences for the raising, the maintenance, the transportation, and comfortable accommodation of these officers and men you shall think necessary you may rely on its being duly reimburs'd you, and such charges as you in honor can offer shall be paid with an adequate reward for so essential a service.

I am, sir,
Your very humble servant

JOHN DALLING

American Regiment for the wilful murder of Ensign Robert Keating of the Prince of Wales's American Regiment. (*Army Lists*; WO 71/93(287) (National Archives, Kew))

[*Subscribed*:]

*As to this paragraph, it is left to Captain Bain's discretion to act for the best.

EDWARD BERRY
Secretary

Enclosure (2)
Order for recruiting the 60th Regiment, 26th January 1780 2(387): C

GEORGE R

To Our Right Trusty and Honoured Counsellor,
Jeffery Lord Amherst KB, General in Our Army
and Colonel in Chief of Our 60th (or Royal
American) Regiment of Foot as to the officer
approved by him to raise men for Our said
regiment

THESE are to authorize you by beat of drum or otherwise to raise so many men in any part of Our Dominions in North America as are or shall be wanting to recruit and fill up the respective companys of Our regiment of foot under your command to the numbers allowed upon the establishment, and all magistrates, justices of the peace, constables and other Our civil officers whom it may concern are hereby required to be assisting unto you in providing quarters, impressing carriages and otherwise as there shall be occasion, and for so doing this Our Order shall be and continue in force for twelve months from the 25th day of March next.

Given at Our Court at St James's
this 26th day of January 1780
in the 20th year of Our Reign

By His Majesty's Command

C JENKINSON[132]

---

[132] Having occupied a variety of public offices, Charles Jenkinson (1729-1808) had succeeded Lord Barrington (see p 52, note 30) as Secretary at War in December 1778, an important post during the revolutionary war and one which brought him into close contact with the King. He was at the very centre of North's group of intimates and, together with John Robinson, the King's other confidential adviser, took on responsibility for sustaining the Prime Minister's morale and reporting to the King. He was indeed thought to be the chief source of that 'secret influence' on the King which the opposition repeatedly condemned. In 1786 he was created Baron Hawkesbury and ten years later Earl of Liverpool. (*ODNB*; Valentine, *The British Establishment*)

Rawdon to Balfour, 21st October 1780　　　　　　　　　　　　　　　　　　　*3(253): C*

Camp between Fishing Creek and the Catawbaw River
October 21st 1780

Lt Colonel Balfour

Sir

Lord Cornwallis being indisposed with a fever, it falls to my share to address you upon the public service. The inveteracy of the inhabitants in Mecklenburg County was so great that during the latter part of our stay there we were totally ignorant of the situation of any of our posts, all our expresses being way laid and many of them murder'd on the road. We had obtained accounts of Major Ferguson's misfortune but we cou'd procure no intelligence of its consequences. We had, however, reason to fear that they might be fatal to the Ninety Six District and from thence might eventually extend yet farther. This consideration, added to our incertitude of co-opperation from the northward, made Lord Cornwallis determine to pass the Catawba and put this country in a proper state of security before he proceeded so far as to be out of reach of being called to its assistance should circumstances require it. We attempted to pass at the ford in the Indian lands but, the river being swollen, were disappointed, and rain coming on, our baggage embarrassed us so much in passing the creeks that we were detain'd for some days in that quarter, still ignorant of all that was passing in any other part of the province. We passed at Lands Ford this morning, and I was joined here by Lt Colonel Doyle, who brought safely the letters from New York[133] to gather[134] with yours and some from Lt Colonel Turnbull[135]. By Lord Cornwallis's direction I open'd the dispatches and your letters to him. The account which you give of affairs in the neighbourhood of Georgetown gives no room to apprehend any thing serious in that quarter, but you do not mention the state of Ninety Six. Turnbull professes himself ignorant about it and I have not yet been able to procure any intelligence. The 63rd (mounted) marched from Camden this morning to join Cruger and I think must be left in that country. The 7th, which is reduced to nothing by sickness, shall be sent immediately to Camden, where Turnbull thinks himself weak. Captains Peacocke and Harrison[136] died on the march from Charlotteburg and the regiment is now commanded by Lieutenant Marshall[137]. It is impossible for me to say directly what measures will be pursued by this army, but if the *Sandwich* etc have not sailed, it will be right to detain them till you hear further from us. In the mean time, more rum, I fancy, will be

---

[133] *the letters from New York*: see pp 48-54.

[134] *to gather*: together.

[135] *some from Lt Colonel Turnbull*: only one dated the 20th, p 256.

[136] John Harrison had been commissioned a lieutenant in the army on 31st March 1763 and entered the 7th Regiment (Royal Fusiliers) some four years later. He was promoted to captain in the regiment on 25th March 1777. He may have died of yellow fever, which had broken out among the troops. (*Army Lists*)

[137] Having entered the 37th Regiment as an ensign on 27th August 1776, Mathew Marshall had been promoted to lieutenant in the 7th Regiment on 7th November 1778. (*Army Lists*)

acceptable at Camden. I will instruct England to write to you about it. I shall be happy to hear from you, as Lord Cornwallis, tho' fortunately recovering fast, is still too weak to attend to business.

I have the honor to be, sir
Your most obedient servant

RAWDON

Rawdon to Balfour, 22nd October 1780   3(255): C

Lands Ford on the Catawba
October 22nd 1780

Sir

I find by reports from the different regiments that this army could not proceed without subjecting itself to much distress unless a supply of necessaries is previously procured for the men. I have on this account directed that each corps shall immediately send to Charlestown for the articles of which they stand in need, and I beg leave to request that you will instruct the Quarter Master General's Department to give every aid towards forwarding this convoy with all expedition. Until its arrival we propose to take some position near Fishing Creek which may communicate easily with both Camden and Ninety Six whilst arrangements are preparing for the better security of those frontiers. I should conceive that this must delay us for a fortnight at least. Lord Cornwallis has desired that I should write to Major General Leslie, as also to the Commander in Chief. The letter to the former[138] will of course require to be forwarded without delay. Possibly you may have some vessel in readiness by the time I send you the dispatch, in which not an hour shall be lost. If you could send up some blankets, stockings and shoes for Colonel Bryan's militia, it would be a very usefull supply. There were some stores at Monk's Corner. If they are there still, I will write to Lt Colonel Turnbull about sending waggons to bring up such as are immediately wanted. Rum, and I believe salt, will be necessary to forward to us.

I have the honor to be etc

RAWDON

[*Subscribed*:]

I have the satisfaction to acquaint you that Lord Cornwallis is much better to day.

There were some split shirts ordered for the militia; about 400 is the number we could wish. There are two rebel prisoners whom Lord Cornwallis desires to have released, viz, John Coker of Surrey County, a Continental, and John (or William) McCulloch of Meclenburg County, North Carolina.

---

[138] *The letter to the former*: of the 24th, p 55.

Rawdon to Balfour, 29th October 1780

3(303): ACS

Wynnesborough
October 29th 1780

Lt Colonel Balfour
Commandant of Charlestown

Sir

I enclose to you a letter for the Commander in Chief[139], which Lord Cornwallis hopes may arrive time enough to go by the *Thames*. The letter is left open for your perusal.

As we shall probably remain fixed here for some time, we hope to have the satisfaction of hearing frequently from Charlestown. The shortest route to us is by the great road across Congaree without touching at Camden.

I have the honor to be, sir,
Your most obedient servant

RAWDON

Rawdon to Balfour, 30th October 1780

3(316): C

Wynnesborough
October 30th 1780

Lt Colonel Balfour
Commandant of Charlestown

Sir

I enclose to you a dispatch for Major General Leslie and another for the Commander in Chief[140]. I hope the latter may be in time for the *Thames*. You are requested to forward the other by the most expeditious conveyance. Both are left open that you may be fully instructed by them of Lord Cornwallis's intentions.

We have learned from Camden this morning that some of our militia from the High Hills of Santee under Colonel Tynes have had some kind of check near the forks of Black River. Lord Cornwallis wishes much to have some account from you of that eastern district.

---

[139] *a letter..*: of the 29th (as sent). See p 57.

[140] For the enclosures, see pp 59-61.

It may be necessary to inform you that Lord Cornwallis has ordered large magazines both of grain and forage to be laid up at Camden, Congaree and Ninety Six.

I understand that Lt Colonel Tarleton with his corps is to cross the Wateree tomorrow and may possibly make a visit to the neighbourhood of Pedee. Lord Cornwallis is very well and recruits his strength rapidly.

I have the honor to be, sir,
Your most obedient servant

RAWDON

Balfour to Cornwallis, 22nd October 1780   3(259): A(in part) LS

Charles Town
October 22nd 1780

My Lord

A fleet from England with victuallers for this and New York is the only occurrence of consequence that has happen'd since I wrote. Captain Symmonds[141] in the *Caron* commands, who begs his best respects to your Lordship. He brings no news but the capture of many of the enemies ships and some frigates by our cruzers. He sail'd the 12th of August from Corke.

My anxiety since the *misfortune* of *Ferguson* you may easily suppose and how *anxiously* I *wait to hear of you*. *A detachment* with Lieutenant Blucke for *Georgetown crossed three days ago* and [I] expect is *this day at their post, which* I mean immediately to make as *strong as we can*. *The vessels* will be ready when *you order them*, with every thing I can *think of*. *Cruger* is much *distress'd at* 96 *about the militia*. In order to make *something* of *them* I have *proposed* the *following plan* upon his own principle: a *draught of* all the *regiments* to be made of *young men* and *volunteers*, which he thinks will amount to *about five hundred men*; the *old men* to be *sent home* to *defend* and cultivate their lands; *Captain Maxwell*, of whom I have a good opinion as a man of sense, temper and, as far as he has *seen service*, a *good officer*, to *command* the *whole* as *major commandant*; his *lieutenant*, an active young man, with his *company* of *grenadiers* to assist him and serve with *them*; *the whole to be paid when* upon duty and *cloathed* in a certain manner by sending up a *quantity* of *cloth*, and *each man*

---

[141] Thomas Symonds (?-1793) had been commissioned a lieutenant in the Royal Navy on 22nd January 1755, rising to commander on 18th February 1762 and post-captain on 18th January 1771. From 1771 to 1774 he commanded the *Captain*, Admiral Montagu's flagship, on the American station, and in the following year was appointed to the *Solebay* under Sir Peter Parker. Now commanding the *Charon*, he would soon proceed with the victuallers destined for New York, from where he would command the fleet which in December conveyed Arnold's expedition to Virginia. During the siege of Yorktown it would be his misfortune to command the ships bottled up in York River, where the *Charon* was blown up by red-hot shot. It fell to him to sign the articles of capitulation on behalf of the navy. He died at Bury St Edmunds. (Syrett and DiNardo ed, *The Commissioned Sea Officers*; Stevens, *Clinton-Cornwallis Controversy*, ii, 459; *The Cornwallis Papers*)

clothes himself; this *corps* to be suppos'd almost always *upon duty* on the *frontier* or where they are *wanted*. This *plan* is upon *Cruger's* own *ideas* and *Maxwell* is the only *man* I know of *here equal to it*, and I really think he will answer the purpose extremely well if he will *accept of it*. I have wrote to *Cruger of it* and desir'd *him* to prepare *matters* for its being put in execution, but wish to know your ideas of it in the first place. Nothing could be so *distressing* as the *dispatches* from *York* being *stopped* at *Camden*. I hope in *God* you have got *them*. Should you want any *messenger* sent to *Leslie*, I can do it *from here by a faithful messenger. As your stay near us*, I concluded, would be longer than expected, a *fresh supply* of *rum is sent*, and shall continue it 'till I *hear from you*. *Westerhagen* begs me to say that his expences being here [are] very high from his situation as *commanding three regiments of Hessians* and begs to know whether it would be possible to make any allowance to him. From the *sickness* and *mortality* of the *garrison* I found the *prisoners* by no means an *easy load* and the *duty so hard* that putting them on *board of ship* was absolutely necessary. The *wharf* at *Gadsden's* being almost so much damaged as to make the *hospital* very *unwholesome*, I have moved the *rebel hospital* to the *barracks*. *Moultrie wrote me* a very *high and violent letter upon the occasion*, which I would *not answer, being wrote in so very improper terms. Is there not a danger of Ferguson's cypher having fallen into the hands of the enemy? Until I hear from you, I shall keep to my own cypher. We get healthier.*

I have sent your watch by Lieutenant Campbell, Quarter Master to the 71st Regiment. I hope it is well mended.[142]

I ever am with the most sincere attachment
Yours etc

NB

Rawdon to Balfour, 31st October 1780   3(333): C

Wynnesborough
October 31st 1780

Lt Colonel Balfour
Commandant of Charlestown

Sir

Lord Cornwallis has just received your letter of the 22nd instant, by which his Lordship sees that you had not at that time learned any thing of our having passed the Catawba River. You will long before this have received instructions to detain the vessels which were destined for Cape Fear and will also have been made acquainted with Lord Cornwallis's further purposes.

---

[142] This paragraph is in Balfour's hand.

The dispersion of Colonel Tynes's militia makes Lord Cornwallis apprehensive for the fate of any stores which may at this time be embarked upon the Santee. Lt Colonel Tarleton will cross the Wateree to morrow and his appearance may repress the audacity of the Pedee plunderers. However, land carriage, if it can be effected, is the only means of conveyance which can be thoroughly depended upon.

Lord Cornwallis cannot coincide in opinion with Lt Colonel Cruger respecting the draft proposed from the Ninety Six militia. Should that body receive cloathing from us, every regiment of militia will expect and demand it. The measure would likewise interfere with Cunningham's regiment, which[143] will be a much more serviceable corps than the other could possibly be rendered, and the aid of the militia will still remain to be called forth in case of exigency. I have written to Lt Colonel Cruger on the subject of militia regulations[144], which from the stationing the 63rd Regiment in that district need not at present be so strict and so tiresome to the inhabitants as was heretofore the case.

I enclose duplicates of the last letters to the Commander in Chief and Major General Leslie, which you will have the goodness to forward. I have the pleasure to inform you that Lord Cornwallis recovers strength surprisingly.

I have the honor to be, sir, etc

RAWDON

Balfour to Rawdon, 26th October 1780   3(289): ALS

Charles Town
26th October 1780

My Lord

I have just now received yours of the 21st of October and most earnestly hope to hear of Lord Cornwallis's recovery by the next messenger. I allways feared for his health from the little care he used to take of it.

I had not heared from Colonel Crugar for some time when I last wrote to his Lordship, but I never apprehended much danger to his post while the army was at Charlotte, and I never doubted of his communicating with Camden by a much shorter rout than this. He has got a stockade made round the town at Ninety Six with block houses and redoubts and has been very active in strengthening his post, so that I would hope there will be but little fear of his being forced by any militia force. I have sent him salt and entrenching tools etc. He has been a good deal allarmed. The arrival of the 63rd will put him entirely at his ease, and, could they be spared, would, I doubt not, secure that district, for without a doubt the

---

[143] In a further copy of this letter (3(338)) there are the following words after 'which': ', if it succeeds,'.

[144] *I have written to Lt Colonel Cruger..*: on 28th and 31st October, pp 203-4.

Provincial troops — officers and men — wish for the support of regulars and, when left to themselves, are diffident and apt to be easily allarmed, a fault infinitely dangerous in this country at present. I have wrote to his Lordship of a plan suggested by Crugar to draft the militia at Ninety Six as the only way to get any kind of benefit from them; and if this takes place, with a small body of cavalry to be formed by Wemyss there, I cannot conceive there could be the least doubt of every thing going well there, especialy when asisted by Colonel Brown's friends[145].

The Pedee, I fear, is totaly in the enemy's posession, and indeed they make inroads into the very banks of the Santee. George Town is posessed by Lieutenant Bluke a few days ago with seventy men composed of the convalescents of your army and Brown's corps, and I mean to reinforce him with some of the same kind of troops to make his party as near a hundred men as I can. He has got into a redoubt made there by Major Wemyss and got two hawitzers from the galley, which, with what he will be able to do in a few days and the galley, I have no apprehensions but will put him in a state of security.

Lieutenant Crosier commanding the gally there has great merit for keeping the place from the enemy and supporting the friends of Government there.

An intermediate post betwixt Camden and George Town is absolutely necessary. If we could afford it as far advanced as the Cheraws, so much the better. If not, Kings Tree Bridge near Black River appears to me by much the best post to hold, and it is thought so by a much better judge, Major Moncrieff.

I know Major Fraser of Colonel Innes's corps to be a very active, sensible and spirited officer, and if he was to take the command of the intermediate post and empowered to raise a troop of horse for that frontier, I should hope it might be soon in a good situation, but works and some troops would be indispensable for him. I have seen Colonel Gray of the Cheraws, who I think will do extremly well and seems a spirited man. I forgot to say that Ballingall's regiment of militia and Lechmere's are on their way to George Town, where I propose them to guard the ferrys over the Pedee and Lynches Creek in front, but I am now clear that (the militia of Orangeburgh and some of the Back Country excepted) we cannot expect the smallest service from any other. In all the districts hereabouts they will not turn out, and if they do, they are not to be depended upon for two days together. If the 7th is left at Camden, and that post can spare to Frazer two hundred men, I think he would soon raise a body of cavalry to asist him and that any post betwixt that and Georgetown would be safe and in all probability the country brought to peace, providing allways that I can keep the convalescents *here* at present for the support of George Town.

The enemy cannot, I should think, send a serious force to this province while the army is on a forward movement, and a very few respectable posts, well commanded with some cavalry, I should hope would effectualy secure us under the shadow of your wings.

The Orangeburgh regiment, I think, should allways be left to guard the Santee.

---

[145] *Colonel Brown's friends*: the Cherokees.

I understand that accoutrements for two or three hundred cavalry are come to Savanah, and for fear of accidents I have sent an express and an official request for them in the name of Lord Cornwallis. Most of them can come in the *Sandwich*, and the others be made use of here.

Being perfectly certain of your want of rum, fifteen hogsheads in addition to the twenty mentioned in my last were sent up, and ten fresh are sent this day, to be carried up by land all the way, as trusting to the river carriage is very precarious indeed; but it is impossible to send the whole way by land as it takes six weeks, and having only one sett of horses, they are totally knocked up by the journey. However, we send ten puncheons now, as we can spare horses for that quantity, and shall continue a weekly supply by water from Nielson's Ferry of ten puncheons. The 2nd convoy sent went from this on the 29th of September.

The *Sandwich* is not sailed and waits your orders. The fleet with Captain Symmonds, the *Thames* and *Iris* are all still here. The weather has been very bad and the wind directly against. The number of vessels captured off this harbour is distressing to the greatest degree. A young man known here to be a friend is just arrived from North Carolina. The amount of his intelligence is: nine hundred Continentals and two thousand militia at Hillsbrough; White[146] with two hundred and fifty light dragoons in Granville County; nothing in Cape Fear River but unarmed prizes taken off this harbour – of this he seems well informed. We are recovering but slowly. The rebell prisoners die faster even than they used to desert. I anxiously wait to hear from you again, and am with great respect

Your Lordship's most obedient humble servant

N BALFOUR

PS

Major Doyle I mean to take charge of all things by the *Sandwich*, etc etc.

Balfour to Rawdon, 27th October 1780   *3(291): ALS*

Charles Town
27th October 1780

My Lord

A few minutes ago I received the letter inclosed from Colonel Crugar, and as I find he does not now communicate with the army, I send it immediately.

---

[146] Born in Brunswick, New Jersey, to wealthy parents, Anthony Walton White (1750-1803) had served as a field officer in the north since 1775, latterly in the 1st Continental Dragoons. Promoted to colonel in his regiment on 16th February 1780, he had been sent south with a detachment of cavalry, only to be routed by Tarleton in the action at Lenud's Ferry on 6th May. White escaped by swimming the Santee. After later recovering from a near-fatal illness at Halifax, he would repair to Virginia and in early 1781 refit there the remains of his men. They would be detained for service with Lafayette. (*Appletons'*; Heitman, *Historical Register*, 585; Tarleton, *Campaigns*, 19, 20; *The Greene Papers*, vi-ix, *passim*)

Last night a messenger came from Colonel Crugar to inform me verbally that he conceived he was in great danger, that the militia to a man would not turn out and semed to wish to be taken prisoners, and that the enemy was advanced to Ennoree River. Nor could he stirr five miles from his post. The reason of his sending the messenger was that he was affraid to trust a letter.

The 63rd Regiment's arrival will, I hope, put him more at his ease. I think you may depend upon not wanting rum in future.

I have the honor to be
Your Lordship's most obedient servant

N BALFOUR

Enclosure
Cruger to Balfour, 22nd October 1780   *3(261): ALS*

96
Sunday morning, October 22nd

Colonel Balfour
Commandant etc etc etc
Charles Town

Dear Sir

No post in yet. Will be prepared, the instant he comes, to send off. Yesterday sent to you by Serjeant Quain a verbal account of matters here. You may rely on what he tells you; it will probably cause new measures to be adopted. Soon after Quain went away yesterday, Pickens, Bowie and Hamilton[147] arrived. They left the rebel army under the command of a Colonel Campbell[148] last Monday at Quakers Meadow in North Carolina with their

---

[147] Born in Augusta County, Virginia, Andrew Hamilton (*c.* 1741-1835) had moved on to the Long Cane area of South Carolina before the revolution. Closely associated with Andrew Pickens, he had served as a captain with him in the action at Ninety Six in November 1775 before going on to serve as a major under him in the engagement at Kettle Creek in February 1779. Now on parole, he would in 1781 continue to serve under Pickens at the siege of Ninety Six and in the Battle of Eutaw Springs. (Moss, *SC Patriots*, 404; Gibbes, *Documentary History*, ii, 105; McCrady, *SC in the Rev 1775-1780*, 90; Auditor General Account Book 1778-1780 (SC Department of Archives and History))

[148] Born in Augusta County, Virginia, William Campbell (1745-1781) migrated over the mountains to the valley of the Holston River and married Elizabeth, the sister of Patrick Henry. By 1780 he had been involved in intermittent warfare against native Americans, had aided in the expulsion of Lord Dunmore, the last royal Governor of Virginia, and, besides being elected to the Virginia revolutionary legislature, had become Colonel of the Washington County revolutionary militia. Persuaded by Isaac Shelby to join the expedition against Ferguson, he had brought 400 men with him and been chosen nominally as the overall commander. Nevertheless, according to some accounts, he personally did not play a prominent part in the ensuing battle. In 1781 he would lead a few of his men in the Battle of Guilford and, having been promoted to brigadier general of militia, would join Lafayette. He would sicken soon afterwards and die on 22nd August. He has been described as a typical pioneer, very tall, of great

prisoners — the number, they were told, 687. The number kill'd they could not ascertain. Our kill'd of British was Colonel Ferguson, and Ensign McGinnis[149] of the Jersey Volunteers, and about 15 or 16 rank and file. The rebels had hang'd nine of their militia prisoners. Colonel Mills and Captain Wilson[150] were two of the unfortunate people that fell a sacrifice to more than savage barbarity. I have every reason to believe that our three ambassadors[151] *faithfully* discharged the trust reposed in them. They were detain'd two days and then told by Colonel Campbell that 'they should carry their arms where ever they pleased, and abhorr'd the idea of plundering'. I am not disappointed in the answer. Pickens tells me that when the mountain army was together they were full 2,000 strong. They had with them Colonels Campbell, Cleaveland[152], Brannon, McDowal[153], Shelvy, Brevard[154], Graham

---

strength and endurance, fair of complexion, grim towards his enemies, with an inveterate hatred of loyalists. (*DAB*; Draper, *King's Mountain, passim*)

[149] John McGinnis had been an ensign in the 3rd Battalion, New Jersey Volunteers, commanded by Isaac Allen. On secondment to Ferguson's corps, he was killed soon after the Battle of King's Mountain began. (Draper, op cit, 255, 481, 510; *The Cornwallis Papers*)

[150] Robert Wilson was a captain in Daniel Plummer's Fair Forest Regiment of the royal militia. After a mock trial at Bickerstaff's Old Fields on 14th October, he and eight other prisoners were summarily hanged by torch light in the evening of the same day. 'Those brave but unfortunate loyalists,' commented Anthony Allaire, who was there, 'all with their last breath and blood held the rebels and their cause as infamous and base and, as they were turning off, extolled their King and the British Government. Mills, Wilson and Chitwood died like Romans.' (Lambert, *SC Loyalists*, 143; Clark, *Loyalists in the Southern Campaign*, i, 329; Draper, op cit, 330-343, 511, 518)

[151] *three ambassadors*: Pickens, Bowie and Hamilton.

[152] Born in Prince William County, Virginia, Benjamin Cleveland (1738-1806) was taken while very young to a border settlement on Blue Run and by early manhood had developed a keen love of hunting, gaming, horse racing, and the wild frolicking common on the frontiers. About 1769 he migrated to Rowan County, North Carolina, settling on the upper Yadkin River. With the onset of the revolution he became a captain in the North Carolina revolutionary militia and took part in the Cherokee expedition of 1776. Afflicted with a serious speech impediment and weighing fully eighteen stones, he began to show a darker side to his nature when suppressing loyalists and was to earn a reputation for summary hangings, floggings, and mutilation. By now Colonel of the Wilkes County revolutionary militia, he had been appointed a Justice of its County Court and had been twice returned to the North Carolina revolutionary legislature. An inspirational leader, he had courageously led his men in the Battle of King's Mountain, but not content with victory, he had been conspicuous in bringing about the mock trial and hanging of prisoners at Bickerstaff's Old Fields, no doubt desiring, in keeping with his character, a little light entertainment. After the war he moved to the Tugaloo region of western South Carolina, where he served for many years as a Justice of the Pendleton (now Oconee) County Court. As a judge he had great contempt for technicalities and for the arguments of lawyers, often sleeping while on the bench. At his death he weighed over thirty-two stones. (Draper, op cit, *passim*; *DAB*; Hunter, *Sketches of Western NC*, 342)

[153] Cruger may be mistaken in referring to Colonel Charles McDowell. Before the Battle of King's Mountain he had departed and left the command of the Burke County militia to his brother, Major Joseph McDowell Jr (Draper, op cit, 471-2 and *passim*)

[154] Of Huguenot descent, Hugh Brevard (1748-1781) was born in North Carolina shortly after his father John (1715-1790) had migrated there from Elk River in Maryland. 'Purgatory', the family homestead, lay in Rowan County not far from Centre Church. In April 1776 Hugh was appointed by the Provincial Congress as major in the 2nd Regiment of the Rowan County revolutionary militia and was later promoted to colonel in Griffith Rutherford's brigade. In 1780 until his untimely death on 30th June 1781 he also served in the North Carolina revolutionary legislature as a Member for Burke County. (Wheeler, *Historical Sketches*, i, 81; Wheeler, *Reminiscences*, 237-8; Hunter, *Sketches of Western NC*, 234; information from Rob Salzman, 25th April 2005)

etc flush'd with their success and confident of doing great things. They are certainly formidable and (I think) require a serious attention, nothing less in my humble opinion than his Lordship's notice.

Last evening I received a letter from Brown. He has begun the work[155] recommended to him. The instruments, he writes, are keen, ready and well disposed. He tells me that he wrote you three weeks ago on this subject. Governor Graham was gone to the Ceded Lands. Robert Cunningham, I imagine, will be with you this week. He will inform you fully the state of the country. The medicine, agreeable to Doctor Ross's[156] return herewith, are much wanted at his hospital, where he has several of the wounded militia who were with Colonel Ferguson, as well as some of his own detachment.

I deliver'd your message to Pickens. I believe he will accompany General Williamson and me to town next week. Our going, however, will depend on circumstances. A pause for the post.

Tattoo beat and no post. I shall therefore close and deliver my letters immediately that they may go off by day light tomorrow for Congarees, assuring you that

I am with the highest esteem very respectfully, my dear sir,
Your obedient humble servant

J H CRUGER
Lt Colonel commanding 96

PS

A week ago Colonel Fisher promised to send me three companies immediately. This evening one company is come consisting of seventeen men, which is all we are to expect.

[*Endorsed*:]

To be forwarded im[mediatel]y from Congarees.

J H CRUGER

---

[155] *the work*: employment of the Cherokees against the overmountain settlers.

[156] George Ross (1746-1801) was a physician who had migrated to South Carolina from Ireland. Between 1774 and 1788 he was granted some 1,105 acres of land near the Enoree River. In 1775 he was a member of the committee to enforce the Continental Association between the Broad and Saluda Rivers and was elected to the first Provincial Congress. In 1776 he was appointed a Justice of the Peace under the temporary revolutionary constitution and in 1778 served the revolutionary militia. Whether, now, he was simply tending loyalists in conformity with his Hippocratic oath or was a fair-weather friend to the revolution is uncertain, but in 1781-2 he would again serve the revolutionary militia. From 1782 to 1784 he would represent the Little River District in the lower house of the legislature. (Bailey and Cooper, *SC House of Representatives*,iii, 618; T W Lipscomb to the editor, 17 and 23 January 2007 ;Bobby Gilmer Moss, *Uzal Johnson, Loyalist Surgeon: a Revolutionary Diary* (Scotia-Hibernia Press, Blacksburg SC, 2000), 54)

To be forwarded immediately from Nielson's Ferry

A MAXWELL

Balfour to Rawdon, 29th October 1780 3(309): ALS

Charles Town
29th October 1780

I am favoured with your Lordship's letters of the 22nd and 24th[157] instant together a few hours ago, in consequence of which I have in Lord Cornwallis's name made a requisition to Captain Dawson[158] commanding the *Iris* to carry the dispatch for General Lessly, which he has most willingly and handsomely agreed to, and I hope he will sail this day.

Lieutenant Gratton of the 64th Regiment, a man of prudence and much attached to General Lessly, carries the letter. Knowing the good opinion the General has of him and that he was well informed of matters here, I thought his being the bearer would be a great satisfaction to the General and a good *channel of communication* to and from that army.

It is with the most sincere satisfaction that I learn Lord Cornwallis gets better fast. We have been all allarmed here about him exceedingly.

I wrote fully my ideas about the posts in the province if the army moves, but as I conceive there will be no forward movement of consequence untill the return of the *Iris*, there will be sufficient time to arrange every thing exactly as his Lordship wishes. Colonel Crugar writes me that he has entred into an agreement with Colonel Kirkland to draft 500 men from the different regiments, to pay them, cloth them, and Kirkland to be lt colonel.

This agreement must have been made before my letter informing him of Captain Maxwell's being chose to command had reached. As to the other parts of the agreement, it is much the same as mentioned in my last[159], but I am clearly of opinion that if an officer, and an active one, is not at the head of militia, nothing can be expected from them. Captain Maxwell with his lieutenant and his company of grenadiers may make them somewhat steady, but no militia officer unasisted ever will. However, if Kirkland drafts them and keeps them complete, and leaves Maxwell to command, there is no great matter in paying him as lt

---

[157] *24th*: the reference is to Rawdon's dispatch of that date to Leslie, p 55.

[158] George Dawson had been commissioned a lieutenant in the Royal Navy on 9th August 1762, rising to commander on 13th May 1776 and post-captain on 9th September 1777. He would be dismissed from the service in 1788. His ship, the *Iris*, was a 28-gun frigate built in Newburyport, Massachusetts, in 1776 and orginally named the *Hancock*. It struck to the Royal Navy in 1777 and was renamed. On 16th March 1781 it would be part of Arbuthnot's squadron in the engagement with Destouches. On 7th September it and the *Richmond* would strike in the Chesapeake to de Grasse's fleet. (Syrett and DiNardo ed, *The Commissioned Sea Officers*; Michael Phillips, *Ships of the Old Navy: A history of the sailing ships of the Royal Navy* (Internet, 26th May 2005))

[159] *as mentioned in my last*: not there, but in his letter of 22nd October, p 129.

colonel if the idea is adopted. At all events something must be determined upon respecting the militia: either the sending them all together home and expecting no duty from them, or paying the young men drafted, under which colour they seem to wish to serve, although they will not enlist in any corps. Lieutenant Bluck is at Georgetown without molestation. I have sent him this day a reinforcement of thirty men, and Balingall's regiment is on the march to support him. I can hear of no force of consequence near him and expect he will strengthen his post in a very short time so much as not to be in any danger. The country betwixt Pedee and Santee is in a truly miserable situation, and I humbly conceive that now is the time to take some intermediate post betwixt Camden and George Town, an officer for which service I mentioned in my last[160], as also a proper situation if the banks of the Pedee was thought to be too much advanced.

The *Thames* being about to sail for New York and a dispatch being mentioned that you intended to send for the Commander in Chief, I have wrote to the captain, begging he would stay a day or two for it as I could not find a safe opportunity when he was gone. I have not received Captain Howe's[161] answer but cannot suppose he will have any objections.

The officers for necessarys are all arrived, and on the 2nd of November they will sett out for Monk's Corner. The best arrangement we could is made for their conveyance, but fear it will be much more tedious than you imagine. Rum and salt shall not be forgot. I have sent some Madeira and spruce etc for Lord Cornwallis, supposing he would want it. The letter now sent is just come by a private ship from England, but a very long passage. The fleet with the *Carron* for New York is sailed. They have left more oat ships than I mentioned, which were, it seems, so dissabled as not to be able to proceed with the fleet. The splitt shirts you mention were sent to Camden and are now with Major England, betwixt six and seven hundred as I am informed. What blanketts can be sent, shoes etc for Colonel Bryan's shall be forwarded, but I fear the want of waggons.

As the police, as well as every other dependents upon Government, want to have their sallarys, I wish to know *what* Lord Cornwallis wishes to allow the Superintendant, which it seems was never fixed here. Forty shillings per day, I am told, is Mr Elliott's[162] sallary at

---

[160] *I mentioned in my last*: not there, but in his letter of 26th October, p 131.

[161] Tyringham Howe (?-1783) had been commissioned a lieutenant in the Royal Navy on 10th September 1765, rising to commander on 28th December 1770 and post-captain on 11th January 1775. Now commanding the *Thames*, he had seen service on the North American station earlier in the war while in command of the *Glasgow*. (Syrett and DiNardo ed, *The Commissioned Sea Officers*; Lossing, *Pictorial Field-Book*, ii, 639)

[162] Andrew Elliott was the third son of Sir Gilbert Elliott Bt, Lord Justice Clerk of Scotland, and was sent while very young to Philadelphia, where he served as an apprentice in a counting house before entering into mercantile life. After marrying his second wife, who possessed a large fortune in Philadelphia, he returned to Britain and obtained through the influence of his brother a place of honour and profit in the household of the Dowager Princess of Wales. In January 1764 he became Receiver General of Quit Rents and Collector of Customs at New York and was to hold these offices till the close of the revolutionary war. Since 4th May 1778 he had also been occupying the post of Superintendent General of Police there (the capacity in which Balfour refers to him), and by 1782 he would occupy the office of Lt Governor. When New York was evacuated in 1783, he sailed for England. He was brother of Captain John Elliott RN, the Governor of Newfoundland from 1786 to 1789, and was an uncle of Gilbert Elliott, 1st Earl Minto, whose only sister married William Eden. One of Andrew's daughters married Lord Cathcart, another Admiral Digby. (*Appletons'*; Boatner, *Encyclopedia*, 345)

New York. Mr Simson, since I have been here, has been of much service and deserves certainly a handsome sallary, but I apprehend his Lordship has some orders fixed for that appointment.

The release of the rebell prisoners[163] shall be attended to immediately. The mortallity amongst them at present is truly shocking. The garrison begins to get up a little but still is very low. Many Hessians, I am convinced, lose their lives from the want of knowledge in their surgeons and the poverty of their hospital establishments.

I hope to hear from your Lordship soon — respecting the militia in particular, who press upon me from all quarters to be drafted, pay'd etc. There is a great deal of woolen goods here, which could be given them in bulk of any colour etc. The jails are now, as well as the ships, quite full. Prisoners from Georgia and the country come in very fast. If a supply of cash does not soon arrive here, we must turn bankrupts.

I have the honor to be
Your Lordship's most obedient servant

N BALFOUR

---

[163] *the rebell prisoners*: the two mentioned by Rawdon in his letter of the 22nd, p 127.

CHAPTER 23

Correspondence between Cornwallis and Ferguson etc

Ferguson to Ross, 19th August 1780   *63(48): ALS*

Colonel Winn's
Little River
August 19th 1780

Captain Ross
Aid de camp

Sir

Colonel Turnbull, who is confined to his bed, directs me to inform you that he has this morning receiv'd your letter of the eighteenth[1] and that he will this evening detach me with most of the King's troops and of the mounted militia on the way up towards Rocky Mount, and we shall endeavour by riding in turn to make all possible haste. Colonel Innes with a part of the garrison of 96, join'd to some militia, are expected this day at Lile's Ford and will, I imagine, advance tomorrow after us.

We are inform'd that Sumpter on the evening of the 16th retreated from Colonel Carry's towards Rocky Mount and march'd all that night and the next, accompany'd by Carry's militia, a party of Graham's light infantry, six of Graham's baggage waggons and twenty seven other waggons from Congaree loaded with some rum and indian corn, all which they had taken on this side of Cambden. Sumpter had some hundreds of Virginia Continentals with him, which, together [with] the prisoners and waggons, it is probable will fall into Colonel Tarleton's hands. His militia horse, being extremely well mounted, will, I fear,

---

[1] *letter of the eighteenth*: no extant copy. It contained orders to pursue Sumter. (Allaire, 'Diary', in Draper, *King's Mountain*, 504)

escape to the mountains.

Besides Sumpter's party there is another which the militia and my detachment drove out of the nieghbourhood of Pacolet over Broad River and were by the last accounts near Cherokee Ford on Broad River. They consisted then of about 450 men (several hundreds after their retreat having abandon'd them) under the command of Colonels Macdowal, Clarke, Graham, Hampton[2], and Major Rutherford, son to the General. We have intelligence that Colonel Pickings of Long Canes, now upon parole and much favor'd and indeed consulted from policy by the commanding officer at 96, has privately sent to Sumpter that he would join him with 500 men if a diversion was made towards Savannah River; wherefore, if in the course of our march we find that Sumpter is dispersed by Colonel Tarleton and that this other party is within our reach, I shall consider it as the spirit altho not the letter of his Lordship's orders to strike at them.

Inclosed is a letter address'd to Lord Rawdon in the absence of Lord Cornwallis relative to the militia, which I beg the favor of you to lay before his Lordship as it is very necessary that some thing is done to enforce the assembling of the militia.

I had the honor of a letter from Lord Cornwallis dated Charles Town, August 5th[3], respecting the militia, to which I have only to say that it shall be my first object to obey and fullfill his intentions and render myself not unworthy of the opinion he is pleased to entertain of my diligence.

I am in haste with great regard, sir,
Your most obedient humble servant

PAT FERGUSON
Major, 71st Regiment

[*Subscribed:*]

Inclosed are the returns of four regiments of militia[4].

---

[2] Born in England, Andrew Hampton (?-1805) migrated to Virginia and sometime before 1751 moved on to Dutchman's Creek on the Catawba, finally settling before the revolution in what became Rutherford County, North Carolina. Having been commissioned a captain in the royal militia in 1770, he was by early 1776 a captain in the revolutionary militia and served against the Scots Highlanders. In the same year he was promoted to lt colonel and three years later to colonel. Now, in 1780, he had been involved in the action at Earle's Ford on North Pacolet, where he lost his son Noah, and in the capture of Thicketty Fort near Goucher Creek, both of which occurred in July. He would soon lead his men in the Battle of King's Mountain and in the action at Blackstock's. In 1782 he became Sheriff of Rutherford County. (Draper, op cit, *passim*)

[3] *a letter..*: see vol I, p 300.

[4] *the returns..*: not extant.

Enclosure (1)
Ferguson to Rawdon, undated 63(95): LS

Lord Rawdon

My Lord

 As the late moves render it probable that a proportion of the militia will be soon wanted for offensive service with the army, I am induced to mention to your Lordship, in the absence of Lord Cornwallis, the difficulties that are in the way and the most effectual means in my opinion of removing them, that such of them as may be approved may be adopted in time to concur with his Lordship's views of acting.

 Notwithstanding the very great proportion of loyalists in the District of 96 between Savannah and Broad Rivers, the men have been so little accustom'd to militiary restraints and become so soon home sick that it is almost impossible to assemble any number of them on a sudden call of danger or to keep them many days together. I have made them sensible of the ruinous consequence of this backwardness of assembling and still more so of the extreme danger to their comrades and the society of quiting camp without leave in time of service, and have lately procured the unanimous votes of all the officers and men to the inclosed resolution, which, if supported, will work some effect upon the men having familys and property but is little regarded by the young batchelors, who, living in their fathers' familys, have no stock of their own, and who in fact are the prime of the militia and can be the best spared from home. These giddy young men frequent camp the least, are very irregular, and desert it the most frequently. One or two who have behaved in a very disgracefull and disorderly manner I have caused to have their hair crop'd, then to be disarmed, turn'd out of camp with ignonimy [sic], and their names erazed from the Militia List, but if every lad who left camp when the whim struck him was to be turn'd out, the militia would soon become very thin.

 Yesterday a circumstance happened which gives me reason to believe that I shall have no difficulty to procure the general approbation of every man now in camp (who have the best and indeed only right to vote, the absentees having been summons'd in vain many days ago). Two lads of loyal familys who had never frequented camp were taken on their way to North Carolina. As they brought evidences to prove their loyalty, I told them the only proof they could give was to stand forth, being young, able and disencumber'd, in defence of their country, and as they had refused and avoided serving in turn in the militia, the choice that now remained, if they realy were subjects, was to serve with the King's troops, otherwise I should send them to 96 jail as traitors escaping to the enemy. Every body approved of the alternative and I have little doubt but all the militia here will concur in a general resolution to the same effect against every obstinate obsconder; and if a regulation of this kind was inforced with moderation and humanity, it would not only enable us to assemble four times the number of men twice as soon but to make them realy fit for service and in half the time, for the men have many qualities to render them, when under a certain degree of discipline with a few real officers, very fit for rough and irregular war, being all excellent woods men, unerring shots, carefull to a degree to prevent waste or damage to their ammunition, patient of hunger and hardship, and almost regardless of blanketts, cloathing, rum and the other indulgences essential to our soldiers. A great proportion of these men have a principle of loyalty and fidelity so very respectable and so thoroughly proved that every honest man must be happy in assisting them and procuring the blessings of real liberty, safety and peace; and it is only necessary to convince them of the necessity of order and of certain regulations to attain those happy ends to procure that general concurrence and concert among them which is essential and alone wanting.

As I feel that these men may be made of infinite importance, I cannot help begging your Lordship will enquire of the officers of Graham's light infantry with regard to their progress in discipline, and I can assure your Lordship that, after a very bloody skirmish of our advanced guard, the militia form'd and advanced some miles in presence of their enemy over very broken ground in as good order as when seen by the light infantry.[5]

I have also inclosed a duplicate of a letter wrote yesterday by order of Colonel Turnbull[6], to which, and this, we hope for a speedy answer.

I have the honor to be with the truest respect
Your Lordship's most obedient humble servant

PAT FERGUSON
Major, 71st Regiment

Enclosure (2)
Resolutions of certain royal militia regiments[7]   *63(97):D*

As the publick safety and preservation of our freedom and property depends upon our acting together in support of the royal cause and in defence of our country against any enemy who may attack us, it is the unanimous opinion of all the officers and men of Gibb's, Plummer's, Cunningham's, Clairy's, King's and Kirkland's battalions of militia, and also of all the officers and men of Colonel Mills' battalion of North Carolinians, assembled under the command of Major Ferguson at Brannon's settlement, August 13th 1780, that every man who does not assemble when required in defence of his country in order to act with the other good subjects serving in the militia exposes his comrades to unnecessary danger, abandons the loyal cause, and acts a treacherous part to the society in which he lives.

And it is also unanimously resolv'd by one and all of us that the man who quits his battalion when on service without leave of the officers commanding is a worse traitor and

---

[5] Ferguson is referring to the action near Cedar Spring on 8th August. His letter of the following day to Cornwallis, vol I, p 301, more fully describes the affair.

[6] *a duplicate of a letter..*: neither is extant.

[7] This document, with minor differences, was published in J G M Ramsey, *Annals of Tennessee* (Charleston, 1853), 216-7. It had been obtained by Colonel John Sevier from a colonel in the royal militia at the Battle of King's Mountain. It was reprinted in part in McCrady, *SC in the Rev 1775-1780*, 712. A potted summary appears in Draper, op cit, 143-4.

enemy to his King and country than those rebels who are again in arms after having taken protection, and deserves to be treated accordingly.

And we do therefore empower the officers commanding in camp as well as the officers commanding our several battalions of militia from time to time to cause the cattle and grain of all such officers and men as basely fail to assemble and muster when required in times of publick danger, or who quits their battalions without leave, to be brought to camp for the use of those who pay their debt to their country by their personal services.

And we do also empower the said commanding officers, and do require of them, that they will secure the arms and horses of such delinquents and put them into the possession of men who are better disposed to use them in defence of their country, and that they will also bring all such delinquents prisoners to the camp in order to be punished as they deserve and turn'd out of the militia with disgrace.

The above resolutions agreed to by every man of the above mention'd regiments, as well as by those of Turner's and Phillips' regiments who were at camp at Edward Moberley's this 16th day of August 1780.

It was also this day unanimously resolv'd by every officer and man now in camp of all the above mention'd regiments that what ever man should neglect to assemble and do his duty in the militia when summons'd for the publick service shall be made to serve in the regular troops, it being the unanimous opinion of every man present that it is the duty of all who call themselves subjects to assist in defence of their country one way or the other.

Ferguson to Ross, 19th August 1780

63(1): ALS

Colonel Winn's
July 19th 1780[8]
10 o'clock at night

Captain Ross
Aid de camp to Lord Cornwallis
Cambden

Sir

In the moment that our detachment was parading in order to march after Sumpter in consequence of your letter of the 18th receiv'd to day, an account arrived from Colonel Innes that, in marching out from Musgrove's Mill on Enoree (above 50 miles from this) this morning in order to support a party of horse he had sent over that river last night, he engaged a body of rebels before whom he was obliged again to cross the river, himself wounded, with

---

[8] Misdated from haste. It was written on 19th August.

Major Fraser of his regiment, Captain Campbell[9], Lieutenant Chew[10] and Lieutenant Camp[11] of Allen's.

He has again taken post at Musgrove's Mill and, as some of the militia have left him, wishes for support.

As Sumpter is certainly by this time several days' march from us unless already overtaken by Colonel Tarleton, and as the reason assign'd in your letter for following him is that there is no other enemy embody'd, and as Colonel Cruger writes that he had detach'd the principle part of his force along with Colonel Innes, it appear'd to Colonel Turnbull, as well as to every other officer whom he advised with, our duty to forgo the pleasanter service of pursuing the retreat of Sumpter in order to oppose this inroad, which is become a little serious both from this advantage and the intelligence receiv'd both by Colonel Turnbull and myself relative to a concerted rising of the rebels of Long Cane under Pickings.

We march this night for Lile's Ford in order either to receive Colonel Innes, if drove a second time, or prevent the march of the rebels towards 96.

I am in haste, sir, etc

PAT FERGUSON
Major, 71st Regiment

---

[9] Peter Campbell (1756-1822) was from Trenton, New Jersey. Commissioned a captain in the 6th Battalion, New Jersey Volunteers, on 20th December 1776, he had been drafted with it into the 3rd Battalion in April 1778. In the action at Musgrove's Mill he had commanded the battalion's light company. At the close of the war he would be placed on the Provincial half-pay list and settle in New Brunswick. He died at Maugersville and was buried at Fredericton. (Draper, op cit, 106, 108-9, 504; Raymond, 'British American Corps'; Treasury 64/23(7), WO 65/164(35), and WO 65/165(6) (National Archives, Kew))

[10] William Chew (1748-1812) had been commissioned a lieutenant in the 3rd Battalion, New Jersey Volunteers, in 1777. He would resign his commission but on 15th August 1782 was recommissioned as a lieutenant in the Royal Garrison Battalion at New York. At the close of the war he retired on half pay to New Brunswick, where he died at Fredericton. (Raymond, 'British American Corps'; Treasury 64/23(7) and WO 65/164(41) (National Archives, Kew); Draper, op cit, 108-9, 505)

[11] John Camp had been commissioned an ensign in the 3rd Battalion, New Jersey Volunteers, on 4th February 1777. Now promoted to lieutenant, he would soon transfer as such to Thomas Brown's King's Rangers and in January 1781 would be granted a Georgia parole, that is to say, he would be killed in cold blood after surrendering to insurgents. (Raymond, 'British American Corps'; *The Cornwallis Papers*)

Ferguson to Cornwallis, 29th August 1780 63(81): ALS

Cambden
August 29th 1780[12]

Lord Cornwallis

My Lord

Concious that I have not express'd myself in so clear a manner as I could have wish'd to have done when your Lordship was pleased to allow me to speak up in favor of the militia, I beg leave to take this last opportunity of submitting my ideas to your Lordship in writing; and the very great use which the rebels derive from a militia (which, altho at present more warlike than ours, is certainly not equal in numbers to the real loyalists of the Carolinas nor establish'd on so good and promising a foundation) may afford some hope that advantage may be made of the many thousand loyalists that are sincerely with us.

General Sumpter with a few militia kept Hanging Rock and Rocky Mount in constant alarm, brought the troops there into danger, and commanded the country round; and on the side of 96 the rebel militia have more than once shown that regular troops have not the same advantage over them in small detachments that they have collectively in an army, being able in the one case to elude the charge of a small front and to wear down the regular troops by distant scatter'd shots from superior marksmen, whilst in large armys both sides must commit themselves in close action along an extensive front where the best charging troops under the best officer must determine the day.

In justice to the militia of 96 I beg your Lordship's indulgence to observe that the different bodys of militia east of Broad River that have behaved so ill with the army were form'd in a hurry without the assistance of any officers of the army to establish order and discipline, employ'd immediately on service, and no scrutiny made into the loyalty of the officers or men, but a great proportion of rebels admitted so as in fact to form (as it has proved) a militia for the enemy, no restraints employ'd to meet skulkers at home and make it the interest of every individual to serve in turn, and the confidence and approach of the rebels inducing many to think theirs the safer side. It was of course to be expected that a mungrill mob, without any regularity or even organisation, without fidelity, without officers and without any previous preparation employ'd against the enemy, would bring the name of militia into discredit.

The militia of 96 that have been admitted to bear arms are certainly loyal, almost to a man. They have been some time under discipline, by their own regulations have given proof that they are convinced of the necessity of order and obedience to their own safety and success, and taken measures to make it the interest of every man to do his duty. Moreover, when in North Carolina, being out of reach of home, they will remain with us, whereas militia

---

[12] Pursuant to Cornwallis's letter of 5th August (vol I, p 300) Ferguson had left Sugar Creek for Camden on 23rd August to discuss the part to be played by the Back Country militia and his corps in future operations. He rejoined his detachment on 1st September near Fair Forest Creek. (Allaire, 'Diary', in Draper, op cit, 505)

in their own province are constantly shifting and old men going and new coming every day.

Their loyalty having made them avoid service, they are, it is true, less warlike than the rebels, but those that accompany our victorious army will soon be inspired with some of its confidence, and those who are detach'd upon offensive service, if once fairly pitted, will also gain confidence.

No officer who is sensible of the difficulty of subsisting and of establishing order among a numerous militia will wish for a large command. For my own part I am thoroughly satisfy'd with the detachment proposed by your Lordship, but I beg leave to submit to your Lordship's consideration whither several such detachments under command of different officers could not (without interfering with the range of one another's subsistance or in the least living upon the tract within reach of the main army) find provisions in the line of their own route, carry on a broad front so as to pervade the whole country, and promote as they proceed that revolution which is more or less necessary in every parish of dethroning the rebels and arming the loyalists, leaving the North Carolina loyalists behind them for that purpose with some officers to form the militia and put that of North Carolina in the same condition to accompany the army into Virginia as that of 96 are now to cooperate in North Carolina. One body of militia marching thus within 4 or 5 leagues of the army on its flank, and another at the same distance on the outward flank of the first, either could reinforce the other in 4 hours should a rebel corps attempt to move on the flank of the army; and the grand army could at any time be reinforced in 12 hours with 2,000 men, who at other times would cover its flanks, in place of exhausting contribute to its subsistance, and give it a very extensive intelligence and command of the country.

With regard to their assistance in firm action I will not presume to say, but with regard to pursuit and rendering a victory decisive I beg leave to observe that, had it been in my power to have arrived in time (as your Lordship's intentions were) either in the rear of General Gates' flank or even in the rear of your army on the day of the action, in all probability every foot soldier and stand of arms of the rebel army would have been gather'd up by our dexterous militia horse men, who would have scatter'd themselves in safety through all the woods and follow'd the pursuit for several days.

I have the honor of inclosing a copy of the memorandums which you was pleased to approve off[13], to which is subjoin'd a cypher.

I am with the truest respect and gratitude
Your Lordship's most obedient servant

PAT FERGUSON

---

[13] *a copy of the memorandums..*: not extant.

Ferguson to Cornwallis, 14th September 1780 64(60): ALS

Gilberton[14]
September 14th 1780

Lord Cornwallis

My Lord

Two days ago I had the honor of your Lordship's letters of the 6th and 7th instant[15] from Cambden and Rugely's.

The six month men having not as yet cross'd the River *Tygar* from the total interruption to their musters by the new levys, and having only with me about *650* old and infirm men (a part of whom neither *arm'd* nor *train'd*) who were detain'd in camp whilst the younger classes were sent home to draw lots and prepare for the campaign, I have proceeded with more caution than would otherwise have been necessary.

On the 8th instant, being satisfy'd by spys from the east that there was no collected force on this side of Catabaw to threaten our flanks and rear, we drew within a march of Gilberton, previously masking the fords of main Broad River, and in the evening push'd on with a hundred mounted militia and fifty soldiers follow'd by two hundred foot into the heart of the supposed cantonments of the rebels, having no certain intelligence of their then situation and being apprehensive that they would withdraw undisgraced to the mountains. We cross'd in the dark within half a mile of Hampton's party on their retreat to Burk's[16] and got about a dozen of his men with their arms and horses. The Georgia party under Colonel Clarke had marched at the same time towards Savannah River in order, as they gave out, to assist in an attempt upon 96 under Pickens.[17]

Clark had only 100 men, and Hampton 60. Macdowal was up in Burk collecting the militia, and Shelby from Nolachuki expected with 200 men, so that they might soon have come to a head and distressed the country.

The next day we fell back to our waggons behind Broad River in the hope that our retreat and the small force we had shown in the rebel settlement of Gilberton might encourage Macdowal to advance if in any force to a gap in the mountains, which they boasted off as impassable; and on the 11th in the evening, understanding that the rebels had actually occupy'd that pass, I march'd by an unexpected detour with 40 soldiers and 100 militia, being

---

[14] Gilbertown consisted of one dwelling house, one barn, a blacksmith's shop, and some outhouses. After the war it was renamed Rutherfordton. (Allaire, 'Diary', in Draper, op cit, 508)

[15] *your Lordship's letters..*: no extant copies.

[16] *Burk's*: Burke County, North Carolina.

[17] In fact, Clark's intention was to attack Augusta, which he proceeded to do on 14th September. Pickens was not persuaded to join him. (McCrady, *SC in the Rev 1775-1780*, 733)

all that we could mount, to turn their rear; but unfortunately they had taken some alarm, and at the instant that my advanced guard was scatter'd on our left in pursuit of a small party, Colonels Macdougals[18] and Hampton appear'd suddenly within 100 yards of our front, descending from a commanding ridge up to which they immediately retreated, and were forming on its top when our mounted men and militia were order'd to turn their right flank, where there was an easy ascent, and the few bayonets we had advanced upon their center, which, after a few idle shots on their part, gave way, and their whole party fled with little loss as our horses were jaded by march of 30 miles and the country cover'd with wood.[19]

We found two dead on the ground and gather'd in 17 prisoners with their arms and horses and one horse loaded with their spare amunition. On our side Captain Dunlap was badly wounded from some skulking shots on the flank, and one soldier kill'd and a militia man wounded.

They gave themselves out for 400 but I know their numbers to a certainty to have been 220, part of whom are skulking in scatter'd partys in the mountains and part at home preparing to avail themselves of the inclosed declaration, which I found necessary to circulate by means of the men of most character and moderation among the prisoners, whom I have sent to their homes upon promise of fidelity to His Majesty's Government. The people here have been kept in total ignorance, and the authority of your Lordship's proclamations would work surprizing effects.

I have also circulated among the loyalists the inclosed instructions, in which I shall be unhappy if there is any thing very improper.

We march to night to Burk's to assist our freinds, *disarm rebels* and procure *rebels' cattle* to send home with our *m[iliti]a, then settle* the *county* and prepare to *join you*.

I am happy to inform your Lordship that our militia have daily gain'd confidence from our petty offensive moves and that the rebels hereabouts are utterly dismay'd.

I have the honor to be with the utmost respect, my Lord,
Your most obedient servant

PAT FERGUSON
Major, 71st Regiment

PS

Unless I receive orders to the contrary I shall march tomorrow to Cherokee Ford on Broad River in order to surprize a Colonel Grahame who is lurking about his own house with 50 or

---

[18] *Macdougals*: McDowell.

[19] Ferguson is describing the action at Cane Creek, 12th September. His account is corroborated by Allaire, 'Diary', in Draper, op cit, 506-7.

60 men.[20]

Enclosure (1)
Ferguson's declaration, 9th September 1780   64(63): C

DECLARATION

Tryon County, Gilbert Town
September 9th 1780

The experience that the deluded inhabitants of the revolted American provinces have had of the falsehoods by which the rebel leaders have artfully excited them, against their duty to God and the King and their best interests, to involve their country in blood and misery will, it is hoped, by degrees open their eyes that they may at last listen to the calm voice of reason and truth.

They have been told that Britain, the land of liberty and toleration and chief support of freedom and the Protestant religion throughout the world, was about to introduce popery and slavery among her American descendents at the very time the rebel Congress was privately forming a league with France and Spain which, had it succeeded to their wish, would have banished real liberty and true religion from the face of the earth.

They were told that the savages were to be solicited to murder and lay waste and that the British troops were to assist them in desolating the country. Now, the only Indians employ'd since the invasion of Carolina are those of Catawbaw by the rebels, and even the Cherokee nation that followed the British troops to Savannah River to revenge the burning of their towns were refused leave and sent back; and the King's troops have exerted themselves to restrain the resentment of the loyalists and prevent the bad men on both sides from aggravating the horrors of war by rapine and outrage.

They were told the King meant to enslave them at a time when He with His Parliament had by a publick Act of the Constitution renounced all right of taxing America for ever and voted a restoration of all their antient rights and libertys to those Americans who should submit; but the chief rebels have industriously conceal'd and suppress'd these advantagious offers, knowing that all reasonable and honest men would gladly receive them.

They were told that all those in South Carolina who had taken protection were forced to inlist, when in fact no protected man was suffer'd, much less compell'd, to bear arms, even in the militia, untill he had given proof of his sincerity.

They were told that the protected men were maltreated and plunder'd by order, when in fact the authority of the King's officers was diligently employ'd to restrain the loyalists from retaliating the injuries that their innocent familys had suffer'd during the rebel government; and altho it is impossible at once to prevent every person amongst a numerous body of men

---

[20] This postscript was intended to deceive if the letter had been intercepted.

irritated by oppression from taking their revenge, yet the good behaviour of our militia at present in Tryon County shows that the King's officers have exerted themselves with success to prevent desolation.

In a word, the King by proclamation, and in consequence of a solemn Act of His Parliament, holds forth to every American who is disposed to return to his duty an offer of the same free and happy government he formerly enjoy'd, with an exemption from taxation and pardon for all offences; and His officers are strictly commanded to protect to the utmost of their power all men who submit and all women and children of every denomination.

Of course no man can have an interest in continuing to his country the miserys of war (particularly after its fate is decided) except those few who have either engross'd all the power or who by their extreme injustice and cruelty to individuals are become detestable to the best men of all partys, or otherwise who, having got a habit of rapine and plunder, wish to continue to rob in the confusion of the times. Under the last description are the partys lately from Georgia, Nolachuki, and some scoundrels of both sides, all of whom it is the duty and interest of every man of honest feelings to surpress and crush.

Wherefore every man that is not conscious of crimes that render him unfit to live in a state of peace in civil society has only to repair to his home and declare his submission, after which his person, his property and just rights as a freeman will be protected to the utmost untill the re-establishment of civil government shall for ever fix and secure his libertys. In the mean time, should the publick service render it necessary to use his cattle, forrage or grain, the same receipts that are in the like case given to the loyalists he will receive from the British commanding officer – not waste paper like the bills of the rebel Congress, but equal to cash, insuring him of full payment in a few weeks.

As to those rebels who continue the waste of human blood in a war without a just object or even a reasonable pretext, whatever fate may befall them and their property, it shall be the endeavour of the King's officers to protect their wives and familys from injury or insult and to pursue with equal vengance those of their own party or of the enemy who shall offer any outrage or insult to the female sex or act the part of house thieves.

Enclosure (2)
Ferguson's instructions to loyalists, undated   *64(64): CS*

The loyalists in Tryon County whose property is not as yet destroyed are to hold themselves ready to join the King's troops at a moment's warning but by no means to rise untill they are called for by proper authority and supported; otherwise they will bring danger and distress upon themselves, at the same time that they hurt the King's cause; but all those who are already ruined or driven from their homes by their rebel oppressors are desired to join the King's troops whenever occasion offers and to endeavour, when they take up arms, to make sure of every leading and obstinate rebel within their reach.

They are strictly enjoined to offer no injury to the persons or propertys of those men that have been of the rebel side who remain at home and shew a disposition for peace and submission, but to afford every protection in their power to them and to women and children of every denomination.

If the loyalists do not by their own voilence [sic] and injustice force every man to take up arms in his own defence, none will have any interest in resisting the King's victorious troops but those rebels who have engrossed all the power, or those who are conscious of crimes that are detestable to the best men of all partys, or others who wish to continue the publick troubles with a view of enriching themselves by plunder and violence, so that the country will in a few weeks be settled in peace and enough of property seized from those rebel chiefs who continue obstinate to indemnify the losses of the loyalists without injuring the quiet and submissive.

On the contrary, those who by plunder and outrage disgrace the name of loyalists will be punished even to death as scoundrels who wish to continue to their country the miserys of war, to distress women and children and other innocent people, to destroy all property on both sides, and to retard the progress of His Majesty's arms.

As intelligence is even of more importance to our success than a reinforcement of men, the loyalists are exhorted to procure every information possible and to send or bring into the King's officers every account of any consequence, particularly what rebel troops are on their march or assembling anywhere, when, at what place, by whom commanded and what number, how many Continental foot, Continental horse, mounted militia or foot militia, what cannon and waggons, where they are collecting flour, forrage or cattle in any quantity for the use of their troops.

Their numbers are best known by the quantity of cattle or flour they fairly eat in a day, and the women and children may from their doors and windows safely count them on their march.

Publish everywhere that whoever by intelligence enables the King's troops or militia to strike a successfull blow will be highly rewarded; and if any rebel deserts from the enemy on the march with good and usefull intelligence, he shall have a considerable sum of money. An officer would be very justifiable in giving 50 or 100 guineas for a piece of intelligence that enabled him to defeat a party of the enemy, and the informer would besides deserve the good offices and thanks of the King's officers and of every faithfull subject.

It is wanted immeadiately to know what rebel militia or Continentals are assembled or assembling in Burk County or about the forks of Catabaw, Ramsoure's, Warlicke's or Fishing Creek or at Charlot or Salsbury, and whether they are preparing to advance or retreat.

PAT FERGUSON
Major, 71st Regiment, commanding in Tryon County

Cornwallis to Ferguson, 20th September 1780   *80(33): ACS*

Waxhaw
September 20th 1780

Sir

I wish you joy of the success of your expedition, which, considering all things, has been as prosperous as we could have expected. I am very much concerned to hear that Captain Dunlap is badly wounded. I approve very much of your instructions and, as soon as our *press* arrives, will endeavour to circulate papers of that kind throughout the country.

I had ordered Tarleton to march to *Charlotte*. He is very *ill*, which *distresses* me very much. Our troops on their march and since their arrival here have been *very sickly* so that we *must* probably *stay here some time*.

I have heard of a rising in the Ceded Lands and that the rebels were going to attack Colonel Brown at Augusta. No arrivals from New York. A packet is come to Charlestown from England; no news; the riots had entirely subsided.

I am, sir,
Your most obedient humble servant

CORNWALLIS

PS

The present recovering state of our troops will enable me to march immediately. I shall send a large detachment of the Legion to Long Canes with orders to pass if necessary to the Ceded Lands.[21]

Ferguson to Cornwallis, 19th September 1780   *64(81): ALS*

Pleasant Gardens
Catabaw
September 19th 1780

Lord Cornwallis

My Lord

By a letter receiv'd today from Colonel Cruger at 96 dated the 15th at noon I am directed to inform your Lordship that on the 14th Colonel Brown was attack'd in Augusta. For the particulars I have inclosed two extracts.

---

[21] see p 150, note 20.

Brown's force — 300 soldiers and *500 Indians*.

Colonel Cruger was preparing on the evening of the 15th to *set out for Augusta* with *120* militia and, *I fear, few* soldiers.

He fears that *Brown* is without *food*.

He writes that, if *Brown is taken, we will be wanted*.

On the evening of the 15th, by a march of our horse round the rear of the rebels, they were reduced to the necessity of retreating through the gap of the mountains to the Western Waters to avoid being intercepted. Their number is about 200, among whom Colonels Macdowal, Hampton, Majors Porter[22], Davison[23] and a very great proportion of officers.

As it appears to me of some importance to settle this corner, through which alone the Back Water plunderers can infest South Carolina or the Georgians either communicate with them or North Carolina, I have avail'd myself of a Mr Cathey[24], who has submitted and has great influence with Macdougle's[25] party, to write a letter by him requiring that Macdowal will do justice to his adherents and their familys by letting them know the easy and advantagious terms upon which they may come in; and as he is said to be a man of a humane and peaceable disposition and will have an opportunity of returning to his family and of putting an end to the ruinous party war here, those who have submitted think that he with most of his followers will return.

The rebel inhabitants here have been kept much in the dark. They are surprized at their treatment and declare that few, if any, would have gone off had we not been misrepresented.

Their arms we are strictly taking and putting into the hands of the loyalists who come in.

As the loyal settlements here are divided by tracts of rebels, and as one part of them must

---

[22] Born in Pennsylvania to Irish immigrants, James Porter (1744-?) had settled early in Tryon County, North Carolina. Now a major in the North Carolina revolutionary militia, he would soon be wounded at the Battle of King's Mountain. In later life he would remove to Greenville County, South Carolina, where he lived many years, dying childless. (Draper, op cit, 475)

[23] Born in Chester County, Pennsylvania, John Davidson (1735-1832) had migrated in colonial days to Mecklenburg County, North Carolina, and settled on the Catawba in Hopewell congregation. Of a very prepossessing appearance, but much esteemed and popular, he became in 1771 a member of the colonial legislature and in 1776 was appointed by the Provincial Congress to a majority in his county's revolutionary militia. The same year he served under Griffith Rutherford in the Cherokee campaign, and recently, in 1780, had taken part in the actions at Rocky Mount and Hanging Rock. After the war he became an enterprising and successful businessman, establishing Vesuvius Furnace and Terza Forge in Lincoln County. Mentally alert to the last, he died at the home of his son-in-law, William Lee Davidson Jr. (Wheeler, *Reminiscences*, 271; Wheeler, *Historical Sketches*, i, 81; Hunter, *Sketches of Western NC*, 49)

[24] *Cathey*: perhaps George Cathey, who had a plantation near Pleasant Garden Ford on the Catawba. (Allaire, 'Diary', in Draper, op cit, 508)

[25] *Macdougle's*: McDowell's.

be opposed to the gaps of the mountains whilst the other has charge of the communication with Georgia, they can not be under one man; and at any rate Colonel Mills, altho very worthy and loyal, is without vigor or exertion and indeed in his dotage; wherefore I shall prevail upon him to come with me and shall, untill your Lordship's pleasure is known, leave some active, steady and faithfull men in authority here.

The reports from Nolachuki are that 800 men are to come over the mountains under a Colonel Selby, but if they come, it is not thought there will be 300.

I beg leave to represent to your Lordship that the militia men of 96 that have really done their duty have been from home so much that they have lost great part of their grain and all their winter fodder to an ammount exceeding tenfold the pay of a soldier exclusive of the distress, whilst those who remain'd at home and avoided their duty have their barns full, and that in other respects the services in which they have been employ'd have not been merely domestic, particularly now in North Carolina and before to support Colonel Turnbull.

Even if their future services should not be so necessary as they may be, I beg leave to submit to your Lordship whither justice and policy do not require that those men who have put themselves forward in the public service should receive some compensation in part for the very great loss they have suffer'd by so doing, and more particularly when it is consider'd that the militia are only paid for the day that they act and without any of those heavy contingencys that encrease the expence of the troops, so that in fact ten militia men do not cost so much as one soldier for every day that each is employ'd in the feild. Moreover the militia are a resource always ready, without expence or preparation – in fact, garrison without pay.

The necessity that appears to me for this at present from what I see of our harrass'd militia occasions this liberty. If allow'd as an indulgence on this very particular occasion, it might be prevented from running into precedent in times of moderate duty.

My Lord, I have the honor to be with the greatest respect
Your most obedient servant

PAT FERGUSON
Major, 71st Regiment

PS

Some printed proclamations are much wish'd for by the inhabitants here, and we shall have opportunitys of circulating them largely.

I shall march in two days by Burk Court House down the Catabaw towards Oliphant's Mills.[26]

---

[26] see p 150, note 20.

Cornwallis to Ferguson, 23rd September 1780

80(43): C

Waxhaw
September 23rd 1780

Major Ferguson etc

Sir

I have just received yours of the 19th and last night had the satisfaction to hear from Lt Colonel Cruger that he had arrived in time to save Brown, had retaken the guns, and totally routed the enemy, who had retired with great precipitation; that the Indians had pursued and scalped many of them.

I have no objection to your making any allowance to the militia you may think they deserve, but had rather it was called gratuity than pay even if it amounts to the same sum. I will desire Lt Colonel Balfour to answer any demand you may make on that head if you have not money enough.

Tarleton is better and was moved today in a litter. His illness *has delayed us*.

I shall *march very soon to Charlotte*.

I heard a report that a Major Davie, who commands a corps of about 80 horse militia, had marched against you. You will know whether that is true before this can possibly reach you.

This report is not true, Davie being gone towards Salisbury.

I am, sir, etc

CORNWALLIS

PS

As soon as I have consumed the provisions in this settlement, I shall march with as much expedition as possible to Cross Creek. I am told the climate will be healthy there by the middle of next month.[27]

---

[27] see p 150, note 20.

Ferguson to Cornwallis, 22nd September 1780   64(100): ALS

Gilberton
September 22nd 1780

Lord Cornwallis

My Lord

The inclosed is a duplicate of a letter I had the honor of sending to your Lordship by express on the 19th instant.

By intelligence from various hands it appears that the rebel party that have withdrawn to the Western Waters from this propose, when reinforced from thence by a Colonel Shelby, *to come out at the Flower Gap* and in *concert with Colonel Cleveland, who with* a few violent rebels are on *the head of Yadkin, to fall upon Campbell and English on the head of New River*.[28]

On this side there are two small partys of rebels *on Pacolet and Bullock Creek*.

According to the accounts *from your Lordship and Augusta I shall proceed* when join'd by the *few young men* that can be *expected now*.

There is a report arrived just now from Holstein that the Canadians and Indians had penetrated to Cane-Tuck and sweep'd all before them. By the rebel accounts previous to this, some partys had shown themselves on that side and made some prisoners, which renders this less improbable. However much regret[29] this rumour may give to your Lordship, it is proper to report it.

I have the honor to be with the greatest respect
Your Lordship's most obedient servant

PAT FERGUSON
Major, 71st Regiment

---

[28] Neither Campbell nor English has been identified. The valley of the upper New River lay in what was then Wilkes County, North Carolina, and had begun to be settled in the mid 1760s. Many of the settlers were loyalists and throughout the war there had been frequent uprisings in support of the Crown. (John E Selby, *The Revolution in Virginia, 1775-1783* (Colonial Williamsburg Foundation, 1988), ch 11; David E Johnston, *A History of the Middle New River Settlements and Contiguous Territory* (Huntingdon VA, 1906), ch IV, part A)

[29] *regret*: as to the use of native Americans.

Cornwallis to Ferguson, 28th September 1780
80(54): ACS

Charlottetown
September 28th 1780

Sir

I received yesterday your letter of the 22nd and inclose a copy of one I sent to you on the 23rd.

Colonel Cruger is marched into the Ceded Lands, where I hope he will have force enough to put every thing into a state of order and security. If *he should want help*, that will be your *first object*. *If not*, when you *are ready*, you will come to the *Dutch Forks* unless some material object should prevent you, of which you will give me notice. Sumter passed the Catawba at Bigger's Ferry and, I believe, is marched up the river.

I am, sir,
Your most obedient humble servant

CORNWALLIS

PS

I shall very soon proceed on my march to Hillsborough.[30]

Cornwallis to Ferguson, 1st October 1780
81(4): C

Charlottetown
October 1st 1780

Major Ferguson

Sir

I am informed that Colonel Williams with part of Sumpter's corps march'd yesterday from Kerrel's Ford[31], giving out that they were going against you. My informant saw only 150, but the enemy told him they had 400 more – that is not good authority. Sumpter has had a quarrel with Williams about command and is gone to Hillsborough to refer it to Gates.

I am, sir, etc

[CORNWALLIS]

---

[30] see p 150, note 20. Cornwallis's plan is described in his letter of 7th October to Wemyss, p 222.

[31] *Kerrel's Ford*: see p 106, note 89.

Ferguson to Cornwallis, 28th September 1780   64(120): CS

Duplicate

Gilbert Town
September 28th 1780

Lord Cornwallis

My Lord

We are here in the center of a variety of rebel partys, who, if their own report were to be believed, *exceed us in number six to one*. In fact, *Colonel Cleveland had advanced two days ago with 300 men to Pleasant Gardens, and* Colonel Bevard is said to be on his march from the Catabaw further south with *300 men*. *Colonel Graham's has also advanced,* considerably reinforced, towards *Broad River*, and there are different arrivals from Nolachuki and Holstein mentioning *800 Back Water men* being on their way, but I believe Hampton and Shelby together will not *bring 300*. We have, moreover, two direct accounts from prisoners taken at different times, who agree that *Clark, loaded with plunder at head of 800 Georgians, is on his march from Pacolet to gain the gap at Munford's Cove to morrow*, and from my intelligence it is probable that we shall cross upon him this evening or to morrow with a number much exceeding his[32], *altho under 800*. It would seem that all these small partys were meant to have join'd and form'd a pretty powerfull diversion towards 96 upon the supposition that the troops there would have had enough ado *on the side of Augusta*, so that their failure against Brown and *my centrical position here* at present are rather lucky. We shall be ready for *to strike at whatever* comes within *our reach*, and situated *centrical as we are*, I shall think *us unfortunate if we do not prevent a general junction and remain masters of the field*; but in the present circumstances it appears to me improper *to turn our backs on this frontier* for some days, and if a *diversion of the Legion and 200 mounted infantry* could be immediately made for three days *towards Little Broad River* in the rear *of Colonel Graham's* without interefering with other views, *it would* probably, with *our movements here, disperse every thing* south of *Pleasant Gardens*, and if I was afterwards to *march upon Cleveland and give some aid* to the numerous *loyalists* near the *head of Yadkin and New River*, would I still gain my *proposed station* in time?

I have muster'd, within 25 miles of this, *500 loyalists, half* of whom are of the first *class and arm'd*, and I believe *200* of the other party have submitted. On the Catabaw, from its head 40 miles downwards, there is *another body nearly as numerous form'd under* Captains *Whitsen*[33] and *Husband*[34], who are now *retiring before Cleveland*, who may possibly

---

[32] *with a number much exceeding his*: intended to deceive in case of the letter's interception. Ferguson's actual number is indicated by the following words in cipher.

[33] It is unlikely that Ferguson is referring to Thomas Whitson of Burke County, North Carolina, who had been returned to the Commons House of Assembly in 1779, but he may be referring to a relative of his. (Hay ed, *Soldiers from NC*, 614)

[34] Like Whitson (see above), Vezey Husband was a captain in the royal militia of Burke County, North Carolina, where he lived near Lower Creek of Catawba. When all was lost at the Battle of King's Mountain, he would attempt to break out with Ferguson through the surrounding revolutionaries but both would be shot and killed.

thereby be encouraged to *come nearer if reinforced from Nolachuki*.

I have the honor to be with the greatest respect
Your Lordship's most obedient servant

PAT FERGUSON
Major, 71st Regiment

[*Endorsed in Money's hand*:]

The original received a few hours after this duplicate.

Ferguson to Cornwallis, 30th September 1780 — 64(128): LS

Between Green River and Pacolet
September 30th 1780

Lord Cornwallis

My Lord

I beg leave to transcribe the following extracts from a letter just receiv'd from Captain Dunlap at Gilbert Town.

> 'Six men arriv'd about an hour ago from Nolachucki. 2 of them were at the rebels' *muster on Monday last*. McDowel and Shelvy were collecting men to return over the mountains. These men think, [fro]m what they themselves saw and heard, that their *two partys will not fall short of 1,000*.

> 'These men left Nolachucki on Tuesday morning and the rebels intended *marching on Thursday*. These men think they will *be on this side the mountain[s] by Sunday*.

> 'By a man arriv'd from Captain Inman[35], who lies on the Catabaw with a party of men, *Cleveland was advancing last night with 500*. He had *taken several* people thereabouts and intends to be to night where I *was wounded*, there to stay 'till *join'd by MacDowal*. Do not make too light of all this, for advancing they certainly are, let

---

Draper, who had no knowledge of Husband, mistakenly refers to him as a colonel. (Draper, op cit, 276, 294, 482)

[35] About 1766 Shadrack Inman (1747-1831) had migrated from England to Limestone, Virginia, accompanied by his brothers Meshack and Abednego. All three moved on to Rowan County, North Carolina, but Meshack was soon to be killed by native Americans while he was on a transmontane expedition. In 1777 the others were to find themselves in hot water with the revolutionary authorities for allegedly making disloyal statements, but made their peace by taking the oath of allegiance. Now, in the autumn of 1780, Shadrack was a captain in the Burke County royal militia, whereas Abednego would soon take part in the Battle of King's Mountain on the revolutionary side. Shadrack died at Dandridge, Tennessee, and is not to be confused with his namesake who was killed in the action at Musgrove's Mill. (William Oliver Inman Jr, 'Some Notes on the Inman Family', http://inman.surnameweb.org/documents/wo-inman.htm, 29th May 2005)

their numbers be what they will.'

Since I receiv'd the above from Captain Dunlap I have examin'd the people from Nolachucki and am of his opinion the accounts are to be credited.

If the *diversion of the Legion* or even one half of it would take place for a few days, the happyest opportunity offers *of crushing the Back Mountain men, who* cannot at other times be *reach'd and* [may] *be a serious thorn in the rear of your army*, and have it at all times in their power to be a *formidable support to the malcontents* and bring this *district into danger*.

2,000 I cannot face. I shall therefore probably incline *eastward* if I do not succeed in my present object[36] *in two days*.

I have the honor to be with the greatest respect
Your Lordship's most obedient servant

PAT FERGUSON
Major, 71st Regiment

Cornwallis to Ferguson, 5th October 1780   81(18): AC

Charlottetown
October 5th 1780

Major Ferguson

Sir

I received your duplicates of the 28th and letter of the 30th and new cypher. I *would have you come to Armer's Ford just below the forks. If we can then fix the enemy, or if they presume to pass on towards Ninety Six*, I will *detach in force against* them. Take *all possible pains to get intelligence* and *let me hear when you arrive at Armer's Ford. Major McArthur* will *meet you there*.

I am etc

[CORNWALLIS]

---

[36] *my present object*: to intercept Clark on his retreat from Augusta. (Allaire, 'Diary', in Draper, op cit, 509)

Ferguson to Cornwallis, 1st October 1780   *3(160): ALS*

October 1st 1780
Denard's Ford, Broad River

The Rt Hon Lt General Earl Cornwallis etc etc etc

My Lord

The men mention'd in the within letter[37] from the Back Waters have already <u>*come to Cataba*</u>. <u>*Two spys I sent*</u> there at different times have return'd seperately within these two days with the best information, having both been <u>*to the musters*</u>. There can be no doubt that <u>*800*</u>[38] <u>*have arriv'd, joined by Cleveland*</u> etc.

I have in vain look'd for Clark, who I beleive has escaped by a difficult pass at the head of Saluda.

I can not <u>*muster half that force*</u> and shall therefore <u>*play off a little and incline eastward if push'd*</u>.

Two old men have been brought in here to day most barbarously maim'd by a party of Cleveland's men, who, after drinking with them in disguise for some time, fell upon them, altho unarm'd, and after butchering two young men, one of whom a son to one of the old, left them for dead and I fear past recovery.

It appears from various accounts that Cleveland gives orders for such cowardly acts of cruelty.

If your Lordship should <u>*detach on this side*</u>, I beg to know by two persons in case of accidents.

I have heard nothing from Colonel Cruger since he left Augusta. I beg your Lordship's pardon for this letter, which I would not send was there a probability of my mending it by a new copy where I am.

I have the honor to be with the greatest respect
Your Lordship's most obedient humble servant

PAT FERGUSON
Major, 71st Regiment

---

[37] *the within letter..*: not extant.

[38] *800*: this number was wrongly deciphered as '301'.

Ferguson to Cornwallis, 3rd October 1780   *3(176): A(in part) LS*

Little Broad River
October 3rd 1780

Lord Cornwallis

My [Lord]

I had the honor of your Lordship's letter of the 28th this morning.

By desire of Colonel Cruger I cross'd upon Clark's retreat but miss'd him, and I am inform'd he went off at the head of Saluda at a gap out of my reach with two hundred men.

The accounts I sent your Lordship respecting the Back Mountain men, MacDowal, Cleveland and Bevard have been confirm'd from various quarters and they are probably by this time *reinforced by Sumter, Grahame's or Clark, if not by all*.

I advanced last night over Broad River *to deceive the enemy* and this day have march'd 20 miles east to Little Broad River *towards any reinforcement your Lordship may send, understanding that the enemy were* to be, as I now find they *are, within twenty five miles of this at Gilbert Town*.

To morrow I shall fall behind Little Broad River towards Cherokee Ford, take a strong ground till I know exactly the amount of the several detachments of the enemy that are join'd, *and, if they insist, at any rate rather give than receive an attack*. They have *flatter'd their followers with a very cheap purchase*, which is much in our favour, and if *their numbers are within bounds, we hope to sell them a bargain*.

400 dragoons, as many mounted infantry, with the loyalists *of the South Forks, would enable us to send them back faster than* they came and *finally settle* Broad River and the Catabaw. As it is, we shall *act with caution* and perhaps rather *allow them to distress a few farms than fight prematurely*.

I have asked *Colonel Cruger* to send me *100 soldiers and some militia*, but they will *come late*.

The position I shall take will *equally favour the communication with your Lordship or* 96.

The constant hurry in which I am kept by the variety of irregularitys and the ignorances of every person belonging to the militia will, I hope, excuse me to your Lordship for the incorrectness of my correspondence, which in any other situation I could not possibly bring myself to address to your Lordship from the respect with which

I have the honor to be, my Lord,
Your most obedient humble servant

PAT FERGUSON, Major, 71st Regiment

Cornwallis to Ferguson, 6th October 1780 81(23): ACS

Charlottetown
6th October 1780

Major Ferguson

Sir

I received your letter of the 3rd and am still of opinion that you should come to Armer's Ford, to which place Major McArthur has orders to proceed from Waxhaw. If the enemy should presume to come down to the lower part of Tryon County, Tarleton shall pass at some of the upper fords and clear the country. For the present both he and his corps want a few days' rest. I hope you will take care that any men coming to you from 96 may not fall into the enemy's hands.

I am, sir,
Your most obedient humble servant

CORNWALLIS

Ferguson to Cornwallis, 5th October 1780 3(189): CS

Duplicate

Bufflow Creek
October 5th 1780

Lord Cornwallis

My Lord

A doubt does not remain with regard to the intelligence I have sent your Lordship. They are since *join'd by Clark and Sumpter* — of courese are become an *object of some consequence*. Happily their leaders are obliged to feed their followers with such storys, and so to flatter them with accounts of our weakness and fear, that, if necessary, *I should hope for success against them myself; but numbers compared, that must be but doubtfull*. I am on my march *towards you by a road leading from Cherokee Ford north of King Mountain*. 3 or 400 *good soldiers, part dragoons, would finish the business*. Some thing *must be done soon*. This is their *last push in this quarter* and they are extreamely desolate *and [low?]*.[39]

I wish for your Lordship's orders.

---

[39] An abbreviated version of this paragraph, ending at '*this quarter*', and with 'hopes' substituted for 'storys', was published without location or date in Almon's *Remembrancer* for 1781, xi, 280. It was reprinted in this form in Tarleton, *Campaigns*, 193, and in Draper, op cit, 207-8. Draper mistakenly inferred that it had been written on the 6th.

If your Lordship should be pleas'd not to supersede me *by sending a superior officer*, it will be an addition to the obligations I owe you, altho not to the gratitude with which

I am, my Lord,
Your Lordship's most obedient servant

PAT FERGUSON
Major, 71st Regiment

Ferguson to Cornwallis, 6th October 1780   3(191): LS

King Mountain
October 6th 1780

Lord Cornwallis

My Lord

I arrived to day at King Mountain and have taken a post where I do not think I can be forced *by a stronger enemy* than that against us.

I have wrote for *2* or *300 militia assembling under Colonel Floyd to join me to morrow evening* if not *destined* for another service.

I understand that we have little *or no reinforcement to expect from Colonel Cruger or his militia* immediately. *2* or *300 good soldiers as reserves behind our riffle men, and a few real dragoons to second with effect* and support *the feints*[40] *of our horse militia upon the enemy's flanks*, would enable us to act decisively and vigorously. As it is, *with Colonel Floyd* we do not think ourselves inferior to the enemy if you are pleas'd to *order us forward*; but help so near at hand, it appear'd *to me improper of myself to commit any thing to hasard*.

I have the honor to be with the greatest respect
Your Lordship's most obedient servant

PAT FERGUSON
Major, 71st Regiment

---

[40] *feints*: this word was wrongly deciphered as 'friends'.

Cornwallis to Ferguson, 8th October 1780

81(31): ADfS

Charlottetown
October 8th 1780

Major Ferguson
71st Regiment

Sir

I had the satisfaction of receiving this day your letters of the 5th and 6th. In regard to what you mention of *being reinforced and advancing upon* the enemy, it appears to me to depend on their situation and the *possibility of getting at them*. Of this you take no notice. I had intelligence from the other side of the Catawba *that Sumpter's corps, Shelby, McDowal* etc were certainly on the 6th instant at and about Bullener's Mill on Clarke's Creek on the south fork of Catawba. If you was *to be reinforced and march towards them*, they would probably *retire to Sherrel's Ford* and pass the river. We are now *surrounded by vast numbers of militia*. Whenever I can *fix any corps so as to have a good chance of getting up* with them, I will endeavour to make a stroke at them. The condition of my cavalry and the continual want of them does not warrant my engaging them in a pursuit from which no very material success can be expected.

I am therefore still of opinion that you *should come to this side of the Catawba* unless you *feel yourself perfectly secure* and see any reason *for continuing a few days longer where you are*. I do not believe that Floyd's militia *consists of forty men*. I shall order McArthur *to join me here*, as I now consider you *perfectly safe*.

I am, sir, etc

CORNWALLIS

DePeyster to Cornwallis, 11th October 1780

3(210): ALS

Camp near Gilbert Town
11th October 1780

Lord Cornwallis

My Lord

I am sorry to acquaint your Lordship that the 7th instant Major Ferguson was attack[ed] near King Mountain by a body of the enemy. Their numbers enabl'd them to surround our post, and ours was only sufficient to form a single line on the top of the hill.

The action lasted an hour and five minuets, when the North Carolina militia who were entyrly commanded by their own officers on the right gave way, which not only discouraged the other regiments but drove them down the hill before them. Our little detachment of soldiers charged the enemy with success and drove the right wing of them back in confusion, but unfortunately Major Ferguson made a signal for us to retreat, being afraid that the enemy would get possession of the highth from the other side. The militia being ignorant of the cause of our retreat, it threw the few that stood their post under the officers from 96 in disorder, tho the officers cut some of them down. They intermix'd themselves with our detachment and broke us in such a manner that we could no longer act, being then reduced to 2 serjeants and 20 rank and file.

The left, on seeing us broke, gave way, got all in a croud on the hill, and, tho' every officer used his endeavours to rally the men, as nothing now offer'd but to make a breach through the enemy, I am sorry to say was not able to get a man to follow them, the chief part being without amunition, excepting four men that followed Major Ferguson while the other officers were doing their best amongst the croud to collect more to follow them; but I am sorry to say that Major Ferguson was kill'd before he advanced 20 yards. Ensign MacGinnes of Colonel Alan's corps was also kill'd soon after the action commenced, which render'd the militia he commanded almost useless. In this situation, and the small body of soldiers we had being cut up, and finding it impossible to rally the militia, I thought proper to surrender as the only means of saving the lives of some brave men still left.

In justice to the officers and men I must beg leave to acquaint your Lordship that they behaved with the greatest gallantry and attention, even to a wish. As to the militia, there was many of them, both officers and men, who, when *then* the enemy was within a hundred yards round us, that behaved with a degree of galantry.

Our wounded are left at one Wilson's, 4 miles this side of the place of action. They are without body cloths or blankets, and I am afraid the man who attends them without mediciens and not sufficiently capable.

I am not allowed to make myself acquainted with the state of the militia, so that I have not it in my power to furnish your Lordship with a state of them.

I enclos'd a state of our detachment, and I cannot help mentioning to your Lordship that the few of them that remains, both officers and men, are without cloaths and shoes, and not a blanket amongest us all.

As this letter is to be read by the commanding officer and I am not allowed to mention particulars, I have only to wish your Lordship may be pleas'd to think of us, particularly of the poor soldiers, who have been a-suffering for some time past.

I have the honor to be with due respect, my Lord,
Your Lordship's most obedient servant

A D'PEYSTER
Captain, King's American Regiment

CHAPTER 24

Correspondence between Cornwallis or Rawdon and Cruger or Innes

---

Innes to Cornwallis, 16th August 1780 — 63(42): ALS

Ninety Six
16th August 1780

Lt General Earl Cornwallis etc etc etc

My Lord

Lt Colonel Cruger and I were honor'd with your Lordship's letter of the 13th[1] late last night, and this evening I shall march with a detachment from this place in consequence of your commands.[2] As I hope soon to have the honor of communicating with your Lordship, I shall defer every particular of our situation here till another opportunity, not thinking this perfectly safe.

I have the honor to be with great respect
Your Lordship's most devoted servant

ALEX INNES
Lt Colonel

---

[1] *letter of the 13th*: no extant copy.

[2] The purpose of the move is summarised by Cruger in his following letter.

Cruger to Cornwallis, 16th August 1780[3]

63(93): ALS

Lt General Earl Cornwallis etc etc etc
Camden

My Lord

By this conveyance Colonel Innes has inform'd your Lordship of our marching from hence a reinforcement for Colonel Ferguson; Colonel Allen's corps being at hand enables us to make it pretty considerable. Colonel Innes goes with the reinforcement; I wait your Lordship's farther orders at 96. Colonel Innes will communicate farther particulars at a more convenient time. The plan proposed in my last letter[4] to your Lordship for Allen must of course be postponed for the present. I am happy at the same time to observe that affairs in that quarter look better now than they did when I wrote last.

The night before last the militia brought into us Colonel Thomas and six more of the prisoners that broke gaol at this place the last week.

Tomorrow will go from hence seven more waggons for Camden, which makes forty two I have sent. I can not promise any more.

I have the honor to be very respectfully
Your Lordship's obedient humble servant

J H CRUGER
Lt Colonel commanding 96

Cornwallis to Cruger, 24th August 1780

79(37): C

Camden
24th August 1780

Lt Colonel Cruger
Commanding at Ninety Six

Sir

I received the favour of your letter with one from Colonel Innes. Yours was without date but I conclude it wrote on the same day with this, the 16th. I am very anxious to hear of Colonel Innes, having been told that he is wounded. It is impossible there can be any enemy openly in arms near the frontier after the total rout of Gates and Sumpter. I inclose to you

---

[3] Although undated, this letter was written on 16th August (see Cornwallis to Cruger, 24th August (this page), and Cruger's reply of the 27th (p 173).

[4] *my last letter*: of 11th August, vol I, p 259.

orders that I have issued to the colonels of militia on the frontier[5]. You will observe it only relates to the second revolt, and will take care that they do not extend it further. I desire that you will direct Major Ferguson to send me as soon as possible the New York Volunteers to this place. I likewise beg that you will let me know as soon as you conveniently can the state of things in your district and towards the Tyger and Ennoree. I am very anxious to march immediately, and as I must leave many sick at this place and shall want convoys of stores to follow me, I must bring Innes's corps and perhaps some militia from your part of the country or I shall be forced to weaken the corps that marches with me too much.

I am, sir,
Your most obedient humble servant

[CORNWALLIS]

[*Subscribed*:]

You will please to direct Major Ferguson to send the five waggons which he detained with the New York Volunteers to this place.

Cruger to Cornwallis, 23rd August 1780

63(62): ALS

Ninety Six
August 23rd 1780

The Rt Hon Earl Cornwallis, Lt General, etc etc etc
Camden

My Lord

I did myself the honor the day before yesterday by express to acquaint your Lordship with my returning with the troops Colonel Innes took from this the last week in consequence of your Lordship's order of the 13th. A return of the killed, wounded and missing I also transmitted.[6] We do not know of above half a dozen of the rebels being killed. They moved off immediately or changed their ground.[7] Colonel Ferguson is looking for them on this side Broad River with the prime of Colonel Turnbull's detachment as he calls it. I yesterday received information that the rebels Colonel Innes met with were a part of a body of 7 or 800 whose object was this place, where they were to have been join'd the begining of this week by the Ceded Lands rebels.

---

[5] *orders..*: see p 332, note 21.

[6] The return, and Cruger's letter of the 21st, are not extant.

[7] Cruger is referring to the action on 19th August at Musgrove's Mill, where Innes was attacked by Clark, Shelby and Williams.

I was only yesterday honor'd with your Lordship's letter of the 5th instant[8] and am very much obliged to you, sir, for your permission to recruit, which indulgence, your Lordship may rest assured, shall not be abused. A fortnight since I received from Charles Town £600 but no advice how to be apply'd. Two hundred guineas I ventured to let General Williamson have a week ago on account of the purchase of beef and flour. Your Lordship will be pleased to let me know if any more of it is to be paid to Williamson. I will give Cunningham's officers and men every assistance in my power. I have made a pretty critical inspection into Kirkland's and King's regiments as I found myself liable to be vastly deceived by their reports or returns. Indeed they knew not themselves what men and arms they had for *service*. Kirkland has short of 100 men with Ferguson, and near 200 at home that he thinks would fight, tho' badly arm'd. King[9] is now assembling his men; I mean to see them myself in a day or two and will then report to your Lordship their situation minutely.

I participate most sincerely in your Lordship's additional success on the 18th and am most respectfully, my Lord,

Your Lordship's obedient and very humble servant

J H CRUGER
Lt Colonel commanding 96

[*Subscribed*:]

Colonel Innes is expected here today; the other wounded gentlemen not worse.

---

[8] *letter of the 5th instant*: see vol I, p 256.

[9] A native of Great Britain, Richard King had migrated to South Carolina in 1763, farming and raising cattle on Turkey Creek, a branch of the Saluda near Ninety Six. Having taken no known part hitherto in the revolutionary war, he had now been commissioned Colonel of the Long Cane Regiment of the royal militia, from whose catchment area Andrew Pickens had previously drawn his men. Not surprisingly, its loyalty was in question. After going to see King to inspect his regiment, Cruger would soon report to Cornwallis, 'He had on the ground 120 men with arms and twenty odd without. He has about sixty in Colonel Ferguson's camp. A great majority of the regiment (formerly Pickens') is certainly disaffect'd, nor do I believe that, should we require their services upon any serious occasion, that 200 would join us.' By late November 100 to 150 of the men would have been in arms for some time past but too cautious ever to go near the enemy. Nevertheless, about fifty or so would perform with spirit when taking part with Isaac Allen some two weeks later in the defeat of Elijah Clark. On the abandonment of the Back Country in the summer of 1781, King fled to Charlestown, where he received pay as a refugee militia officer until its evacuation. By that time he had been subjected to banishment and confiscation by act of the revolutionary assembly at Jacksonborough. (Lambert, *SC Loyalists*, 110; *The Cornwallis Papers*; Clark, *Loyalists in the Southern Campaign*, i, *passim*; The SC Banishment and Confiscation Act 1782)

Cornwallis to Cruger, 27th August 1780   79(39): C

Camden
August 27th 1780

Lt Colonel Cruger

Sir

I received this morning your letter of the 23rd by Colonel Kirkland. Major Ferguson is now here. I have directed him to send the light company of the Prince of Wales's Regiment and the New York Volunteers to this place and then to proceed with his own corps and the militia towards Tryon County and Gilbertown, as I think the militia are more likely to be kept in spirits and together by the appearance of offensive operations. I shall be glad to know whether you think you shall be safe at Ninety Six without James's corps[10], as I wish much to post that corps and the York Volunteers for a time at this place when we move forward. You can in my opinion have no enemy to fear, except those of the Ceded Lands and the disaffected of the late militia of Pickens, as every thing towards North Carolina would be occupied by us when we move. I therefore hope, by continuing Brown's corps at Augusta and by encouraging our militia colonels to great vigilance and activity, that it may be done without risk. By what I hear of Pickens I should think him worth getting. However, it may not be safe to enter into any treaty with him without the approbation of General Williamson, to whom I shall always pay the greatest attention and gratify in every thing that would fix him to our interests in the firmest manner.

I sent the £600 by Colonel Cunningham, £300 of which I desired him to give to Major Ferguson, to whom I wrote at that time[11] to direct the disposal of it. I likewise wrote to you on the 5th of August. How the letter miscarried I cannot conceive. I transmit, however, a copy of it, by which you will find that you disposed of the £200 perfectly according to my wishes.

As every thing in this country is exaggerated and misrepresented by ill disposed persons, I think it right to tell you that the first division of the rebel prisoners consisting of 150 under the escort of 36 men, regulars, Provincials and militia, were attacked in the night of the 24th at Sumpter's house near Nelson['s] Ferry and taken by a Colonel Marion with 150 militia from Kings Tree Bridge on Black River. All but twelve of the escort afterwards made their escape from them, and to our great surprise 85 of the prisoners, all Continentals, refused to go with them and insisted on proceeding to Charlestown. This is a pretty good proof of the affection of their army, and I think the accident a very fortunate one. I inclose the orders to the militia colonels, but if there was any district in which there was no insurrection or defection on this occasion, there will be no occasion to give it to the colonel of that district. You will continue to keep up a constant correspondence with Colonel Balfour and consult with him upon matters relative to General Williamson and Pickens and the principal persons

---

[10] *James's corps*: a copying error. The reference should be to Innes's.

[11] Cornwallis to Ferguson, 5th August, vol I, p 300.

in your district, the perfect security of which I consider of the utmost importance. I hope Colonel Innes is doing well. Be so kind as to present my best compliments to him and assure him that I was much concerned at his accident and sincerely wish him a speedy recovery.

I am, sir,
Your most obedient humble servant

CORNWALLIS

Cruger to Cornwallis, 27th August 1780   *63(68): ALS*

Ninety Six
August 27th 1780
Sunday afternoon

Lt General Earl Cornwallis etc etc etc

My Lord

I am just now honor'd with your Lordship's letter of the 24th. I have wrote to Captain DePeyster commanding the troops at Fair Forrest (Major Ferguson being gone to Camden) to send as soon as possible the New York Voluntiers and their five waggons to Camden. I have wrote to Captain DePeyster for a return of his strength. I have not yet received it but was told yesterday by a militia officer from his camp that he had between 5 and 600 men and lay undisturb'd. By different accounts I learn since the 19th instant that the rebels on the frontiers (part of whom fought Colonel Innes) consisted of from five to seven hundred. Two Negroes are come in here, one yesterday, the other the day before, and report that they had just run from the rebels and that they were encampt ten miles beyond the iron works on the frontiers. I have desired DePeyster to be attentive to them and find out if possible their intentions. They were intended, as I am inform'd, in case Mr Gates had succeeded, in conjunction with the Ceded Lands rebels of Georgia and probably part of Sumpter's detachment, to have fallen on this part of the country. My intelligence is such that I can make no doubt of it. Yesterday evening I received the inclosed letter from a captain of the militia[12] and this morning early order'd Major King with fifty men of his regiment to Long Cane settlement to check them from making farther inroads into this province, with directions to call for more assistance if necessary and to give me the earliest advices. Previous to my dismissing Major King I went to see his regiment. He had on the ground 120 men with arms and twenty odd without. He has about sixty in Colonel Ferguson's camp. A great majority of the regiment (formerly Pickens') is certainly disaffect'd, nor do I believe that, should we require their services upon any serious occasion, that 200 would join us. I am also clear in opinion that a large majority of Kirkland's regiment are still in their hearts rebels. He thinks 300 would serve with him. *I do not.* I am induced to be thus particular on a subject I humbly conceive very momentous, as I have hitherto understood that the strength of the militia in this part of the province was much more considerable than what I find it. My duty

---

[12] *the inclosed letter..*: not extant.

and zeal are the best apologies I can make to your Lordship for so minutely entering upon a business that has already been in abler hands. The rebels in Georgia, I am convinced, want only opportunity to act against us; the information of between 2 and 300 being in arms I gave your Lordship[13], I think, may be relied on. I shall pay the strictest attention to your Lordship's orders issued to the militia colonels on the frontiers.

Colonel Innes is at a house four miles from this. His wound is through the back part of his neck. It's healing fast and I am in hopes in very few days he will be able to ride out. The other wounded gentlemen and soldiers are also recruiting.

Since my last respects to your Lordship of the 21st, Colonel Allen has received 12 of his men, convalescents, from Augusta.

I beg your Lordship's pardon for omitting to date my letter of the 16th, and have the honor to be with the greatest deference very much, my Lord,

Your Lordship's most obedient humble servant

J H CRUGER
Lt Colonel commanding 96

Cornwallis to Cruger, 31st August 1780   79(50): C

Camden
August 31st 1780

Lt Colonel Cruger
Commanding at Ninety Six

Sir

I last night received yours of the 27th and have no doubt that the rising in the Ceded Lands was part of General Gates's general plan of an insurrection and that they had not received the accompt of his and Sumpter's total defeat. Favorable accounts for us circulate very slowly, whilst the most improbable lies fly like lightning through the province. Notwithstanding my order for the immediate march of Colonel Innis's corps, if any imminent danger appears you will of course keep them untill it is over. As the inhabitants of the Ceded Lands have never fairly submitted, I leave it to your judgement what course to take with them, as you can have the best information concerning them; but the protectioners, as the captain of militia calls them, must be dealt with in the most severe manner. As I am sure that you have only one motive for your actions, which is the real happiness and welfare of your country, I give my sanction to any act of rigour you may think necessary. The disarming all suspicious persons in the whole district is absolutely necessary, and the punishing the propagators of falsehoods tending to encourage our enemys and discourage our friends is

---

[13] *the information..*: presumably in Cruger's letter of the 21st, which is not extant.

likewise of great consequence. I trust to your sending Colonel Innis's corps as soon as you can do it with safety. I hope to be able to move forward with my first division in the course of next week. If I should be under the necessity of detaining any of the horses belonging to Ninety Six, I will send the waggons back with horses out of condition and unfit for our use, and I will pay the owners a fair price for the horses so detained. You will do well to keep as much of the militia that you can depend on as possible embodied untill we march, and after that a certain proportion to be regularly relieved. I consent to your keeping the Florida Rangers as long as you please at Augusta. I shall be glad to hear frequently from you and am, sir,

Your most obedient and most humble servant

CORNWALLIS

[*Subscribed*:]

My best compliments to Colonel Innis. I am glad to hear a good account of his wound.

Cruger to Cornwallis, 1st September 1780   64(5): ALS

Ninety Six
September 1st 1780

Rt Hon Earl Cornwallis etc etc etc

My Lord

The evening before the last I was honor'd with your Lordship's letter of the 27th ultimo, and this instant with what you were pleased to write me the 28th[14], in consequence of which Colonel Innes's corps is under marching orders. Four officers and four serjeants, agreeable to your Lordship's directions, will go from hence tomorrow to join Major Ferguson. In answer to your Lordship's question respecting the safety of this post, I think it stands thus: not much danger is to be apprehended from the rebels on the Ceded Lands or from the disaffected in Pickens' regiment unless, when your Lordship moves forward into North Carolina, they should be encouraged and supported by those rebels who have gone from Georgia and this province with Clark, Twiggs and several other desperate villains, and some North Carolinians who are in the mountains, west and north west of us, and who will most probably avoid our advancing troops by retiring to the west and avail themselves of your absence. I have industriously cultivated a very good understanding with Williamson. I believe him an honest man and friendly disposed, but his grand object is a state of neutrality. His neighbour, the colonel[15], is favorably reported. The sentiments of the people in general in that quarter, as far as I was able to learn them, I have already communicated to your

---

[14] *the 28th*: no copy of this letter is extant.

[15] *the colonel*: Pickens.

Lordship. One thing more in regard to them I have to observe, the result of a conversation with Williamson: the cause of those men not turning out when order'd is their being disarm'd, as it's called. Here, with submission to your Lordship, arises the important question whether those men (Pickens's) can be trusted and may be arm'd. If answer'd in the negative, and consequently a distrust and diffidence shewn, is there not an impropriety in calling them out? The use they would make of arms, in my opinion, would depend entirely on circumstances.

Edghill's impair'd health will not admit of his holding any longer the command of the regiment late Cunningham's. I have prevail'd on Patrick Cunningham[16] to take charge of it, provided your Lordship thinks proper to appoint him the lt colonel. He wishes for a major that, when one field officer is out, the other at home may be hunting up and sending the deserters and delinquents of every sort to camp. Give me leave, my Lord, to mention the inconveniencies that are like to attend Lt Colonel Cunningham's recruiting business[17]: the *few good* officers the militia have, particularly their field officers, he has taken for his own regiment; a number of the best men will be taken from active service; the militia service must inevitably suffer, I think, exceedingly if he goes on. He is sensible of it and has promised me to wait immediately on your Lordship on the subject.

Colonel Innes desires me to return his very respectful compliments to your Lordship. He continues mending, tho' slow. The other wounded officers are pretty much in the same situation. One of my wounded is dead.

The present state of this garrison your Lordship will see by the return herewith[18].

The 27th last month I did myself the honor to write to your Lordship.

---

[16] Accompanied by Robert and two other brothers (see vol I, p 117, note 13), Patrick Cuningham (1743-1796) had migrated to the Back Country of South Carolina in 1769. Acquiring several tracts of land, he established himself as a planter in the Little River area of the Dutch Fork besides receiving a steady income from fees earned as a surveyor. Apparently deferring to Robert in political matters, he too had become a leader of the Back Country non-associators in 1775 and, like Robert, had been consigned to Charlestown jail. In 1780 he was commissioned major in command of the Little River Regiment of the royal militia, whose catchment area lay not only on Little River but also on Beaverdam, Cane and Bush Creeks as well as on the north bank of the Saluda itself. Interestingly, he would in November support Moses Kirkland instead of Robert for the post of brigadier general in overall charge of the Ninety Six District militia. With the loss of the Back Country in the summer of 1781 he would flee to Charlestown, where he was promoted to lt colonel and received pay as a refugee militia officer until its evacuation. In the meantime he had been subjected to banishment and confiscation by act of the revolutionary assembly at Jacksonborough. Moving on with some thirty slaves to East Florida, he engaged in preparing lumber from live-oak timber before persuading the South Carolina legislature in 1784 to annul his banishment and confiscation and to subject him instead to an amercement of twelve per cent. Prospering on his return, he owned forty-six slaves by 1790 and was elected to the South Carolina House of Representatives. He signed himself with a single 'n' in his surname, whereas his brother Robert signed himself with two. (Lambert, *SC Loyalists, passim*; *The Cornwallis Papers*; Clark, *Loyalists in the Southern Campaign*, i, *passim*; The SC Banishment and Confiscation Act 1782)

[17] *Lt Colonel Cunningham's recruiting business*: Robert Cunningham's attempt to raise a Provincial corps.

[18] *the return..*: not extant.

I am, my Lord, most respectfully
Your Lordship's obedient and very humble servant

J H CRUGER
Lt Colonel commanding 96

PS

I beg your Lordship's answer and orders to the inclosed letter from Mr Brown, contractor for provision for the post of 96[19].

Cornwallis to Cruger, 4th September 1780

80(5): C

Camden
September 4th 1780

Lt Colonel Cruger
Commanding at Ninety Six

Sir

I this morning recieved your letter of the 1st. As I mean, before I take the troops out of this province, to disarm all doubtful characters and punish in the most rigourous manner all who joined in this second revolt, I am inclined to hope that you will not be much disturbed. I intend to leave the New York Volunteers, with the addition of their light company, and Colonel Innes's regiment here until every thing belonging to the hospital etc is removed. I shall then perhaps move them as far as Waxhaw or Charlottesburgh, but no farther. I hope to raise troops enough amongst the Highlanders of Bladen, Cumberland and Anson Counties to awe the country from the Cheraws to Georgetown after that country has been properly disarmed and reduced to subjection, and I then think that, if our affairs go on well in North Carolina, that the frontiers of this province will be in a state of tolerable security.

The question you state of Pickens's men and other doubtful persons is certainly of importance, but I am clearly of opinion that in a civil war there is no admitting of neutral characters and that those who are not clearly with us must be so far considered against us as to be disarmed and every measure taken to prevent their being able to do mischief. At the

---

[19] The enclosed letter is not extant. It is possible that Cruger is referring to Hugh Brown, a leader of the loyalist uprising in autumn 1775 and now a captain in the Little River Regiment of the royal militia, but if so, it is odd that Cruger does not use his military appellation. More likely he is referring to Archibald Brown, a Charlestown merchant who owned lands in the Back Country and who may well have contracted to supply the post of Ninety Six. Both would be banished and have their property confiscated by act of the revolutionary assembly at Jacksonborough in January 1782, but after the war both secured relief and were subjected instead to amercement. After moving for a time to East Florida, Hugh settled in Camden County, Georgia, where he became a leader of the community, a Justice of the Peace, and a representative of the county in the legislature. (Sally Jr, *Orangeburg County*, 297, 300, 317, 428; Clark, *Loyalists in the Southern Campaign*, i, 297; Lambert, *SC Loyalists*, 291, 295, 301; The SC Banishment and Confiscation Act 1782; Marguerite M E Mathews, 'The Brown Family of the Sand Hills, Camden County, Georgia' (np, 1999))

same time, if they have been guilty of no new offences, I would do it by the gentlest methods which the nature of that business will admit of, but I would do it effectually. The absurdity of calling out those men to serve in our militia who are disarmed for being our enemies is too glaring to need my troubling you with any instructions on that head.

From what you say of Mr Cunningham and from the ill success which has attended all attempts to raise Provincial corps in this country I think we shall run a risk of greatly hurting our militia without being sure of a regiment from which any important services may be derived. I therefore decide for Mr Cunningham's adhering to the militia. As he is a very loyal man and has a great property at stake, I have no doubt of his acquiesing chearfully in any measures that may be thought essential to the good of the cause.

I should hope from what Colonel Balfour told me that General Williamson will be rather better than a neutral, having already expressed my opinion of that character. As Colonel Balfour made the agreement about the supply of the 96 garrison, and as all the internal regulations of this province will naturally fall into his hands, I shall refer Mr Brown's letter to him.

It is true we took a vast number of waggons in the late action, but in many cases the drivers cut the gear and fled into the woods with the horses; many of the horses were likewise stole by the militia and followers of the army; and many, by the length of the enemies march, were rendered totally unserviceable — so that our want of horses and of gear has been very little relieved by our success. The total want of provisions in which we found ourselves after the action, by Mr Sumpter's breaking in on our communication and the additional mouths we had to feed, obliged us to work our horses so hard that we are now in as great distress as ever. I wish you could send 12 or 15 waggons with four good horses in each as soon as possible to this place loaded with flour. The owners shall have their choice of receiving an equal number of horses which are at present unserviceable to us and ten pounds hard money to be paid in Charles Town for the exchange of each horse, or they shall be paid the full Government allowance for the hire of each waggon and horses, being 12 shillings stirling a day, for which they shall have an order to be paid monthly at Charles Town as long as I shall find it necessary to detain them in the service of Government. I trust you will be kind enough to exert yourself to accomplish this very important piece of service. I propose moving with a part of the troops in a few days to Waxhaw, but the 2nd division will not leave this place until the end of the month.

I am, sir,
Your most obedient and most humble servant

[CORNWALLIS]

[*Endorsed*:]

Dispatched by express, September 5th.

Cruger to Cornwallis, 3rd September 1780 64(9): ALS

Ninety Six
September 3rd 1780

My Lord

The 1st instant I did myself the honor to write your Lordship in answer to your letters of the 27th and 28th last month. I gave your Lordship my opinion on the situation of this post but omitt'd to mention our attempting some kind of works of defence. We have thrown up two redoubts and are building a block house, but having only a dozen axes to work with, we go on exceeding slow. The ideas of an engineer would not injure us.

Lt Colonel Cunningham waits on your Lordship on the subject of his recruiting business. I took the liberty in my last letter to mention that matter to your Lordship. Cunningham is a zealous man and very well inclined but stands in need, from what I can learn, of some pay. Since my last respects nothing material has occurr'd here.

With the greatest respect I am very much, my Lord,
Your Lordship's obedient humble servant

J H CRUGER
Lt Colonel commanding 96

Cruger to Cornwallis, 4th September 1780 64(15): ALS

September 4th 1780

Lt General Earl Cornwallis etc etc etc

My Lord

The preceeding is a copy of my last respects to your Lordship, which, for fear of a miscarriage, I beg to trouble your Lordship with by Major McLaurin, since which time nothing material has occurr'd. Colonel Innes wrote your Lordship yesterday on the subject of his regiment's marching, which he means to be on Friday next. I know at present of no impediment. If any should happen, we will take our measures accordingly, I hope to your Lordship's satisfaction.

With the highest respect and deference I am, my Lord,
Your Lordship's obedient and very humble servant

J H CRUGER
Lt Colonel commanding 96

Cornwallis to Innes, 6th September 1780

80(11): C

Camden
September 6th 1780

Lt Colonel Innes

Dear Innes

I have just received your letter of the 3rd[20] and am sorry to find you are still in pain. I will appoint Captain Fraser[21] major to your corps and desire you will prepare his commission. Cunningham at my request has given up for the present his attempt to raise a corps as I found it would totally destroy the militia, who, however bad, are still a necessary evil.

I shall move with part of the troops tomorrow to Waxhaw, and Tarleton will be stationed between the Catawba and Broad River. I shall probably remain there some days. Had I known that it would have been material for your regiment to have remained a week longer at 96, I could have allowed it without much inconvenience. They will be left here for some time with the New York Volunteers under Lt Colonel Turnbull, so that they cannot suffer any material inconvenience as the appointments may follow them hither as well as the furlough'd men.

Your friend Ross has sailed. If I should be too far advanced for you to come to me, I have only to say that, after taking the proper time to settle your business in this province, you will proceed according to the General's directions to New York, remembring that there are no Provincial stores or appointments whatsoever in the Southern District. Tarleton says his boots would not fit a boy of seven years old. In short, if you come here, you will hear grievances in plenty.

The Highlanders of Anson, Bladen and Cumberland have offered to form a battalion and have desired to have Governor Martin for their colonel. What appointments we can get for them must go by the vessels which are to carry provisions to the Cape Fear River. I intend to purchase for them some plaids belonging to the 71st for which they have no use. McArthur tells me they are ordered to be sent from Savannah to Charles Town and he supposes them arrived by this time. Accept my best wishes for your speedy recovery and believe me

etc etc etc

[CORNWALLIS]

---

[20] *your letter..*: not extant.

[21] Thomas Fraser. See vol I, p 243, note 11.

Innes to Cornwallis, 5th September 1780
64(29): LS

September 5th 1780

Lt General Earl Cornwallis etc etc etc

My Lord

Major McLaurin has shewed me a memorial he means to present to your Lordship praying a warrant to raise a battalion of South Carolinians. His pretensions to this mark of your Lordship's favor will appear by his memorial. I shall only in justice to Major McLaurin say that his delicacy and constant attention he paid to the publick business in this country ever since the arrival of Colonel Balfour to take the command was the only reason why he did not sooner put in his claim, as he certainly had a superior plea to any man of this part of the province. I am certainly sorry to be under a necessity of differing in opinion with those gentlemen who wou'd sacrifice or postpone new levies least they shou'd prove detrimental to the militia. I look upon it that every man inlisted to serve in a Provincial corps during the war is a usefull soldier gain'd to the King's Service, and I am well convinced the militia on their present plan will ever prove a useless, disorderly, destructive banditti. It may seem extraordinary that the same people of which the militia are composed shou'd be such different men in a regular Provincial corps, but as a proof, my Lord, of the fifty men of my detachment that belonged to the South Carolina Royalists, thirty five were recruits inlisted since last June and no men cou'd behave with greater spirit than they did in the late affair of the 19th ultimo, notwithstanding they saw their late associates behave in so dastardly and cowardly a manner. Your Lordship will, I hope, excuse my taking this liberty and believe it is dictated solely by zeal for the service. If Major McLaurin, who is the bearer of this, has the honor of seeing your Lordship, he will fully explain the state of this country and communicate some particulars relative to the leading men in it which wou'd not be prudent to commit to writing.

I have the honor to be with the highest respect, my Lord,
Your Lordship's most obedient and most devoted servant

ALEX INNES
Lt Colonel

Cornwallis to Innes, 11th September 1780
80(15): C

Forster's Plantation, Waxhaw
September 11th 1780

Lt Colonel Innes

Dear Innis

I have just received yours of the 5th by Major McLaurin but am so circumstanced that it is at present out of my power to do what he desires. I have stopped the raising of

Cunningham's corps on the representation that it would entirely ruin the militia of Ninety Six. At the same time I assured Cunningham that if the measure of raising new corps should be again adopted, he should undoubtedly stand first. By the account Major McLaurin gives of your wound I do not think it probable that I shall see you, in which case I beg you will accept my very sincere good wishes.

I am
Faithfully yours

CORNWALLIS

Cruger to Cornwallis, 7th September 1780   64(30): ALS

Ninety Six
September 7th 1780

Earl Cornwallis etc etc etc

My Lord

Since I had the honor of writing your Lordship by Major McLaurin, I have received your Lordship's two letters of the 31st August and 4th instant. Your Lordship's instructions respecting our internal enemies shall be minutely attended to. The militia your Lordship mentions to be embody'd, I conceive, are to be promised pay and to be, I presume, posted in the neighbourhood of Tyger or Enoree, from two to three hundred men, countenanced and supported by 40 or 50 red coats from this post, to be regularly [relieved][22] once a month. The Florida Rangers will be absolutely necessary at Augusta.

Colonel Innes's corps will march early on Saturday morning, and with them I shall send 3 or 4 waggons. The remainder order'd by your Lordship shall follow as soon as possible. I have sent for one of the ablest men in the country to collect them, tho' dispair of getting the full complement, and as to flour I am sorry to inform your Lordship that it will not, I am afraid, be in my power to send any. It is so scarce an article about this country that with the utmost industry our contractors have been only able to furnish it to the troops here from hand to mouth, nor is there more, from what I can learn from Williamson, than will serve us till the corn (indian) is ready to grind.

I am much pleased to find your Lordship will admit of no neutral characters amongst us. My plan of proceeding then with the inhabitants on this side the Saluda in 96 District, provided your Lordship has no objections, will be immediately to call them together and tell them that the aid and military exertions of every man in the country is required against the common enemy, and that, if they will readily engage to make use of arms for the defence of the country (this is also Williamson's idea), that arms shall be given them, and that, if any should refuse, we shall look upon them inimical and not entitled to protection or the common

---

[22] *[relieved]*: the missing word is supplied in the copy letter (64(32)).

benifits of citizens. My present opinion is that they will accede and defend the country against the common *plunderers* and *horse thieves*, but how far they would stand by us, in case [of] a formal army invading the province by authority, is what I can't answer for. In their present situation they enjoy every advantage without contributing or bearing any part of the burthens of war, and, by being kept deprived of arms, look upon themselves as an acknowledged enemy and therefore at liberty to join the rebels when ever they find it their interest. By engaging those people against one sett of rebels, may it not introduce the division, jeaulosy and animosity we wish?

Lt Colonel Brown's situation and the conduct of the Governor and Council I can't make so fully known to your Lordship as it may be requisite but by forwarding the letters etc received from him this day which your Lordship will be pleased receive herewith. Mr Oldfield, the commissary, remain'd here but one day and went to Charles Town.

I have the honor to be most respectfully, my Lord,
Your Lordship's obedient humble servant

J H CRUGER
Lt Colonel commanding 96

Enclosure (1)
Brown to Cruger, 5th September 1780   62(8): ALS

Augusta
September 5th 1780

Colonel Cruger
Commanding His Majesty's troops at Ninety Six etc etc etc

Sir

An Act of Assembly[23] having passed in this province to disqualify and render incapable several persons from holding any offices of trust, honor or profit and for other purposes as particularly specified in the Act:

This Act requires that all persons shall take and subscribe an oath of allegiance and fidelity to His Majesty and abjuration of the Congress, and, in case of refusal, it may be lawful for any Justice to apprehend and confine in the common gaol such persons for the term of three months unless they comply with the terms of the Act or [agree] to serve His Majesty as private soldiers during the war.

The Governor and Council being of opinion that the prisoners are not to be exempted who are now on their parole, and the Justices being directed to administer the oaths and in case of a refusal to subject them to the pains and penalties prescribed by the Act, I should be

---

[23] See vol I, p 283, note 70.

obliged to you to enquire of Lord Cornwallis whether it is his Lordship's pleasure that I permit the oaths before mentioned to be tendered etc to the Continental and militia prisoners of war, civil or military, and if his Lordship purposes that they should remain at their respective places of abode agreable to the tenor of their paroles or how and in what manner I am to act relative to them.

It certainly would be attended with a good effect if the Continental and militia officers were ordered to some other part of the country, as I have every reason to believe, in violation of their paroles, they carry on a regular correspondence with the rebels to the essential prejudice of the peace of this province and His Majesty's Service.

Some few exceptions in justice ought to be made, which I can point out whenever his Lordship signifies his pleasure.

As to the lower class of people (Continental soldiers excepted), if Lord Cornwallis does not chuse to claim them as prisoners of war, I think for the good of the province they ought to be subjected to the civil authority, as there are 6 or 700 prisoners.

I should be obliged to you for your answer as soon as convenient.

I am, sir, with just regard
Your most obedient and most humble servant

THO^S BROWN
Lt Colonel commanding King's Rangers

PS

I have just received the Act above mentioned, which I inclose for your perusal[24] with the form of the parole given by the prisoners.

Enclosure (2)
Form of parole in Georgia   *62(8): C*

I, AB, hereby acknowledge myself to be a prisoner of war upon my parole to his Excellency the Commander in Chief of His Majesties Forces, and that I am hereby engaged, until I shall be exchanged or otherways released therefrom, to remain at my home in the Parish of St Paul's in the Province of Georgia, and that I shall not in the mean time do or cause to be done anything prejudicial to His Majesties arms or have intercourse or hold correspondence with His enemies, and that I will surrender myself and my arms to him or any other officer of the King's troops at such time and place as shall be hereafter required.

Witness my hand
this [*blank*] day of June in the year 1780

---

[24] The Act was forwarded to Balfour.

Cornwallis to Cruger, 12th September 1780 80(18): C

Camp at Crawford's on Waxhaw Creek
12th September 1780

Lt Colonel Cruger
Commanding at Ninety Six

Sir

I received yours of the 7th. It will certainly be right to keep two or three hundred militia constantly embodied to prevent partys coming down from the mountains. As I have given the fullest directions to Lt Colonel Balfour relative to the affairs of this province, and as he will have the management of all the posts when I move into North Carolina, you will please to keep up a constant correspondence with him that he may be able to secure every part of the frontier. In regard to regular pay, I should think it had better be avoided if possible unless the militia should be called out to a distant march. Whilst they are only defending their own district, I should think that provisions, some salt, which might be brought for that purpose from Charlestown, and handsome gratuitys given occasionally, when they are diligent and behave well, would answer the purpose. You will, however, concert this with Lt Colonel Balfour, as it must depend on the practise which he finds himself under the necessity of pursuing in the other districts. What I mentioned in regard to neutrals went only to my own opinion of them, but I hardly think it can be right to arm them. I would have them paroled in the strictest manner, by which their lives would be forfeited if they ever joined or were detected in carrying on correspondence with the enemy. I would oblige them to furnish some contribution either in clothing, provision or liquor to the militia whilst embodied, but with such moderation as not to make them desperate, and after some of the best of them shewed signs of sincere repentance, they should be armed and restored to the rights of citizens, but this should be done with great caution. I have enclosed Lt Colonel Brown's letters, and the papers contained in them with my opinion on the subject, to Lt Colonel Balfour[25], as I should be too much employed and at too great a distance to carry on a correspondence with the Governor and Council of Georgia on that subject. I have found this settlement pretty well supplied with wheat, but we find it difficult to supply Camden, and as it is essential to the sick and wounded to have wheat flour instead of indian meal, I should be glad if you would take every possible means to send even a small quantity.

I am, sir,
Your most obedient and most humble servant

CORNWALLIS

---

[25] See Cornwallis to Balfour, 12th September, p 79.

Cruger to Cornwallis, 13th September 1780 64(52): *ALS*

Ninety Six
September 13th 1780

Lt General Earl Cornwallis etc etc etc

My Lord

Since my last respects of the 7th instant I have not been honor'd with any of your Lordship's commands. Rather sooner than I expect'd, Clark has return'd to Georgia with about 200 men. He there meets the Ceded Lands people in arms. An insurrection through this country is one of their objects. I have been much perplex'd what to do. My own small garrison and the inactivity and want of spirit in the militia, to say no worse of them, have put me under the necessity of calling on General Williamson, who has just given me his opinion to march into the heart of Long Canes to stop the people there from rising, who, if left alone by us, would most probably join upon our few friends there being drove off. I have therefore determin'd to go immediately with my whole garrison, sick and convalescents except'd, and such of the militia as I can get together about 20 or 25 miles into Long Canes and there call upon all the principal people to meet me and prevent their rising if possible. I have also order'd, or rather desired, Colonel Robert Cunningham to follow me with 100 of his own in case I find it necessary to cross into Georgia. He has promised me they are men I can put some dependence on. The situation of this country, your Lordship may be assured, is alarming. If we lay still, the rebels will become formidable, daring and dangerous. The more formidable we are, the more easily and the more effectually will the business be done. I have also intelligence of a farther reinforcement into the Ceded Lands from the rebels in the mountains under a Colonel Shelby. I wish to God there was a second Legion in those parts for the benefit of this country, which wants a deal of purging yet and I am afraid will not be soon reconciled to His Majesty's Government. I was very apprehensive the rebels would play this game but imagin'd they would have waited till your Lordship had got at a greater distance.

I will intrude no farther on your Lordship's time than to promise doing every thing in my power to extinguish as speedily as possible the present dangerous insurrection, being with the greatest respect and deference, my Lord,

Your Lordship's obedient and very humble servant

J H CRUGER
Lt Colonel commanding 96

Cornwallis to Cruger, 18th September 1780   80(27): C

Camp at Waxhaw
September 18th 1780

Lt Colonel Cruger
Commanding at Ninety Six

Sir

I received this morning yours of the 13th, and by this time mine of the 12th will probably have reached you. It is undoubtedly the wisest measure you can pursue to take the most vigorous means of quelling the disturbances and insurrections in the Long Canes. This is the most favourable moment for your doing it as no real danger can threaten Ninety Six from any other quarter, and I shall hope very soon to hear good accounts from you. On considering maturely the situation of this country, I have determined to fix a considerable post at Charlottesburgh, which, with the assistance of a corps that I am endeavouring to raise in Tryon County to be commanded by Captain Dunlap, added to all the other precautions taken by me and Colonel Balfour towards settling the eastern part of the province, will, I hope, perfectly secure you on this side. I should hope that you would be able to strengthen your corps by some recruits, which will render you more independent of the militia.

I am, sir,
Your most obedient and most humble servant

[CORNWALLIS]

Cruger to Cornwallis, 15th and 16th September 1780   64(67): A(in part) LS

Ninety Six
September 15th 1780

Rt Hon Earl Cornwallis etc etc etc

My Lord

Two persons of credit and veracity just came in to me and report that yesterday between 12 and 1 o'clock they were on a hill this side the Savannah opposite to the house in Augusta in which Colonel Brown has his Indians' stores; they saw the rebels at this house attack Brown; the firing continued at a distance for about an hour and an half; they then came off, but, 'till they got out of hearing, heard a few shot now and then; that neither party, while they were present, advanc'd. Brown lay under the disadvantage of being confin'd to the spot where his house stands, which is to the extreem part of the town west. His force, by a return I got from him yesterday, is : fit for duty, 3 captains, 2 lieutenants, 2 ensigns, 12 serjeants, 180 rank and file; Indian Department, 2 commissaries, 30 traders, 3 interpreters, 500 Indians; convalasents of the New Jersey Volunteers and his own, 100. I have not yet heard from

Colonel Browne. If I do not verry soon, I shall think him in a bad way. I believe he has no stores of provissions. I am ready to move in an instant but have not yet been able to collect here 100 militia.

The day before yesterday I did myself the honor to inform your Lordship of my apprehensions of the traitors of the Ceded Lands, and of the aid they were to receive from Clark and his confederates. I don't find that their success in the Long Cane settlements has been more than seducing off some of the young men. Every means has been taken to prevent a general insurrection in that quarter, but the fate of things will depend much upon the present opperations at Augusta, from whence I expect momently to hear, and shall defer troubling your Lordship any farther.

96
9 o'clock am
September 16th

The preceeding I did myself the honor to write your Lordship yesterday. This moment I received the inclosed from Colonel Brown, for whom march'd off a force sufficient an hour ago to save him, I flatter myself. I have much more in view absoluetly necessary, but it depends on the assistance of the militia, who are slow to the greatest degree and exceeding distressing. I must observe to your Lordship that I apprehend difficulty in holding these posts this winter. I look upon Clark and his present army fixt for Georgia. They will not go north of it, but rather south, when push'd. I gave yesterday an account of the Augusta business to Ferguson, which desired him to communicate to your Lordship, conceiving you were nearer to him than to us.[26] I find Brown has not had so many kill'd as was reported yesterday. I go off this instant and beg your Lordship will pardon this hurry'd scrawl.

J H CRUGER
Lt Colonel commanding 96

PS

I sent 4 waggons with Colonel Innes's corps to Camden. Seven or eight have since gone from the other side Saluda. ½ dozen were engaged and coming from Long Canes, but lost in consequence of the present confusion. I had also engaged beyond Saluda between 20 and 30 barrels flour and order'd to Camden.

---

[26] See Ferguson to Cornwallis, 19th September, p 153.

Enclosure
Brown to Cruger, 15th September 1780   64(65): LS

                                                                        Augusta
                                                               15th September 1780

Colonel Cruger
Commanding His Majesty's troops at Ninety Six

Sir

Yesterday morning about nine o'clock intelligence was brought me that the Ind[i]an camp was attack'd by a strong body of rebels of whose march or movements I had not received the smallest intimation till that moment.

I immediately drew my force and marched with two field pieces to attack the enemy and sicure the Indians, then about three miles distant from my encampment, but immediately upon my effecting a junction with the Indians, intelligence was brought me that the enemy had entered the town by a back road which leads into the main road from Savannah – on which we returned instantly to give them battle. After a smart conflict of upwards an hour we drove them from their ground and from amongst the houses where the Indian stores are lodged and of which we instantly took possession. Here we continued engaged with them for, I suppose, full two hours longer, when they thought proper to retire, and we have had verry little annoyance from them since. By the best information I have yet collected, their force is upwards six hundred men, but am told they give it out to be *thirteen* hundred. Here (at the Indian store) we stand fast, but from the number that I have had killed and wounded I do not think myself sufficiently strong to march out and attack them in their present position, viz, at Grierson's Fort, where, I am inform'd, they are at work mounting some of the cannon which they have carried from our encampment. I make no manner of doubt but that your own ideas of my present situation will readily lead you to give such aid as you may judge to be effectual, till which time I shall maintain my post to the last extremity. Yesterday, soon after the action commenced, I find Captain Smith[27] of yours set off for 96, and after the action I sent you a verbal message by [*blank*]. I hope both are arrived safe before this time. You may safely communicate your intentions to me by the bearer, to whom I beg leave to refer you for some particulars.

---

[27] Born on Long Island, New York, at a place known as Stoney Brook, Jacob Smith (1749-1837) was a committed loyalist who had been commissioned a captain in the 1st Battalion, De Lancey's Brigade, on 21st October 1776. When the battalion, commanded by Cruger, came south to Savannah in December 1778, Smith accompanied it and was now part of the garrison at Ninety Six. On the disbandment of the battalion at the close of the war he would be placed on the Provincial half-pay list and settle at Woodstock, New Brunswick, where he was granted 550 acres, to which he added 350 acres by the turn of the century, together with an island shortly afterwards which lay opposite in the St John River. 'Smith was a man of spirit and resolution, fond of good horses, which he rode at a great pace over very rough roads. It is said that he broke in a colt to harness when in his 88th year. He traded considerably with the Indians and had some pretty hard bouts with them when they were under the influence of liquor...' (W O Raymond, 'The Woodstock Pioneers: Captain Jacob Smith and Some of his Comrades in Arms' and 'The First English Proprietors of the Parish of Woodstock', *The Dispatch* (Woodstock), 1894-6 (available on Fort Havoc Archives CD, vol i); Treasury 64/23(9), WO 65/164(33), and WO 65/165(7) (National Archives, Kew))

I have the pleasure to be, dear sir,
Yours verry sincerely

THO[S] BROWN
Lt Colonel commanding King's Rangers

[*Subscribed:*]

Grierson[28] is with me and desires to be remembered to you, but he had not time to call out any of his militia.

Cruger to Cornwallis, 19th September 1780   *64(77): ALS*

Augusta
September 19th 1780

Rt Hon Lt General Earl Cornwallis etc etc etc

My Lord

The 16th instant I did myself the honor from 96 to inform your Lordship that on the 14th Colonel Brown was attack'd by Clark with about 700 rebels, about one half from the Ceded Lands and that neighbourhood. Many of this also join'd him. I got here yesterday morning. The rebels, hearing very early of us, prepared for a retreat and only gave us the chance of a few shot at them on the wing, as they went off in the most precipitate manner. We took a few prisoners, retook a brass field piece and one mounted iron gun four pounder, all the rest of the iron ordnance, some ammunition, five or 6 waggons and carts, and four punchions of rum, saved the town from being burnt, and stopt a most dangerous and daring insurrection that would have been pretty general in this part of the world had Mr Clark succeeded. The inhabitants of the country on both sides the river, being yet amazingly disaffect'd, would have been in arms and like a torrent bore down the friends to Government. Nothing but a prudent timidity restrain'd their joining immediately. A return of Colonel Brown's kill'd and

---

[28] A planter, James Grierson (?-1781) had been a resident of Georgia since 1762 and possessed six slaves and a landed estate of 1,350 acres, mostly (if not all) in St Paul's Parish. Between 1768 and 1773 he occupied the office of a collector and assessor under the Tax Acts and acted as surveyor of the local roads. In 1772 he was commissioned a Justice of the Peace, and in 1774 he became Colonel of the Augusta Regiment of the royal militia. With the coming of the revolution he supported the Crown, but was allowed by the revolutionary authorities to continue as a Justice of the Peace and in 1778 was appointed a tax assessor. Now, in 1780, he had been reappointed Colonel of the Augusta Regiment of the royal militia and would continue actively to support Thomas Brown throughout the British occupation of the village. After the post had capitulated to Pickens and Lee on 6th June 1781, he was promptly granted a Georgia parole, that is to say, he was murdered in a dastardly way by Captain James Alexander, one of Pickens' men. Entering the room where Grierson was held captive, Alexander shot him fatally before the eyes of his three children. According to Thomas Brown, neither the sentinel at the door nor the main guard attempted to interfere with the murder, after which Grierson's body was mutilated and thrown into a ditch. In 1782 the Georgia revolutionary assembly confiscated Grierson's estate. (*DGB*)

wounded I inclose your Lordship[29]. The number of rebels kill'd and wounded I can't ascertain. In their hurry they left a dozen unbury'd on the field, and by the surgeon who dress'd their wounded on the first day of the attack I learn that upwards of 50 were brought into him. I am now sending out parties of horse to pick up the traiterous rebels of this neighbourhood, who I purpose to send to Charles Town. The audacious scoundrels have sent to me to sue for pardon. Brown has with [him] about 300 Indians. They behaved very well. They brought in several scalps got by sallying out from the house and out houses in which they threw themselves, cover'd by a brast work, that contain'd most of the Indian goods, tho' many were lost at his barracks a mile and an half distence, with all the King's stores, an account of which I have not yet got.

I beg leave to observe to your Lordship that from the very defenceless situation of Colonel Brown's small garrison his resistance was a very gallant one. They were so effectually surrounded by the enemy as to be entirely cut off from water for upwards of two days, and severely cannonaded within 100 yards of their house with the guns and ammunition they took from him.

As soon as I get matters properly arranged here, I shall sett out (tomorrow evening I expect) for 96, and I fancy from thence immediately to be under the necessity of going up through Long Canes to the Ceded Lands.

I have the honor to be with the greatest deference most respectfully, my Lord,
Your Lordship's obedient and very humble servant

J H CRUGER
Lt Colonel

PS

Clark, I am told, cross'd Little River last night with 100 men. Some doubt it and imagine he will endeavour to rally.

Cornwallis to Cruger, 23rd September 1780   80(41): C

Waxhaw
September 23rd 1780

Lt Colonel Cruger
Commanding at Ninety Six

Sir

I received last night with great pleasure your letter of the 19th and beg you will accept my warmest thanks for your spirited conduct and activity in the very trying situation in which the

---

[29] *A return..*: not extant.

unexpected insurrection in the Ceded Lands had placed you, and I most heartily congratulate you on your success. You will please to communicate my thanks to the officers and men under your command, and to Lt Colonel Brown and the garrison of Augusta, whose gallant defence does them the greatest honor. I shall not fail to represent the merit of the officers and soldiers to his Excellency the Commander in Chief. Lt Colonel Brown will likewise say something civil from me to the Indians. As soon as your hurry is a little over, you will please to let me know what addition either of men or works you think absolutely necessary for the preservation of the posts under your command. I will give every assistance in my power. Of course you would not wish to have more men than are absolutely necessary, considering the great want of men elsewhere, and I think the additional post[30] mentioned to you will greatly contribute to the security of all that country.

I am, sir,
Your most obedient and faithfull servant

[CORNWALLIS]

Cruger to Cornwallis, 23rd September 1780

64(104): ALS

Georgia
September 23rd 1780

The Rt Hon Earl Cornwallis, Lt General etc etc etc
Waxhaw camp

My Lord

The 19th I did myself the honor to advise your Lordship of my being at Augusta and had relieved Colonel Brown, retook his cannon of different kinds, some prisoners etc and that I should return as soon as possible to 96, but on the 20th heard that Clark had stopt in this neighbourhood and was collecting his dispersed troops, probably with an intent to return to Augusta when we left it, destroy the few friends of Government and keep up this new insurrection till they could establish a formidable body in this quarter. Under these circumstances I determin'd it most advisable to march immediately up the country on the south side the Savannah, sending about 100 Georgia loyalists, which was all we could collect, up the Wrightsborough road parallel with our march. I am just come to Colonel Dooly's house 45 miles above Augusta. The rebels have cross'd Broad River. They give out that they will make a stand there and fight us, which they must either do, or run away, very soon. If they escape us with their booty, I am in hopes Ferguson may cross upon them. I have given him notice. I meant by this march also to settle all the Ceded Lands business, which I flatter myself will not be very difficult, especially if we drive Clark out of the country, as all or very near the whole of the inhabitants are with him.

---

[30] *the additional post*: Charlotte. See Cornwallis to Cruger, 18th September, p 187.

I have a letter this day from Colonel Kirkland, who I left in command at 96. They are there for the present very easy.

I shall do myself the honor of writing your Lordship as soon again as any thing worthy your notice occurs, and am most respectfully, my Lord,

Your Lordship's very humble servant

J H CRUGER
Lt Colonel

Cornwallis to Cruger, 1st October 1780   81(3): C

Charlottetown
October 1st 1780

Lt Colonel Cruger
Commanding at Ninety Six

Sir

I received last night your letter of the 23rd and sincerely hope that by this time you have put an end to all disturbances in your part of the province. I inclose to you a proclamation which I have issued here[31] and I should advise you to do the same, making perhaps a few exceptions. It is the only way of disarming the disaffected, and indeed as long as they are prevented from returning to their homes, they must be troublesome. I should apprehend they will for the future pay more attention to a parole as they have found that we treated the breach of it so seriously. I have written to Colonel Balfour about raising a troop of dragoons[32] to consist of 60 men for your district and thought of Cunningham for the command of it. I wish you would transmit your sentiments on that subject to Colonel Balfour. As I have no view in this business but the publick utility, I can have no partiality to persons and only mentioned Cunningham as the man most likely to succeed.

I am with great regard etc

[CORNWALLIS]

---

[31] *a proclamation..*: see p 331, note 20.

[32] See Cornwallis to Balfour, 1st October, p 105.

Cruger to Cornwallis, 28th September 1780
64(116): LS

Ceded Lands, Georgia
September 28th 1780

Lt General Earl Cornwallis etc etc etc

My Lord

The 23rd instant from Dooly's house I did myself the honor to inform your Lordship of my motives for moving into the Ceded Lands, which I shou'd be happy to find meets with your Lordship's approbation. Last Monday morning we cross'd Broad River about 60 miles above Augusta, when we found that Clark and his booty had moved on so fast as to get beyond our reach. They crossed the Savannah some distance above the Cherokee Ford last Saturday and Sunday. We have every reason to hope that they may yet be interupted as their rout appears to be for North Carolina. Since my entering upon the Ceded Lands, our militia horse have been very busily employed in scouring the country. The rebel court house, forts, and some private houses belonging to the most notorious villains are burnt, their cattle driven off, and their property in general paying the price of their treachery. I have call'd in all the inhabitants who are on parole and have not violated them, and administred the inclosed oath, which they affect to be very hearty and sincere in. Such arms as I can get from them I shall carry to Ninety Six, for which I purpose crossing the Savannah to morrow, having laid very sufficiently the foundation for the Georgians to work on as they please. They have *now* here and in this neighbourhood upwards of 200 militia, which will do to remove and devour what property the absconding rebels may leave. Upwards of 200 of them (many with their families) have gone off with Clark. A more particular account of this business I will furnish your Lordship with as soon as I get to Ninety Six. The rebels who were at Augusta with Clark in violation of their paroles and have not left this country lay so conceal'd in swamps that it has not been in our power to discover more than two or three of them, but upon some small hope of pardon thirty odd have surrender'd themselves and arms to me, who I have bound by the inclosed bond and oath, most of them poor wretches who were carried down by force and threats from Clark and his adherents. Unfortunately for us, almost every capital scoundrel is gone off. I inclose your Lordship a return of the kill'd, wounded, missing and prisoners of the Jersey Volunteers who were at Augusta at the time of Clark's attack. I had also a captain and his servant (a soldier). They were all left on parole. I wish to know your Lordship's pleasure respecting them.

I have the honor to be with the greatest diference most respectfully, my Lord,
Your Lordship's obedient and very humble servant

J H CRUGER
Lt Colonel

PS, Thursday evening

Since finishing this letter this morning, the number of rebels who were at Augusta in arms come into me are 68. 45 I have released for the present on bond and oath, and 23 of the worst characters shall send under guard in the morning for Charles Town. Those released have but little except their lives spared them. They are certainly for the present fully humbled and execrate Mr Clark as the author of all their misfortunes and distresses.

Enclosure (1)
Oath by persons not having broken their parole   64(118): C

Dartmouth, Georgia
September 25th 1780

We, the subscribers, do solemnly swear upon the Holy Evangelist of Almighty GOD that we will bear true faith and allegiance to His Majesty George the 3rd, King of Great Britain etc, and that we will to the utmost of our power support His Government, Crown and dignity; and we do further swear that we have deliver'd up all the fire arms that we had in possession, that we have none concealed or conveyed to any person for our use, and that we do not know of any that are concealed belonging to any other person.

SO HELP US GOD

Sworn before me, John Howard[33], Justice of the Peace

[*Subscribed in Cruger's hand:*]

Sign'd by the inhabitants of Georgia above Augusta who were on parole and have not broke them in the late revolt with Clark, to the number before me, on the 25th, 26th, 27th and 28th September, of 106.

J H CRUGER
Lt Colonel

Enclosure (2)
Oath by persons having broken their parole   64(119): C

We, the subscribers, do solemnly swear upon the Holy Evangelist of Almighty GOD that we will remain quietly and peaceably at our respective places of abode, and that we will not give intelligence, countenance and support to His Majesty's enemies, and that we will deliver our selves up to the Commander in Chief of the Southern Army or the Governor or Commander in Chief of the Province of Georgia when call'd upon, and that we will deliver

---

[33] Of John Howard little is known. He may have migrated to Georgia from Rowan County, North Carolina, where a John Howard was residing in the 1760s. Be that as it may, he would pay the price for his loyalism in 1782, when the revolutionary assembly banished him from Georgia and confiscated his property. (Jo White Linn, *Abstracts of the Deeds of Rowan County, North Carolina, 1753-1785* (Salisbury NC, 1983); The Georgia Banishment and Confiscation Act 1782)

to Major Moore[34] of the Georgia militia all fire arms and plunder that we now have in possession, and that we have no arms or plunder conceal'd nor know of any conceal'd, the property of any other person.

SO HELP US GOD

Enclosure (3)
Bond entered into by persons having broken their parole 64(119): C

We do acknowledge our selves held firmly bound joyntly and severally unto our sovereign lord the King, his heirs and successors in the sum of one thousand pounds sterling to be levied on our respective goods and chattles on failure of the following conditions, viz, that we and each of us do remain quietly and peaceably at our respective places of abode and that we will not give intelligence, countenance or support to His Majesty's enemies. For the performance of these conditions we do promise and engage each for himself and one for the other, and that we will deliver our selves up to the Commander in Chief of the southern army or to the Governor or Commander in Chief of the province of Georgia when call'd upon.

In witness where of we have here unto set our hands
this 28th day of September 1780

Enclosure (4)
Return as to the New Jersey Volunteers 103(4): DS

A Return of Killed, Wounded, Missing and Prisoners of the 3rd Battalion, New Jersey Volunteers, in an Action with the Rebels at Augusta, 14th September 1780

	Killed	Wounded	Missing	Prisoners
Lt Colonel	-	-	-	-
Major	-	-	-	1
Captains	-	-	-	-
Lieutenants	-	-	-	1
Ensigns	-	-	-	-
Surgeon	-	-	-	1
Serjeants	-	1	-	-

---

[34] Andrew Moore, James Grierson and Thomas Waters, all of the Georgia royal militia, were named as the men most active in searching the Ceded Lands for members of Clark's band. Their searches were marked by instances of brutality. In 1782 Andrew would be banished, and his property confiscated, by act of the Georgia revolutionary assembly. (Cashin, *The King's Ranger*, 119; The Georgia Banishment and Confiscation Act 1782)

Drummers	-	-	-	-
Rank and file	1	5	1	16
TOTAL	1	6	1	19

ISAAC ALLEN
Lt Colonel commanding

Cruger to Cornwallis, 2nd October 1780   *3(170): ALS*

Ninety Six
October 2nd 1780

Rt Hon Earl Cornwallis etc etc etc

My Lord

The 28th of last month I did myself the honor to inform your Lordship fully of my proceedings in Georgia, to which I have but little to add at present, as march'd the day after for Long Canes, through which we made our rout to this place, where we came the last evening, having previously dismiss'd the militia on the Savannah. I left between 2 and 300 Georgia militia on the Ceded Land, who have promised me faithfully to accomplish very speedily the work we cut out for them. They will not meet with interruption, are very equal to the task, and exceedingly well inclined.

I have now by me the honor of [your] Lordship's letters of the 12th, 18th and 23rd ultimo and shall pay full attention to their contents. The honor of your Lordship's approbation of my late proceedings is very flattering. I have communicated to Colonel Brown your Lordship's letter of the 23rd and to those more immediately concern'd with me, who are made happy with the honor your Lordship is pleased to do them. Lt Colonel Hamilton of North Carolinians has made an offer of a company in his regiment to Ensign Jn° Wormley[35] of General DeLancey's 1st Battalion. Mr Wormley has served with me near three years. His merit is such as to entitle him to my recommendation to your Lordship, and altho' I can but ill spare a good officer at this time on account of the several sick and absent, yet shall readily acquiesce if it's your Lordship's pleasure to promote him. I am sorry to say we are unlucky in picking up recruits. The country lads will not inlist. I have not yet been able to get half a dozen. The rebels collecting and imbodying in and about the mountains pretty formidable your Lordship will undoubtedly hear before this gets to hand. I am humbly of opinion that they will make a very respectable body of our troops absolutely necessary in the country between Broad and Saluda Rivers, the ground hitherto occupy'd by Major Ferguson. The

---

[35] John Wormley (1761-?) would be promoted to captain in the Royal North Carolina Regiment with effect from 10th November. Remaining on duty in Charlestown, he would not take part in the winter campaign or see service in Wilmington or Virginia. At the close of the war he was placed on the Provincial half-pay list. (Treasury 64/23(17) and WO 65/165(11) (National Archives, Kew); Clark, *Loyalists in the Southern Campaign*, i, 370, 403, 409, 425)

militia turn out reluctantly. I took the liberty to give my opinion to your Lordship some time since respecting what would be the rebel system from the mountains when your Lordship moved forward. That opinion is rather strengthen'd than weaken'd. The post at Charlottesburg, I am afraid, is too remote to have any effect on this quarter, tho' answering in other respects many good purposes. Horse is the thing to cover this country. Your Lordship will be good enough to pardon my presuming thus far, and I will intrude no farther for the present than to assure your Lordship that I am most respectfully, my Lord,

Your Lordship's obedient and very humble servant

J H CRUGER
Lt Colonel commanding 96

PS

Since my first coming to 96 with Colonel Allen's and my corps, we are only strengthen'd by Allen's with about 50 men. This will point out to your Lordship the strength of our garrison.

Five waggons loaded with flour were sent the last week from hence to Camden.

Cornwallis to Cruger, 6th October 1780   81(22): C

Charlottetown
6th October 1780

Lt Colonel Cruger
Commanding at 96

Sir

I received your letter of the 28th and am very glad that every thing has gone so well in your district. A large body of rebels are come over the mountain[s] upon Ferguson. He has sent to you for assistance. I hope, however, that you will not risk the safety of your own post. If any thing in force marches your way, I will take care to be soon after them. I cannot help again repeating my obligations to you for the spirit, zeal and capacity which you have shewn in the conduct of the late business in Georgia, and am, sir, with great esteem

Your most obedient humble servant

CORNWALLIS

[*Subscribed*:]

I have just received yours of the 2nd, but have nothing at present to add in consequence.

From the experience I have lately had of the militia I am convinced we must try to raise Provincial corps and am therefore determined to let Cunningham go on if he thinks he can manage it. I shall certainly consent to the promotion of Ensign Wormley after what you have said of him.

Innes to Cornwallis, 10th October 1780   3(203): ALS

Charles Town
10th October 1780

My Lord

I came down to this place about ten days ago much recovered and take the earliest opportunity of returning my most sincere and grateful thanks to your Lordship for all your goodness to me.

I am preparing to proceed to New York as soon as I can put the affairs of the department in some order here[36], altho I cannot think there is near so much to do to the northward as in Carolina. The arrangement I proposed to make in Nova Scotia, which was approved of by the General, referr'd to General McLean[37], and approved also by him, is totally overset by the remonstrances of Mr Wm Bayard[38] on the part of his son, and the finishing stroke seems to be put to the few wretched corps in New York province by a draught from each to form a corps of light infantry for Colonel Watson[39] of the Guards. I am now preparing as correct

---

[36] Besides commanding the South Carolina Royalists, Innes was Inspector General of Provincial Forces.

[37] Francis MacLean was Colonel of the 82nd Regiment. With the local rank of brigadier general he commanded British land forces in Nova Scotia. (Boatner, *Encyclopedia*, 668)

[38] William Bayard (1729-1804) was one of the most prominent and wealthy merchants in New York. While sympathising with the grievances of the colonists, he did not go so far as to support a constitutional break with the Crown. Indeed, so opposed was he to the rupture that in December 1776 he formed the King's Orange Rangers on the Provincial establishment, a corps whose catchment area lay in Orange County, New York, where he had been colonel of the militia. While he went on to depart for Southampton, England, his son John was appointed to the lt colonelcy of the corps and another son Samuel to the majority. The corps was to play an insignificant part in operations around New York until 1778, when it was struck by a severe outbreak of small pox and a total breakdown in discipline. Reduced to perhaps 200 men on the verge of mutiny, it was transferred in October to Halifax, Nova Scotia, where it slowly recruited, garrisoning Halifax and other smaller towns till its disbandment at the close of the war. For his sins William Bayard's estate at Castle Point, which included almost all the land on which Hoboken was built, was confiscated by the revolutionaries, but by marriage it again passed into the possession of a Bayard. His third son William became the head of a leading New York mercantile house in the early 19th century. (*Appletons'*; Treasury 64/23(12) (National Archives, Kew); information from Todd Braisted, 7th June 2005)

[39] Born in London, John Watson Tadwell Watson (1748-1826) was a captain in the 3rd Regiment of Foot Guards (the Scots Guards), a rank which carried with it a lt colonelcy. While still a lieutenant in the regiment, he began to serve in North America in 1777, and forming part of a Brigade of Guards, he went on to command its light company. Promoted to captain in November 1778, he commanded four flank companies of the Brigade during Mathew's Virginia raid the following May. On the Charlestown expedition he served as an aide-de-camp to Clinton and afterwards returned to New York. Now destined to command a corps of Provincial light infantry, he

a state of the Provincials under your Lordship's command as their dispersed situation will admit. Brigadier General Brown's, Wright's and the 2nd Battalion of Delancy's do not deserve the name of corps. The cloathing for the New York Volunteers and South Carolina Royalists is gone to Camden, that for the North Carolinians is packing up, and blue jackets are making as fast as possible for such new levies as Governor Martin may raise, which, with the plaids of the 71st, will at least keep them comfortable till the proper cloathing arrives from England, as the stores at New York are as badly supplied as we are here. I am happy in thinking no blame on this account can fall on me, as my requisitions were made so early that compleat cloathing for 5,000 men was embarked in February, three thousand of which I have directed Rooke[40] to send to Charles Town. I am greatly at a loss how to forward the cloathing for Governor Martin, the distance by land is so great and exposed to such risk. I must therefore entreat your Lordship's commands on that subject. General Paterson is so much recovered as to propose joining your Lordship by the next opportunity from New York. I have a few lines from Bruen[41] in which he desires his most dutiful respects to your Lordship, and a letter intended for Captain Ross I take the liberty to inclose.

I have the honor to be with the most perfect gratitude and respect
Your Lordship's most obedient and devoted humble servant

ALEX INNES

---

would arrive with them at Charlestown in mid December as part of Leslie's reinforcement. While his men were welcome, he was not. Seemingly puffed up with self-importance and reluctant to obey or cooperate with ranking officers whom he considered his professional inferiors (such as Rawdon, Balfour and Tarleton), he presented a problem for Cornwallis, who decided not to take him and his light troops on the winter campaign because 'there would be a constant difficulty of command between him and Tarleton'. In advising Tarleton of his decision, Cornwallis remarked, 'Lord Rawdon has very readily agreed to undertake Watson, so that we shall be relieved from that plague.' To Rawdon he observed, 'Now your Lordship can make him obey you,' to which Rawdon replied, 'He certainly shall neither disgrace nor injure the service with impunity,' but whether or not Watson obeyed orders at a critical juncture is debatable. Detached to the Pee Dee in March 1781 with 500 men comprising his corps and the 64th Regiment, he failed to return and reinforce Rawdon before the Battle of Hobkirk's Hill. He may have disobeyed orders, they may have miscarried, or he may have been unavoidably delayed by Balfour's stopping him for a short time to cover the ferries needed for Cornwallis's possible return from Wilmington to South Carolina. At the beginning of June he was recalled to New York, an event which precluded his taking overall command should Rawdon have fallen ill – in Balfour's words, 'a horrid idea'. After the war he rose to be a full general but never saw active service again. He was typical of many a Guards officer down the ages. (*Army Lists*; *The Cornwallis Papers*; Margaret Baskin, 'John Watson Tadwell Watson (1748-1826) (www.banastretarleton.org, 29th June 2005))

[40] Captain Henry Rooke had been a Deputy Inspector General of Provincial Forces since at least June 1778, when he was present as such at the Battle of Monmouth. In 1783 he would be occupying the same post with the rank of major and at the end of the war was placed on the Provincial half-pay list. (The Clinton Papers, vol 36(5); CO 5/96(77), WO 65/164(6), and Treasury 64/23(21) (National Archives, Kew)

[41] Perhaps Major Henry Bruen, who was a Deputy Quartermaster General.

Rawdon to Cruger, 26th October 1780　　　　　　　　　　　　　　　*3(285): ACS*

Rockey Creek
October 26th 1780

Lt Colonel Cruger
Commanding at Ninety Six

Sir

Mr O'Neil, whom you sent to Lord Cornwallis, has this day joined us. Our movements will have convinced you that Lord Cornwallis's opinion of the danger to which the District of Ninety Six was exposed concurred with yours. I hope, however, that [with] the addition of the 63rd Regiment (which I imagine will be left with you during the winter) not only your post will be secure but you may be enabled to punish any party which may attempt to trouble your frontier. You may place the fullest dependance on Major Wemyss's activity and judgement, and I am persuaded you will find cause to approve his zeal upon every occasion. Lt Colonel Balfour was desired by Lord Cornwallis to establish a troop of light horse for the service of your district. I know not if he has yet taken any steps in it, but I hope it may soon be effected. Lord Cornwallis desires that you will lose no time in collecting as large magazines as possible both of grain and forage at Ninety Six. Of course you will endeavor principally to get in what lies in your front and might hereafter be liable to interruption in collecting. I should hope that promises of immediate payment in ready money would induce the inhabitants to be zealous in supplying you. This army will probably remain between the Wateree and Broad River for some time. Its position will be determined by the conveniency of supplying it with flour and forage. Lord Cornwallis not being yet thoroughly recovered from a severe fever, I must request that you will have the goodness to communicate as frequently as you conveniently can with, sir,

Your most obedient etc

RAWDON

[*Subscribed*:]

I beg to know if Captain Dunlap has any prospect of raising men.

Cruger to Cornwallis, 13th October 1780   3(220): ALS

Ninety Six
October 13th 1780

Earl Cornwallis etc etc etc

My Lord

Last Tuesday morning I did myself the honor to write your Lordship by Tim McKenny[42], to whom I took the liberty to refer your Lordship for an account of matters in this neighbourhood that it would not be prudent to commit to paper. I must again beg your Lordship's referrence to the bearer, Captain Gibbs (the major's brother)[43].

I have been very busey for three days past securing this post against a superior number or rather force which, from the intelligence I get, I have reason very soon to expect. I have palisadoed the court house and the principal houses in, about one hundred yards square, with block house flankers. I have provided and got in a quantity of indian corn, which in case of siege must be our principle support, and which, and less, we will chearfully live on till we have the pleasure of your Lordship's relief. I shall object to two points with our enemy, which if granted, I shall hold them cheap till by *your Lordship* relieved, for relief I can not look to any other quarter for. The militia are always ready and willing to receive my support, but should I require theirs in consequence of a considerable force coming into the country, they would behave ill. It is now above a week since I have been using every argument in my power to get them together to save their country, themselves and their families. How they behaved the bearer will inform your Lordship.

Last Monday I sent to Charles Town the prisoners I brought from the Ceded Lands, and this morning sent the same way sixteen others with Colonel Thomas at their head, who might prove a burthen to us in more respects than feeding.

I am, my Lord,
Your Lordship's most obedient and very humble servant

J H CRUGER
Lt Colonel commanding 96

---

[42] The letter of the 10th is not extant. It may have miscarried.

[43] James Gibbs, who had settled on Fair Forest, was a captain in his brother Zacharias's Spartan Regiment of the royal militia. When the Back Country was abandoned in the summer of 1781, he would accompany his brother and the remains of the regiment to Charlestown, where he would be employed as an inspector of refugees. (Clark, *Loyalists in the Southern Campaign*, i, 278-9, 282, 505; *The Cornwallis Papers*)

Cruger to Rawdon, 20th October 1780 3(247): ALS

Ninety Six
October 20th 1780

The Rt Hon Lord Rawdon etc etc etc

My Lord

I should have done myself the honor to have answer'd your Lordship's letter of the 1st instant[44] earlier but only received it four days ago. I should always be happy to have it in my power to comply with any requisition your Lordship might make of me. Kelly is at present sick in country quarters. I will propose to him joining the Volunteers of Ireland, and if he chooses it, he shall go; and as he is a very good, sure and well disciplined soldier, our weak state obliges me to ask in return for him a soldier of equal merit.

Your Lordship will pardon my being so particular. Our poverty, I beg, may plead my excuse.

I have the honor to be most respectfully, my Lord,
Your Lordship's obedient and very humble servant

J H CRUGER
Lt Colonel, 1st Battalion, General De Lancey's Brigade

Rawdon to Cruger, 28th October 1780 3(295): AC

October 28th 1780

Lt Colonel Cruger
Commanding at Ninety Six

Sir

Mr Gibbs has arrived this day with your letter dated the 13th instant and has verbally given me information similar to that which I received from Mr O'Neil. You may assure the militia who have been called forth into active service this campaign that it is Lord Cornwallis's intention to order them immediate recompence for their zeal and trouble. I hope the reinforcement which has been sent to you may greatly ease the loyal subjects in their militia duty. The army will move tomorrow to Wynnesborough, where we shall probably make a considerable halt. I shall have the pleasure of writing to you from thence respecting some points which Mr Gibbs mentioned to me, and I shall be happy to have your ideas with regard to the best means of securing your district from inroads. I am told that the regulations established by Major Ferguson are thought too strict by the militia. It is Lord Cornwallis's

---

[44] *letter of the 1st instant*: no extant copy.

wish that such measures may be adopted as will be most agreable to the inhabitants, who will naturally consider what is requisite for their own security. Lord Cornwallis hopes that Colonel Cunningham proceeds in raising his regiment on the Provincial establishment and desires that every assistance may be given to the attempt. As long as we remain at Wynnesborough, I hope you will use your best endeavors to procure and transmit early intelligence of any rebel parties which may attempt to break in upon our communication with you, for, if we can get a good blow at any of them, it will save us much trouble by discouraging others from such enterprizes. In my letter to you by Mr O'Neil I desired that you would immediately lay up at Ninety Six as large a magazine of grain, flour and forage as you may be able to collect. Lest that letter should fail, I now beg leave to repeat the instruction.

I have the honor etc

[RAWDON]

Rawdon to Cruger, 31st October 1780

3(332): C

Wynnesborough
October 31st 1780

Lt Colonel Cruger
Commanding at Ninety Six

Sir

When the 63rd Regiment received orders to join you it was in consequence of our not being able to pass with the army at the Old Nation Ford; and Lord Cornwallis's apprehensions for the safety of Ninety Six made it necessary to send to you such troops as might arrive there with the greatest dispatch.

It will certainly be necessary that your garrison should be strong if occurrences call the army from this quarter, but the present state of affairs does not seem to require that you should restrict yourself to an absolute defence. Lord Cornwallis wishes that Major Wemyss should keep the field, moving occasionally, as he shall see reason, between Ninety Six and Broad River. He will by that means secure our supplies of grain from being interrupted by small parties of the enemy, and the duty of the militia in that tract may in some degree be lightened. Major Wemyss will of course communicate to us any intelligence which he may receive of any consequence, and it will always be in your power to recall him without difficulty should the circumstances of your post demand it.

I have the honor to be, sir,
Your most obedient servant

RAWDON

Cruger to Rawdon, 30th October 1780

3(324): ALS

Ninety Six
October 30th 1780

Rt Hon Lord Rawdon

My Lord

Yesterday I was honor'd with your Lordship's letter of the 26th by Mr O'Neil, and this instant with that of the 28th by Captain Gibbs. Major Wemyss came to this post on Saturday last as he himself informs your Lordship[45], which will not only add greatly to our strength but will give confidence and spirits to our desponding friends and essentially affect our internal enemies. It is a circumstance I must declare myself very happy in, as am fully persuaded that good consequences will result from it.

Lord Cornwallis may be assured that I will exert myself in collecting as large magazines as possible of grain, flour and forage at 96, for which purpose am now sending to proper persons in the country called the Dutch Fork. When I found the militia in the state described to your Lordship by O'Neil and Gibbs, I adopted the only alternative that I conceived would render them of any use to us. I beg leave to trouble your Lordship with my ideas on that point as communicated to Colonel Balfour the 24th instant (when I imagined my Lord Cornwallis was out of this province), a copy of which you'll be pleased to receive herewith. An answer I expect tomorrow.

The troop of horse consisting of 60 men proposed by his Lordship to be raised in this neighbourhood I have sett a-going with this alteration, of raising two troop each of 40 men, which Major Clary of the militia, a very clever, spirited man, has undertaken, and for fear of failure in our militia infantry I would humbly propose a third troop of 40 men; and those men to be mounted as *dragoons* would be very useful, but this as well as my infantry scheme, I have let the officers know, is wholly subject to the controul of my superiors, who, as they see proper, will condemn or confirm. I shall immediately communicate my Lord Cornwallis's benevolent sentiments to the militia. Cunningham declines for the present attempting to raise a corps.

Your Lordship may depend on the best intelligence I can procure being immediately transmitted to you. Plundering parties of one or two hundred rebels are now about Pacolet. I have direct'd Captain Gibbs, who will be with your Lordship in a day or two after this letter, to ascertain as near as possible their number and situation.

The 20th instant I answer'd your Lordship's letter of the 1st, which I only received the 16th.

---

[45] See Wemyss to Cornwallis, 29th October, p 224.

I have the honor to be most respectfully with great deference, my Lord,
Your Lordship's obedient humble servant

J H CRUGER
Lt Colonel commanding 96

Enclosure
Cruger to Balfour, 24th October 1780

3(311): C

Ninety Six
24th October 1780

Colonel Balfour

Sir

In consequence of the defenceless state of the country and other good reasons I have just agreed and engaged with Colonel Kirkland to raise immediately from four to five hundred men to serve for twelve months in any part of South Carolina, at present to fortify and take post at Musgrove's Mills or the iron works. I have engaged Colonel Kirkland the pay of lt colonel and his men British pay, provisions and cloathing, for the want of which none of them can serve in cold weather. I flatter myself you will not only confirm but approve of what I have done[46]. I am sure it's right and absolutely necessary. At the same time I must confess that your acquiescence will add much to the satisfaction I feel in having done thus much. And now, my good sir, as the men are almost naked, they will require 200 blankets, 200 pair shoes, 200 pair coarse cloth trowses, 200 cloth jackets, and 200 shirts and some camp kettles to be sent them up immediately from Charles Town to begin with. The colonel's zeal and readiness to engage immediately in this necessary business does him great honor, especially when almost every other man in this country seems in a lethargy. I have presumed no farther than the outlines of this work. The nice touches and compleat arangement of things will be left to your judgment. Cunningham I don't find will do any thing. If he goes on with his regiment, this plan will not interfere with him.

J H CRUGER
Lt Colonel commanding at 96

---

[46] Balfour commented on the plan in his letters of 22nd and 29th October, pp 129 and 137. Cornwallis refused his consent, as conveyed to Balfour in Rawdon's letter of the 31st, p 130.

Cruger to Money, 30th October 1780 3(318): LS

Ninety Six
October 30th 1780

Captain Money
Aid de camp to Earl Cornwallis
Head Quarters

Sir

I am this day favoured with yours of the 28th[47] and am now giving orders for waggons from this destrict to be sent to the army immediately. I have just received directions from Colonel Balfour to make payment of the £300 that was intended for the militia. I have paid some days ago to Major Gibbs and the other commanding officers of corps each twelve guineas in part untill I should hear farther from Colonel Balfour, as 100 dollors to each commanding officer and 50 dollors then to be paid to some others would leave a great majority without any compensation. Under these circumstances I have presumed to defer farther payment till the dividend might be reconsider'd, as I conceived paying few pretty handsomely and giving the majority nothing, tho' of equal merit, would not answer the benevolent intentions of his Lordship. Your letter to Major Wemyss[48] I have deliver'd to him.

I have the honor to be very much, sir,
Your obedient humble servant

J H CRUGER
Lt Colonel commanding 96

---

[47] *yours of the 28th*: no extant copy.

[48] *Your letter..*: no extant copy.

CHAPTER 25

Correspondence with Wemyss, De Peyster, Gray and Hamilton

1 - With Wemyss, De Peyster and Gray

Cornwallis to Wemyss, 28th August 1780　　　　　　　　　　　79(43): C

Camden
August 28th 1780

Major Wemyss
63rd Regiment

Sir

　I would have you now set out as soon as you conveniently can for your expedition. Lt Colonel Hamilton will have orders to detach one hundred of his best men to join you and Colonel Bryan with his corps (Colonel Bryan is only a nominal colonel and consequently has no interference in command) and Major Harrison with whatever he can collect of his corps. I should suppose you would order them to meet you at Kings Tree Bridge; however, you will do in that as you think best. I should advise your sweeping the country entirely from Kings Tree Bridge to Pedee and returning by the Cheraws. I would have you disarm in the most rigid manner all persons who cannot be depended on and punish the concealment of arms and ammunition with a total demolition of the plantation. All those who were enrolled voluntarily in Colonel Mills' militia, or by Lt Colonel Gaillard, and afterwards joined the rebels must be instantly hanged up, unless you should seize a very great number, in which case you will please to select the properest objects of mercy. All who have either submitted themselves or have lived quietly at their plantations in an apparent acquiescence to the King's Government, and have since joined in this second revolt, must have their property entirely taken from them or destroy'd and themselves be taken as prisoners of war. Let me hear from you constantly. Don't stay longer in that country than is absolutely necessary to do your business effectually, and take care to procure constant intelligence, especially towards Anson County. The part of the 63rd whom you do not think it necessary to take with you you will order to assemble at this place, where you will join them after performing the service on which you are now going, and where you will receive orders from me how to proceed if I should have left Camden. When you are ready to march, you will immediately acquaint Colonel Balfour, who will order the militia under Colonels Ball and Wigfall to proceed directly to George Town. I would not, however, have them remain on the east of Santee after your return, of which you will give them notice. I cannot send rum with you without disgusting the militia, refugees etc, but you may promise your men three days' double allowance when they get to Camden. If you find that you have more people than you want, you may send back the 100 men of Hamilton's corps, and when the service is performed, I wish you would inspect what Harrison has got by way of corps. If he has 150 good men, I would have them formed into three companys and sent to Monk's Corner to be provided with necessarys and cloathing. The Deputy Inspector of Provincials shall receive orders for that purpose. I am sorry to see the state of the 63rd. It is nearly neighbours' fare. We must do the best we can.

I am
Your most obedient humble servant

CORNWALLIS

PS

Colonel Mills will come to you with Mr Campbell[1], and you will give him any directions and employ him in such manner as you think proper.

Wemyss to Cornwallis, 28th August 1780   *63(79): ALS*

High Hills of Santee
August 28th 1780

The Rt Hon Earl Cornwallis etc etc etc
Cambden

My Lord

I was honored with yours of this day by Mr Campbell and shall proceed without loss of time to execute with the greatest pleasure every part of your Lordship's commands. The weakness of the detachment now with me, and the impossibility of getting horses before the return of the partys sent with the prisoners, will make my stay here for four or five days absolutely necessary. If I can get horses enough, I propose taking with me eighty or a

---

[1] David Campbell had been commissioned a lieutenant in the 63rd Regiment on 13th June 1778. (*Army Lists*)

hundred men. The rest I shall send to Cambden, where I beg your Lordship will give the necessary orders for the reception of the sick. I will do myself the pleasure of letting you know from time to time where I am and shall take every means of sending you intelligence. When I am ready to march, I will let you know. I am sorry to tell you that Captain Croker[2] died this morning of a billious fever.

I am with the greatest respect
Your most obedient and most humble servant

J WEMYSS

[*Subscribed*:]

As I have expended most of my ready money in the publick service, I will be obliged to your Lordship if you will order the Quarter Master General to answer any draft of mine on that head, should I find it necessary.

Cornwallis to Wemyss, 31st August 1780   79(54): C

Camden
August 31st 1780

Major Wemyss
63rd Regiment

Sir

I send Captain De Peister to you, who acts as deputy to Ferguson[3]. He has my directions to try to model the militia of Major Tynes and of Colonel Mills. He is an active young man and may be possibly usefull to you. You will be pleased to order back the mounted men of the Legion when they return from escorting the prisoners. I must likewise desire that you will order one hundred able Negroes furnished with spades to be collected from the plantations in your neighbourhood and send them to Camden under an escort of militia. You will order receipts to be given for them by the commanding officer of the militia with assurance that they shall be returned to their owners in about a fortnight. The infamous falsehoods so industriously circulated by our enemys have done us infinite mischief. I desire that you will order the commanding officers of militia to seize the busy retailers of those pernicious lies and order them a whipping in some publick place of their district.

---

[2] John Croker had spent his entire service in the 63rd Regiment. Commissioned an ensign on 14th March 1772, he was promoted to lieutenant on 11th July 1775 and to captain on 20th April 1778. (*Army Lists*)

[3] Frederick De Peyster was to accompany Wemyss. It was his brother, Captain Abraham De Peyster, who was second to Ferguson.

I am, sir,
Your most obedient humble servant

CORNWALLIS

[*Subscribed*:]

I shall be glad to hear that you have begun your march.

Cornwallis to De Peyster, 31st August 1780   79(52): C

Camden
31st August 1780

Captain De Peister
Acting as Deputy Inspector of Militia

Sir

You will please to join Major Wemyss on the High Hills of Santee and, untill he moves, endeavour to make something of the militia under Major Tynes by regulating the few honest loyalists under the officers of the best characters and disarming the rest in the most rigid manner. Major Tynes is a weak, well intentioned man. Captain Moore[4] may be treated with civility, but not trusted on account of his connexion with the Singletons[5]. Captain

---

[4] Isham Moore, who was married to Nancy (or Ann), a daughter of Matthew Singleton (see below), had migrated to the High Hills of Santee from Johnston County, North Carolina, about 1768. Rapidly establishing himself as a planter, he had by mid 1771 also become the Crown Surveyor for Camden District, a post which he was to occupy until the fall of the royal government. Allying himself with the nascent revolutionaries, he was a member of the Grand Jury for Camden District which in November 1774 issued a stirring call to resist attempts by Parliament to tax or otherwise bind by law the American colonies. By autumn of the following year he had been appointed a lieutenant in Matthew Singleton's troop of revolutionary light horse but has left no record of active involvement in military operations during the next five years. A wealthy man by 1780, he may have been content to sit for the time being on the sidelines, uncertain as to which party to the conflict would prevail, and too untrustworthy to be offered a commission in the royal militia. He would soon begin to vacillate more actively, first coming down firmly on the side of the Crown (which led to an aborted proposal to commission him), and then, as the tide turned in 1781, saving his reputation with the revolutionaries by going off to join Marion. After the war he would continue as a planter and become a Deputy Surveyor General for South Carolina. He died sometime after 1800. (Virginia Eliza Green Singleton, *Genealogy of the Singletons after their Emigration to America* (Columbia SC, 1914); Clara A Langley, *South Carolina Deed Abstracts 1719-1772* (Southern Historical reprint, 1984), iv, 153; Thomas J Kirkland and Robert M Kennedy, *Historic Camden* (Columbia SC, 1905), i, 106-8; *SCHGM*, i (1901), 184, 262; *The Cornwallis Papers*; Lambert, *SC Loyalists*, 158n)

[5] Of the Singletons now residing on the High Hills of Santee, Cornwallis has principally in mind Matthew (1735-1787), his son John (1754-1820), and Matthew's nephews John (?-1824) and Joseph. Matthew, who was born in Isle of Wight County, Virginia, migrated to South Carolina about 1753 and became in 1775 a member of the committee in St Mark's Parish for putting into effect the Continental Association subversive of the Crown. In the same year he was also appointed captain of a troop of revolutionary light horse under Colonel Richard Richardson - a troop in which his son John served as a lieutenant and his nephew Joseph as a trooper. Now, in 1780, Matthew and the two Johns either were serving in Marion's Brigade or would soon be so, Matthew with the rank of colonel.

Bromfield[6] is an active and I believe well affected man, but rather more intent on private plunder than the King's Service. You may perhaps get more particular information on the spot and from Major Wemyss. You will afterwards attend on Major Wemyss on his march, and endeavour if possible to establish some trusty militia under Colonel Mills at the Cheraws, and above all give the strictest order against admitting men of suspicious characters into the militia. Those of that description are all to be disarmed, and Major Wemyss will please to publish that if any man who is order'd to be disarmed shall be discover'd to have fire arms in his possession, the informer shall have five guineas and the delinquent shall forfeit all his property and be confin'd during the pleasure of the commanding officer of His Majesty's forces in this province.

I am, sir,
Your most obedient humble servant

CORNWALLIS

Memorial from Wemyss concerning succession in the 63rd Regiment, 2nd September 1780   *3(29): ADS*

To his Excellency Sir Henry Clinton, Knight of the Bath, Commander in Chief etc etc etc

The Memorial of Major James Wemyss commanding the 63rd Regiment

That in consequence of the death of Captain Croker of said regiment (the 28th August) a company is now vacant. Your memorialist begs leave to recommend Captain Lieutenant Jonathan Roberts to succeed to the company and Lieutenant John Money to the captain lieutenancy, your memorialist not thinking it consistant with his duty to recommend Lieutenant Marshall[7] (the only senior to Lieutenant Money) as he has never joined the regiment but has been constant[l]y employ'd as an assistant engineer.

J WEMYSS   High Hills of Santee
Major commanding 63rd Regiment   2nd September 1780

(Information in part from Don and George Lightfoot Singleton, 30th July and 3rd November 1999; Virginia Eliza Green Singleton, op cit; Anne King Gregorie, *History of Sumter County, South Carolina* (Sumter County Library Board, 1974); *SCHGM*, i (1901), 184, 262; Moss, *SC Patriots*, 867)

[6] Bromfield has not been positively identified. He may have been Watson Bromfield, who was soon to be recorded as owning land near the High Hills of Santee, having earlier taken up land on Black River. If so, he had fallen foul of the law in North Carolina, where in December 1770 he was conveyed to Salisbury jail as a felon. (T W Lipscomb to the editor, 14th February 2008; Clark ed, *State Records of NC,* xxii, 861)

[7] William Marshall had been appointed a lieutenant in the army as long ago as 17th December 1762. He entered the 63rd Regiment on 16th August 1775. On 26th June 1779, shortly after Stony Point on the Hudson was occupied by the British, he was appointed acting engineer there. Some three weeks later the post was subject to Wayne's *coup de main*, and the garrison, including Marshall, was captured. He would spend over eighteen months in captivity at Lancaster, Pennsylvania. (*Army Lists*)

Wemyss to Cornwallis, 3rd September 1780 64(11): *ALS*

High Hills of Santee
September 3rd 1780

The Rt Hon Earl Cornwallis etc etc etc
Camden

My Lord

Mallom[8] is just now arrived with about half the detachment that marched from Cambden. The other half are either dead or almost as bad. I sent yesterday a memorial in favor of Roberts and Money for the succession of Captain Croker's company to your Lordship to be transmitted to Sir Henry Clinton. I must now beg that you will not send it as I think from my information Captain Roberts' conduct must first be enquired into. I will not pretend to give my own opinion on the matter but am afraid upon an examination things will not appear to be so right as could be wished. One thing is certain, that Captain Roberts's party, the night that they were surprised, lay not only without their accoutrements but without their coats. They were so compleatly surprised that about a 100 infamous militia siezed most of their arms without any opposition. Under those circumstances I hope your Lordship will see the propriety of my stopping the succession untill the whole of Captain Roberts' conduct during the march is enquired into. I am afraid negligence will mark the whole of it. The militia have deceived me in my horses, but as they are to be assembled here tomorrow, I shall provide myself from the horses they will then bring with them and shall march on Tuesday.

I have the honor to be
Your Lordship's most obedient and most humble servant

J WEMYSS

De Peyster to Cornwallis, 5th September 1780 64(26): *ALS*

High Hills of Santee
5th of September 1780

The Rt Hon Lt General Earl Cornwallis

My Lord

I have the honor to inform your Lordship that a part of Major Tynes' regiment of militia, agreeable to the enclos'd return[9], assembled yesterday. I communicated your Lordship's

---

[8] Having been commissioned a lieutenant in the 57th Regiment on 3rd June 1767, John Mallom was promoted to captain in the 63rd some ten years later. At the beginning of 1781 Cornwallis would permit him to go to England for the recovery of his health. He would be charged with Cornwallis's and Balfour's dispatches. He was, according to Balfour, 'an officer of merit'. (*Army Lists*; *The Cornwallis Papers*)

[9] *the enclos'd return*: not extant.

orders and gave Major Tynes copys of some arrangements for the militia as well as returns for his regiment.

I beg to acquaint your Lordship that not a third that assembled had arms, and those, the officers assures me, where men to be trusted. Those men that had no arms observ'd that they where disarm'd by your Lordship and my Lord Rawdon on your Lordship's march to Camden.

The resolutions agreed to by all the officers and men of the several regiments of militia assembled under Major Ferguson at Brannon's and Moblese settlements I communicated to the officers and men of Major Tynes' regiment. They one and all unanimously agreed and approved of the same and Major Tynes in behalf of the regiment sign'd it, which I have the honor to transmit to your Lordship[10].

With the most perfect respect I have the honor to be
Your Lordship's most devoted and obedient servant

FRED[K] DE PEYSTER

Wemyss to Cornwallis, 20th September 1780   *3(80): ALS*

Cheraw Court House
September 20th 1780

The Rt Hon Earl Cornwallis etc etc etc

My Lord

I would have done myself the honor of writing to you some time ago but till now could not get a man to carry my letter. On my arrival at Kings Tree Bridge I was joined by the detachment of Colonel Hamilton's corps, Harrisson's of 50, and about 50 militia.

I have done every thing in my power to get at Mr Merrion, who with Giles[11] commanded about 150 men on my arrival in this part of country. Altho I never could come up with them,

---

[10] The resolutions agreed to (64(28)) are dated 4th September and signed by 'SAM[L] TYNES Colonel'. They are identical to those contained in enclosure (2), Ferguson to Ross, 19th August, p 143.

[11] Hugh Giles (1750-1802) was the son of Samuel, whose family migrated from England about 1735 and settled with others in Britton's Neck, twenty miles below Mars Bluff on the Pee Dee and forty miles above Georgetown. In mid 1775, as the revolution began, Hugh was elected 1st lieutenant in a company of subversive militia and at the same time became a member of the committee for Prince Frederick charged with putting into execution the Continental Association. By mid 1780 he had risen to be Colonel of the Britton's Neck revolutionary militia and had now placed himself and his men under the command of Marion. Little record remains of their service. After the war he owned and occupied a plantation which came to lie a little to the south of Marion District Courthouse. The hamlet of Gilesborough was named after him, but it was renamed Marion some years later. (Moss, op cit, 355; Gregg, *The Old Cheraws*, 68-70, 326-7, 589, 590; Rogers Jr, *Georgetown County*, 115, 128, 134; James, *Marion*, 44; Rankin, *Marion, passim*)

yet I pushed them so hard as in a great measure to break them up. The few that still continue together have retreated over the Litle Pedee.

It is impossible for me to give your Lordship an idea of the dissaffection of this country. Every inhabitant has been or is concerned in the rebellion, and most of them very deeply. Wherever I have gone, the houses were deserted by the men. Even their Negroes and effects were in general carry'd away. I have taken about 20 prisoners, one of whom, a notorious villain, I mean to hang to morrow[12]. The rest are poor ignorant people. Many of them are objects of compassion, notwithstanding their crimes are of such a nature as to put their lives in my power.

To give Colonel Mills an opportunity of attempting to embody his militia I had fixed upon this neighbourhood as a place to halt at for two or three days, but upon trial find it impossible. Few turned out, and even most of them of such suspicious characters as to convince both him and me of impracticability of such a scheme. He is therefore determined to leave this part of the country at least for a time, and as his house and plantation will in all probability be destroy'd as soon as I move, he begs that your Lordship will permit him to remove his family and effects to some rebell plantation on Savannah River untill he can otherwise provide for them. He has been of great use to me from his general knowledge of the country and is indeed the only man I have met with who is not afraid of taking an active part.

It is with great satisfaction that I inform your Lordship of the very healthy state of my detachment, notwithstanding the very severe fatigue they have some times undergone. We are pretty well mounted, so much so as to be able to march 56 miles without halting. This I did yesterday with a view to surprise a party of rebels on the other side of the Pedee. I shall expect to receive your orders where to proceed to by the bearer. We begin to be in want of shoes and trowsers.

I have the honor to be with the greatest respect
Your Lordship's most obedient and most humble servant

J WEMYSS
Major, 63rd Regiment

[*Subscribed*:]

I forgot to tell your Lordship that I have burnt and laid waste about 50 houses and plantations mostly belonging to people who have either broke their paroles or oath of allegiance and are now in arms against us.

---

[12] *a notorious villain..*: a reference to Adam Cusack, a native of England, who had formerly served as a bo'sun's mate in a British man of war and deserted. Now a prominent local revolutionary, he would be executed after conviction by court martial for cruelly persecuting loyalists, perhaps in breach of a parole. (Margaret Baskin, 'James Wemyss (1748-1833)' (www.banastretarleton.org, 29th June 2005) Contrary accounts of the event, tinged by partiality, are given in James, op cit, 58; Gregg, op cit, 303; and Ramsay, *Rev of SC*, ii, 188-9, where exception is implied to the fact that in their view Cusack was condemned on the evidence of a black man.

Cornwallis to Wemyss, 26th September 1780   *80(47): C*

Charlottetown
September 26th 1780

Sir

I receiv'd this day your letter of the 20th dated at Cheraw Court House. It gives me great pleasure to hear that your detachment is healthy; in other respects your accounts are not so agreeable. I enclose to you a letter from Moncrief to Balfour[13], and I must absolutely try to raise some kind of militia at the Cheraws. It is impossible to leave all that frontier entirely open to the enemy. I wou'd have you return directly to Camden with the detachments of the 63rd and Hamilton's corps and leave Harrison and the militia to keep some kind of hold of the country. I will order Major Fraser of Innes's corps to mount fifty men on some of the horses you bring back and to go and join Harrison and try to form some militia, or some independent companies if he can get only 100 or even fifty men. If Colonel Mills cannot undertake it, some body must — Colonel Gray or any person who can be prevailed on by persuasion or by more forceble arguments of interest. You will receive directions about your moving with the 63rd when you arrive at Camden. I wish you to publish to the country that all persons except those actually concern'd in the seizeing the field officers of the militia may return to their habitations, where they will be suffered to live quietly, provided they deliver up their arms and give their military parole neither to say or do any thing contrary to His Majesty's interest untill they are releas'd from that parole by the commanding officer of His Majesty's forces in South Carolina or Commandant of Charlestown.

I am, sir,
Your most obedient and faithfull servant

CORNWALLIS

Wemyss to Cornwallis, 30th September 1780   *64(134): ALS*

Cheraw Hill
September 30th 1780

The Rt Hon Earl Cornwallis etc etc etc

My Lord

I had the honor of receiving your letter of the 26th last night and, agreable to your orders, shall march for Camden to morrow morning with the detachment under my command, presuming in regard to Harrisson's corps to dissobey your directions, being convinced, were they to be left here, that they would dissperse in two or three days. They are if possible worse than militia, their whole desire being to plunder and steal and, when they have got as much as their horses will carry, to run home.

---

[13] *a letter..*: of 20th September, p 98.

I think I may safely venture to assure your Lordship that as long as this country continues a frontier it cannot be kept by militia, altho assisted by a small detachment of Innes's or Harrisson's corps. My opinion is the same as to the militia that have been arranged by Major Moncrieff and Cassillis's regiment. Merrion, Giles, a Colonel Ford from Cape Fear with several other leading men are assembl'd at Drowning Creek with about 400 men and are increasing daily. They are burning houses and disstressing the well affected in a most severe manner. Several people from that country have been with me to represent their disstressed situation. The Highlanders in particular, who are very numerous there, have been treated with such cruelty and oppression as almost exceeds belief. Some of them are now with me, who say that their country men to a man would turn out if they had the least countenance or support. They are dissarmed.

I have offered pardon to all people now in arms who have not broke their paroles or oath of allegiance that will surrender themselves, but without any effect. They are deluded in a most extraordinary manner by reports of a large army coming from the northward, the arrival of a French fleet and army etc etc.

Believe me to be with the greatest respect
Your Lordship's most obedient and most humble servant

J WEMYSS
Major, 63rd Regiment

Gray to Cornwallis, 30th September 1780   64(130): ALS

Cheraw Hill
30th September 1780

My Lord

I arrived here with the detachment under Major Wemyss in order to assist Colonel Mills in embodying the militia here and am sorry to inform you we found it to be impossible for the following reasons.

The second rebellion had been so general in this district that at least three fourths of the inhabitants upon this river had taken active parts in it, and in this number must be included almost every person of influence or popularity here. These upon the approach of Major Wemyss retired in arms to Cross Creek under the command of their respective leaders, where they find countenance and protection from the rebel post established there. The others that remained were so few in number that they were able to effect nothing, and even of these many had their nearest connections among the rebel refugees and could not be trusted.

The only well affected part of the district, exclusive of the inhabitants on Black and Lynch's Creek, lies on Little Peedee constituting the frontier towards North Carolina. Few of the people from thence turned out because by coming so far from their homes they exposed their families and property to the resentment of the rebels from Cape Fear, who have been indefatigable in persecuting them upon every occasion. Neither will it be possible to protect them from the incursions of the rebels unless Cape Fear River was the boundary, because the country there is so barren that it is impossible to find provisions for a sufficient number of men if it was found necessary to establish a post there.

No dependance therefore can be placed upon the militia here, but as the restoration of the British Government in this district is a measure highly necessary for the security of the province in general, as well as of many well affected subjects here, I beg leave to state my ideas on that subject (Colonel Mills having retired to the southward), assuring your Lordship that my freedom on this subject proceeds only from my zeal for His Majesty's Service.

To effect this it will be necessary to have a force, independant of the militia, established here untill Cape Fear River is the boundary. This, I suppose, will at least require a hundred regular troops well mounted with three hundred well affected militia from some other part of the province, including Harrisson's corps. With this number a force might be spared to scour the frontiers occasionally and to secure the different ferries on Peedee betwixt this and the George Town District, but as there are two ferries, Port's and Britton's, in that district, it were to be wished they were occupied by the lower regiment because they command the passes to North Carolina and I apprehend would effectually cover and overawe Williamsburg Township and King's Tree. Port's Ferry is near the confluence of Lynch's Creek with Peedee and a detachment of twenty men from the post established there would be sufficient to keep possession of Witherspoon's Ferry over that creek, it not being above four miles distant and is a pass of the last importance as it entirely commands the communication on the south side of this river betwixt the two regiments, that creek not being passable for twenty four miles above that place.

If your Lordship judges these arrangements proper, I make no doubt but that, with a sufficiency of arms and ammunition for the well affected, the publick peace may be restored; but as many of the loyal inhabitants on the frontiers have had their houses burnt lately by the rebels and now talk of going to Georgia, perhaps they could still be retained here if leave was granted to the proper officers to put them in possession of the vacant rebel plantations in this and George Town District untill your Lordship's pleasure was known.

As the few militia who were embodied here have gone to Camden for arms and ammunition and Major Wemyss marches for that place tomorrow, I shall proceed with him and there wait your Lordship's further commands.

As I am almost destitute of cloaths and other necessaries, having lost my baggage when I made my escape from the rebels, I beg your Lordship's permission to sell a Negro and to have leave of absence for twelve days or a fortnight to go to Charlestown to purchase necessaries.

I am with great respect, my Lord,
Your Lordship's most obedient humble servant

ROBERT GRAY
Lt Colonel of the Cheraw Militia

Cornwallis to Gray, 2nd October 1780   81(6): C

Charlottetown
October 2nd 1780

Lt Colonel Grey

Sir

I received the favor of your letter of the 30th from Cheraw Hill, for which I am much obliged to you. It always gives me the greatest satisfaction to hear the opinion of the gentlemen of the country, but yours is so very clear and sensible that every officer must receive it with pleasure.

I have directed Lt Colonel Turnbull to send Major Frazer with eighty mounted men, old soldiers, and Harrison's and the best militia he can get, and hope he will be able with the help of the militia in the lower districts to secure the country tolerably well untill the march of our army shall oblige the enemy to quit the country between the Pedee and Crosscreek. You will use your discretion about the suffering inhabitants and have my full permission to put those whose plantations have been burnt into possession of those belonging to the rebels. You will likewise sell a Negro to help to provide yourself. I must beg that you will make your stay at Charlestown as short as possible. Lt Colonel Balfour, on your shewing him this letter, will give you a commission of colonel in the room of Colonel Mills and advance to you one hundred dollars, which gratuity has been given to most of the commanding officers of militia.

I am, sir, etc

[CORNWALLIS]

Wemyss to Cornwallis, 4th October 1780   3(184): ALS

Camden
October 4th 1780

My Lord

Finding that an express is just going to set off for Charlotte Town, I take the opportunity of acquainting you of my arrival here. I am sorry to hear that Merrion has drove the militia from Georgetown and is now there. I very much fear that all the posts established by Major Moncrieff will share the same fate.

I hope your Lordship will not look upon it as presumption in me when I say that Cape Fear River ought to be the frontier of this country and that, untill such a movement is made, the rebels must be the masters of the Pedee etc except a force is constantly kept there of at least 200 regular troops independant of militia etc. With litle more than that number of good men mounted I think that the whole of the Cape Fear River from Cross Creek to Willmington might in a month be in our possession, as from the best information I can get I believe that the Highland settlers on that river would to a man rize in our favour. As they are all dissarmed, should your Lordship think such a movement at any time necessary, arms and ammunition will be much wanted. If this plan should be try'd and succeed, the militia of George Town and the Cheraws (bad as they are) would under the direction of a prudent man settle the whole of that country in a permanent manner.

Nothing but an absolute want of necessarys makes me wish to remain here for a few days, in the getting of which I shall not loose a moment. Colonel Turnbull has desired me to keep both the horses of my detachment and Hamilton's untill he hears from you.

I am with the greatest respect
Your Lordship's most obedient and most humble servant

J WEMYSS

De Peyster to Cornwallis, undated[14]   3(16): ALS

The Rt Hon Lt General Earl Cornwallis

My Lord

At the time Major Wemyss wrote your Lordship from the Cheraws, my indisposition prevented me that honor.

Having now recover'd, I beg leave to inform your Lordship that on our march to the Cheraws Major Wemyss inform'd me the militia where to assemble at George Town, in consequence of which I attended Major Moncreiffe at that place. Their was part of three regiments, viz, Colonel Cassells', Colonel Wigfall's and Colonel Ball's. There returns I have the honor to enclose your Lordship[15]. After this I join'd Major Wemyss and attended him, agreeable to your Lordship's directions, to the Cheraws, at which place the inhabitants are very rebellious and very few of them at their habitations.

In that part of the country their are rebel partys commanded by Gyles, Marrian, Harrington[16], Cupp[17] and Wayne[18].

---

[14] Internal evidence suggests that this letter was written on or after 4th October at Camden after De Peyster's arrival there with Wemyss.

[15] *There returns..*: not extant.

[16] Born in England, Henry William Harrington (1748-1809) had migrated via Jamaica to the Pee Dee, settling firstly at Cheraw Hill and soon after in the Welch Neck. In August 1775 he was commissioned captain of a subversive militia company in St David's Parish, and although in June 1776 he came down with it to Haddrell's Point, he did not take part in repulsing the British. Later in the year he was returned to the South Carolina revolutionary assembly in a by-election. About the end of 1778 he removed to North Carolina and on 25th November 1779 was commissioned a colonel in the North Carolina revolutionary militia. Having six months later been promoted to

On our arrival Major Wemyss directed a muster of every man, and out of that very large district there was not above one hundred men, and Major Wemyss' observation and opinion was that he was fearfull many of the number assembled was doubtfull characters, and the whole unprovided with arms and ammunition. Under those circumstances he thought I should not interfere with them at all. Major Wemyss also observ'd that a very few days would disperse them again, notwithstanding every endeavour to the contrary might have been used.

With permission I beg leave to trouble your Lordship by informing you that I have had the misfortune of having my servant and all my baggage taken on the 13th ultimo by the rebels, in consequence of which I have made application to Colonel Turnbull for permission to go to Charles Town to get myself some necessarys, which he has been pleas'd to grant, and this afternoon I set out and shall return to Camden in the course of 16 or 18 days, at which time I shall be infinitely proud to receive your Lordship's commands.

Major Harrison, who I believe has your Lordship's permission to raise men, informs me he has more than his compliment, and if I can obtain your Lordship's approbation, he will permit [me] to have 25 for my company in the New York Volunteers, [with] which your Lordship has been pleas'd to honor me with your countenance.

I beg your Lordship's pardon for this interruption and have the honor to be with the most perfect respect

Your Lordship's most obedient and very humble servant

FRED[K] DE PEYSTER

Money to Wemyss, 6th October 1780 81(24): ACS

Head Quarters, Charlottetown
October 6th 1780

Major Wemyss
Commanding the 63rd Regiment

Dear Sir

Lord Cornwallis desires me to acquaint you that he has received your letter and requests you will equip the 63rd Regiment as speedily as possible with the appointments they are

---

brigadier general *pro tempore* by the North Carolina Board of War, he had now established his headquarters at Cross Creek but would soon move to the Pee Dee opposite the Cheraws. Concurrently a member of the North Carolina revolutionary assembly, he would resign his command on 2nd December when the assembly refused to confirm his rank of brigadier general. (Gregg, *The Old Cheraws, passim*; *The Greene Papers*, vi, 519n)

[17] Abel Kolb (Culp) was a colonel of the revolutionary militia on the upper Pee Dee. An active partisan who had a reputation for severity, he would be killed by loyalists when his house at the public ferry near Society Hill was surrounded on 28th April 1781. (Gregg, op cit, *passim*; Rankin, *Marion*, 197-8)

[18] Amos Windham was a captain under Abel Kolb. (Gregg, op cit, 414)

deficient in and be in readiness to march on the shortest notice. You will detain all the horses you brought in and collect as many from Colonel Hamilton's corps as possible. His Lordship will send you further directions in two or three days.

I have the honor to be, dear sir,
Your most obedient and most humble servant

J MONEY
Aid de camp

Cornwallis to Wemyss, 7th October 1780   81(26A): ADfS

Charlottetown
October 7th 1780

Major Wemys
63rd Regiment
Camden

Sir

The state of the lower country, and the absolute necessity of preventing the enemy from being in quiet possession of the east bank of Santee, obliges me to change the destination of the 63rd Regiment. I will therefore explain my plan to you and the part you are to bear in it. *The object of marching into North* Carolina *is only to raise men*, which, from every account I have received of *the number of our friends*, there is great reason to hope may be done *to a very considerable amount*. For this purpose I shall *move in about ten or twelve days to Salisbury and from thence invite all loyalists of the neighbouring countys to repair to our standard* to be formed into Provincial corps and armed, clothed and appointed as soon as we can do it. From *thence I mean to move my whole force down to Cross Creek*. As it will then be *about the middle of November, I hope* the *lower country will be healthy*. I shall then be in *full communication with our shipping and shall receive all the arms and clothing that Charlestown can afford*.

I would have you *mount your whole regiment and, if you think yourself too weak, take thirty men from Turnbull, desiring him* to detain in *their place* as many of our convalescents, and proceed into *the country* as soon as possible. I can give you *no particular directions*. *My object is to prevent the enemy from being thoroughly masters* of the country *you have left*. *You will therefore act, according to your discretion and the intelligence* you may *receive, either offensively or defensively untill you hear of my march to Cross Creek, when you will join me*. We may correspond by means of the cypher. You will please to give a copy of the cypher to Turnbull and send another by a safe conveyance to Balfour. Tell Turnbull that I address this letter to you as he is ill, and shew him the contents. You will of course take Harrison's corps and what militia you please.

I am, sir,
Your most obedient humble servant

CORNWALLIS

[*Subscribed*:]

You will send a copy of this letter to Balfour, which you may, I suppose, venture without cypher as the only danger is near this place, and you will afterwards correspond with him when you think it necessary.

Gray to Cornwallis, 7th October 1780   *3(197): ALS*

Camden
7th October 1780

My Lord

I am this day honoured with your Lordship's letter of the 2nd current and beg leave to return you my warmest acknowledgements for the order on Colonel Balfour and for the honour you have done me in appointing me Colonel of the Cheraw Regiment of militia.

The disaster that has befallen the lower parts of Peedee occasions me again to obtrude upon your Lordship my thoughts on the situation of the northern frontier.

The rebel partisans who infest that country command a number of desperadoes who are kept together by the hopes of plunder. As they are incapable of opposing any regular force, they will upon this as the former occasion retire to Cross Creek upon the approach of any body of men that may be sent against them and invade the country again by a number of different routs when the troops retire. It would therefore, I apprehend, be attended with the best effects if the troops who are sent to scour that part of the country should penetrate immediately into North Carolina, seize Wilmington and drive them beyond Cape Fear River, carrying with them arms and ammunition to give the inhabitants on the frontiers, who are in general well affected.

As I passed through that part of the country lately when I made my escape from the rebels, I had an opportunity of learning their sentiments and found Colonel Hamilton to be extremely popular there. I should conclude, if he had the command of that expedition, the happiest consequences might be presaged for the above as well as the following reasons.

His connections extend from Wilmington to Halifax. The greater part of his regiment has been recruited from the frontiers among the natives and Scotch. Himself and almost all his officers being from North Britain will give him great influence among the latter from their national attachment, which is carried to a greater length among them than is common and seems to be owing to the unremitting persecution they have suffered from the rebels for these last six years, to which must be added the openess of his temper and extreme affability of his manners, so indispensably necessary in conciliating the affections of the people, especially in this country, where all ranks are so much upon a level.

I have the honour to be, my Lord,
Your Lordship's most obedient most humble servant

ROBERT GRAY

Money to Wemyss, 10th October 1780[19]   3(208): ALS

Charlottetown
October 10th 1780

Major Wemyss
63rd Regiment
Camden

Dear Sir

I am favor'd with yours of the 8th[20]. Lord Cornwallis desires me to acquaint you that *the sick and convalescents of the regiment must be left at Camden* and if *you can spare an officer to remain with them, so much the better*.

I should imagine *Mallom would answer the purpose*. I am *sorry you will be so weak*. *We have a report of Ferguson having been routed and killed*. *Something has certainly happened with his corps*.

I am, dear major,
Very faithfully yours

J MONEY
Aid de camp

Wemyss to Cornwallis, 29th October 1780   3(307): ALS

Ninety Six
October 29th 1780

The Rt Hon Earl Cornwallis etc etc etc

My Lord

I do myself the honor of informing you that I arrived here yesterday forenoon, when I found every thing perfectly *quiet* and *safe*. Colonel Cruger has *enclosed the court house* and *some other houses that joined it within a square stockade flanked by block houses*. He is now

---

[19] This letter may not have been sent. The cover containing the addressee and address is extant (3(207)).

[20] *yours of the 8th*: not extant.

making a ditch, which, when finished, will make him very strong. This *work with the jail* and *a small block house holds all his people*. He has near *three hundred men fit for duty*. As report does not *even allow a rebel to be in this part of the country*, I am to *request you will be good enough* [to permit me] *to join you or to go on the expedition formerly intended*, as I can by no means add to the *strength of* [this] *post. Should they be attacked, their numbers are equal to its defence*. I shall with impatience wait for your Lordship's answer, being in a very uncomfortable situation, laying in the open fields some distance from hence, and, as forrage is very scarce, must move about from place to place on account of our horses.

I am with the greatest respect
Your Lordship's most obedient and most humble servant

J WEMYSS

Rawdon to Wemyss, 31st October 1780   3(337): C

Wynnesborough
October 31st 1780

Major Wemyss
63rd Regiment

My dear Sir

By Lord Cornwallis's orders I have this day written to Lt Colonel Cruger[21], desiring that you may still keep the field between Ninety Six and Broad River. The great object is to prevent the supplies of corn which we expect from the other side of Broad River from being interrupted by scouting partys of the enemy. Therefore it will be adviseable for you to keep near to Broad River as long as we remain in our present position. Lord Cornwallis would even wish you to cross it in case you should learn that any parties attempt to come down to the mills upon this side of it. We shall be happy to hear from you constantly, for tho' you may not have any thing material to say, it will be a satisfaction to learn that all remains quiet, and we will in return give you what intelligence we receive from the rest of the world.

I am, dear sir, with great esteem and regard
Very faithfully yours

RAWDON

§ - §

---

[21] See p 204.

2 - With Hamilton

Cornwallis to Hamilton, 28th August 1780 *79(41): C*

Camden
August 28th 1780

Lt Colonel Hamilton
Ratcliffe's Bridge

Sir

I have ordered Major Wemys to march as soon as he conveniently can for the purpose of punishing and disarming the country between Santee and Pedee. You will please to form a detachment of one hundred of your most healthy men and best marchers to join him under a careful officer. He will send to you when he is ready and let you know at what place he is desirous of being joined by your detachment of the 100 men, by Colonel Bryan's corps and by whatever Harrison has collected, as that is the detachment which I have allotted for that service. Whenever Major Wemys sends his directions relative to them, you will please to order them to march accordingly and return yourself with the remainder of your corps to Camden for the purpose of putting it into the best order possible against our march.

I am, sir,
Your most obedient humble servant

[CORNWALLIS]

Hamilton to Cornwallis, undated[22] *63(74): ALS*

My Lord

I have this moment received certain intelligence from Kings Tree that the rebell party who retook the rebell prisoners consisted of 150 men under the command of Colonel Marrion, pass'd over Lynches Creeck last Saturday towards Pee Dee, which place they were to cross at Britain's Ferry.

84 of the Continentalls had made their escape, and they had only 12 British prisoners with them.

---

[22] According to the endorsement, the letter was written on 28th August.

I can here of no other body of rebells except 100 light horse under the command of a Captain McCorterie[23]. They are gone to George Town in order to procure a supply of salt and it is said they are to return up Saint tee. I have sent out severall parties of mounted militia in order to gain intelligence and to take prisoners any of the noted rebells they may fall in with.

I have the honor to be with the greatest respect, my Lord,
Your Lordship's most obedient and very humble servant

JN HAMILTON
Lt Colonel Commandant, Royal North Carolina Volunteers

Hamilton to Cornwallis, 28th August 1780   63(76): ALS

Camp, Ratcliff's Bridge
August 28th 1780

My Lord

I have the honor to enclose your Lordship the report of Joshua Garret[24] just arrived from North Carolina. It is of no great consequence, yet it may be satisfactory to your Lordship to hear so late intelligence from that quarter.

A party of the militia are just come in and brought four prisoners, to wit: Josiah Clemens[25], an arch rebell, and has acknowledged to have been in arms, and warn'd the militia in[26] during the late insurrection; Samuel Baccoat[27] and Peter Alston[28], both noted

---

[23] William McCottry was an inhabitant of Williamsburg Township, some thirty miles above Georgetown, and like most of its population was almost certainly of Scotch-Irish extraction. When John James returned there in June from meeting John Plummer Ardesoif at Georgetown (see vol I, p 306, note 3), he had been chosen by those of the revolutionary persuasion to be major of an irregular band of militia. He in turn chose McCottry to be one of his captains. When in mid August Francis Marion assumed command of the band, he appointed McCottry as captain of an independent company of sharpshooters. In 1781 they would distinguish themselves in the action at the lower bridge on Black River and in the capture of Fort Watson. Later in the year McCottry would be returned from Prince Frederick to the revolutionary assembly which met at Jacksonborough. (Gregg, *The Old Cheraws*, appendix, 580; Rankin, *Marion*, 50-2, 59, 60, 148, 168-170, 187-9; McCrady, *SC in the Rev 1780-1783*, 558)

[24] Joshua Garrett (1758-?) was a South Carolina loyalist who would go on to be commissioned an ensign in the King's Rangers. He was placed on the Provincial half-pay list at the close of the war. (Treasury 64/23(16) and WO 65/165(11) (National Archives, Kew); Clark, *Loyalists in the Southern Campaign*, i, 466)

[25] Josiah Clements would soon escape or otherwise obtain his release. He would go on to serve as a sergeant and lieutenant in Marion's Brigade for the next two years. (Moss, *SC Patriots*, 177)

[26] *warn'd the militia in*: an expression (now obsolete) meaning 'ordered the militia to come in'.

[27] Of Huguenot descent, Samuel Bacot (1745-1797) came to the Pee Dee in 1769, settling on Black River not far from the present town of Darlington. He would soon be conveyed a prisoner to Camden and from there be sent on with others to Charlestown. On the way he would lead his fellow captives in overpowering the escort, who were

rebells; Jacob Ferby, a Continentall soldier, who made his escape from Saint Mark's Church on the way to Charles Town.

I have the honor to be, my Lord,
Your Lordship's most obedient and very humble servant

JN HAMILTON
Lt Colonel Commandant, Royal North Carolina Volunteers

Enclosure
Report of Joshua Garrett, 28th August 1780   63(78): D

A detachment of troops from Edenton, New Bern and Bute marched from these places the last of July under the command of Colonel Sewel[29], Jarvis[30] and Major Pasteur[31], said in all to consist of 800 men. He left them last Tuesday 15 miles the other side of Coles Bridge on Drowning Creeck.

---

paroled, and return homeward. He would go on to serve as a lieutenant in Marion's Brigade. (Gregg, op cit, 105-6, 328-9, 405; Moss, op cit, 35)

[28] Peter Allston (1743-?) had accompanied Samuel Bacot (see above) to the Pee Dee in 1769. Both were married in that year, Peter to Samuel's sister Mary, and Samuel to Peter's sister Margaret. In a by-election in March 1783 Peter would be returned to the lower house of the legislature as a Representative for St David's Parish. (Gregg, op cit, 105, 416)

[29] Born in Brunswick County, Virginia, Benjamin Seawell Jr (1741-1821) migrated to Bute County, North Carolina, in the early 1770s. Like Samuel Jarvis (see below), he was of the revolutionary persuasion and in 1775 sat on the Bute County Committee of Safety. The following year he was a delegate from Bute to the Provincial Congress which, on convening in November, went on to adopt a revolutionary constitution for North Carolina. He was then returned as a Senator for Bute in the revolutionary assembly of 1777 and, when Bute was divided, as a Senator for Franklin in the assembly of 1779. Now, in 1780, he was colonel of his county's revolutionary militia but would play little if no part in forthcoming military operations. In 1785 he became Sheriff of Franklin County before moving on to Tennessee, where he was licensed to practise as an attorney at law on 6th April 1798. He took up residence in what became Wilson County and died there at Hot Springs. (Powell ed, *Dictionary of NC Biography*; Wheeler, *Historical Sketches*, i, 85; Revolutionary army accounts, ix, 101(2) (North Carolina State Archives, Raleigh, NC); Commission Book of Governor John Sevier, April 2nd - June 16th, 1801 (Archives Division, Tennessee State Library and Archives), 5)

[30] Samuel Jarvis (?-c. 1807) was an inhabitant of Currituck County, North Carolina, and about 1767 had been a captain in his county's royal militia. Of the revolutionary persuasion, he had become a delegate from Currituck County to the Provincial Congresses of 1774 and 1776 besides being appointed Colonel of the Currituck County revolutionary militia in September 1775. Now, in 1780, he was Colonel of the 1st North Carolina Regiment of revolutionary militia and would go on to command the 2nd Regiment formerly commanded by Colonel Benjamin Exum. Like Benjamin Seawell Jr (see above), he would play little or no part in forthcoming military operations. (Return of militia officers *c.* 1767 (North Carolina State Archives, Raleigh, NC); Wheeler, *Historical Sketches*, i, 65, 78, 85; Hay ed, *Soldiers from NC*, 502; *State Records of NC*, xvii, 1054, 1057-8)

[31] Pasteur has not been positively identified. He may have been John Pasteur, who in July 1776 was commissioned a lieutenant in the 6th North Carolina Continental Regiment. If so, he would at some stage have transferred to the North Carolina revolutionary militia. (Heitman, *Historical Register*, 428)

Says that Gates and Caswell were at Charlote, collecting the remains of their army; that the troops under Sewel etc were order'd to Charlote; from thence the whole were to march to Hillsborough to cover the Assembley, which is now sitting at that place for the purpose of raising a new army.

He further relates that the Torries have disarmed a great many of the militia; that the country about Cross Creek and Drowning Creek is totally laid waste; that the rebells in North Carolina are distressed for ammunition, having taken off the lead from the Palace at New Bern to make into bullets.

21 of the 71st Regiment sent to Hillsborough. Garret cross'd at Cheraw Hill last Thursday. Not a man in that quarter, but says a party are imbodiing at the Long Bluff.

No other troops imbodiing in North Carolina nor any expected from the northward, as he heard of.

Hamilton to Cornwallis, 28th August 1780

63(72): ALS

Monday evening
August 28th 1780

My Lord

I had the honor to receive your Lordship's letter of this date.

The detachment from my regiment, Bryan's corps etc shall be in readiness to join Major Wymes when ever he may direct.

When that is accomplished, I shall fullfill your Lordship's orders in returning to Camden with the remainder of my regiment.

I have sent out a party of militia, mounted, for the purpose of collecting horses. Would be glad to know whither your Lordship means to take the horses from Harrisson['s] corps and militia who are on duty or only from the rebell plantations etc.

I have just heard the rebells are all dispers'd and moved over Pee Dee. Numbers have left their famalies on Lynches Creek and Black River and gone off with the rebells.

I have the honor to be, my Lord,
Your Lordship's most obedient and very humble servant

JN HAMILTON
Lt Colonel

Hamilton to Money, 31st August 1780　　　　　　　　　　　　　　　　　　*3(14): ALS*

Camp, Ratcliff's Bridge
August 31st 1780

John Mony Esquire
Aid de camp
Head Quarters

Dear Mony

I have this moment received accounts from North Carolina: Generall Gates is most certainly at Hillsborough; Generals Smallwood and Guess and Colonel Armang are on the Yadkin River about 7 miles the other side of Salisbury, where they are to remain, untill further orders from Mr Gates, with the remains of their army; the militia are imbodying at Charlote and they expect a reinforcement from Virginia; Gates has sent for the cannon he had left at General Person's[32] in Granville County. I suppose he intends making another tryall on Camden.

A report prevailes in the rebell camp that 3,000 French are landed at Petersburg in Virginia, but this wants confirmation.

You'll please communicate this intelligence to Lord Cornwallis.

I am, dear Mony,
Yours most sincerly

JN HAMILTON
Lt Colonel Commandant, Royal North Carolina Volunteers

Hamilton to Cornwallis, 4th October 1780　　　　　　　　　　　　　　　　*3(182): ALS*

Camden
October 4th 1780

My Lord

Major Wymess is just return'd with the detachment under his command.

---

[32] Thomas Person's plantation lay near present-day Berea. Probably born in Brunswick County, Virginia, Person (1733-1800) had lived from infancy in Granville County, North Carolina, and in the course of years acquired a landed estate of more than 82,000 acres. A prominent and influential figure politically, he was now a member for his county in the revolutionary legislature and had previously served in the colonial legislature and the Provincial Congresses. In addition he had been appointed in 1776 to the rank of brigadier general in the North Carolina revolutionary militia, but there is no record that he ever saw active service at any time in the war. At its close he would continue to play a prominent part in public affairs. (Robinson, *NC Guide*, 425; *DAB*; *Appletons'*)

I must entreat your Lordship may order my self and regiment to join the army under your command, or detach us on any other service your Lordship may think proper, so that the whole regiment may be together, as a young regiment being detach'd prevents it from being of real service.

Wishing your Lordship all manner of success, I remain with the honor of being with the greatest respect, my Lord,
Your Lordship's most obedient and very humble servant

JN HAMILTON
Lt Colonel

Rawdon to Hamilton, 15th October 1780[33]   3(230): ACS

October 15th
Ten in the morning

To Lt Colonel Hamilton

Sir

Should you by chance have begun your march before this note reaches you, Lord Cornwallis directs that you shall immediately return to Camden, where you will wait for further orders. Forward this note without delay to Lt Colonel Turnbull, who is hereby instructed to detach (as soon as possible) Major Wemyss with the 63rd Regiment, *mounted*, to Ninety Six. Major Wemyss will there put himself under the command of Lt Colonel Cruger. If the 63rd have marched towards Pedee, they must be recalled directly and must proceed to Ninety Six with as little loss of time as possible.

RAWDON

[*Superscribed:*]

Sent from the Old Nation Ford before twelve on the 15th.

§ - §

---

[33] This letter miscarried. See Turnbull to Rawdon, 20th October, p 256.

CHAPTER 26

Letters to or from Camden or the Waxhaws etc

1 - To or from Turnbull

Cornwallis to Turnbull, 11th September 1780 *80(16): C*

Forster's Plantation, Waxhaw
September 11th 80

Lt Colonel Turnbull
Commanding at Camden

Sir

I propose marching to morrow to Captain Crawford's plantation on Waxhaw Creek[1], which will entirely cover all this settlement. I have found a considerable quantity of wheat in the different plantations; the threshing, cleaning and collecting it at the mills is a work of some trouble. The 71st may march in five days easily to Crawford's, halting one day at Berkley's. I do not think we can manage to send any flour to them on the road. Therefore they must provide themselves for five days. When we are at Crawford's, the road on both sides of the river will be equally secure. Should you have any dispatches of great consequence to forward, it may be right to send two or three mounted men with them. Innis's regiment march'd from Ninety Six on Friday last, so that it will arrive at Camden in two or three days. The account of the 63rd gives me the greatest concern. I hope that care and

---

[1] Robert Crawford's plantation lay on the north side of Waxhaw Creek. He was a major in the South Carolina revolutionary militia and a distant relative of Andrew Jackson. His house was occupied by Cornwallis as a temporary headquarters. (Robinson, *Davie*, 44, 67; Moss, *SC Patriots*, 214)

being kept dry and taking a great deal of bark will soon reestablish the regiment and render it fit for service. I am not without my apprehensions for the 7th. Everything is perfectly quiet in this part of the world. The inhabitants are mostly fled.

I am, sir,
Your most obedient and faithfull servant

CORNWALLIS

Turnbull to Cornwallis, 11th September 1780   *64(42): ALS*

Camden
September 11th 1780

Earl of Cornwallis

My Lord

There is very little happned here worth your notice. A detachment of the 63rd Regiment under the command of Captain Mallom arrived three days ago. He has brought thirty eight men fit for duty, and in the state of the regiment I find their totall sick amounts to one hundred and sixty seven.

The 71st recover fast. McArthur says, if he was not wanted immediately, he could bring a great many more men with him.

Captain McKinnon, I dare say, has reported the quantity of stores he is bringing from Charlestown. Some of the waggons, I believe, are arrived.

The greatest difficulty I find is about the prisoners. The Provoost is a stupid, drunken fellow. He has made such a confusion and has not even guarded the courts of inquiry upon the people mark'd try'd; and some he has without a crime at all.

Some days ago a flag of truce came here from Hilsborough and was a day and a night here without my knowing any thing about him. When I sent for him, he insisted that I was not the commanding officer.

If your Lordship intends that Major England shall command the district, I must say it wou'd give me a great deal of pleasure.

I am ready at all times to obey your Lordship's commands, and believe me to be with the greatest respect

Your Lordship's most obedient humble servant

GEO TURNBULL

Cornwallis to Turnbull, 13th September 1780   80(22): C

Camp on Waxhaw Creek
September 13th 1780

Lt Colonel Turnbull
Commanding at Camden

Sir

I have just received the favor of your letter of the 11th. The state of the 63rd is truly distressing. It gives me great pleasure to hear so good an account of the 71st. You will please to order Major McArthur to march on Monday next, the 18th instant, to Crawford's plantation on Waxhaw Creek. They must have five or six days' flour and they must bring up a large proportion of rum and salt.

I beg you will believe that the addressing the rebel surgeon to England was only an inadvertency and no intended neglect to you, a thought of which is very far from my heart. The room we were in had hardly any roof, and as it rained very hard, there was not more than one or two spots where it was possible to keep the paper dry enough to write. As Money was writing to England, I requested him to mention the rebel surgeon.

If you can find a proper person for a Provost, I wish you would appoint one and send the serjeant who acts in that capacity to join his regiment.

It is difficult to know what to do about the prisoners. I found it in many cases impossible to get either their crimes or prosecutors. If there are still several who were in our militia and afterwards joined the enemy, another example or two would be very proper. A certain number of the most violent and most capable of doing mischief such as Alexander etc should be kept in prison to awe the enemy from putting any of our friends to death. The rest you will please either to parole or to send to Charlestown as prisoners of war whenever any more of the wounded prisoners are fit to proceed thither. In chusing the proper objects for each, I trust totally to your discretion.

I am, sir, with great regard
Your most obedient and faithfull servant

CORNWALLIS

[*Subscribed:*]

You will please to continue sending the expresses on the west side of the river, directing them to pass the Catawbaw at Blair's Mill.

Turnbull to Cornwallis, 12th September 1780 64(48): ALS

Camden
September 12th 1780

Lord Cornwallis

My Lord

I have had the honor to receive your letter of yesterday, and as you don't fix any time for their departure and as Major McArthur has wrote to Despard[2] on that subject, he means to wait his answer.

I hear nothing of the 7th Regiment. We have had some good supplys of flour and cattle lately.

Captain King brings your Lordship's dispatches from England. I have mounted three dragoons out of Major England's yard, as I dislike that of pressing if it can be avoided.

Two men from North Carolina and one from Lynches Creek bring some confused acount of Captain Kemble's company being defeated by the rebels. They cou'd not tell any thing about killed or wounded, but they say that Kemble[3] run of[4] before it began.

Two other gentlemen from North Carolina mention that our militia in that quarter do a great deal of mischief. We shall hear more of this matter soon. A detachment of Lord Rawden's and the 23rd will leave this on Thursday morning. I forgot to mention that a Mr McDonald[5], an assistant commissary, arrived some days ago.

---

[2] John Despard (1745-1829) entered the 12th Regiment as an ensign in 1760 and became a lieutenant in the army in 1762. After serving in Germany, he transferred to the 7th Regiment (Royal Fusiliers) and came with them to Quebec in March 1773. Taken prisoner at St Johns in November 1775, he was exchanged in December 1776 and joined the army at New York. He went on to take part in the capture of Fort Montgomery on 6th October 1777 and, perhaps for some act of bravery there, was promoted to captain in his regiment with effect from the following day. In June 1778 he transferred to the Provincial establishment, becoming major in Rawdon's newly forming Volunteers of Ireland. Eighteen months later he was appointed a deputy adjutant general and, having been present at the capture of Charlestown, would accompany Cornwallis throughout his campaigns. After the war he served on the staff of the army and was promoted to colonel in 1795 and to major general three years later. From 1800 to 1807 he was Governor of Cape Breton and in 1814 became a full general. He is said to have been in twenty-four engagements and to have been shipwrecked three times. He died at Oswestry. (*Appletons'*; *Army Lists*)

[3] Perhaps John Kimble, who resided in the neighbourhood of Lynches Creek. (Joan A Inabinet, 'Local Revolutionary Kin? Search a list from "Clermont" (Rugeley's)', *Newsletter of the Catawba-Wateree Genealogical Society* (Camden SC), January 2002)

[4] *run of*: ran off.

[5] McDonald was to serve as an assistant commissary at Camden until its evacuation in May 1781. He was still serving in South Carolina ten months later. (*The Cornwallis Papers*)

I am with the greatest respect
Your Lordship's most obedient humble servant

GEO TURNBULL

Cary to Turnbull, 18th September 1780[6] 64(70): ALS

18th September 1780
Monday, 1 o'clock afternoon

Lt Colonel Geo Turnbull
Commandant etc at Camden

Sir

I have just now received intelligence that Colonel Brown at Augusta is attacked by a great number of rebels from the uper part of Georgia and is drove from the barrocks to the sand barr about three miles from the barrocks.

I understand the inhabitants of the uper parts of Georgia called the New Purchase are all intirely imbodied themselves and come down on him. I believe the intelligence to be true or nearly so.

I am, sir,
Your most obedient humble servant

JA[S] CARY
Colonel of Royal Militia

Turnbull to Cornwallis, 22nd September 1780 64(102): ALS

Camden
September 22nd 1780

The Rt Hon Earl of Cornwallis

My Lord

I send you some newspapers which I received last night from Charlestown.

Doctor Hill persuaded me to change my quarters three days ago and am now with Major England and Mr Haldane, and whither it is change of air or cheerfull company I cannot say, but I find myself amazingly alter'd for the better.

---

[6] Apparently forwarded by Turnbull without an accompanying letter.

Our works goes on tolerably well but we can't prevent the Negroes from deserting.

Colonel Innes's regiment makes but a very sorry appearance. I have never been able to get a state, which I shall forward as soon I receive, but they do duty for one hundred and sixty rank and file.

Major Pinckney has apply'd for a pass for his servant to bring your Lordship some memorial about his making a longer stay than fourteen days at his father in law's at the Congarees.

I have told him whatever dispatches he had to send shou'd be most faithfully forwarded, but cou'd not consent to give his servant a pass to the British Army.

I have the honor to be with the greatest respect
Your Lordship's most obedient humble servant

GEO TURNBULL

Pinckney to Money, 22nd September 1780[7]   3(84): ALS

Camden
September 22nd 1780

Major Money

Sir

The favors which your politeness and humanity have already induced you to confer on myself and family encourage me to give you this additional trouble.

It may be almost needless, sir, to remind you that in the action of the 16th ultimo I received a wound in my left leg from a musquet ball which broke both the bones and splinter'd them very considerably. From the nature and situation of this wound the cure will necessarily be very tedious (Dr Hayes informs me it will require 3 or 4 months) and I am at present much reduced by the discharge from it and the confinement to my bed. The unhealthiness of this place and the impracticability of procuring necessaries proper for the sick here must, sir, be well known to you, sir, and it was these considerations which I apprehend induced Dr Hayes to recommend my removal by water, which he did in the strongest terms and was joined in opinion by the gentleman who now attends me.

Under these circumstances I applied to Colonel Turnbull for permission to be removed for the completion of my cure to my father in law Mr Motte's plantation, to which place I can be removed in my bed by water. There I may have a surgeon (who lives in the neighbourhood) to attend me, may expect to have the greatest attention paid me, and to be

---

[7] Forwarded by Turnbull on 23rd September with its enclosure. He did not write an accompanying letter.

supplied with necessaries which this place does not afford. Colonel Turnbul did not think proper to grant this permission 'till he should be acquainted with Lord Cornwallis's pleasure, of which he this day apprized me, informing me that his Lordship 'had no objections to my going to my father in law's at the Congarees but limited *this visit* to fourteen days, after which I must join the other field officers on parole at Orangeburg'.[8] From this, sir, I fear it is understood that I am either perfectly or nearly recover'd and only wish to pay a visit of convenience or pleasure to my family, but you may be assured, sir, that it is principally a measure taken for the recovery of my health. Of the state of my wound I will endeavor to procure and enclose a certificate from the gentleman of the faculty who now attends me, and am very sorry that Dr Hayes being absent in Charles Town prevents my conveying to you his sentiments on my case.

What I have therefore, sir, to request of you is that you will make the above representation of my case to Lord Cornwallis and endeavor to procure his Lordship's permission for me to remain at Mr Motte's 'till my wound shall be cured, immediately after which I will join the other field officers at Orangeburg. Within a fortnight I fear it will be impossible for me to be removed by land, which is the only way I can go to Orangeburg, and even if I could get there I should be destitute of the assistance of a surgeon and of those necessaries and attendance of which I absolutely stand in need. Be assured, sir, that I do not mean to stay longer from the place appointed for my confinement than my health will require and than the surgeons shall be willing to certify the necessity of.

I have many apologies to make, sir, to you for giving you this trouble and have to request the favor of an answer by the first opportunity. In the meantime I remain with sentiments of personal esteem, sir,

Your much obliged and most obedient servant

THOMAS PINCKNEY[9]

---

[8] See England to Cornwallis, 18th September, and Cornwallis's reply of the 20th, pp 271-3.

[9] Educated in England like his brother Charles Cotesworth (p 111, note 103), and like him admitted to the Middle Temple there, Thomas Pinckney (1750-1828) was a major in the 1st South Carolina Continental Regiment and a member of the South Carolina revolutionary assembly. Sent out of Charlestown before the capitulation to hasten troops for its relief, he had joined Gates in North Carolina and been employed by him as an aide-de-camp. Cornwallis would now permit him to repair to the home of his father-in-law, Jacob Motte, where he would slowly recover, but his wound was to trouble him for years to come. In June 1781 he would be exchanged under the cartel with Greene and be elected to the revolutionary assembly which met at Jacksonborough. After the war he would play a prominent role in public affairs, being elected Governor of South Carolina before being appointed Minister to the Court of St James and Envoy Extraordinary to Spain. He was then elected to Congress. In 1822 he published a pamphlet in which, among other things, he attacked the movement for the abolition of slavery. He is described as tall and spare in figure, poised and self-controlled, with great personal dignity, but with delightfully easy and courteous manners. Charles Pinckney (vol I, p 311, note 8) was his cousin. (*DAB*; McCrady, *SC in the Rev 1775-1780* and *1780-1783, passim*; Heitman, *Historical Register*, 442)

Enclosure
Medical certificate pertaining to Thomas Pinckney　　　　　　　　*3(86): ADS*

Camden
September 23rd 1780

This is to certify that Major Thomas Pinkny is unable to be removed to Orangeburgh on account of his wound which he received on the 16th of August. At the same time I think change of air will conduce greatly to his recovery if it can be done by water carrage. I likewise am of opinion that it will be two or three months before he can have the use of his leg so as to be conveyed any distance by land.

THO^S GIBB[10]
Surgeon, New York Volunteers

Cornwallis to Turnbull, 24th September 1780　　　　　　　　*80(45): C*

Waxhaw
September 24th 1780

Lt Colonel Turnbull
Commanding at Camden

Dear Sir

I received by Captain Kinlock your letter of the 22nd and am sincerely glad to hear that you are so much better. May I beg to trouble you to give the inclosed[11] to Major Moncrief.

I am told the rebel prisoners desert from their hospital very fast. As all those men are going to fight against us, I trust you will do every thing in your power to prevent it [by] the sending them in small divisions as fast as they recover under militia guard and paying the militia so much a head for every one they deliver up to the Commandant of Charlestown. You will please to allow them as much as you think will be an inducement for them to take care of them.

You will please to take every opportunity of send[ing] convalescents to us.

I consent to Major Pinkney's going as soon as he can be removed to his father in law's. He will report his arrival there to Colonel Balfour and will inform him that he has my permission to remain there untill his wound is well enough to allow him to travel unless Colonel Balfour should see cause to alter it.

---

[10] Thomas Gibb would resign before the close of the war, being succeeded by Francis Brindley, and therefore was not placed on the Provincial half-pay list. (Treasury 64/23(1) (National Archives, Kew))

[11] *the inclosed*: no extant copy. It contained orders to return to Charlestown.

I am, sir,
Your most obedient and faithful servant

CORNWALLIS

Cornwallis to Turnbull, 27th September 1780   80(52): C

Charlottetown
September 27th 1780

Lt Colonel Turnbull
Commanding at Camden

Dear Sir

Major Wemyss writes me word[12] that he has failed in raising a militia at Cheraws and that Colonel Mills had entirely given it up. It is absolutely necessary that we should leave no means untried to establish some force in that country to keep the balance if possible and not leave all the tract east of Santee to the mercy of the enemy. Moncrieff has established a militia at George Town under Colonel Cassels. I am sure by the appearance of those persons who came with Harrison that we must have some friends in that quarter. I therefore desire that when Wemyss arrives at Camden, you will order Major Frazer with 50 of the eldest soldiers of Innes's corps to be mounted on some of the horses which Wemyss's detachment or the 7th Regiment may bring in, but not on any that would do for the Legion; to march into that country and to get Harrison to join him with what he can collect; and to endeavour to form either a militia under Lt Colonel Grey, who was in Mills's regiment, or to raise two or three independent companys under Harrison, or in short by any means to get two or three hundred men in arms to cooperate with Colonel Cassels and with the militia which Colonel Balfour has ordered on both sides of the Santee. I send you an extract of his letter[13] that you may the better understand his plan. I would have the 7th Regiment sent up to the army as soon as possible. The 63rd and Hamilton's corps will require some time at Camden, especially the latter. I desired Colonel Balfour to send up twenty puncheons more of rum and I would have Colonel Hamilton stay to bring it up unless he hears further from me. I have likewise requested that Colonel Balfour would continue to send rum up to Camden as the post here must be supplied from thence. By the assistance of the militia, some mounted men and the post which, after the business of the Ceded Lands is over, Cruger will establish on the Tyger or Ennoree, the communication between Camden and Charlottetown will, I hope, be tolerably safe for convoys of no great value. We must now and then expect accidents in this complicated and difficult service. I would have a few days' interval between the march of the 7th and 63rd, and Colonel Hamilton will not march untill he hears from me. Major England will come up either with the 7th or 63rd. The 71st remain still at Waxhaw, to which place their convalescents should be sent by every opportunity as it will contribute

---

[12] *Wemyss writes me word*: on 20th September, p 214.

[13] *his letter*: Balfour to Cornwallis, 20th September, p 90.

to their health and to ease you at Camden.

I am, sir,
Your most obedient and faithfull servant

CORNWALLIS

PS

Sumpter with about 300 mounted men passed the Catawbaw at Bigger's Ferry. I am not yet sure whether he is gone up or down the river, but I think up. You will do all you can to procure intelligence from all quarters. I am never economical on that head.

Turnbull to Cornwallis, 25th September 1780   *64(110): ALS*

Camden
September 25th 1780

Lord Cornwallis

My Lord

A number of letters having arrived to day from Charlestown, we agreed it was best to send them forward.

Colonel Innes has seized all the Provincial cloathing in store at Charlestown for his own corps, so that we must wait untill a fleet arrives from New York.

Mr Treville arrived here last night and we had an acount from Augusta by one Allen, a trader, that Colonel Cruger had reinstated Mr Brown in his command or in other words had drove the rebels from that quarter.

We have heard of Wemyss by a deserter who came in to day. He is at Long Bluff upon Pedee.

I have the honor to be with much respect
Your Lordship's most obedient humble servant

GEO TURNBULL

Cornwallis to Turnbull, 29th September 1780   80(57): C

Charlottetown
September 29th 1780

Lt Colonel Turnbull
Commanding at Camden

Sir

In my letter of the 27th relative to the march of the troops I did not mention the two six pounders and the artillery stores. I wish you to send them by the 63rd Regiment, and to give me notice of their march, and to direct Major Wemyss to halt with Major McArthur at Waxhaw unless he receives orders from me. The 7th Regiment you will send on immediately to Charlottetown according to former orders. Dr Harper has been a great sufferer and very active and zealous in our service. If he makes any application to you for some provisions, you will please to comply with his request. If the artillery wants horses, you will give them every assistance.

I am, sir,
Your very obedient etc

CORNWALLIS

Turnbull to Cornwallis, 28th September 1780   64(124): ALS

Camden
September 28th 1780

My Lord

I had the honor to receive your letter of the 24th instant two days ago.

Major Moncrief is not yet arrived, nor do we know where he and the 7th Regiment are.

Major England had a letter from Major Wemyss yesterday. He talks of being here in about eight days.

With regard to the rebell prisoners, I have fixed a place for those who are recovering and able to walk and keep a constant guard upon them. They are too weak yet to march, but we propose sending as many of[14] as we can the first boats which arrives.

I can assure your Lordship that there has been no desertion among them this fourtnight. There was indeed a considerable desertion between the 6th instant and the day which Mr

---

[14] *of..*: off.

Booth[15] left this, which was, I think, about the 11th or 12th.

He never came nigh me untill he was booted and spurr'd ready to set off, and then gave me a return of the number of rebell prisoners dated the 6th. Perhaps the man might have been sick, and it was very unlucky that I was so much indisposed that that affair never ocurred untill the return was put into my hand by Mr Booth. We have still remaining about eighty and I believe about one hundred had made their escape.

In a couple of days we shall be able to send forward a great number of convalescents.

By a letter from a Captain Youman[16] of Colonel Innes's, acting lt colonel of militia at Coosahatchie: that about twenty of the inhabitants of that district had endeavour'd to join the rebels of Augusta, but upon hearing of Colonel Cruger's driving them of, they have return'd and lye out in the bushes; that he had embody'd his militia, trying to catch them; that they had killed one but were at a loss how to victual their militia. I have order'd him to give receipts for their provisions while on such duty and every two months to bring those receipts to the Commandant of Charlestown, who wou'd examine them and cancel them.

While I am writing, Moncrief has arrived. He will write your Lordship[17].

I am with the utmost respect
Your Lordship's most obedient humble servant

GEO TURNBULL

Cornwallis to Turnbull, 1st October 1780

81(5): C

Charlottetown
October 1st 1780

Lt Colonel Turnbull
Commanding at Camden

Dear Sir

I last night received yours of the 28th and am glad to hear of the arrival of the 7th Regiment. I must desire that you will lose no time in sending out the detachment under

---

[15] Having left Camden as a commissary of prisoners, Booth would soon resurface at Winnsborough as a commissary of captures. As such he would accompany Cornwallis into Virginia and fall captive with him at Yorktown. While there, he wrote interesting guidance for the conduct of his assistants, a copy of which appears later in these Papers. (*The Cornwallis Papers*)

[16] Levi Youman(s) had been commissioned a captain in the South Carolina Royalist Regiment on 24th August 1779. By September 1782, when he was a refugee in Charlestown, he would have resigned his commission and consequently was not placed on the Provincial half-pay list at the close of the war. (Clark, *Loyalists in the Southern Campaign*, i, 39, 525-6)

[17] Moncrief to Cornwallis, 28th September, p 266.

Major Frazer, which I mentioned in my letter of the 27th, after the arrival of Major Wemyss. If Major Frazer should be sick or unable to go, you will chuse some other officer. You will receive a copy of a proclamation[18] which I would have circulated in that country, it being the only means of disarming the people who have fled, and who will be constantly troublesome as long as they are kept from home. You will please to forward the letter to Lt Colonel Cruger[19].

I am, sir,
Your most obedient and most faithfull servant

[CORNWALLIS]

Cornwallis to Turnbull, 2nd October 1780

81(8): C

Charlottetown
October 2nd 1780

Lt Colonel Turnbull
Commanding at Camden

Dear Sir

By a letter which I received this day from Major Wemyss[20] I am very uneasy about all the lower country and am much afraid that the two regiments of militia of Ball and Wigfall and that lately embodied by Colonel Cassels will meet with some serious disaster which will be exceedingly prejudicial to His Majesty's Service. I must therefore beg that you will add thirty good men of the New York Volunteers to the fifty which I directed you to detach under Major Frazer and order Harrison and some of the best militia you can get to go with him. His object must be to prevent the enemy from undertaking any thing against our militia posts, for which purpose he should keep constantly moving, spare no pains or expence to get intelligence of the enemy, and always give them a blow when he can do it with advantage. By conversing with Major Wemyss and Colonel Grey he will get a better idea of the country and the service than I can give him. As soon as Colonel Grey returns from Charlestown, he will assist him in embodying a militia.

As this addition to Major Frazer's detachment will considerably weaken your post, I would have you, when Lt Colonel Hamilton leaves Camden, detain thirty of the convalescents belonging to the different corps here of those that appear to be the least able to go through long and severe marches, and let it fall as equally as possible amongst the corps. Major Frazer's detachment will of course be all mounted, and I must again recommend that no time

---

[18] *a proclamation*: see p 331, note 20.

[19] *the letter to Lt Colonel Cruger*: of 1st October, p 193.

[20] *a letter..*: of 30th September, p 216.

may be lost in their moving. As I have heard a very good character of Major Frazer, I have no doubt of his acquitting himself well in this difficult command. It will be necessary that he should pay attention to the health of his men and not place himself in low and swampy ground unless it is absolutely necessary.

I am, sir, etc

[CORNWALLIS]

Turnbull to Cornwallis, 1st October 1780

3(164): ALS

Camden
October 1st 1780

The Earl Cornwallis

My Lord

I was favour'd with your letter of the 27th September two days ago, when Moncrief and the 7th Regiment arrived. Moncrief sets out this day for Charlestown, and the 7th Regiment with about 160 convalescents will march tomorrow for the army. They will bring up eight puncheons of rum.

Colonel Mills from the Cheraws came in last night, demanding arms for his militia, which I am afraid I will have but very few to give him. I imagin'd that we had 200 French muskets in store when your Lordship march't, and I find there was only 100. Sixty I have given to Phillips' regiment and some to the Rocky Mount people, nine to Lord Rawdern.

Mills says that Major Wemyss waits your Lordship's orders at Cheraws.

Major Moncrief says he thinks that Black River wou'd be far enough for us to extend our troops, that Pedee is such a distance and so very extensive that a party cou'd have no support.

Major Fraser is still very ill of his wound[21], but fifty men of Innes's shall be sent with Harrison's corps agreable to your Lordship's orders.

I have superceeded Colonel Turner for absenting himself from his duty. It seems he had been at Charlestown selling tobacco, and never made his appearance till last night. It makes me blush to think I recommended such a man.

I have just received intelligence of a small party of 20 rebels at Water Eye[22] Creek about twenty five miles from this and have sent a party of Carey's militia after them.

---

[21] *his wound*: received in the action at Musgrove's Mill on 19th August.

[22] *Water Eye*: Wateree.

Yesterday I received a letter from Messrs Ancrum and Lord at the Congarees with a copy of an order they had received from Colonel Balfour the 13th of June empowring them to take charge of all publick stores. They complain that the commissary took away corn without giving receipts. I answer'd that he never took corn on that footing except rebell property, and even that he cou'd give a certificate of the quantity [for].

These gentlemen have got on the right side of Colonel Balfour and Colonel Innes. Colonel Carey is sent for to town, which we suppose is on a complaint of Lord and Ancrum. From Innes's letter to me I am pretty sure it is so.

I have the honor to be with the greatest respect
Your Lordship's most obedient humble servant

GEO TURNBULL

Cornwallis to Turnbull, 3rd October 1780

81(15): C

Charlottetown
October 3rd 1780

Lt Colonel Turnbull
Commanding at Camden

Dear Sir

I have this instant received yours of the 1st and am very sorry that Major Frazer is too ill to undertake the service I intended for him. If Captain Coffin of your corps is at Camden, he may probably be a proper person to command the party. If not, I trust to your appointing the best man that you can. My chief object is to prevent any affront or misfortune happening to our militia on the east of Santee. The more of the country we can safely keep, the better, but if the Pedee is thought too far, I shall be satisfied with the protection of our militia and of the Santee, to which their partys must never advance with impunity if we can help it. If Captain Coffin undertakes this service, I beg you will assure him that I shall endeavour to make it turn out to his advantage.

I have taken care to represent the characters of Lord, Ancrum and Carey in their proper colours[23]. Carey is now gone to Balfour to settle the best mode of forming some plan of militia on the Congarees, where we are very defective, and which is at a great distance from Carey.

I have an exceeding good opinion of Carey's honesty and loyalty and will support him against all malicious attacks.

I am, sir, etc

[CORNWALLIS]

---

[23] See Cornwallis to Balfour, 3rd and 6th September, p 71.

Turnbull to Cornwallis, 2nd October 1780 *3(172): ALS*

Camden
October 2nd 1780

The Earl Cornwallis

My Lord

This morning the 7th Regiment has marched with about one hundred and sixty convalescents. The reason that those of the Legion were not of the number: Captain Hovenden[24] told me that he expected some of their appointments dayly from Charlestown, so that I think they have a chance to come with Wemyss, who is, by the by, still at the Cheraws.

I went to the store and found sixty one French muskets, which I deliver'd to Colonel Mills and gave him ammunition for one hundred and eighty men. Colonel Mills thinks that a post at Port's Ferry, five miles above the mouth of Lynches Creek and forty miles from Georgetown, will be the properest place at least for a commencement, and he has got a Major Ford[25], who I have order'd to take post there untill your Lordship's pleasure is known.

When Harrison's corps comes in, we shall try to fit them out as well as we can, and Major Fraser is getting much better. I hope in a few weeks he will be able to take that command. They are expecting a large number of men dayly to join them. Your Lordship will see, by the return[26] I send to Major Despard of the state of the troops at Camden, that regiment[27] has only ninety one fit for duty. There is a number down of the small pox.

---

[24] At the outbreak of the war Richard Hovenden (*c.* 1750-*c.* 1810) was a trader living in Newton Township, Bucks County, Pennsylvania. At the beginning of 1778 he commanded a loyalist unit known as the Pennsylvania Light Dragoons. When it was absorbed later in the year into the cavalry of the British Legion, he accompanied it and was commissioned a captain on the Provincial establishment with effect from 25th August 1778. When last noticed in these Papers, which occurs on 8th November, Cornwallis remarks, 'Captain Hovenden is very ill and I fear will never be fit for any service.' He nevertheless went on to serve in North Carolina and Virginia and was among the troops who capitulated at Yorktown. After the war he was placed on the British half-pay list and migrated to Ireland. In 1798 he was promoted to lt colonel on the active list, moved to England, and served for about three years as recruiting officer for the 21st Light Dragoons. Retiring again to Ireland, he became a Justice of the Peace for Queen's County. During his service in the British Legion a younger brother Moore was a lieutenant in his troop of horse. (Margaret Baskin, 'Richard, Moore and John Hovenden', *Banastre Tarleton and the British Legion: Friends, Comrades and Enemies* (www.banastretarleton.org, 30th June 2005); Donald J Gara, 'Biographical Sketches on Cavalry Officers of the British Legion 1778-1782' (*The On-Line Institute for Advanced Loyalist Studies*, 24th June 2005); WO 65/164(38) (National Archives, Kew); *The Cornwallis Papers*)

[25] James Ford was a major of militia from the Cheraws. By June 1781 he would have fled to Charlestown, where he remained until at least the early summer of 1782. (Clark, *Loyalists in the Southern Campaign*, i, 492-5) According to Moss (*SC Patriots*, 323), a James Ford was a captain in the revolutionary militia of St David's Parish in 1776. If he was the same man, Moss appears to be mistaken in stating that he served in Marion's Brigade as a captain.

[26] *the return*: not extant.

[27] *that regiment*: the South Carolina Royalist Regiment.

I mention'd in my last my having superceded Colonel Turner for absenting himself from his duty. He saw Colonel Balfour at Charlestown, who gave him a number of blank commissions for justices of the peace. It is a matter I don't well undestand. Besides, I know severall districts where there are not a single man fit for such an office, particularly that where Turner commanded.

Our commissary branch at this place has been but very badly carry'd on. We can scarcely get flour for the sick. The indian meal, it seems, gives them a looseness. Mr Kneght has set out to join your Lordship. I think he is either a fool or a knave.

Poor Captain Cotton[28] of the 33rd died Saturday evening and we buried him yesterday with every mark of honor.

I am with the utmost respect
Your Lordship's most obedient humble servant

GEO TURNBULL

Cornwallis to Turnbull, 5th October 1780   81(21): C

Charlottetown
October 5th 1780

Lt Colonel Turnbull
Commanding at Camden

Dear Sir

I am sorry to find that you are distressed for flour at Camden. I was assured positively that should not be the case. What was coming to us from Broad River is now ordered to you. In the affair of Colonel Turner you will do as you think fit and supercede him if he deserves it. You will, however, acquaint Colonel Balfour and correspond constantly with him about all business, military as well as civil. You will of course give me every military intelligence, but it is impossible for me, in the distant service in which I am engaged, to direct the civil regulations. I have fully explained my general ideas on those subjects to Colonel Balfour. I understand from Wemyss that Mills had given up all hopes of forming a militia and had desired to go with his family to a distant part of the country, in consequence of which I had desired Colonel Balfour to give a colonel's commission to Lt Colonel Grey, who did not seem inclined to give the matter up. You will be kind enough to have this matter explained. At any rate I am sorry that you let them have any French firelocks. I am convinced it is throwing away good arms or, what is worse, helping the enemy by giving them to the militia. As I have removed the 1st Battalion of the 71st from Waxhaw to Armer's Ford, our

---

[28] Richard Cotton had spent his entire service in the 33rd Regiment. Commissioned an ensign on 17th March 1769, he was promoted to lieutenant on 27th January 1774 and to captain on 25th December 1776. He died of wounds received at the Battle of Camden. (*Army Lists*)

communication will be more uncertain. You will therefore be the more carefull about letters of consequence.

I am, sir, etc

[CORNWALLIS]

Turnbull to Cornwallis, 4th October 1780   3(178): ALS

Camden
October 4th 1780

Earl Cornwallis

My Lord

I am to acknowledge the receipt of your letters of the 1st, 2nd and 3rd instant.

Major Wemyss arrived this forenoon. He has wrote your Lordship[29]. Colonel Balfour's ideas of militia, I am afraid, goes too high. We have a recent instance of that and the indulgence shown to rebels who were in the last revolt.

About fourteen of the most noted rebels were muster'd at Georgetown by officers of militia, who, I suppose, wanted to be popular; but Captain De Peyster told Moncrief that severall of the militia which he had muster'd were noted rebels, broke their parole, and Wemyss had burnt their houses. He said he hoped it wou'd be for the good of the service.

By this and other misfortunes George Town is abandon'd. Balfour recommends a movement from this quarter, not knowing our strength or the situation of the Cheraws.

Wemyss says positively that three out of four inhabitants are rebels in that country. Mr Marion, who took posession of Georgetown, has about 400. Mr Wade upon Pedee has as many.

Harrison's corps, Wemyss says, are not worth any thing. There is but fifty of them, irregular and plunderers, and are all dispersed. He is now gone to assemble them, and in a week, I suppose, we may see him.

Major Fraser can't set a foot to the ground as yet. Captain Coffin is gone to Charlestown to try to get cloathing for the regiment. Colonel Mills is gone some where with his family, and his militia is not collected. When Major Wemyss cou'd not establish a militia when he was there with a force, I don't know what eighty Provincials wou'd do. I should look upon myself as highly culpable at present were I to send out any small detachment to be sacrificed; therefore shall wait your Lordship's further orders.

---

[29] On 4th October, p 219.

Depend upon it, militia will never do any good without regular troops.

Your Lordship will be pleased to observe that Colonel Innes's corps and ours makes only 247 men fit for duty. The rest of the troops here are all attached to your Lordship's army.

Major Wemyss has mention'd to me that if two or three hundred regulars cou'd be spared, he thinks it practicable, with the asisstance of some militia, to take posession of Cape Fare and Cross Creek. There are a number of Scots inhabitants who wish to join us but they have no arms. If we once got there, the Cheraws and Pedee wou'd be hemm'd in. This is an idea of Major Wemyss. I have seen Colonel Grey, who I think a good kind of man – much better than Mills.

His ideas and Major Wemyss' correspond very much about establishing a militia at the Cheraws. The people are running away bag and baggidge.

Balfour talks of retaking posession of Georgetown in three or four days. If he sends all militia, I doubt very much his success. He is puffed up with the number of regiments of militia and does not consider that our officers of militia in general are not near so active as the rebels, and great numbers of their privates are ready to turn against us when an opportunity offers.

A quantity of rum etc will be here in a few days.

I have been unlucky enough to have a third attack of the fever and it is even with pain now that I write.

I am with the utmost respect
Your Lordship's most obedient humble servant

GEO TURNBULL

Cornwallis to Turnbull, 7th October 1780   81(30): A(in part) C

Charlottetown
October 7th 1780

Lt Colonel Turnbull
Commanding at Camden

Sir

I received yesterday your letter of the 4th. Unluckily, by some mistake my letters for Charles Town were sent back to this place. It gives me great concern to hear of your relapse. I have written very fully to Wemyss[30] about the principal business and directed him to shew

---

[30] On 7th October, p 222.

the contents to you. As soon as the medicines and rum arrive, I would have Hamilton's corps proceed to this place with the two six pounders. You will please to give me notice two days before they set out that I may take precautions in case I apprehend any risk. As you will soon get a fresh supply of rum from Charlestown, you will please to send as much as possible to us. Colonel Cruger writes me word[31] that he has sent five waggons loaded with flour to Camden. You had better detain those waggons to help to bring up the stores.

I am, sir,
Your most obedient humble servant

[CORNWALLIS]

[*Subscribed*:]

As I find the duplicate of this letter has fallen into the enemy's hands, you will please to send duplicates in cypher of the intended march of Hamilton's corps and at the same time send a letter not written in cypher to mention their march at least ten days distant from the real time and to say that for fear of parties coming over the Catawba they will march the old Salisbury road. You will write this in a separate letter.

Money to Turnbull, 11th October 1780 *81(37): ACS*

Charlottetown
October 11th 1780

Lt Colonel Turnbull
Commanding at Camden

Sir

Lord Cornwallis desires you *will order Lt Colonel Hamilton to march with his corps to this place as soon after the arrival of the stores from Charlestown as possible.* You will *send by this opportunity the two six pounders as formerly mentioned by his Lordship* and *all the recovered men who are able to march belonging to the regiments here excepting thirty*, which you will *detain in the room of that number of the* New York Volunteers *to be sent with Major Wemyss, taking them as equally as possible from* the *different regiments. You will also send a quantity of salt, as you will have an opportunity of being* immediately *supplied with that article from Charlestown. If Lt Colonel Hamilton wants any of the Provincial stores for his regiment which were intended for Major Harrison's corps, you will be pleased to give orders for his* receiving them.

I am, sir, etc

JM

---

[31] On 2nd October, p 197.

PS

Lord Cornwallis consents to Dr Williamson's[32] returning if you have no objection and to Colonel Porterfield's sending out for a chair and horse by the 1st flag.

JM

Since writing the above, his Lordship has determined that *the sick of the 7th Regiment should remain at Camden*. You will not therefore *detain thirty convalescents as first ordered*.

The recovered men of the *Fuzileers will most likely be more than equal to that number*.

JM

Money to Turnbull, 12th October 1780   81(39): ACS

Charlottetown
October 12th 1780
Ten in the morning

Lt Colonel Turnbull
Commanding at Camden

Sir

Lord Cornwallis desires me to inform you that Colonel Hamilton's corps is not to march from Camden till further orders. If Major Wemyss has left Camden, you will immediately send him orders to return. If he has not marched, you will acquaint him that the 63rd Regiment is to remain at Camden till further orders.

I am etc

[JM]

PS

You will be pleased to communicate the contents of this letter to Lt Colonel Balfour at Charlestown as soon as possible.

JM

---

[32] Of Scottish descent, Hugh Williamson MD LLD (1735-1819) was born in Philadelphia and had been educated there and in Edinburgh and Holland. Now a physician in the service of North Carolina, he had in August been sent into Camden by Richard Caswell to attend the wounded revolutionary prisoners there. He would go on to represent North Carolina in Congress and in the convention which framed the Federal Constitution, of which he was a staunch advocate. He published *Observations on the Climate of America*, a *History of North Carolina* (3 vols), and other works. (D MacDougall ed, *Scots and Scots' Descendants in America* (New York, 1917); Mary C Gillett, *The Army Medical Department 1775-1818* (University Press of the Pacific, 2002); *The Cornwallis Papers*)

Turnbull to Cornwallis, 12th October 1780
3(214): ALS

Camden
October 12th 1780

Earl Cornwallis

My Lord

I am to acknowledge the receipt of your letters of the 5th and 7th instant and shall take very particular care to report to Colonel Balfour every thing worth his notice.

I find that a Major Ford, who came here with Mills, has assembled about one hundred and fifty militia. I have sent him orders to fall back to Ractliff's Bridge, where he will be very safe untill a reinforcement arrives.

With regard to Mills, I think the mistake is lucky. He has thrown himself out by giving up the matter. Mills' character is very doubtfull and not popular. Grey's is good and I think will answer our purpose better.

The rum and salt I am told is on the road but they advance slowly owing, I suppose, to the weakness of the horses.

A reports prevaills since last night that General Somner is assembling a number of men at the Cheraws. If so, it must be intended against us. I shall send out some people immediately for intelligence, and your Lordship may be assured that I shall take every precaution in my power for the defence of this place.

Believe me to be with the greatest respect
Your Lordship's most obedient humble servant

GEO TURNBULL

Rawdon to Turnbull, 16th October 1780[33]
3(233) ACS

October 16th 1780

Lt Colonel Turnbull
Commanding at Camden

Sir

In a note which I yesterday addressed to Lt Colonel Hamilton[34] I signified to him Lord Cornwallis's directions that untill further orders he should remain at Camden with the

---

[33] According to Turnbull's letter of 20th October (p 256), this letter and the note to which it refers miscarried.

[34] *a note..*: see p 231.

detachment etc which was to have marched under his command. In the same note (which was ordered to be forwarded to you) it was prescribed that you should send the 63rd Regiment, *mounted*, as soon as possible to put themselves under the command of Lt Colonel Cruger at Ninety Six. Lest the note should have failed, I now repeat by Lord Cornwallis's orders the above directions, and have the honor to be, sir, with great regard

Your most obedient servant

RAWDON

[*Superscribed*:]

Dispatched from Steel Creek on the 16th at eight at night.

Turnbull to Cornwallis, 17th October 1780

3(237): ALS

Camden
October 17th 1780

Earl Cornwallis

My Lord

I am to acknowledge the receipt of your letter of the 12th instant by your servant.

The adjutant of the 23rd has likewise come in here. *We have a large packet of letters from the Commander in Chief for you, and report says that an embarkation was to take place for Cheaseapeak under the command of General Leslie.*

Poor Stapleton[35] died some days ago.

I am with the utmost respect
Your Lordship's most obedient humble servant

GEO TURNBULL

---

[35] Wynne Stapleton, surgeon to the British Legion. See vol I, p 207, note 33.

Rawdon to Turnbull, 19th October 1780

3(241): C

Waxhaw
October 19th 1780

Lt Colonel Turnbull
Commanding at Camden

Dear Sir

We propose to encamp to morrow near Blair's Mill on the Catawba River in this district. I request that you will send to me thither, with as much dispatch as possible, all the information you can respecting Charlestown, New York and Ninety Six, concerning all which we are perfectly ignorant. You had better send expresses to me by both sides of the river. Those whom you send by the Rockey Mount road may cross at a ford close to Blair's. I hope you have received instructions which were sent to you directing that the march of Lt Colonel Hamilton with the stores etc should be postpon'd. Let them, however, be held in readiness to move upon the shortest orders, and inform me whether they can with safety be spared from your garrison.

I likewise sent you directions that Major Wemyss should immediately march with the 63rd Regiment (mounted) to put himself under the command of Cruger at Ninety Six, which movement I hope has taken place.

We do not know of any enemy near us and I believe they certainly are not collected any where in force, but our present possessions must be thoroughly secured before we aim at further acquisitions.

Lord Cornwallis is indisposed with a fever — not violent, however. You shall hear from me to morrow, and I again request that you will lose no time in communicating with, dear sir,

Your very faithfull servant

RAWDON

[*Endorsed*:]

Dispatched on the night of the 19th.

Rawdon to Turnbull, 20th October 1780   3(245): CS

Blair's Mill on the Catawba
October 20th 1780

Lt Colonel Turnbull
Commanding at Camden

Dear Sir

The weather bears so much appearance of rain that I think it necessary to pass the river to morrow lest I should not be able to do it hereafter, and my incertitude relative to the condition of the Ninety Six District makes me anxious to get within reach of succouring that post should it prove needfull. To morrow I shall halt on the opposite bank. The day after I shall proceed to Fishing Creek, but to what particular part of it I cannot yet ascertain as it will depend upon the accounts I receive of wheat and forage. You may, however, dispatch some rum for us under escort of such convalescents as you may think sufficient for its guard, as I can always send to meet it and order it back should I be obliged to push for the relief of Ninety Six. You may send forward, at any rate, Captain Hovenden with his party of the Legion. I would not wish them to accompany the convoy, but to join us with as much expedition as may be convenient, and they may bring any letters that have arrived either from New York or England. From Fishing Creek I shall probably send to Camden a number of sick, who at present greatly retard our movements. I mention this that you may be prepared for them. Lord Cornwallis is a good deal better.

I have the honor to be, dear sir, with great regard
Your very humble servant

RAWDON

[*Subscribed:*]

Do not send any convalescents of the 7th Regiment without further directions, as I have some thoughts of proposing to Lord Cornwallis to send that corps to Camden.

Turnbull to Rawdon, 20th October 1780   3(249): ALS

Camden
October 20th 1780
Five o'clock pm

The Rt Hon Lord Rawdon

My Lord

I have this moment been favour'd with your letter and dupplicate of yesterday.

Lord Cornwallis's groom and a corporal of the Legion who left Charlotte express the 12th instant for this place — the groom arrived here next morning before day. He met an officer with twelve dragoons carrying Lord Cornwallis's dispatches from New York and turn'd him back, saying that it was his orders to turn every thing back and that we shou'd send nothing forward untill we shou'd hear from his Lordship.

The corporal was killed at Sugar Creek.

Colonel Doyle is now here. He proposes carrying forward the dispatches with a strong escort of dragoons. We are trying to copy over what is most material in case of accidents, but finding the cypher differ from Lord Cornwallis', we have kept some dupplicates of the same cypher sent by Balfour.

All at New York was well the 23rd of September, as likewise Charlestown the 15th instant.

Ninety Six we can say little about, only that Cruger expected to be attack't, that he was fortifying.

Wemyss's horses are a few miles at grass. He shall march tomorrow morning. I never received any order prior to this concerning him.

There is a small detachment of recover'd men with militia sent to reposess Georgetown. We have not as yet heard of their success.

Ever since Wemyss left the Cheraws, the rebells have been plundering the horses and cattle and dispersing the few militia that were well disposed from Pedee round all that country, Black Mingo, Black River etc. We are more apprehensive from that quarter than any other.

The salt and rum will soon be up and Hamilton shall have orders to hold himself in readyness to march on the shortest notice, but our garrison wou'd be rather too much weakned if he was to leave us. The three Provincial regiments does not afford more than three hundred men fit for duty and our works are not altogether finished.

I had a great complaint this morning from Captain Maxwell of the Prince of Wales's Volunteers (who had cross'd the Santee with one hundred militia and took post at Sumter's house to protect the communication, expecting to be join'd by Colonel Tynes' militia) that he had waited for many days and been constantly dissappointed and, hearing of Marion with four hundred men being this side of Black River, that he had a mind to repass the Santee.

I am with much esteem
Your Lordship's most devoted humble servant

GEO TURNBULL

Rawdon to Turnbull, 21st October 1780   3(251): C

>   Camp between the Catawba and Fishing Creek
>   October 21st 1780

Lt Colonel Turnbull
Commanding at Camden

Dear Sir

We passed the river this morning according to the intention specified in a letter dispatched last night, the duplicate of which I now enclose to you. Lt Colonel Doyle joined me here safely with the dispatches. I find that neither you nor Lt Colonel Balfour know exactly the situation of Ninety Six and I have not yet been able to get any information respecting it. I believe I shall be obliged to halt here to morrow. The next day I think of proceeding to Fishing Creek. I shall give you notice should I change my plan. When I quit this ground, I shall dispatch a number of sick to Camden under escort of the 7th Regiment, which will probably be left with you. Be so good as to send the letters for the army under the care of Captain Hovenden. Major England may come up to us either by that opportunity or with the rum as he shall think convenient, since he can easily return should his presence be necessary at Camden.

Sumner is certainly above Salisbury. Sumpter is somewhere near McAlpine's Creek. Morgan and Smallwood in Salisbury. This is late information and I believe exact. You shall hear from me to morrow.

In the mean time I have the honor to be, dear sir, very truly
Your faithfull humble servant

RAWDON

[*Subscribed*:]

I have the satisfaction to tell you that Lord Cornwallis is recovering fast.

Pray dispatch the letter for Balfour[36] as quick as possible.

---

[36] *letter for Balfour*: of 21st October, p 126.

Rawdon to Turnbull, 22nd October 1780   3(257): ACS

Lands Ford on the Catawba
October 22nd 1780

Lt Colonel Turnbull
Commanding at Camden

Dear Sir

We shall march tomorrow towards Fishing Creek and shall send our sick with the Seventh Regiment to you. I beg to know what your number fit for duty (including the 7th) will be should there be occasion to withdraw the Royal North Carolina Regiment from Camden. I am sure Lord Cornwallis would wish your post to be left in a condition not for a bare defensive alone, but such as may enable you to detach in support of the friendly militia upon any inroad from the quarter of Pedee. As to any attack upon Camden, I think you never can have any thing to apprehend but from surprize, and against that I am certain your vigilance will take every precaution. We shall be obliged to remain upon Fishing Creek or its neighborhood for some time, waiting for some supplies from Charlestown. If you could send any waggons to receive stores at Monk's Corner and afterwards bring them up by Congaree, it would expedite us exceedingly. You must have the goodness to forward some rum to us with all dispatch. I have written to Lt Colonel Balfour[37], requesting him to send up a further supply. I send some of Bryan's militia to the hospital at Camden. As they have no officer to look into their situation there, let me request that you will have the goodness to give such directions as you may think expedient for their welfare. I have the happiness to tell you that Lord Cornwallis is much better.

I have the honor to be etc

RAWDON

Haldane to Turnbull, 22nd October 1780   81(42): ACS

Head Quarters
October 22nd 1780

Lt Colonel Turnbull

Sir

Lord Cornwallis has directed me to acquaint you that he wishes <u>*all prisoners may be sent to Charlestown under a guard of militia, and to promise them a reasonable allowance for each when delivered*</u>.

---

[37] On 22nd October, p 127.

I have the honour to be etc

HH

Turnbull to Rawdon, 23rd October 1780 — 3(263): ALS

Camden
October 23rd 1780

Lord Rawdon

My Lord

I had the honor to receive your letters of the 19th and 21st and was very happy to find that Colonel Doyle had arrived safe with the dispatches; but every one rejoiced to hear that Lord Cornwallis was on the way of recovery.

Your letters for Balfour were forwarded without delay. Major England will acquaint you of the rum and salt which arrived this evening. We shall wait your orders for the quantity to be forwarded, as likewise the escort. Balfour writes me that there is a good deal of more rum on the way.

A Cork fleet bound to New York with a good many London ships called in last week at Charlestown. Their first appearance was alarming, and while the Commandant and Major Moncrief was viewing the works to see that every thing was compleat, some rebells could not help showing their cloven foot.

Wemyss, I dare say, is across Broad River by this time. Hovenden leaves only a corporal and six; we keep their infantry untill the rum and salt goes.

Towards Black River and the Cheraws it is the same as I mention'd some time ago. Major Harrison with sixty of his men are encamped about six miles from town. He has apply'd for cloathing for them. Major England and I intend taking a ride tomorrow to look at them.

A Mr Coates[38] arrived here some days ago from North Carolina. Lord Cornwallis had sent him to buy horses for the army. He assures us that Gates had left Hilsborough and gone into Virginia and that all the people who were rebelling had taken that rout with their Negroes and effects. Strong reports prevaill'd that a fleet was at Cape Fare.

Another man from Cross Creek who came in to escort a Mrs McCarlie, whose husband is with our army, says that a report prevailled that the siedge of New York was raised and that the French troops were marching back to Rhode Island.

---

[38] Perhaps William Coats (*c.* 1752-*c.* 1826) of Camden District, who was also resident in Rowan County, North Carolina, where he would remain for many years after the war. He died in Lincoln County, Tennessee. (Clark, *Loyalists in the Southern Campaign*, i, 162-4; information from Larry D Hamilton Coats, 3rd December 1998)

I am with much esteem
Your Lordship's most obedient humble servant

GEO TURNBULL

Rawdon to Turnbull, 26th October 1780   3(279): ACS

Cross Roads
October 26th 1780

Lt Colonel Turnbull etc

Dear Sir

I have just received your letter by Captain Hovenden. I was in hopes the rum would have arrived here by this time as I requested some to be sent without delay. We have now been two days without it. I request you to send ten puncheons with all expedition to meet me near Lee's Mill on Rocky Creek. I find we cannot be supplied with flour in this position. Therefore I shall fall back this afternoon. You shall hear further from me tonight.

I have the honor etc

RAWDON

Rawdon to Turnbull, 26th October 1780   3(283): ACS

October 26th 1780

Lt Colonel Turnbull etc

Dear Sir

I dispatched a letter to you this morning informing you that I had received yours by Captain Hovenden. I likewise pressed your sending to us with all expedition ten puncheons of rum as we have been two days without any. I was in hopes you would have forwarded some in consequence of my former letters and I must beg you not to lose a moment in it. We are now on our way to Lee's Mill on Rockey Creek or that neighborhood, having found it impossible to be supplied properly at the Cross Roads. Should the prospect of better supplies induce us to change our destination, I will take care that the convoy of rum shall be met and guided to us and I will send you notice.

I have the honor to be, dear sir, with great regard
Your very humble servant

RAWDON

[*Endorsed*:]

10 at night.

Rawdon to Turnbull, 27th October 1780   *3(293): C*

McClarkin's near Lee's Mill
October 27th 1780

Lt Colonel Turnbull
Commanding at Camden

Dear Sir

    We arrived here this day, and very fortunately I met Colonel Phillips here. His knowledge of the country will be very usefull to us. I find by his account that Wynnesborough is the most eligible post for us at present, as our communications with you and Ninety Six will be easy, we shall cover Congarees, and may be readily and very plentifully supplied with flour or meal. We think of moving the day after to morrow. I hope by that time we shall hear of some rum. Our route lies directly down the great Charlestown road. If you can induce the people about Lynches Creek or towards the High Hills to bring you in indian corn (or wheat if it is to be procured) for ready money, I wish you to collect as large a quantity as possible at Camden. Once more let me request you to forward rum to us with all dispatch.

I have the honor to be, dear sir,
Your faithfull servant

RAWDON

Rawdon to Turnbull, 29th October 1780   *3(305): AC*

Wynnesborough
October 29th 1780

Lt Colonel Turnbull
Commanding at Camden

Dear Sir

    Since the arrival of Captain Hovenden we have not had the pleasure of hearing from you; neither have we had any intelligence of our rum. It will be a satisfaction to us to learn frequently the state of your post, and as we have now taken a decided position, I hope we shall have constant intercourse with you. Our distance from you is rather short of forty miles and it is a good waggon road the whole way. We have received information that Smallwood had advanced to Twelve Mile Creek just above Waxhaw. Washington's dragoons were with him. Lord Cornwallis therefore requests you to be vigilant. His Lordship wishes that a redoubt should be immediately thrown up on your side of the ferry to secure the passage for reinforcement to you in case of necessity. Could you send us timely notice of the approach of any enemy towards you, it might probably be in our power to make them pay for the attempt. I hope you will have no difficulty in finding a person qualified to inspect the construction of the redoubt. Mr Haldane has the ague, otherwise he would visit you for the purpose. Hoping that I shall soon hear from you,

I have the honor etc

[RAWDON]

Turnbull to Rawdon, 29th October 1780

3(312): ALS

Camden
October 29th 1780

Lord Rawdon

My Lord

I am to acknowledge the receipt of your letters of the 22nd, two of the 26th, and one of the 27th.

The rum will set out *this day*[39].

Colonel Tynes has been surprized and defeated on the forks of Black River — lost all his arms — so that we are much exposed to the east and north, which will prevent our collecting provisions in these quarters.

I have brought Major Harrison with his people within a few miles of Camden. Major England has seen them. He will report their state and condition.

Dragoons or mounted men must be got to check these rebells which lays waste the country and murders the well affected in cold blood.

I am with much esteem
Your Lordship's most obedient humble servant

GEO TURNBULL

---

[39] A duplicate of this letter (3(314)) adds: 'This water carriadge becomes too tedious. We must fall upon some method of getting our supplies intirely by land as we have reason at this season of the year to expect freshes in the river, when boats cannot stir against the stream.'

PS

Inclosed is a petition of a Major Harris. Doctor Williamson returned some time ago.

Enclosure
Harris to Turnbull, 28th October 1780   3(301): ALS

Camden
28th October 1780

Colonel Turnbull
Commandant, Camden

Sir

    I must beg leave to trouble you for a few minutes with the relation of my disagreeable situation, not doubting but your humanity and generosity will plead so far in my favour as to grant my request. An unfortunate wound received on the sixteenth of August has taken away almost the use of my limbs and I am in such a low state that 'tis the opinion of Doctor Johnson[40] I cannot recover if I am detained here. I have no commission and am but a volunteer and acted as aid to General Rutherford. I am without any necessarys, nor do I see any probability of procuring any from the State. Could I be permitted to go home upon parole, I might possibly recover my health and furnish myself with necessaries and shall observe my parole in all respects with utmost exactness, not failling to return precisely at the time appointed.

I am, sir,
Your obedient servant

THOMAS HARRIS[41]

---

[40] Born in Pennsylvania, Robert Johnston (?-1808) had seen service early in the war as a regimental surgeon before being promoted to the rank of senior surgeon and Assistant Director General in the Continental hospitals. At the request of Gates he had been permitted in September to go to Camden and attend the wounded revolutionary prisoners there. After the war he would take up residence in Franklin County, Pennsylvania. (Heitman, *Historical Register*, 322; *The Cornwallis Papers*)

[41] A native of Cabarrus, Thomas Harris (1737-1826) had accepted a captain's commission in the 4th North Carolina Continental Regiment in April 1776, having concurrently received from Josiah Martin, the deposed Governor, the offer of a captain's commission in the royal service. He reputedly went on to take part in the Battle of Monmouth. His letter to Turnbull suggests that by mid 1780 he had resigned his Continental commission, having risen to the rank of major, whether in the Continental line or in the North Carolina revolutionary militia. At the end of the war he was awarded 1,000 acres for his Continental service and in 1806 received an invalidity pension. He died in Iredell County, North Carolina. (*The Carolina Observer* (Fayetteville, NC), 13th September 1826; Wheeler, *Historical Sketches*, i, 79; Wheeler, *Reminiscences*, 97; Hay ed, *Soldiers from NC*, 262, 437)

Turnbull to Rawdon, 30th October 1780 3(322): ALS

Camden
October 30th 1780

Lord Rawdon

My Lord

I had the honor of writing to you yesterday by the return of your express. Twelve puncheons of rum will be with you on Wednesday.

Your Lordship was pleased to desire me to order the commissary to buy corn, wheat etc for ready money. He has been very active in bargaining for a good deal of corn, but he is not entrusted with any cash. The greatest quantity was to come from Santee. Unless we can make those rebells retreat, we shall not be able to get it in. Sending foot against them is doing nothing. Dragoons or mounted men, and so swell the train.

Wood and forage will be necessary to be prepared for this post. I don't find we shall get any salt meat before the end of January. Mr Tounsend will not send us any. A trader on the Congarees has contracted with the commissary for two hundred barrels to be deliver'd at that time.

Hamilton has left his taylors and convalescents, expecting his cloathing; and as you said nothing about the six pounders, I have kept them here.

Major England can tell you every thing about this post.

I am, my Lord,
Most faithfully yours

GEO TURNBULL

Turnbull to Rawdon, 31st October 1780 3(328): ALS

Camden
October 31st 1780

Lord Rawdon

My Lord

I have received your letter of the 29th instant. We shall set about making <u>a redoubt on this side of the ferry and be as vigilant as we can. Tynes' regiment is dispersed, and so the greatest part of Rudgely's. The Colonel himself I don't know where. In short, my Lord, I do not like my situation. We are intirely exposed unless from your quarter, our fortifications not</u>

near compleated, and not horse men enough to keep up proper patroles. Depend upon it, this is the place they aim at. The inclosed letters[42] came to my hand last evening.

I am, my Lord,
Most faithfully yours

GEO TURNBULL

§ - §

2 - From Moncrief

Moncrief to Cornwallis, 28th September 1780　　　　　　　　*64(122): ALS*

Camden
28th September 1780

My Lord

I have the honor to inform your Lordship that upon my arrival at George Town Colonel Cassels' militia was ordered to be mustered at different parts of that district that those suspected of being our enemies might be known. Such as I thought were not to be trusted were ordered down to Charlestown to be disposed of as the Commandant thinks proper — in all, about thirty. Such of the inhabitants as were concerned in the revolt, I destroyed their property; the Negroes are sent to Charlestown; and the horses are here, about 200 marked thus: ↑.

The passes necessary for covering this part of the country I think are along Black River, which is only passable at Rag's, North's and Potatoe Ferrys and at Kingstree and lower bridges. I have therfore ordered Wigfall's and Ball's to take up the three ferrys, and the two other regiments expected from the southward the upper part of the river. Cassels's regiment I have left to patrole between Pedee and Black River with orders to fall back to Black River if any considerable force should cross Pedee. The country between these rivers is all an open pine wood, so that I think no small party will venture between them.

I shall with pleasure obey your Lordship's commands by returning to morrow morning to Charlestown.

I have the honor to be with the utmost respect, my Lord,
Your Lordship's most obedient and most humble servant

JAMES MONCRIEF
Major of Engineers

---

[42] *The inclosed letters*: perhaps Balfour's of 26th and 27th October, pp 131 and 133.

Moncrief to Cornwallis, 1st October 1780 64(136): ALS

Camden
1st October 1780

My Lord

I should have reported to your Lordship, upon my arrival at Charlestown from the southward, the state of the garrisons of Savannah and St Augustine, but I was in hopes at that time of having the honour of waiting upon your Lordship at Camden.

The fort ordered by General Prevost at Savannah was in great forwardness on my arrival. Colonel Clark and I thought it best to let it go on. The batteries upon Coxpur Island are compleated, which are all the works necessary for Georgia at present.

The fort of St Augustine is in very tolerable repair but wants a number of platforms and other little matters, which I have ordered. Colonel Clark is of opinion that this is the likliest place in his district of being attacked, and if Pensacola should fall into the hands of the enemy, I think it is very probable. I have ordered frames and materials to be got ready for four or five redouts with an eighteen pounder carronade in each, so that, should Colonel Clark order them to be put up, with the assistance of the inhabitants of the place, they may be done in a few days and the abatis laid in the intervals. The post may be made very respectable before an enemy can get near him, as he must see them at least eight days before they can make a landing good upon the main. One galley will be absolutly necessary to be kept under the fort to guard the passage up the North River, as the fort is only within random shot of the channel.

I shall beg leave to refer your Lordship to Mr Haldane, to whom I have explained the whole.

Colonel Fuser[43] at the time of the siege of Savannah laid out about £2,000 sterling and is not paid. The account was laid before me. I cannot help thinking it reasonable and what I would have done if I had been in his situation.

I have the honour to be with the utmost respect, my Lord,
Your Lordship's most obedient and most humble servant

JAMES MONCRIEF
Major of Engineers

§ - §

---

[43] An officer of long standing, Lewis Valentine Fuser had been Lt Colonel of the 4th Battalion, 60th (or Royal American) Regiment, during its service in East Florida. Moncrief does not appear to be aware that Fuser was now dead, a fact which Prevost related to Germain in February 1780. (*Army Lists*; Cashin, *The King's Ranger*, 313n)

3 - To or from England, Hill or Macleod

Macleod to Cornwallis, 12th September 1780   *64(46): ALS*

Camden
September 12th 1780

My Lord

I take the opportunity of Mr Cruden to assure you no effort has been wanting to arrange my department to your Lordship's intentions and that I feel no small degree of pleasure in declaring every thing meant to be forwarded under escort of the 71st is ready and I hope completed to your Lordship's approbation.

I cannot, however, omit mentioning, my Lord, a defect in the number, and some diffidence in the quality, of my horses. The last, tho, need not alarm your Lordship, since I confess it proceeds more from apprehension of promising *too* much than any apparent danger of failing in competition with other departments, but the first distresses me a good deal from the impossibility of supplying upon a spot (so drain'd by the Legion and others) a proportion adequate to a train and distance so unusually great.

The arms I have applied to Major England about. I think myself oxen, as accustom'd to heavy draughts, are best adapted for them, and as there are some in his department, I am in hopes of his assistance. If your Lordship should approve, the 7th upon their arrival might, from the number of horses collected in the country, be perhaps able to supply the guns and waggons order'd to be left for them. In that case I think I may say I can join your Lordship with a heart at ease.

I do not enter into a detail of particulars least some accident might attend my letter, but must assure your Lordship to the best of my abilities no contingency or circumstance is left unprovided for.

I have the honor to be, my Lord.
Your most obedient and obliged humble servant

J MACLEOD

England to Cornwallis, 14th September 1780   64(57): ALS

Camden
September 14th 1780

Lord Cornwallis etc etc etc

My Lord

I have the honor to inclose to you an invoice of Provincial cloathing and appointments arrived here this day. I have stored them in my quarters untill some person receives your Lordship's orders to take them under their charge. I shall send a large proportion of rum and salt by the 71st Regiment on Monday. I doubt my being able to accompany them, as the wounded won't leave this untill Wednesday and I wish to settle the arrangement for them both here and at Nelson's Ferry to Doctor Hill's satisfaction before I leave this. Shou'd I not go, I shall send Lieutenant Oldfield with the care of the rum etc with directions to remain at Head Quarters and receive your Lordship's commands. The port wine arrived here has suffered very considerably by lakage. Half on't is reported by the commissary to have been wasted. It seems a doubt to what department it is consigned as no invoice or direction is arrived with it, and both the commissary and Doctor Hill claim it. Colonel Innis's corps is not yet arrived, nor is there yet any account from the 7th Regiment. The 63rd sick are at a stand; no amendment[44] yet of any consequence. I shall send your Lordship's money by Major McArthur. There are hourly people coming in from Peedee giving dreadful accounts of the depredations committing there by the rebels. They bring in with them all their family, Negroes etc.

I have the honor to be, my Lord, with great esteem
Your Lordship's very obedient and very humble servant

R^D ENGLAND

Enclosure (1)
Invoice of clothing, accoutrements etc   64(58): ADS

Monk's Corner
the 8th September 1780

INVOICE of clothing, accoutrements etc sent under the care of Richard Dickie, Conductor of Waggons, for Major Harrison's corps at Cambden:

    Hogshead N° 10   containing Russia drill jackets

    Cask N° 25   containing 49 pair overalls

---

[44] *amendment*: improvement.

Case Nº 3 containing 25 coats for the officers

Hogshead Nº 33 containing 372 pair shoes }
} Total 720 pair
Ditto Nº 60 containing 348 pair ditto }

Casks Nºˢ 18, 20, 23, 34, 42, 48, 49, 41 —

being 8 casks of accoutrements of 50 each, is 400 setts accoutrements

309 canteens.

H FLIEGER
Provincial Storekeeper

Enclosure (2)
Invoice of clothing   *64(59): ADS*

Monk's Corner
the 8th September 1780

INVOICE of clothing sent under the care of Gabº Irenmonger of Collington County for Major Harrison's corps at Cambden:

Case Nº 1   containing 132 Russia drill jackets in materials, with trimmings for other clothing

Cask Nº 17 }
}
Ditto Nº 19 } containing 231 pair of overalls and 148 split shirts.
}
Ditto Nº 23 }

H FLIEGER
Provincial Storekeeper

NB

The above 148 split shirts, being intended for the North Carolina Refugees, but being packed with the overalls, could not be easely separated.

Cornwallis to England, 17th September 1780 — 80(24): C

Camp at Waxhaw
September 17th 1780

Major England
Deputy Quarter Master General

Dear England

I this day received yours of the 14th. I had written to stop the Provincial cloathing. I do not believe that Harrison has got 50 men and had directed Major Wemyss, when his expedition was over, if Harrison had collected men enough to form two or three companys, to send them to Monk's Corner to be equipp'd. You will please to send to Major Wemyss to revoke that order. Lt Colonel Hamilton will want many of the appointments. I am glad to find that you mean to pay all possible attention to the removal of the wounded. The port wine is intended for the use of the hospital and wounded officers and of course is in Mr Hill's department. I would have those rascals who tapp'd it severely punish'd. Lt Colonel Innis's corps marched from Ninety Six on Saturday last and must consequently be at or very near Camden. I shall write to Lt Colonel Balfour to send some more rum up as soon as possible with the last division. If you think there is more rum and salt at Camden, exclusive of a few days' for the garrison, than your waggons can bring up, I will send down some empty waggons to assist you. The march of Major Wemyss will, I hope, put a stop to the depredations of the enemy on Pedee.

I am
Your most obedient and faithfull servant

CORNWALLIS

England to Cornwallis, 18th September 1780 — 64(71): ALS

Camden
September 18th 1780

Lt General Earl Cornwallis

My Lord

I have the honor of acquainting you that this morning I forwarded to your camp sixteen puncheons of rum and forty bushels of salt escorted by the 71st battallions and under the care of Lieutenant Oldfield. A detachment of artillery with two six pounders, a few pioneers, and the convalescents of the 33rd Regiment have marched at the same time. Major McArthur has received directions, according to your Lordship's orders, to march in six days[45] and has

---

[45] *to march in six days*: i.e to take six days in completing his march to the Waxhaws.

taken provisions accordingly. I have also sent under Mr Oldfield's care the nine hundred pounds sent me from Charlestown, as reported before.

On Lieutenant Oldfield's arrival at Head Quarters he will have thirty eight waggons belonging to the department under his direction, exclusive of those attached to battallions, and I have at this post twenty five, which number I can increase if necessary. Shou'd your Lordship consider those sufficient at present, beg your permission to dismiss either the Orangeburg waggons or those from Ninety Six, particularly as they seem much wanted in their districts and many applications made here for them. Shou'd your Lordship think proper to order them to be dismissed, I will either pay them here or give certificates to them to be paid at Charlestown. Their demands are, I believe, considerable.

I am desired by Lt Colonel Turnbull to inform you that Major Pinkney (a rebel prisoner) has applied to him for permission to go to his wife's father's house on the Congaree when he is sufficiently recovered of his wound. As he does not consider himself at liberty to grant him permission without your Lordship's consent, he has desired me mention the circumstance to you and beg your Lordship's answer.

Lt Colonel Innis's corps arrived here last night. The Lt Colonel is expected in a week. The 71st Regiment relapsed two days before their march and many returned to the hospital. The flux prevails much and is fatal to those who have been weakened by *agues*. The 63rd *rather* mend. No account yet of the 7th Regiment or of Major Wemys. All the wounded are to embark on Wednesday the 20th.

Shou'd your Lordship soon move from your present ground, hope you will grant me permission to join you, and Lieutenant Oldfield may return here. I am now perfectly recovered and Mr Haldane mends fast.

I have the honor to be with great esteem
Your Lordship's very obedient humble servant

R^D ENGLAND
Deputy Quarter Master General

PS

The inclosed[46], authenticated by the evidence of several, has been just sent me.

---

[46] *The inclosed*: not extant.

Cornwallis to England, 20th September 1780   *80(31): C*

Camp at Waxhaw
September 20th 1780

To Major England
Deputy Quarter Master General at Camden

Dear England

I find it difficult to decide immediately about the waggons. I have desired Balfour to send up more rum and salt for the use of the troops at Camden and I should wish to carry with us every drop of rum that is now there if we can get conveyance for it. Of the quantity you will be able to judge and will proportion the carriages accordingly, but the difficult point to ascertain is the conveyance of the sick. We have now above 120 here and they are daily increasing; the 71st will add considerably to that list. The disposal of all these sick will be a matter very maturely to be considered, but whether we move them forward or send them back, waggons will be equally necessary. I think at present of fixing a post under Wemyss at Charlottetown if I find that it can be supplied with provisions. Tarleton was to have gone thither to have ascertained that point, but unfortunately he is exceedingly ill at White's on Fishing Creek. He cannot be removed and I am obliged to leave his corps there for his protection. Should the post at Charlotte be found practicable, that will be the best place for the sick of whose recovery within these six weeks or two months we have any hopes. They will soon become a considerable addition of strength to Wemyss and may afterwards, very possibly, be brought up to the army.

Make my best compliments to Colonel Turnbull, who I hope is recovering, and tell him that when Major Pinkney is able to travel, I will allow him to pass fourteen days at his wife's father's at the Congarees. He must then join the other field officers on parole, who are at Orangeburgh unless otherwise disposed of by Colonel Balfour, and report his doing so to the Commandant.[47]

Colonel Cruger informed me of the rising in the Ceded Lands in Georgia and has march[ed] with his whole force, which, by the bye, is not very great. Ferguson, who has made rather a successful expedition to the mountains above Gilbertown, has, I hope, stopped some of the rebel parties who were going to the assistance of the Georgia insurgents. I most sincerely hope that Colonel Cruger will be able to settle that business without obliging me to detach, which will be very inconvenient.

Pray talk over the arrangement of the mates and medecines very fully with Hill. We certainly must take a great stock of the latter with us, and a very considerable quantity must be left at Charlottetown if it should be found expedient to establish the post I talk of. You may depend on my not leaving you behind.

---

[47] For Pinckney's response and Cornwallis's reply, see pp 237-9.

I am
Faithfully yours

CORNWALLIS

[*Subscribed*:]

If you find that more medecines are wanted from Charlestown, send an express to Colonel Balfour without losing time by writing to me.

England to Cornwallis, 19th September 1780 64(79): ALS

Camden
September 19th 1780

Lt General Earl Cornwallis

My Lord

I beg to report to you the arrival of your printing press, some stationary from Robertson[48], a chest marked with your Lordship's name (contents unknown), also some mollasses and other articles sent for by a soldier of the 33rd Regiment. Serjeant Crabtree is not yet arrived, but a sutler has just brought to camp the articles I inclose[49], but least your Lordship may have occasion for them or any part of them, I have forbid him breaking bulk[50] untill I receive your Lordship's commands. I was this day honored with yours of the 17th and have wrote by express to Major Wemys, forbidding him to send Harrisson's corps to Monck's Corner. Lt Colonel Hamilton's corps want many of the appointments arrived, but he wishes to defer taking them untill he is under orders to move, as he expects his own appointments soon.

There still remain here twenty five puncheons of rum and a quantity of salt. As there will be a quantity of wine and stores belonging to the hospital necessary to be carried to the army and other articles belonging to the last division of an army, I will thank you for the assistance you mention and shall write to have ten waggons sent from the militia if you think proper,

---

[48] James Robertson (1740-?) was born in Edinburgh, Scotland, where he learned the printing trade from his father. Having migrated to North America by 1766, he began briefly to publish a newspaper in New York City before going on to publish ones in Albany and Norwich, Connecticut. When the British occupied New York City, he, being a royalist, moved there and in January 1777 began the *Royal American Gazette*, which continued in publication for over six and a half years. Now, in 1780, he had come south to Charlestown with two fellow Scots, Donald MacDonald and Alexander Cameron, and together they had set themselves up at 20 Broad Street as general printers and publishers of the *Royal South Carolina Gazette*. At the close of the war Robertson would move to Shelburne, Nova Scotia, where he continued to publish a newspaper for several years. Eventually he returned to his native city of Edinburgh, engaging in the printing trade until 1810 or later. (*DAB*)

[49] The enclosure is not extant.

[50] *breaking bulk*: beginning to unload.

as they probably will be afterwards discharged.

I forward to your Lordship a letter from Lt Colonel Cruger[51] and have the honor to be with great esteem

Your Lordship's very obedient servant

R^D ENGLAND
Deputy Quarter Master General

Hill to Cornwallis, 21st September 1780

64(93): ALS

Camden
September 21st 1780

My Lord

I have the pleasure to inform your Lordship that seventy eight wounded men were embarked yesterday and fell down the river at eleven o'clock. The boats were well covered with tents, and plenty of good straw for them to lay on. For those supplies I am much indebted to the friendly assistance of Major England. The men are very comfortably placed, not crouded. They have two hospital mates to attend them, furnished with proper dressings, medicines etc. Wine, rum, bread, flour, sugar and every other necessary were amply supplied for ten days subsisting them. I hope they will have a pleasant and expeditious passage. I have this day inspected Lord Rawdon's sick left in regimental hospital. I have ordered twenty four to the general hospital and thirty two convalescents with the surgeon to join the regiment, understanding they are in want of his assistance. I shall send by this opportunity returns[52] of the general hospital, the rebel wounded in hospitals, and the different regiments who have wounded men sent yesterday to Charlestown to the Deputy Adjutant General, to whom I beg leave to refer your Lordship for any farther information.

I have the honour to remain with the truest respect, my Lord,
Your Lordship's most obedient and most faithful servant

WEST HILL

---

[51] *a letter..*: of 15th and 16th September, p 187.

[52] *returns*: not extant.

England to Cornwallis, 22nd September 1780   64(98): ALS

Camden
September 22nd 1780

Lt General Earl Cornwallis

My Lord

I have the pleasure to report to you that all the wounded left this last Wednesday morning in as comfortable a manner as their situation wou'd admit of. They were supplied by Doctor Hill with a proper allowance of bread, biscuit, wine, medicine and attendants. Their boats were well covered, floored, lined, dry, and a sufficiency of straw and room. In short, they seemed very happy and much pleased.

I have spoke to Doctor Hill about the arrangement of mates, stores and medicines. I forward to your Lordship his report and shall this night write to Colonel Balfour to expedite the demand he makes on Doctor Hayes. He informs me that he will require ten waggons to remove the hospital stores with, which obliges me to demand twenty waggons from Head Quarters. I have wrote fully to Lieutenant Oldfield on this subject and have desired him acquaint your Lordship with the purport of my letter. I mentioned poor Tarleton's situation to Captain Kinloch, who in consequence on't sets out to join the corps and receive your Lordship's commands. I have wrote to Major Money and shall forward tomorrow by the Volunteers of Ireland (sixty) the sutler I mentioned.

I have the honor to be
Your Lordship's most obedient humble servant

R^D ENGLAND

Enclosure
Hill to Cornwallis, 23rd September 1780   64(106): ALS

Camden
23rd September 1780

My Lord

Since I had the honour of writing my last to your Lordship, Major England has informed me of your Lordship's wishes that a good supply of medicines may be brought with me to the army. I shall take care to bring as good an assortment as our present stock at Camden will admit of. This day I have written to Dr Hayes for a very good supply to be sent hither from Charlestown, which will be forwarded by Major England this evening to Colonel Balfour agreeable to your Lordship's orders.

Mates I am fearful I shall not be able to bring so many as my intentions proposed for the expedition. One died a few days since, and two at present very ill. However, I hope to be able to bring up four or five. In the mean time I shall request of Dr Hayes to send up two to the assistance of Mr Huddleston[53], who will be left with the care of the sick at this place. I hope they will arrive, with the medicines, before I join.

This morning has brought me a letter from the Isle of Wight of the 10th of July. My brother desires me to present his most respectful compliments to your Lordship. He has informed me of some recommendations having been sent very lately from England by a friend of his to Sir Henry Clinton in my favour, requesting his Excellency's appointing me physician to the General Hospital. He says he has written also at the same time and desires likewise that I would acquaint your Lordship of this circumstance and that he hopes for your Lordship's interest on this occasion. On my own part I owe so much to your Lordship for the many acts of friendship which I have already received[54] that I am at a loss what to say on this subject. I can only assure your Lordship that if I am honoured with your Lordship's support, I must ever remain, as I always have,

Your Lordship's most grateful and most faithful servant

WEST HILL

England to Cornwallis, 1st October 1780   3(162): ALS

Camden
October 1st 1780

Lt General Earl Cornwallis

My Lord

I have the honor to report to your Lordship that I have this evening put on waggons for Charlotte ten puncheons of rum and fifty six bushells of salt. They are to proceed early to morrow under escort of the Royal Fuzileers. A detachment of convalescents move at the same time, some for the 71st Regiment, some for the 23rd, and some for the 33rd Regiments, the whole of the convalescents amounting to one hundred and fifty. The Fuzileers leave here one hundred and six men sick, most of which have fallen down here. However, I hope, with

---

[53] Richard Huddleston (?-1806) was an apothecary at the General Hospital in North America, the department responsible for hospitals other than small regimental ones. He had taken up his post on 29th April 1780, having served for more than nine years as surgeon to the 7th Regiment. He would not be long in charge of the general hospital at Camden, being obliged to leave by mid November due to his reduced state of health. In April 1782 he was placed on the half-pay list but was recalled to active service as a staff surgeon eleven years later, again retiring on half pay in August 1802. (Johnston, *Commissioned Officers in the Medical Service*, 44; *The Cornwallis Papers*)

[54] *I owe so much to your Lordship..*: before Hill's appointment as a surgeon on the staff of the General Hospital in North America he had been surgeon to the 33rd Regiment, of which Cornwallis was Colonel. The rank of physician, which he now sought, was senior to that of surgeon.

the assistance of Doctor Hill and bark, that many of them will be able to join the army with the 63rd Regiment. I have not heared from Major Wemys since the 23rd of last month, at which time he wrote me from Cheraws, saying that he waited your Lordship's orders either to return here or proceed to you. Notwithstanding your Lordship's indulgence, I think it better for the regulation of the different departments to remain here untill the 63rd Regiment marches, at which time I suppose your Lordship wou'd wish the hospital stores wou'd move. Should you chuse, I will undertake to bring forward all the men that Doctor Hill thinks are able to be moved. I am already making preparations for them; and all the bad amputated cases that cou'd not be sent to Charlestown with the last cargoe will be sent by the boats expected here every day. We have not heard any thing of the rum ordered from Charlestown but what is mentioned in your Lordship's letters. There now remains at this post six puncheons, which I dare say will hold out untill a supply arrives. Major Moncrieffe returned to Charlestown this day. He left fifty very elegant horses for the Legion with Captain Hovenden, twenty for the artillery, and fourteen for me, exclusive of seventy young colts with sore backs and lame that I have taken charge of for the public service and turned to grass to recover. I send *by this convoy* your Lordship's baggage under Crabtree and one hundred pounds in dollars sent me for your use by Colonel Balfour.

I have the honor to be, my Lord, with great esteem and respect
Your Lordship's most obedient and very humble servant

R^D ENGLAND

England to Haldane, 6th October 1780   93(5): ALS

Camden
October 6th

Lieutenant Haldane etc

Dear Haldane

The requisition from the fair lady mentioned in the inclosed note directed to me is humbly submitted to you, and I request *some* answer relative to it. I am very anxious to join you and eagerly wait your summons.

The Commandant[55] is confined to his bed — even port won't cure him. His reprimands are more severe than usual.

Make my compliments to his Excellency[56], who I expect to see at the head of his battalion when I join, and assure yourself of the sincere regards of

R^D ENGLAND
Deputy Quarter Master General

---

[55] Turnbull.

[56] Governor Martin.

Enclosure
Mrs Habersham's note, 5th October 1780   *93(6): D*

Thursdy morning

Mrs Habersham presents her compliments to Major England and begs the favor of him to use his interest with Lord Cornwallis to get permission for Major Habersham[57], her husband's brother, a Continental officer on parole at Hadderril's Point, to make her a visit in Camden, which favor she will ever remember with gratitude; and from the character she has had of his Lordship's humanity and great goodness of heart she flatters herself he will not refuse her request.

England to Haldane, 8th October 1780   *64(138): ALS*

Camden
October 8th 1780

Lieutenant Haldane etc

My dear Haldane

Our Commandant here desires me to acknowledge the receipt of the dispatches of the sixth instant, and I beg to report that those directed to Lt Colonel Balfour were instantly forwarded. Turnbull continues very ill (tho not, I believe, dangerously so) and totally incapable of attending to any public business, which you may *hint* to his Lordship if you think proper.

I shall be totally prepared to *start* in two days and hope I may by that time receive permission. Many people have fallen ill here since your departure.

I am with best respects, compliments and good wishes, my dear friend,
Very faithfully yours

R^D ENGLAND

Haldane to England, 22nd October 1780   *81(40): ACS*

Camp, Lands Ford
October 22nd 1780

Dear England

I had the pleasure of receiving your letters of the 6th and 8th and have presented Mrs Habersham's request to Lord Cornwallis, but his Lordship can not possibly consent to Major

---

[57] John Habersham (?-1799) was a major in the 1st Georgia Continental Regiment. He had been taken prisoner, first at Savannah in December 1778, and then in the action at Briar Creek in March 1779. Two years later he would get into hot water for allegedly breaking his parole by corresponding with the enemy and be placed in close confinement. (Heitman, *Historical Register*, 265; McCrady, *SC in the Rev 1780-1783*, 354-5)

Habersham coming to Camden. If the commanding officer at Camden has no objection, Lord Cornwallis will allow Dr Williamson to return[58] and Colonel Porterfield to send by that opportunity for his chaise and horses. I was rather unfortunate in my waggons. The small one broke down and I was obliged to leave it on the road, and one of the horses died. I answered your letters some time ago but have not had an opportunity of sending it. I hope it will not be long before you will be enabled to join us.

Believe me ever, dear England,
Yours most sincerely

HH

§ - §

4 - To or from McArthur

Cornwallis to McArthur, 29th September 1780   80(56): C

Charlottetown
29th September 1780

Major McArthur
71st Regiment

Dear Sir

I am sorry to find that, by the mistake of the commissaries and by the men of Bryan's corps coming away who were left to trash, you have been distressed for provision. I now send you Mr Carr with 20 trashers. As I have great reason to think there are no partys of the enemy in our rear and that Sumpter is gone up the Catawbaw in order to pass and join the militia corps near Salisbury, there can be no reason for your being so strong at Waxhaw. I therefore desire that you will send up the 2nd Battalion of the 71st with the six pounder and ammunition waggons on Sunday next, the 1st October, and all the convalescents belonging to the regiments here that are fit to move. You will please to remain on Waxhaw Creek with the First Battalion and try to form a little magazine of flour for the regiments as they come up. You will soon, I believe, receive some flour from Broad River. By your account of Tarleton[59] I shall hope to see him very soon.

I am, sir,
Your most obedient humble servant

CORNWALLIS

---

[58] See Williamson to Cornwallis, 2nd October, p 289.

[59] *your account..*: in a letter not extant.

[*Subscribed*:]

You will please to forward the inclosed to Lt Colonel Turnbull[60].

McArthur to Cornwallis, 30th September 1780   64(132): ALS

Camp at Waxhaw
September 30th 1780

The Rt Hon Lt General Earl Cornwallis
Head Quarters

My Lord

I have been honored with your Lordship's letter of yesterday. The 2nd Battalion of the 71st with the cannon, waggons and convalescents shall march tomorrow. I shall use all possible means to collect flour and form a litle magazine for the regiments that are to come up. I have wrote to Colonel Rugely to send a sufficient party of his militia to receive the prisoners at Barclay's House. I am sorry to inform your Lordship that one of those left here when the army march'd made his escape the night before last. His name is Northington Hunt. I shall forward the letter for Colonel Turnbull immediately.

I have the honor to be, my Lord,
Your Lordship's most obedient and most humble servant

ARCH[D] McARTHUR

McArthur to Cornwallis, 2nd October 1780   3(174): ALS

Camp at Waxhaw
October 2nd 1780

The Rt Hon Lt General Earl Cornwallis

My Lord

I have by this bearer received a letter from Mr Knecht desiring I would stop the eighteen waggons here that are now on their way from Broad River with flour till your Lordship's pleasure is known, which I shall take care to do; and after his letter was sealed, he has wrote on the outside: 'If it can be effected, the waggons will be stopped before they can reach you, Colonel Turnbull thinking it very unsafe to let them go on.'[61] We are busy preparing flour

---

[60] *the inclosed..*: a letter of 29th September, p 242.

[61] See Knecht to Cornwallis, 1st October, p 287.

and don't doubt to have a sufficient quantity for the 7th against their arrival.

I have the honor to be, my Lord,
Your Lordship's most obedient humble servant

ARCH[D] McARTHUR

[*Subscribed*:]

The prisoners go off tomorrow morning.

Cornwallis to McArthur, 5th October 1780   81(20): C

Charlottetown
October 5th 1780

Major McArthur
71st Regiment

Sir

I desire that you will march with the 1st Battalion of the 71st Regiment to Armer's Ford, where you will please to take post and inform me of your arrival. It is possible that you may meet with, or hear of, Ferguson. You will take your threshers of corn along with you and, if you can, leave a few barrels of flower under the care of Colonel Harpur[62] for the troops coming up from Camden. You may march either on the 7th or 8th.

I am, sir,
Your most obedient humble servant

CORNWALLIS

[*Subscribed*:]

I send six waggons under a militia guard to bring up the sick. If more are wanted, you will try to press them. They had better come up with the 7th Regiment, who may halt a day for them if they are not ready.

---

[62] Possibly Daniel Harper (see vol I, p 217, note 46). Residing in the Waxhaws, he may have just been commissioned a colonel in the royal militia even though the prospect of enlisting men in his locality was faint.

McArthur to Cornwallis, 7th October 1780 3(199): ALS

Camp at Waxhaw
October 7th 1780
8 o'clock am

The Rt Hon Lt General Earl Cornwallis

My Lord

I have been honored with your Lordship's letter of the 5th and the duplicate. I informed you the day before yesterday[63] that the 7th were arrived here and would halt yesterday. They are now just setting off for Charlotte. The six waggons for the sick not being yet come, the convalescents and sick of the regiments at Charlotte are unable to proceed. I have therefore kept here Lieutenant Cameron[64] of the 2nd Battalion 71st and 12 convalescents of that battalion, which, with near thirty of the Volunteers of Ireland able to carry arms, will be a sufficient guard for the sick, which I hope the six waggons will be able to convey. If nine men of Colonel Bryen's threshers had not gone off without leave the day before yesterday, I would have been able to leave some flour here, but the consumption by the number of convalescents has been more than I expected and I purpose if possible to carry three days' flour with me for the 1st Battalion that moves tomorrow. None of our threshers or foragers have been disturbed till last night, when the sentry of a serjeant's covering guard at Wauchop's, where Bryen's men were threshing, was fired at by three men, who attempted to carry him off, but the guard came to his assistance. He is shott through the hand. Mr Carr, the commissary, has been sick ever since he came here, so that I have had no assistance from him. Colonel Harper promises me to send the cattle to Camden and to get some flour ground for the use of such as may pass this way. I take the sick of the 1st Battalion with me and shall not fail to inform your Lordship of my arrival at Armer's.

I have the honor to be, my Lord,
Your Lordship's most obedient humble servant

ARCH{D} McARTHUR

---

[63] The letter is not extant.

[64] Donald Cameron had been commissioned an ensign in the 2nd Battalion, 71st (Highland) Regiment, on 2nd December 1775. He was promoted to lieutenant on 3rd August 1778. (*Army Lists*)

Money to McArthur, 8th October 1780   *81(33): AC*

Head Quarters, Charlottetown
October 8th 1780

Major McArthur
71st Regiment

Sir

I am directed by Lord Cornwallis to desire you will march with the 1st Battalion of the 71st Regiment to this place instead of Armer's Ford as mentioned in his Lordship's letter of the 5th instant.

I am, sir, etc

[J MONEY]

§ - §

5 - To or concerning Tarleton

Cornwallis to Campbell, 20th September 1780   *80(29): C*

Waxhaw
September 20th 1780

Lieutenant Archibald Campbell[65]
71st Regiment

Sir

I have written to Major McArthur, who is at Hanging Rock, to send if possible Mr Stewart[66] of the 71st to assist Mr Smith[67]. I am very anxious for the next accounts of Colonel Tarleton and beg you will send twice a day at least.

---

[65] Lt Archibald Campbell commanded a detachment of the 71st on secondment to the British Legion. One of three lieutenants in the 71st who bore his name, he was with Tarleton, who was very ill, at White's Mill on Fishing Creek. (*The Cornwallis Papers*; *Army Lists*)

[66] John Stewart had been appointed surgeon to the 1st Battalion, 71st (Highland) Regiment, on 5th April 1778. He would transfer to the Royal Horse Guards in January 1782 and retire on half pay in October 1785. (Johnston, *Commissioned Officers in the Medical Service*, 50)

[67] Edward Smith was surgeon to the British Legion cavalry. (W O Raymond, 'British American Corps')

I enclose a letter for Major Ferguson[68]. I understand there is a man waiting at Colonel Tarleton's to carry it to him.

This will be a favourable time to disarm the men in whom Colonel Floyd of the militia has no confidence. You will please to inform the officer next in command to Lt Colonel Tarleton that I wish he would concert measures with Colonel Floyd for doing this in as quiet a manner and as effectually as possible. The men so disarmed must be put on parole. If any serviceable arms can be procured from them which are not wanted for Lt Colonel Tarleton's corps, I would have them sent hither and, on receiving notice from the commanding officer, will send waggons to meet them at Blair's Mill.

I am, sir,
Your most obedient humble servant

CORNWALLIS

Rawdon to Tarleton, 26th October 1780   3(281): AC

Brown's House near the Cross Roads
October 26th 1780
10 in the morning

My dear Sir

I dispatched a letter to you yesterday evening[69] informing you that Lord Cornwallis thought it necessary that your proposed march should for the present be postponed. As I have received no answer from you, I fear that the letter may have missed you. Therefore I am now to repeat the above instruction. Till it shall be judged expedient to let you proceed, I should of course wish to have you either with us or as near us at least as forage will admit. I see plainly that we cannot possibly be supplied with flour or meal in this post and I am convinced that this situation for the army was recommended to you by the militia merely because it was such as would cover them from the enemy's incursions, no matter at what expence of convenience to the troops. We are too far likewise from Camden; the business of getting up our rum would be a perpetual weight and distress to us. From these reasons Lord Cornwallis judges it best to fall back to the neighborhood of Lee's Mill, in which situation I am informed we shall likewise be able to draw supplies from the Dutch Forks. I think we shall march this evening as I only wait for some meal which we have been long expecting from Walker's. We shall proceed as far as Grimes's, where I should be glad to see you if it should not be inconvenient. I refer the bearer to you respecting the feasibility of breaking up a nest of plunderers who infest the neighborhood and very much distress the loyal subjects.

---

[68] *a letter..*: of 20th September, p 153.

[69] *a letter..*: no extant copy.

Captain Hovenden has arrived with forty-five dragoons.

[RAWDON]

§ - §

6 - To or from commissaries

Knecht to Cornwallis, undated[70]   63(99): ALS

Rt Hon Earl Cornwallis

My Lord

I have now the pleasure to inform your Lordship that by tomorrow night I expect to have loaded fifteen waggons with wheat flour, and the day after ten more, all from the neighbouring mills. If waggons could be got, I could load in the course of this week thirty more waggons.

The Dutch vrous (whilst their husbands were in camp with Colonel Innis to fight the battles) applied themselves with a most remarkable industry to raise wheat for our support. This year's crop in the Dutch settlement on Broad River is but little inferior to those years when peace reigned in the country, and I have the pleasure to find that the Germans here are sincere and firm in their loyalty!

Tomorrow, after settling matters here for future supplies for Colonel Ferguson as well as for the troops at Camden, I purpose going down as far as Friday's Ferry to know what resource[71] I may have to that place in case of need and hope to reach Camden by Wednesday morning.

There is a report in this settlement that Colonel Ferguson had by a forced march gained upon the rebels and took back from them the prisoners they made in their late skirmish with Colonel Innis, but I see nothing authentic in it. I cannot traze[72] any thing how they go on in the settlements of Charlotte!

I have the honour to be, my Lord,
Your Lordship's most obedient and most humble servant

A KNECHT
Acting Assistant Commissary General

---

[70] Written from Broad River, this letter was received by Cornwallis on 14th September. (Money, Journal, p 363)

[71] *resource*: used either mistakenly for 'recourse' or in the archaic sense of 'possibility of assistance'.

[72] *traze*: archaic form of 'trace', meaning 'find out' or 'discover'.

[*Subscribed*:]

My chief motive for going to Congeree is to get teams. This settlement cannot furnish above 12 or 15. I impressed nine waggons going empty to Ninety Six, but not having any soldiers with me to detach, and the militia being all gone up to Colonel Ferguson, I am afraid they will give me the slip!

Knecht to Cornwallis, 1st October 1780   3(166): *ALS*

Camden
the 1st October 1780

Rt Hon Earl Cornwallis

My Lord

I am under the disagreeable necessity of informing your Lordship that yesterday, when the express left Camden, I had a severe fit of the ague upon me, which deprived me of the honor of writing to your Lordship by that opportunity.

Mr McDonald (whom I had the honor to mention to your Lordship in my last letter[73]) is come back from the Congerees, has engaged there about 110 barrels flour and upwards, informs me that eighteen waggons with flour were setting off as yesterday from Broad River for the Waxaws. I take the liberty to observe to your Lordship that the consumption of flour is here unavoidably great, and if that transport now moving to the main army was to be ordered for this place, more benefit would be reap'd from it. The officers who are more or less indisposed and the sick in the general and regimental hospitals, being latterly used to flour, press hard for its continuance to them. I have had the pleasure to hear that wheat and cattle is in abundance brought into camp. I have in consequence of this intelligence requested of Major McArthur to stop them eighteen waggons till your Lordship's pleasure on that head was made known to him[74]. If the cattle, which I understand was chiefly left at the Waxaws, was to be order'd hither, it would be acceptable! – the people hitherto employ'd in bringing in cattle being most of them confined to their homes by sickness.

Mr Tounsend desires me to notice to your Lordship that he hopes for your Lordship's commands, if any provisions are to be sent round by sea. Though I have no advice of Mr Tounsend regarding his forwarding rum for this place, yet cannot doubt of shortly being here by land carriage the 20 or 30 puncheons I wrote for by Mr Cruden.

---

[73]   *my last letter*: not extant.

[74]   See McArthur to Cornwallis, 2nd October, p 281.

Tomorrow I purpose leaving this sickly place to wait on your Lordship, having the honour to be with due respect, my Lord,

Your Lordship's most obliged and most humble servant

A KNECHT
Acting Assistant Commissary General

[*Subscribed*:]

On communicating the above to Colonel Turnbull, he advised me by all means to stop the above waggons and have them brought here under an escort of militia, having advice of rebel parties collecting up that way, and does by no means think it safe to suffer them to go on towards Waxaws. Accordingly I sent off an express with the proper instructions.

Rawdon to Stedman, 31st October 1780   3(340): C

Wynnesborough
31st October 1780

Mr Charles Stedman
Commissary

Sir

You will proceed to Congarees without delay. In the spot there which appears most secure and at the same time easy of access, both for boats and waggons, you will cause a magazine both of grain and forage to be collected with all possible dispatch. From what general idea I have of the country I imagine the neighbourhood of Friday's Ferry will be the most eligible situation. The magazine should consist of sixty thousand bushels of grain at least, but of as much more as you can possibly collect, and the store of forage should be proportionable. Part of the grain may be rice. Whatsoever corn is growing upon the deserted plantations of rebels you will of course secure for His Majesty's Service. And that the magazine may be the more readily formed, you may make an allowance to such of the loyal subjects as will collect and bring to you the crops under that predicament[75].

Whatever is supplied to you by any person under the King's protection must be paid for immediately by an order for the exact amount upon the Deputy Commissary General in Charlestown. He shall have instructions to be punctual in honoring such orders. You may contract with Messieurs Lord and Ancrum for such quantity of grain and forage as they will undertake to furnish, and you will have the goodness to report from time to time in what manner you proceed.

---

[75] *that predicament*: used in the archaic sense of 'that category'.

Lord Cornwallis wishes particularly that you would endeavour to inform yourself what is the stock of corn at present in Camden and that you would take care to send an ample supply thither with all expedition.

I have the honor to be etc

RAWDON

§ - §

7 - To or from physicians attending the enemy

Williamson to Cornwallis, 2nd October 1780 *93(3): ALS*

Cambden
2nd October 1780

Rt Hon Earl Cornwallis
Headquarters
Carolina

My Lord

The commanding officer in this town informs me that, tho on his part he shall not object to my departure, it is necessary that I should apply to your Lordship for a flag.

From the annexed state of the American hospital your Lordship will perceive that there is not the least occasion for my longer stay in this place. The business is now so contracted that Dr Johnson and Dr Kelty, American surgeons, or either of them, can discharge it with ease. There are but 29 wounded or sick who require the particular attention of a surgeon. There are 42 convalescents who are in such a state of recovery that they are drafted for removal, and we daily expect they will be removed to Charles Town. Some of the convalescents are just [recovering] from the small pox by inoculation, for notwithstanding our utmost exertions we have not been so fortunate as to save more than 2 or 3 who were seized by that disease in the natural way.

I am urged by the present state of my health, which is greatly impair'd, to request your Lordship would be so good as to name an early day for my departure.

I have the honor to be
Your Lordship's most obedient and most humble servant

HU WILLIAMSON

Annex

*Extract from the Return of sick and wounded Prisoners in Camden
October 1st 1780*

Patients

12	very ill
17	ill
42	recovering
71	

ROB[T] JOHNSTON
Senior Surgeon and Assistant Director General, American Hospitals

Haldane to Williamson, 10th October 1780[76]

81(35): ACS

Charlotte Town
October 10th 1780

Hugh Williamson Esq
Surgeon

Sir

Lord Cornwallis has directed me to acquaint you that you have his permission to return if the commanding officer at Camden has no objection.

I am, sir,
Your most obedient and humble servant

HH

---

[76] This letter may have miscarried. Haldane wrote to England on 22nd October, p 279, repeating its terms.

Kilty to Cornwallis, 13th October 1780   *93(8): ALS*

Camden
October 13th 1780

Rt Hon Earl Cornwallis

My Lord

The earnest desire I have to exchange my present situation induces me to apply once more to your Lordship on the subject. I understand the surgeon's mate of the 71st Regiment who was lately captivated is come to this place on parole and is extremely desirous of being exchanged. I have wrote to General Gates, who I expect will at my request shortly propose the matter. In order to facilitate an event so desirable to myself I beg leave to lay before your Lordship the real state of the matter. In my parole I have signed myself as surgeon owing to my having been muster'd as such for some months previous to my captivity, but as I had no commission or appointment higher than a mate's on account of the absence of the proper officers, I am in hopes I may still be considered and exchanged in that capacity. Should your Lordship not concur in this opinion, my only hope must rest on your Lordship's indulgence, which I flatter myself will be extended so far as to grant me a parole for a term equal to that granted to the above mentioned gentleman.

My ill state of health may perhaps plead also in my behalf.

I have the honour to be
Your Lordship's most obedient humble servant

W KILTY[77]
5th Maryland Regiment

§ - §

---

[77] Appointed a surgeon's mate in the 5th Maryland Continental Regiment on 5th March 1778, William Kilty sets out here the anomalous situation in which he finds himself. Presumably exchanged, he would transfer to the 4th Maryland Continental Regiment on 1st January 1781. (Heitman, *Historical Register*, 331)

CHAPTER 27

Letters to or from Savannah, St Augustine and Pensacola

1 - To or from Savannah

Clarke to Cornwallis, 20th August 1780   63(50): ALS

Savannah
August 20th 1780

Lt General Earl Cornwallis etc etc etc

My Lord

I am just returned from St Augustine, which place, with the addition of a few redoubts (to be constructed only in case of necessity) and a supply of such ordnance stores as appear deficient in the enclosed return, will in my opinion be in as good a state of defence as the nature of its situation, with the garrison that can be afforded, will admit of. Major Moncrief has ordered the frames to be prepared for the redoubts immediately so that no time may be lost in throwing them up on the appearance of an enemy, and as carronades seem best calculated for the defence of them, I am to request your Lordship will let me have such from Charles Town as Moncrief shall point out to be necessary. In justice to the troops that at present compose the garrison I cannot omit informing your Lordship that their appearance is infinitely beyond what I expected. They are extremely clean, well dressed, do their duty with great attention and exactness, and the French deserters they enlisted have almost all left them, which has determined me not to remove them; but as their numbers are inadequate to the defence of the fort and redoubts necessary to protect the town, it will be proper to reinforce them from hence, and, the Provincials in this place being totally undisciplined and in other respects not the most trusty, I am afraid, when it takes place, it must be by sending as many of the Regiment of Wiessenbach as will make the garrison five hundred men, to which Governor Tonyn seems to think he can make an addition of a hundred and fifty volunteers from amongst the inhabitants of the place. Some of them may be useful, but I confess I shall not have any great reliance on their fidelity in general, as many must be Minorceans[1], with which the town is crowded. Orders have been sent to the Governor for dismantling the galleys and gun boats, which have hitherto been under his directions, and they were to be sold accordingly, but as two of the latter *or a block house* seems absolutely requisite for the defence of the entrance of the harbour, which is too far from the fort for the guns to have much effect, I have desired Lieutenant Mowbray of the navy not to dispose of them 'till he hears further from Charles Town. Must therefore request your Lordship will give such directions as will ensure us the use of them, which would be of the most essential service if the place should be attacked.

Hoping your Lordship's opinion of me will remove all doubts of my having any other motive than the good of the service, I shall without hesitation express my wish that you would adopt some mode of preventing any difficulties that might otherwise arrise between Governor Tonyn and myself relative to the command in East Florida, for, though nothing but the greatest kindness and civility has yet taken place between us, nor could there if things remained in the same inactive state they are at present, I foresee it is an event that may happen, for on my arrival at Augustine the *parole* was brought to me from him, which occasioned my enquiring into the mode of service in that instance, and I was informed it was customary for the Governor to take the command when a brigadier was not in the province in consequence of a letter from the Secretary of State to General Gage, a copy of which I transmit your Lordship as explaining the matter more fully, and thinking it may point out some manner of obviating difficulties which an undecided command must ever be liable to. I have begged Major Moncrief to explain my motives and ideas more clearly than I can possibly do by writing and express my anxiety for your determination concerning it, as your Lordship's feelings will immediately suggest the unpleasant sensation of assuming a command which is disputed by another, and which on an emergency I should think it my duty to do in order to execute the trust with which you have been pleased to honor me. I cannot conclude this subject without saying that Governor Tonyn's civility and kindness to me was such as would demand every return in my power, and I should think it my duty to pay all possible respect and attention to the situation in which he is placed.

I have the honor to enclose your Lordship a letter from Major Glasier[2], who requests me so to do as he is so unfortunate as not to be known to you. I likewise enclose one from Captain Wickham to myself. He commands the débris of three companies of the 2nd Battalion of the 60th, as you will see by the return annexed. I promised him to represent to your Lordship the unpleasant predicament that he and his officers are in, being exempted from promotion in this army by the absence of their battalion, in hopes of your consent for them to go to the West Indies by the first opportunity that offers. I should not propose this to your Lordship if there was not a large proportion of officers that would still remain at Augustine.

---

[1] The British had brought a number of Minorcans and Greeks into East Florida. See Philip Schaff ed, *Schaff-Herzog Encyclopaedia of Religious Knowledge* (New York, 1882), iii, 2065.

[2] *a letter..*: not extant.

An express arrived yesterday from Pensacola and I opened a letter[3] directed to your Lordship agreeable to the superscription. General Cambell seems confident of the Spaniards attacking him, which I have no doubt of if they should not think it more feasible and endeavour to get to Augustine on a supposition of finding it more unprovided. I own this idea makes me anxious to have that garrison speedily and properly supplied with every thing, but in particular it is absolutely necessary that provisions for one thousand men for four months should constantly be in store there, as the country affords little or nothing. Lt Colonel Allen's battalion marched in obedience to your orders during my absence, and I hope Lt Colonel Brown's will soon arrive here, there being very few men fit for duty in any of the corps, occasioned by the extreme unhealthiness of the climate, and I am aware that Sir James Wright would be very tenacious and uneasy should I send more troops from hence to Florida.

Major Wright, who seems much distressed by a letter he received from your Lordship, says he has discovered the imposition of his recruiting officer and wrote to you on the subject[4]. I am sorry your Lordship found it necessary to move during this hot weather, but hope you will not suffer from it and that your present success may facilitate your future operations.

I have the honor to remain with the utmost regard and respect, my Lord,
Your Lordship's most obedient and most faithful humble servant

ALURED CLARKE
Lt Colonel

PS

By a letter which Mr Dunford has just received from Captain McKinnon I am informed that your Lordship did not assent to paying me the forage money of a brigadier. I therefore think it my duty to acquaint your Lordship that I should not have made such a requisition had not his Excellency, the Commander in Chief, on my being ordered to this command, told me that I should receive the emoluments of a brigadier and particularly mentioned an extra pay of thirty shillings a day in my letter of service, which Lt Colonel Campbell likewise had whilst employed here. I chiefly mention this in my own justification, as I should be extremely sorry your Lordship should conceive me capable of demanding more than seemed just. Lieutenant Cliffe[5] came with me by permission of the Commander in Chief, and as he has been the only *publick officer* employed in the province, as major of brigade, since my arrival and really has had a great deal of business to do, I am in hopes that his receiving that emolument may not be thought improper.

---

[3] *a letter*: not extant.

[4] Wright Jr to Cornwallis, 20th August, p 300.

[5] Commissioned an ensign in the 28th Regiment on 22nd December 1776, Walter Cliffe had been promoted to lieutenant in the 7th Regiment (Royal Fusiliers) eighteen months later. He was now serving on secondment to the Adjutant General's Department as a major of brigade. (*Army Lists*; WO 65/164(3) (National Archives, Kew))

Enclosure (1)
Return of ordnance and ammunition in East Florida   **63(57): DS**

OFFICE OF ORDNANCE
EAST FLORIDA
8th August 1780

RETURN of Ordnance and Ammunition in the Garrison of St Augustine and Outposts				
Species of Stores			*In store this day*	*Want-ing*
LAND STORES				
Ordnance, iron:		24 pounders	28	-
		18 ditto	1	-
		12 ditto	7	-
		6 ditto	4	-
		4 ditto	4	-
		3 ditto	3	-
Ordnance, brass:		6 pounders	2	-
	Mortars:	5½ inch	3	-
		42/5 ditto[6]	5	
Bayonets:			34	-
Cartridges, paper:		24 pounders	4,385	300
		18 ditto	-	250
		12 ditto	1,612	150
		6 ditto	534	666
		4 ditto	172	828
		3 ditto	-	750
Cartridges, flannel:		24 pounders	36	605
		18 ditto	-	100
		12 ditto	-	1,065

---

[6] *42/5 inch mortar*: otherwise known as a cohorn.

	6 ditto		439	300
	4 ditto		-	228
	3 ditto		-	80
Corn'd powder:	WB		502	-
	½ ditto		51	-
Flints:	Carbine		2,468	-
	Musquet		9,393	-
Fuzes, fix'd for mortars:	5½ inch		472	1,028
	42/5 ditto		118	2,382
Hangranadoes:	Fix'd		196	500
Musquets:	Bright		10	-
Musquet ball cartridges:			44,156	-
Shells empty for mortars:	5½ inch		414	1,086
	42/5 ditto		189	2,311
Shot, round:	24 pounders	loose	2,621	179
	18 ditto	ditto	50	200
	12 ditto	ditto	728	1,022
	6 ditto	ditto	390	1,110
	4 ditto	ditto	148	852
	3 ditto	ditto	94	656
	6 ditto:	fix'd	96	-
		unfix'd	335	500
Shot, doubleheaded:	4 pounders		19	181
Shot, grape:	Ditto		40	160
Shot, case:	24 pounders:	fix'd	17	-
		unfix'd	324	300
	18 ditto	ditto	-	100
	12 ditto:	fix'd	45	-
		unfix'd	20	1,000

	6 ditto:	fix'd	115	-
		unfix'd	51	500
	4 pounders:	fix'd	36	-
		unfix'd	42	150
	3 ditto	ditto	-	80
Shot, musquet:	Tons, cwts, qrs, lbs		3 ton, 6 cwt, 2 qrs, 24 lbs	-
	Loose		11,729	-
Shot, carbine:	Cwts, qrs, lbs		10 cwt, 1 qr, 20 lbs	-
LABORATORY STORES				
Match, slow:	Cwts, qrs, lbs		3 cwt, 3 qrs, 4 lbs	5 cwt
Portfires:			119	100
Sheepskins:			-	60
Tin Tubes for:	24 pounders	fix'd	-	300
	18 ditto	ditto	-	100
	12 ditto	ditto	-	600
	6 ditto	ditto	600	800
	4 ditto	ditto	-	100
	Mortars: 5½ inch	ditto	400	1,100
	4 2/5 ditto	ditto	500	2,000

THO^S WILLI^M BURLY HALL
Ordnance Storekeeper

Enclosure (2)
Secretary of State to Gage, 9th February 1765   *63(54): C*

The Power and Authority of the Civil Governors over His Majesty's Forces station'd in the respective Provinces

His Majesty's intentions are that, according to His commissions granted for that purpose, the orders of His Commander in Chief, and under him of the brigadiers general commanding in the Northern and Southern Departments, in all military affairs shall be supreme and must be obey'd by the troops as such in all the civil governments in America.

That in cases where no specifick orders have been given by the Commander in Chief or by the brigadier general in the district, the Civil Governor in Council, and, where no Council shall subsist, the Civil Governor, may for the benefit of his government give orders for the marching of troops, the disposition of them, for making and marching detachments, escorts, and such purely military services within his government to the commanding officer of the troops, who is to give proper orders for carrying the same into execution, provided they are not contradictory to, or incompatible with, any orders he may have receiv'd from the Commander in Chief or the brigadier general of the district.

And the commanding officer is from time to time duly to report with all convenient expedition to the Commander in Chief or brigadier general such orders as he shall have receiv'd from the Civil Governor.

That the Civil Governor shall give the word in all places where he shall be within his province, except when the Commander in Chief or brigadier general shall be in the same place.

That the return of the state and condition of the troops, magazine and fortification shall be made to the Governors as well as to the Commander in Chief and the brigadier general.

That the civil government is not to interfere with the detail of the military regimental duty and discipline, the report concerning which is to be made to the commanding officer, who is to make his general report to the Civil Governor.

When the Commander in Chief or brigadier general shall be present, all military orders are to be issued by them only.

Enclosure (3)
Wickham to Clarke, 9th August 1780   *63(56): LS*

St Augustine
9th of August 1780

Colonel Clark
Commanding in Georgia and East Florida

Sir

I have had the happiness to hear that His Majesty's troops in Georgia and East Florida is now under your command. I must beg leave to trouble you in behalf of the officers and men of three companies of the Second Battalion, Sixtieth Regiment, under my command, the whole consisting of thirty five rank and file, which you will please to observe by the annexed return. We were ordered from St Vincents in April 1776, by an order from Lord Amherst, to assist in forming the recruits of the new battalions with great expectation of returning to the regiment in twelve months, and it is now five years. We think it exceedingly hard (!) to be kept from the battalion with so small a number of men at a time when we have reason to think the regiment is on service, by which means we are deprived of promotion or any thing else that might turn to our advantage. As officers never can be more happy than with the regiment, we most sincerely beg of you, sir, as a particular favour you will represent our present situation to the Commander in Chief that something may be done in our behalf.

I am, sir,
Your most obedient and most humble servant

BENJ WICKHAM[7]

Enclosure (4)
Companies of the 60th Regiment serving in St Augustine   63(56): DS

A Return of three companies of the 2nd Battalion, 60th Regiment, doing duty in St Augustine 9th August 1780	
Officers present	
Commissioned	
Captains	1
Lieutenants	2
Ensigns	1
Staff	
Chaplain	-
Adjutant	-
Quarter Master	-
Surgeon	-
Mate	-
Serjeants present	8
Drummers and fifers present	6
Effective rank and file	
Present fitt for duty	28
Sick in quarters	2
Sick in hospital	2

---

[7] Commissioned a lieutenant in the 2nd Battalion, 60th (or Royal American) Regiment, on 3rd June 1772, Benjamin Wickham had been promoted to captain in the battalion on 10th August 1777. (*Army Lists*)

On command	3
On furlough	-
Recruiting	-
TOTAL	35
Wanting to complete	
Serjeants	-
Drummers	2
Rank and file	187
Alterations since last return	
Inlisted	-
Dead	-
Discharged and recommended	-
Discharged and not recommended	-
Deserted	-

BENJ WICKHAM
Captain commanding 3 companys, 2nd Battalion, 60th

Wright Jr to Cornwallis, 20th August 1780

63(59): ALS

Savannah
20th August 1780

Rt Hon Earl Cornwallis
Commander in Chief etc etc etc
South Carolina

By Major Moncrieff

My Lord

I had the honor to receive yours of the 21st July[8] during our march from Augusta to Savannah and have experienced infinite pain and chagrin therefrom. I trust to your Lordship's pardon for presuming on your time by giving a short account of my corps since its commencment and for assuring you that my whole attention, time and purse have been

---

[8] *yours of the 21st July*: see p vol I, 277.

constantly employed to promote the same. In June twelvemonths[9], several of my officers pressed me for permission to inlist from the prison ships at Cockspur, which I for a time objected to; but on seeing other corps admit them, I made application to Colonel Prevost[10] for such prisoners as were *inhabitants* of the Province of Georgia and in consequence of his assent recruited 50, of which number 15 have since diserted, 20 died, 5 were killed during the siege, and 10 are at present with me, being the whole amount of prisoners now in my corps, and whose behaviour has been irreproachable for 14 months past.

I may within bounds say that I lost in the last year by deseases not less than 70 men, tho I daily visited them myself.

When General Leslie was at Savannah, he did me the honor to inspect my corps to regulate my number of officers and companies, by which I have since been guided, hopeful of the approbation of my superiors.

My corps was the first ordered on service from this garrison after the siege, nor did I undress myself from the beginning of September [but] ten nights until General Patterson marched from hence for Charles Town in March last, keeping constant patroles between Ebenezer and Abercorn by order of General Prevost, and was frequently out in search of plunderers, who then infested the province.

In consequence of your Lordship's commands I have made the strictest scrutiny into my recruits from Charles Town, in number 37, of which 4 are dead, and I have discovered 17 to have been prisoners of war and shall return them to Charles Town by the first opportunity. I have ordered my recruiting officer under arrest, to whom I assure your Lordship I had given written instructions and a verbal injunction not to recruit a single prisoner, being the proviso on which Sir Henry Clinton gave me leave to recruit. I am disappointed at Lieutenant Obman's conduct, yet wou'd feign by leave to recommend him to clemency, being an old officer and throwing the blame, not uncommon, upon his serjeant. His zeal, not intention, lead him astray.

I am to acquaint your Lordship that I inlisted only 5 men at Augusta, 3 of which joined me having brothers in the corps.

---

[9] *twelvemonths*: of last year.

[10] Jacques Marc (anglicised to James Mark) Prevost (1736-1781) was a younger brother of Major General Augustine Prevost, to whom Wright refers later. Born in Geneva, Switzerland, he was commissioned a captain in the newly forming 60th (Royal American) Regiment in 1756 and saw action in the Seven Years' War, being wounded at Ticonderoga. After the close of the war he was placed on the half-pay list and took up farming in Bergen County, New Jersey, about 25 miles from New York City on the post road to Albany. In 1772 he returned to active service and rejoined the 60th in Jamaica. From there he repaired with the 3rd or 4th Battalion to East Florida in 1777 and attained the local rank of lt colonel in August of the same year. In March 1779 he went on to play a distinguished part in the victory at Briar Creek, Georgia, before being involved in breaking the siege of Savannah seven months later. Now, in 1780, he had returned with a detachment to Jamaica to put down disturbances there and was wounded. His poor health, exacerbated by the debilitating climate, led to an untimely death in October of the following year. ('The Prevosts: Late Colonial and Revolutionary War Era'(http://www.thehermitage.org/prevosts _text.html, 5th February 2006); *Army Lists*)

I have the honor to be with all respect
Your Lordship's most obedient humble servant

JAMES WRIGHT JUN[R]

Cornwallis to Clarke, 5th September 1780   80(7): C

Camden
September 5th 1780

Lt Colonel Clarke
Commanding His Majesty's forces in Georgia and East Florida

Dear Sir

I this morning received your letter of the 20th of last month and am glad to find upon the whole that both the place and garrison of St Augustine were in a tolerable state. I shall direct Balfour to pay all attention in his power to the requisition of Moncrief. I have read over with attention the paper which you inclosed to me relative to the right of command in East Florida and am convinced that there can be no doubt of its being vested in you. The right of military command given by His Majesty to the Civil Governor is expressed in the clearest terms to extend only to such cases where no specifick orders have been given by the Commander in Chief or by the brigadier general in the district. I consider myself as standing at present in the situation of the brigadier general of the district, and of course that my appointment of you to command must be valid. The giving the parole, unless where the Commander in Chief or the brigadier of the district is present, is particularly mentioned to belong to the Governor. I beg you will please to express these my sentiments to Governor Tonyn, for whose person and character I have great esteem and towards whom I would by no means be thought to have acted improperly.

I have received Major Glazier's letters. You can with truth assure him that I have ever declined taking any part in the promotions of this army. I think Captain Wickham's request so reasonable that I desire you will please to permit him and the officers of his battalion to join their corps by the first opportunity.

The great events which have happened in this province make it absolutely necessary for me to march immediately into North Carolina, but you will have every attention and possible assistance from your friend Balfour. I fear Cruger will not be able to spare Brown's corps very soon from Augusta. I have no ill will to Major Wright. I am convinced his officers have deceived him, but I am very credibly informed that his corps inlisted above 200 men last year out of the prison ships, and he even pleads guilty to 17 prisoners taken from Charles Town contrary to the most possitive orders. I have no objection to your releasing his officers if you think proper. McKinnon totally misunderstood me about the pay. I told him that, notwithstanding his assurances to you and Webster, Sir Henry had left no instructions with me about you and I therefore doubted whether I should venture to pay you before I heard from him but I had not the smallest doubt of your receiving it then. I have, however, ordered pay for you both and for Major Cliffe. Your friend Ross is sailed in the *Providence* with the account of our success. I sincerely hope it may prove useful to him. I shall desire the commanding officer of the navy at Charles Town to write to Lieutenant Mowbray about the gun boats. I beg you will accept my very sincere good wishes, and believe me to be with great regard

Your most obedient and faithful servant

[CORNWALLIS]

Cornwallis to Clarke, 6th September 1780   *80(9): C*

Camden
September 6th 1780

To Lt Colonel Clarke
Commanding in Georgia and East Florida

Dear Sir

Doctor Hayes informs me that Mr Edwards[11] has represented to him that there is no occasion for a general hospital at Savannah as there have not been for several months more than twelve patients. I therefore submit it to you whether it will not be for the good of the service that the hospital there should be broke up and the regimental surgeons well supplied with medicines, which Doctor Hayes has my directions to pay particular attention to. If you see no objection, you will please to order the hospital to be broke up. If, on the contrary, you see any reasons against it, you will communicate them to me.

I am
Your most obedient and faithfull servant

CORNWALLIS

---

[11] Arthur Edwards was a master apothecary at the General Hospital in North America, the department responsible for hospitals other than small regimental ones. He had taken up his post on 8th October 1778, having served for more than thirteen years as surgeon to the 10th Regiment. He would resign on 4th May 1782. He appears to have been the last master apothecary appointed in the army medical service, a post apparently assigned to the senior apothecary in a hospital or to the senior apothecary attached to a force in the field. (Johnston, *Commissioned Officers in the Medical Service*, xxxiv and 41)

Clarke to Cornwallis, 30th August 1780   63(83): ALS

Savannah
August 30th 1780

Earl Cornwallis etc etc etc

My Lord

It is with the most heartfelt satisfaction that I have the honor to congratulate your Lordship on the signal and glorious victory you have obtained over the rebel army. Mr Gates's former success seems to have inspired him and the people he commanded with sufficient confidence to give your Lordship an opportunity of proving to the world what British troops are equal to performing when commanded by a general for whom they feel a strong personal regard, in addition to the more necessary qualifications of abilities and determined perseverance which, (even at the risque of being suspected of flattery) I must beg leave to say, have been strongly manifested in your Lordship's recent success, which is a happy presage, and I sincerely hope will prove the forerunner, of many similar actions that must terminate in honor to your Lordship and permanent advantage to your grateful country.

Major Moncrief will, I hope, have had the honor of delivering my letters to you before this arrives, as he seemed extremely anxious lest you should be under the necessity of moving during his absence. I begged the favor of him to explain some things to your Lordship more fully than I could possibly do by letter, particularly my inclination to move to St Augustine if you had the slightest wish for me so to do. I was much mortified to find by a letter from Lt Colonel Cruger that an unfortunate affair[12] had happened in the neighbourhood of Ninety Six, but I hope the consequences will not extend beyond the loss we have sustained and the sufferings of Colonel Innes and the rest of the unfortunate wounded people.

I have repeatedly applications from Lt Colonel Browne on the subject of money for supplying the Indians, to which I as often give negatives. I am apprehensive the intended congress will cause a heavy expence. The troops in this place are so sickly that I have desired Colonel Cruger will send Browne's corps down as soon as they can possibly be spared. Indeed, I think many reasons might be assigned why this would be a more proper situation for it.

I have the honor to be with great respect and regard, my Lord,
Your Lordship's most obedient and most faithful humble servant

ALURED CLARKE

PS

I have just received an account that the *Ceres*, an armed transport, is ashore on the Grenadier Bank, and as in all probability she will be lost, I have sent all the boats we could

---

[12] *an unfortunate affair*: the action at Musgrove's Mill on 19th August.

collect to take out her stores. She was sent from Charles Town to dismantle the *Vigilant*.

I am, my Lord, etc

ALURED CLARKE

Clarke to Cornwallis, 5th October 1780   3(186): ALS

Savannah
October 5th 1780

Lt General Earl Cornwallis etc etc etc

My Lord

I take it for granted your Lordship has long before this been informed of the particulars of the attack made on Lt Colonel Brown's post at Augusta; therefore shall not trespass further on your Lordship's time than to do that justice to him and his corps which the very spirited defence they made merits by recommending them to your Lordship's notice. Lt Colonel Brown was wounded in the beginning of the action, yet persevered in the execution of his duty, although for the two last days they had not a drop of water, which was extremily distressing to the wounded, a return of which and the killed I have enclosed to the Deputy Adjutant General for your Lordship's inspection.

When Major Moncrief came here from Charles Town, he said your Lordship had consented to a stockade and some redoubts being constructed for the security of the town if Sir James Wright wished it and the province would furnish labourers etc so that the expence to Government might not exceed three or four hundred pounds. And on the late alarm, before we knew the event of the attack on Augusta, the Governor and inhabitants seemed so greatly apprehensive for the security of this place that Sir James Wright applied to me, stated the proposals made to him by Major Moncrief, and pressed so very earnestly about it that (knowing your Lordship had no objection) I was induced to give my consent and Lieutenant Dunford is now in the execution of it upon Moncrief's plan. And your Lordship may be assured the expence shall not exceed the sum proposed.

Our suffering from sickness in this vile climate is terrible, and I am sorry to inform your Lordship that it continues in a very great degree. The Regiment of Wiessenbach has lost many men and some officers and at present has not really above sixty men fit for duty. I have myself been extremely ill, and Mr Cliffe at death's door, but we are now almost well again.

I was sorry to hear of the death of Lieutenant Prideaux[13] and Quarter Master Taylor[14]

---

[13] Edmund Prideaux had been commissioned a lieutenant in the 7th Regiment (Royal Fusiliers) on 6th November 1778. (*Army Lists*)

of the Fusiliers. Previous to General Prescott's[15] leaving America he informed me that Sir Henry Clinton had promised the first vacant lieutenantcy in the regiment to his nephew, Mr Richard Prescott, and when an opportunity offered, he desired me to remind the Commander in Chief of it. I therefore take the liberty of recommending my colonel's cause to your Lordship's protection and friendly assistance. And I have in my own behalf and that of the regiment to recommend Serjeant Nathaniel Taylor[16] to succeed to the quartermastership vacated by the death of his brother, the success of which I feel much interested in, as he is a very honest, deserving man and greatly attached to the corps from having been born in it.

A much smaller some[17] of money having been left with me by Major General Prevost than Sir Henry Clinton expected, it is very near exhausted. I have therefore written to Lt Colonel Balfour, desiring him to adopt some mode of sending me a supply, which I hope he will do soon.

This accompanies some dispatches for your Lordship which arrived here in the *Galatea* from New York[18]. She was drove past Charles Town and came in here last night, and as her getting there was very uncertain, Captain Reade[19] desired me to send an express with the letters.

I must beg your Lordship will excuse the badness of my writing, which is occasioned by the weakness left by my illness. I cannot conclude without acknowledging the receipt of your Lordship's letter of the 5th of September, expressing my anxious wishes that success may crown all your undertakings, and assuring your Lordship that I have the honor to remain with the utmost respect, my Lord,

Your Lordship's most obedient and most faithful humble servant

ALURED CLARKE

---

[14] Thomas Taylor had been appointed quartermaster of the 7th on 29th November 1777. (*Army Lists*)

[15] Richard Prescott (1725-1788) was Colonel of the 7th, with which he had come to Canada in 1773. Now a major general, he was an unlucky officer, having been twice captured, first at Montreal and then at Rhode Island, and twice exchanged. (*Appletons'*; Boatner, *Encyclopedia*, 886-7; *Army Lists*)

[16] Clarke's recommendation would be accepted. Nathaniel Taylor was appointed quartermaster of the 7th with effect from 22nd September 1781. (*Army Lists*)

[17] *some*: sum.

[18] *some dispatches..*: the originals of those conveyed to Charlestown in the *Thames*. See pp 48-54 and 117.

[19] James Reid (?-1798) had been commissioned a lieutenant in the Royal Navy on 16th September 1755, rising to commander on 25th June 1773 and post-captain on 5th July 1776. Now commanding the *Galatea*, he would, according to Balfour, prefer to cruise for prizes rather than carry on the more important service of convoying some provision vessels to St Augustine. (Syrett and DiNardo ed, *The Commissioned Sea Officers*; *The Cornwallis Papers*)

PS

In a letter some time ago I inclosed your Lordship a memorial of one Mr Young[20], to which I received no answer. I am now, at the frequent instigation of the sufferer and his friends, together with General Prevost's recommendation, induced to enclose you one of Phillip Alman's[21], as without your Lordship's directions I neither can nor will do any thing in it.

I must beg your Lordship will excuse some scratching in the first page, which happened by accident after the letter was wrote.

§ - §

2 - From St Augustine

Tonyn to Cornwallis, 13th August 1780　　　　　　　　　　　　　　　*63(40): ALS*

St Augustine
13th August 1780

Earl of Cornwallis

My Lord

I had the honour of receiving your letter of the 18th ultimo[22] by Major Moncrief, and it is very pleasing and very flattering to me that your Lordship retains a remembrance of our former days.

I shall have great satisfaction in faithfully discharging whatever business you may think proper to trust to my care, and it is fortunate on this occasion that I may mention to your Lordship that it is my earnest ambition to serve our royal master in any capacity, especially

---

[20] See Clarke to Cornwallis, 13th July, vol I, pp 340-2.

[21] The memorial (3(188)) makes a claim for £360 sterling to cover property taken down in September 1779 to fortify the lines in Savannah at the time of the siege. The claimant, Phillip Alman (?-1781), had arrived in Savannah in 1745. Apparently a carpenter by trade, he had set up in business and appears to have become a prominent member of the community, if only from the fact that he was one of the members of the Provincial Congress in 1775. Whether he opposed the constitutional break with the Crown or was a fair-weather friend to the revolutionaries is uncertain, but what is clear is that he had sufficiently ingratiated himself with Augustine Prevost, Clarke's predecessor, to obtain his recommendation that the claim be paid. (Information in part from Bonnie Treon, a descendant of Alman's second wife, 29th February 2000)

[22] *your letter..*: see vol I, p 354.

in that wherein I had the honour of being first known to your Lordship, and I should be happy to renew my natural profession under your Lordship's auspices.

In my last letter[23] I had the honour of mentioning that Sir Henry Clinton had acquainted me of your Lordship's taking the command of the King's forces in the southern provinces, which would consequently give full employment; and should the future operations carry your Lordship to a greater distance from hence, I still trust, for the security of the province, to your watchful care over it; and I hope, in case of an attack by an enemy, it will be previously put into a proper state of making a vigorous defence, which situation I have indeed long wished to see effectuated, and then, should even a misfortune happen at Pensacola, the bad effect will not be so much felt here; but I am not now so apprehensive of a misfortune in West Florida, as I depend upon the vigilence of our general and admiral at Jamaica, who must be rendered very respectable by the successes of His Majesty's fleet in the West Indies.

It will be, however, necessary that the Superintendents preserve a cordial disposition in the Indian nations inhabiting the country immediately between this province and West Florida, and it will be my constant attention to keep in harmony and good humour with the Siminoly Indians, who domiciliate within this province.

Lt Colonel Clerk[24] and Major Moncrief, who leave this to day, will acquaint your Lordship of the state of this province, and to whom I beg leave to refer you for other particulars.

I am sorry that some imprudences committed by the soldiers, in which they are alone to blame, should have given rise to many other falsities which have been industriously propagated abroad. As Mr Younge[25], our Attorney General, will pay his respects to your Lordship, he can acquaint you of the particulars.[26]

---

[23] *my last letter*: not extant.

[24] *Clerk*: pronounced 'Clark' in the English manner.

[25] A son of Henry Yonge (see vol I, p 342, note 15), Henry Yonge Jr (*c*. 1750-1789) had been forced to flee Georgia like his father on account of support for the Crown. On 24th June 1779 he was appointed Attorney General of East Florida, where he had been involved in commanding royal militia and would continue to be so. He would remain in the province until its cession to Spain in 1784, when ill health caused him to move to the Bahamas, where he hoped to establish himself as a lawyer. Having presented extensive claims to the royal commission in respect of lost property in Georgia and South Carolina, he would die at sea while on passage from the Bahamas to England. (Coldham, *Loyalist Claims*, i, 543)

[26] Tonyn may be referring to events which began on 5th June when soldiers went to a house – apparently a rum shop – of a Minorcan, Lorenzo Capo. They allegedly carried off his wife, Mary Magdalen Capo, to the guard room and raped her. After a grand jury ruling, an Ensign John Manning of the 60th Regiment shot himself, an event which so enraged the soldiery that they rioted and pulled down Lorenzo's house. Tonyn and Glasier offered a reward for discovery of the guilty parties, but the offer did not sway a grand jury from bringing a presentment against Glasier for not trying to prevent the riot. By 26th November no one would have come forward to claim the reward. (Daniel Schafer to the editor, 28th November 2005; Tonyn to Germain, CO 5/560 (National Archives, Kew))

As Colonel Clerk's departure is more sudden than I expected, I beg leave to assure you that I have always the honour to be with the greatest respect and attention, my Lord,

Your Lordship's most obedient and most humble servant

PAT TONYN

Tonyn to Cornwallis, 18th August 1780   63(44): ALS

St Augustine
18th August 1780

Rt Hon the Earl of Cornwallis

My Lord

Not having been honoured with an answer to my letter of the 6th June last to Admiral Arbuthnot by his being removed to a greater distance, I take the liberty to enclose for your Lordship's information a copy of that letter.

Since the Admiral's departure Captain Henry sent Mr Mowbray with directions to discharge all vessels employed for the protection of the province. This situation, my Lord, lays open all our plantations to the incursions of the enemies privateers; the settlements in general are upon the rivers, which, if not guarded, the rovers can easily enter. I doubt not your Lordship will see the necessity of a permanent marine establishment for the protection of the rivers. It would be cruel and very vexatious, after the great expence which has enabled us hitherto to baffle all the attempts and efforts of our enemies, the province should be striped of every marine resource and the settlements thereby endangered to total ruin.

As the copy of my letter to the Admiral expresses my ideas of a proper arangement for the security of the province, I shall not presume to trouble your Lordship further by this opportunity.

A commissary for the care of prisoners of war has been at the Provincial charges at five shillings per day, and it is necessary should be continued. Mr William Brown[27], a worthy gentleman and an old officer, though out of the army, has punctually executed that duty. He is an old acquaintance. Permit me therefore to recommend him to be continued in that office, as I have to request of your Lordship to take that charge from the province, having now no Provincial fund to provide for it.

---

[27] The son of a judge, William Browne was from Salem, Massachusetts. By late 1762 a lieutenant in the army, he entered the 14th Regiment on 6th June 1766 and was promoted to captain in the 52nd five years later. Both regiments were serving in North America. In 1778 or 1779 he ceased to be an officer. Having 'suffered much during the rebellion', presumably from banishment and confiscation, he now occupied three public posts at St Augustine: Commissary of Prisoners, Deputy Commissary of Stores and Provisions, and Stores Cooper. He would be in England in 1784 following the cession of East Florida to Spain. (Sabine, *Biographical Sketches*, i, 268; *Army Lists*; *The Cornwallis Papers*)

When affairs of no greater moment intervene than the important service of this province, I hope to receive the honour of your Lordship's sentiments upon a general system of measures adopted for its defence.

I have the honour to be with the greatest respect and esteem, my Lord,
Your Lordship's most obedient and most humble servant

PAT TONYN

Enclosure
Tonyn to Arbuthnot, 6th June 1780   *63(46): C*

St Augustine
6th June 1780

Dear Sir

A report has circulated a few days past that Charlestown has surrendered to His Majesty's arms on the 12th ultimo, of which event I most heartily congratulate your Excellency although I have no certainty of the fact.

In former letters I had the honour to acquaint you of the state of the Provincial marine, and your Excellency gave me reason to hope that proper measures would be taken respecting it when the operations against Carolina offered a favorable opportunity for it. As my situation in defraying the expences incurred by the Provincial armament is of a very delicate nature, having solicited since 29th May 1779 to be relieved of these charges, I hope you will excuse my earnestly requesting it, and that Captain Mowbray may be sent with your instructions to settle his own account and all other collateral marine expences and to fix a permanent establishment for the protection of the province.

Early in the spring 1779 several armed vessels employed in our defence were discharged, and the *Dreadnought* galley continued for the protection of St John's River. Upon Count d'Estaing's arrival on the coast it was indispensably necessary to arm again, which measure has been approved of by His Majesty as signified to me by Lord George Germain, and I beg leave to transmit a further extract of his Lordship's letter to me upon that subject, viz:

> 'And as that danger is now happily over, and I trust the reduction of Charlestown has been effected, which must remove all apprehensions of a future attack from the rebels, it [is] His Majesty's pleasure that you do put a stop to every extraordinary expence which the grant of Parliament does not enable you to defray or the Commander in Chief of His Majesty's Land or Sea Forces does not authorise you to incur and at the same time provide funds for their payment. The vessels you have purchased or hired must therefore be discharged or delivered over to the officer commanding His Majesty's ships on the southern station, but if you judge it absolutely necessary for the safety of the province that either those or others should continue in the province, you will apply to Vice Admiral Arbuthnott for such assistance, who has orders to pay all proper attention to your representations.'

Although the happy successes of His Majesty's arms give a more certain security from depredations of the rebels, this province is open to the attacks of the Spaniards and must necessarily be protected from the incursions of their rovers. I have erected a block house to guard the entrance of the Moskito's, which, cooperating with the *Prince of Wales* galley, will effect that object in that district. The *Dreadnought* and *Thunderer* galleys are for the protection of St John's River, and the *King* and *Queen's Galleys* are in this harbour to guard the North and South Rivers. It would also be of very great advantage if a proper armament was fixed for the protection of St Mary's River, the northern district of the province, and which is well inhabited.

A privateer from Havannah lately entered Indian River in this province. Fourteen of the people got on shore and have been taken by the troops that are posted in the block house at the Moskito's and the sailors of the *Prince of Wales* galley.

I have sent this express on purpose to have the honour of your commands, and

I have the honour to be with the most perfect respect and esteem, dear sir,
Your Excellency's most obedient and most humble servant

PAT TONYN

Tonyn to Cornwallis, 24th August 1780   63(64): ALS

St Augustine
24th August 80

Rt Hon Earl of Cornwallis

My Lord

Since I had the honour of writing to your Lordship on the 18th instant, duplicates of which are inclosed, the *Hydra* man of war and a provision brig arrived off this bar. It has blown a storm for several days, which has prevented the vessel geting into port.

This will be a great relief to the garrison, which has been too scantily provided with supplies and in general has had great reason for complaint on that score. I hope the contractors will be obliged to be more diligent in the performance of their contracts and that we shall not feel the like scarcity for the future.

Trusting to your Lordship's due attention for the protection of the province, and that a permanent marine will be established by the Admiral to guard our rivers, which I have earnestly wished to see accomplished and hope your Lordship will support my request in it, we shall then have many anxieties removed and consequently be less troublesome to your Lordship.

May perfect good health and every happiness always attend you.

I have the honour to be with the greatest respect and esteem, my Lord,
Your Lordship's most obedient and most humble servant

PAT TONYN

Tonyn to Cornwallis, 8th September 1780 64(36): ALS

St Augustine
8th September 80

Rt Hon Earl Cornwallis

My Lord

In the first transports of joy I am impelled most heartily to congratulate your Lordship upon the glorious victory obtained over the rebel army by His Majesty's forces under your command.

This happy event must be attended with the most important consequences in the scale of American affairs, and must throw a transcendant brightness on the fame of your Lordship's conduct that will have an exalted place in the British annals amidst the most remarkable and renowned actions, and cannot fail of crowning your Lordship with the high approbation of our gracious Sovereign and the love and admiration of our country.

I had not the honour of receiving your Lordship's favour of the 3rd August[28] untill after the departure of the *Hydra* frigate and have this moment received a letter from Lt Colonel Balfour transmitting the printed account of the battle and a list of atrocious rebel prisoners in a vessel now off this bar, sent for St Augustine by your Lordship's commands, and I have the honour to inclose a copy of my answer to the colonel for your satisfaction.

These are the very wicked men who raised the superstruction of rebellion in South Carolina and whose vile machinations held up the horrid spectre to adoration throughout the land. They are proper examples of stigmatizing with infamy and punishing in just detestation of hellish rebellion, and Colonel Glazier shall have every assistance in keeping them within decent bounds.

I have the honour to be with the greatest respect and esteem, my Lord,
Your Lordship's most obedient and most humble servant

PAT TONYN

---

[28] *favour of the 3rd August*: see vol I, p 360.

Enclosure
Tonyn to Balfour, 9th September 1780

64(40): C

St Augustine
9th September 1780

Lt Colonel Nesbit Balfour

Sir

I had the honour of receiving your letter of the 4th instant acquainting me of the glorious victory obtained over the rebel forces near Camden and the successes of Colonel Tarlton, which have given the greatest satisfaction.

The measures previously taken to the battle throw a meritted lustre upon the conduct of Earl Cornwallis, and the intrepid valour with which they were carried into execution is equal to any thing met with in history performed by the most renowned generals, and I am very happy Lord Cornwallis has had this fair opportunity of proving his great military capacity.

It will always afford me pleasure to concur in whatever may answer to relieve his Lordship's anxiety in any situation, and you may rely upon every assistance to Colonel Glazier in a watchfull care over the rebel prisoners sent to this province.

These men have been, from the first of the disturbances, the most mischievous and flagitious and the very demagogues of sedition in South Carolina. They are the fittest objects to hold out as examples to the people in conscious horror of rebellion, and their residence here would have less bad effect in close confinement than in the indulgent permission of a district, which they have abused in Carolina and will probably do so again. The recent aggravation of their former black crimes justified such treatment towards them, and I should have less apprehensions of their pestiferous counselling being of any weight here in poisoning the minds of the people, for I have been of opinion from the begining that a proper use of hemp must be applied to this infernal disease, as such deep and latent venom cannot be radically cured by more gentle remedies.

Lt Colonel Glazier, I imagine, will send a state of provisions in the King's Stores since those came by the order of Earl Cornwallis, and if a further supply could be spared it would be very convenient. I also refer you to the colonel for the treatment the rebel prisoners are to have here.

In hopes of fresh occasions of congratulating you upon repeated successes of Lord Cornwallis,

I have the honour to be with perfect regard and esteem, sir,
Your most obedient and most humble servant

PAT TONYN

§ - §

3 - From Pensacola

Campbell to Cornwallis, 21st September 1780 *3(82): LS*

Head Quarters
Pensacola
21st September 1780

The Rt Hon Earl Cornwallis, Lt General etc etc

My Lord

On the 12th instant I received by express from Lt Colonel Browne, Superintendant of Indian Affairs at Augusta, the pleasing, grateful and important news that your Lordship had obtained a signal victory over the rebel army in Carolina under the command of Gates, whereon I beg leave most heartily and sincerely to congratulate your Lordship and to rejoice at an event productive of such glory and advantage to your country and highly honorable to yourself.

Our state here, my Lord, is that of uncertainty and suspense (whether of receiving aid from our friends or the degree of danger we are in from our enemies). In short, we are threatned with a speedy attack by Spain, and no answer as yet received to any one of my repeated and reiterated applications to Sir Henry Clinton, General Dalling and Sir Peter Parker for reinforcements.

I have the honor to be with respect, my Lord,
Your Lordship's most obedient and most humble servant

JOHN CAMPBELL
Major General

§ - §

CHAPTER 28

Miscellaneous papers

1 - Correspondence with Simpson

Simpson to Cornwallis, 4th September 1780　　　　　　*64(18): ALS*

Charles Town
September 4th 1780

My Lord

I am honor'd with your Lordship's letter of the 27th of last month[1] incloseing the proclamation[2], which will be return'd, as you have desired, by Captain McKinnon, who is to set out from Charles Town tomorrow.

Inclosed are copies of the papers relative to the land and Negroes at Hobcaw, three fourths of which are forfeited to the Crown, being the publick property of the rebels.

---

[1] *letter of the 27th..*: no extant copy.

[2] *the proclamation*: a draft. It dealt with sequestration.

I have been much importuned by Messrs Begby and Manson[3] to have them put into possession of it, but as your Lordship never gave me explicit orders about it, nothing hath hitherto been done in it. Besides, they seem to expect it as a matter of justice for their losses and sufferings in adhereing to the cause of Goverment, for which I most sincerely wish they and every other sufferer had a proper compensation, but it is not in my opinion a proper moment to open such a bussiness as it would produce a number of claims that would not be easily satisfied. If your Lordship should therefore think proper to give them possession, it, I presume, will only be as trustees for the Crown, to whose Receiver they must be accountable for the proffits of it.

I sincerely wish your Lordship happiness and success and am with all possible regard

Your Lordship's most obedient and faithfull humble servant

J SIMPSON

[*Subscribed*:]

Upon examination in consequence of Mr Pritchard's letter the Board of Police were satisfied the effects have been appraised at their full value and there is no foundation for the complaints set forth by Mr Pritchard.

Enclosure (1)
Begbie and Manson to Simpson, 29th August 1780   64(20): C

Charles Town
29th August 1780

Hon James Simpson Esq

Dear Sir

I called upon you yesterday in order to receive authority for taking possession of the ship yard at Hobcaw consistent with the award of the arbitrators and umpire delivered in at the

---

[3] James and William Begbie, like Daniel Manson (see vol I, p 21, note 21), were Scottish shipwrights who had migrated to Charlestown, where in 1769 all three jointly purchased a shipyard founded in 1753 by two other Scots, John Rose and James Stewart. Situated on the south side of Hobcaw Creek off the Wando River, it was the largest shipyard in South Carolina. Being loyalists like Daniel Manson, James and William had been obliged, like him, to sell up in 1778 and sail into exile, from where they had now returned to reclaim possession of the shipyard. In the meantime it had been purchased by Paul Pritchard before control was acquired by the Commissioners of the South Carolina (revolutionary) Navy, who used the yard to refit vessels for their purposes. The situation since the capitulation is set out in Simpson's present letter, together with its enclosures, and in Cornwallis's reply. After the war ownership of the yard would revert to Paul Pritchard and remain with the Pritchard family until 1831. (P C Coker III, *Charleston's Maritime Heritage, 1670-1865: An Illustrated History* (CokerCraft Press, 1987); C D Crowse, 'Shipowning and Shipbuilding in Colonial South Carolina: An Overview', *The American Neptune*, xliv (1984), No 4, 221-244; A S Salley Jr, *Journal of the Commissioners of the Navy of South Carolina* (Historical Commission of South Carolina, 1913 and 1914); Lambert, *SC Loyalists*, 27, 187)

Office of the Honorable Board of Police with an inventory annexed of the articles so appraised. As I had not the pleasure of finding you at home, I called at the Office of the Board, where Mr Winstanley[4] shewed me a letter from Paul Pritchard wherein he offers a greater sum for the place than it is valued at in the award, which is an illiberal reflection thrown on the judgment and candour of the gentlemen arbitrators and a contempt of the authority of the Honorable Board and intended as an evasive shift to answer purposes of his own and deprive us of our just claims upon the place, which we are still unpaid for.

As the arbitrators were duly chosen by his own consent and voluntary offer before you, and the gentlemen so chosen approved of by the Honorable Board, and an umpire nominated by them and acted by authority of their warrant, the award is and ought to be binding and decisive and humbly requests your Honours will order us by authority possession of the place as we are ready and willing to comply with the award and conform to every reasonable and just measure towards a settlement with him on our part. We look to you, sir, for that justice and impartiality your honour and candour gives us hopes to expect and justice and humanity for our great losses on account of our attachment to Government intitles us to.

We are with the greatest esteem, dear sir,
Your most obedient servants

BEGBIE AND MANSON

Enclosure (2)
Pritchard to Phepoe, undated   *64(22): C*

Thomas Phepoe Esq[5]

Sir

Am informed the matter relative to the ship yard is to be determined this forenoon. Have already seen the award delivered by the arbitrators, nor did anything ever surprize me more.

---

[4] Thomas Winstanley was a turncoat. Now Clerk of the Board of Police, he had been Clerk of the Charlestown revolutionary militia before the capitulation. In January 1782 the revolutionary assembly at Jacksonborough would subject him to banishment and confiscation of his property. (McCowen Jr, *Charleston, 1780-82*, 75)

[5] Thomas Phepoe was a lawyer who, arriving from Ireland with Chief Justice Gordon in 1771, was promptly admitted to the Charlestown bar. A loyalist by inclination, he has been described as 'the classic case of a professional man who was able to carry water on both shoulders'. While professedly bearing allegiance to the revolutionary state and even serving from 1778 to 1780 in the revolutionary legislature, he made it his speciality to defend persons charged with sedition, thereby achieving notoriety as 'the Tory lawyer'. After the capitulation of Charlestown he began openly to support the Crown, and, from Simpson's enclosures (1) and (2) above, it appears that he was now connected with the Board of Police. Contrary to Bailey's and Cooper's assertion, it is doubtful whether he ever served as a captain in the royal militia. In January 1782 the revolutionary assembly at Jacksonborough would subject him to banishment and confiscation of his property. On the evacuation of Charlestown some eleven months later, he would sail for England and present a claim to the royal commission with respect to his confiscated property, which included a house in Broad Street, Charlestown, and some 3,800 uncultivated acres. In 1788 he was living in Dublin. (Lambert, *SC Loyalists*, 66; Bailey and Cooper, *SC House of Representatives*, iii, 551-2; The SC Banishment and Confiscation Act 1782; Coldham, *Loyalist Claims*, 390)

The plantation containing three hundred and forty acres within four miles of Charles Town, with all the wharves and buildings (the greater part of which are rebuilt a year ago), are valued at only £1,500 with all the utensils belonging to the yard. Now, sir, I do assure you that I would chearfully give two thousand five hundred guineas for the ¾ of this plantation and the other articles annexed thereto by the arbitrators. You'll please observe they value the timber, mahogany and other lumber at £175, whereas I am also ready and willing to give for said articles five hundred guineas.

Now, sir, as matters has gone in this way, I must declare to you that I am quite indifferent about the trifle allowed me, as I confess I look upon myself to be compleatly ruined. Have now only to request that I may be allowed a reasonable time for removing my crop, which I planted entirely at my own expence, also my own working utensils, which are my own private property, with some timber, planks and spars which I brought to the ship yard since I was put in possession of the same by Admiral Arbuthnot, whom I then looked upon to have power for doing so, nor can I yet pretend to say or think any thing to the contrary.

I beg leave to observe to you that, being concerned with the Commissioners of the Navy and possessed of their three fourths of the ship yard and half the utensils belonging to it, I've suffered them to fall in my debt one hundred and fifteen thousand pounds of our late Continental currency, which I thought was secure to me, having possession of their ¾ of the yard as before, also of ¾ of the Negroes. Nor do I yet doubt, if you'll please represent these different matters to the Honorable Board of Police, but you'll be able to have justice done me.

I am, sir,
Your obedient servant

PAUL PRITCHARD

Cornwallis to Simpson, 8th September 1780 — 80(13): C

Camp at Hanging Rock
September 8th 1780

James Simpson Esq

Dear Sir

I this morning received your letter of the 4th. Unless my memory fails me, I am pretty certain that it was finally settled sometime before I left Charlestown that Messrs Begbee and Manson should be put into possession of the property at Hobcaw until some settlement should take place, but they must certainly be accountable to the Receiver of the Crown. I have no authority to give them any other possession. Their case is certainly hard and will, I hope, in future be properly considered. You see we have got out of Camden; that is some satisfaction.

I am
Your most obedient and faithfull servant

CORNWALLIS

Simpson to Cornwallis, 11th September 1780 64(44): ALS

Charles Town
September 11th 1780

The Earl Cornwallis

My Lord

The day before yesterday the *Grenville* packet arrived here after fifty three days' passage from Falmouth, but I have received no letters except those that were private, and in them I have very little intelligence. I could not indeed expect any publick dispatches, for my letters were sent under the care of General Prevost, who was arrived at Falmouth but had not got to London when the mail was made up.

I have received a copy of the Act of Parliament regulateing the trade of America[6]. If it had been before me when I drew up the restrictions under which your Lordship opened the trade of this country, I could not have followed it more exactly. The identical sums mentioned in it occurr'd to me, and it authorizes your Lordship to make the appointments which you have done, so there is not the least cause for a deviation from the present regulations unless it shall hereafter become expedient to permit exportation to the West Indies. Captain Gardner hath fixed the 26th for the convoy to sail. The value of the several cargoes will amount, as I am well informed, to above one hundred thousand pounds sterling.

My letters contain very little news. The papers, pamphlets etc that are usually sent out to me are gone to New York. From the letters of other people I have learn'd that our Cork fleet are safe and were to sail soon after the packet, and several of the Saint Domingo fleet, which I mentioned to be taken in the last letters[7] I wrote to your Lordship, were arrived. The minds of the people were not quite settled after the very unprecedented riots which had lasted so long in London. Several people had been executed near the places where the devastations were committed, but they all seem to be of inferior condition; and the bill against Lord George Gordon had not been given out. It is perhaps intended to try him and some others for high treason. Those who have already suffered were indicted for felonies only. Wedderburn is Chief Justice of the Common Pleas and gone to the House of Peers with the title of Lord Loughborough[8]. I am inform'd his charge to the grand jury at the opening the

---

[6] The Act, which received royal assent on 23rd June, was 20 GEO III c 46. According to its long title, it was 'An Act to allow the exportation of provisions, goods, wares, and merchandize from Great Britain to certain towns, ports or places in North America which are or may be under the protection of His Majesty's arms, and from such towns, ports or places to Great Britain and other parts of His Majesty's dominions'.

[7] *last letters*: not extant.

[8] Alexander Wedderburn (1733-1805) was a Scot who, like many of his countrymen, saw his fairest prospect as the high road to England. Admitted to the Inner Temple in 1753, he became a Member of Parliament in 1761 and a King's counsel by 1763. Eight years later he entered the North ministry as Solicitor General and was soon a valued Government speaker in the House of Commons during the difficult years of the American revolutionary war. Using his position to pressure North into advancing his political career, he was made Attorney General in 1778 and became in 1780 Chief Justice of the Court of Common Pleas with the title of Lord Loughborough. In later life

special commission was a masterpiece.

I am surprized we have no arrivals from New York. The winds have been constantly fair these three weeks. I would gladly flatter myself some important expedition that will favour your Lordship's operations is the reason of our being neglected and that we shall soon receive satisfactory accounts.

I wish your Lordship every possible happiness and success, and

I am with great truth and regard
Your Lordship's most faithfull and obedient humble servant

J SIMPSON

[*Subscribed*:]

There are reports that there will be a coalition of parties and a peace with Spain, but I do not know what foundation there is for them.

§ - §

2 - From or relating to Cruden

Cruden's commission concerning the sequestration of property,   7(22): C
   16th September 1780

BY The Rt Hon Charles Earl Cornwallis,
Lt General of His Majesty's forces etc etc etc

TO JOHN CRUDEN Esquire

WHEREAS it appears to me to be a measure dictated as well by justice as good policy to seize the estates real and personal of all such rebels and adherents to, and abettors of, rebellion as are particularly described by my proclamation of this date, for the publick benefit and advantage, and that[9] it is expedient to appoint immediately a person of fidelity and capacity to carry this purpose into execution in the manner most conducive to His Majesty's Service, *I, REPOSING* especial trust and confidence in your loyalty, integrity, skill and

---

he would be appointed Lord Chancellor and be created Earl of Rosslyn. A man of great application, he attained considerable repute as a public speaker, whether in the law courts or Parliament, and served as a judge for more than twenty years without discredit. He is buried in St Paul's Cathedral. (*ODNB*)

[9] *that*: the meaning is 'whereas'. See vol I, p 108, note 12.

abilities, *DO* hereby nominate, constitute and appoint you, the said John Cruden, during my pleasure, or untill other appointment be made, to be Commissioner for the seizure, superintendance, care, custody and management of all property of whatever denomination that shall be liable to be taken and seized by virtue of this commission and my proclamation aforesaid.

AND you are accordingly hereby invested with full power and authority, on receipt of a warrant or order under my hand or under the hand of the officer commanding the British forces in this province or the Commandant of Charlestown (and not otherwise), to proceed to seize and take into your custody the estate and property real and personal that shall be mentioned or described in every such warrant or order respectively, taking, or causing to be taken by your deputy or deputies, whom you are hereby authorized to appoint in such number as you shall find to be necessary, immediately and upon the spot an exact inventory of the property seized, (if in the country) in the presence of two persons of the district where the property shall lie acting either as field officers or captains of militia under His Majesty's Government, and (if in town) in the presence of two creditable freeholders, who are required to sign the same, which inventory together with the warrant or order of seizure is to be kept and produced by you as a voucher on the exhibition of your accounts.

AND you are carefully in each and every case of the seizure of property whether real or personal to cause notice thereof to be published in three successive news papers within the term of twenty one days after the seizure that no person may plead ignorance of the same; and no sale or disposal is to be made of the property so seized until the expiration of the said term of twenty one days, which term you are also to allow for the removal of persons from the premisses seized.

AND WHEREAS the property which makes the object of this commission will be of divers nature and kinds, consisting of lands, slaves, houses, cattle, horses, household furniture, plate and of the various produce of lands and other articles not necessary to be particularly enumerated, *I DO* hereby direct and require you to continue, according to your judgment, under the most profitable culture for the publick advantage all settled lands and plantations and to employ all slaves who shall come to your hands and are not attached or belonging to landed estates either in aid of their improvement and cultivation, where there shall be a deficiency of slaves, or in clearing and planting new lands or such as have been stripped of their slaves or in any other manner or way that you shall deem most for the publick profit and advantage.

AND you are hereby empowered and directed to sell and dispose, in the like manner as may be most for the publick emolument, of the issues and produce of all lands and of the labour of all slaves from time to time and all perishable articles of property, as you shall see fit and most conducive to the publick interest.

KEEPING and preserving always entire and in the best state of improvement and increase the capital stock consisting of lands and Negroes, and after taking due care that the plantations under your guardianship be sufficiently stocked with cattle, horses etc, you are to sell or keep, as you shall see most profitable, any surplusage or overstock that may be, for the publick benefit as aforesaid.

AND where the proprietors are present and resident, you are, in the case of their being possessed of plate and household furniture not exceeding such moderate quantity as may be necessary for the ordinary occasions of a family, to suffer the same to remain in their possession, taking inventories thereof as above directed that it may appear how every article of property is disposed of or preserved.

AND as compassion and humanity dictate that due and reasonable consideration be had for the families of the traiterous offenders whose property is the object of this commission, *I DO* hereby authorize and require you to pay one fourth part of the neat annual product of estates for the support and maintenance of the wife and children and one sixth part where there is a wife and no children, as the case may be, provided they are resident and continue to be resident within this province, and their receipts or acquittances for the same shall be your sufficient discharge at the settlement of your accounts.

AND to the end that it may be made constantly manifest and apparent that this trust of so great extent and importance hereby commited to and reposed in you be duly and faithfully administered for the publick benefit, *I DO* hereby strictly require and direct you to keep, in the most clear and distinct manner possible, particular and separate accounts of all estates and property real and personal of whatever nature that shall be seized by virtue of this commission and my proclamation of this date, under the respective names of the persons who were supposed and acknowledged to be the proprietors at the time of seizure.

AND I do in like manner further direct and require you to make up a full and general account of the expence of the management, and of the amount of the sale and of the disposal, of all property whatsoever that shall come into your hands and to lay the same before the Commandant and Board of Police of Charlestown on the first day of January and the first day of July in every year, or oftner if it shall be thought necessary and practicable and you shall be thereunto required.

AND on receipt of a certificate which the Commandant and Board of Police are authorized and directed to give you at each time of their passing and approving your accounts, being satisfied therewith, you shall forthwith pay the ballance stated in the said certificate to be due and remaining in your hands to the Paymaster General of His Majesty's Forces or his deputy, whose acquittance shall be your sufficient discharge for the amount of the respective ballances you shall from time to time pay into his hands.

AND WHEREAS it is necessary to direct how the charges accruing in the management of this great publick concern and trust committed to you shall be defrayed, *I DO HEREBY* direct and allow that all fair, reasonable, customary and necessary contingent expence for the culture and management of landed estates and plantations (comprehending the wages of overseers, the cloathing and sustenance of slaves, the surgeons' care of their health, the necessary supply of cattle and horses, of all implements of husbandry and manufacture, the repair and erection of necessary buildings and the transportation of produce and personal property to the usual market at Charlestown, and all rewards directed by my proclamation of this date to be allowed for information and discovery of property whether real or personal) shall be charged to and defrayed out of the produce and profits of each respective estate or property real or personal.

AND in consideration and full compensation of your trouble and charge in executing the great trust hereby reposed in you, *I DO* allow you to charge upon, and deduct from, the amount of sales of all such issues and produce of lands and all other property you shall from time to time sell and dispose of, agreeable to the direction of this commission and my proclamation of this date, the commission of [*blank*] heretofore allowed to merchants by the custom and usage of Charlestown on the transaction of business of like nature, which said commission etc is to be understood to be in full compensation for your own care and superintendance and to defray all charges of your deputies, clerks, assistants etc and all other charges not herein provided for to be incurr'd in the management of this great concern committed to your direction; and the publick shall be liable to no other charge on this behalf whatsoever.

IN pursuance of this trust hereby reposed in *YOU*

GIVEN under my hand and seal
at Head Quarters in Waxhaw in the Province of South Carolina
this 16th day of September Anno Domini 1780
and in the twentieth year of His Majesty's reign

CORNWALLIS ○

By his Lordship's command

J MONEY
Aid de camp

Preliminary sketch of the sequestration proclamation made on 16th September 1780[10]   *1(37): ADf*

Whereas, notwithstanding the unparalel'd lenity of the British Government, many of the inhabitants of this province persist in an obstinate resistance to the reestablishment of good order and lawfull authority, and others by abandoning their plantations or an open avowal of attachment to the rebel Congress have render'd themselves unworthy of His Majesty's protection or indulgence, and whereas it appears to me to be expedient and just that the property of such persons should, untill final regulations can take place, be applied towards defraying part of the expences of this unnatural war, I have thought fit to order the same to be sequestered and to appoint [*blank*] Commissioner for the management of it for the purpose above mentioned, and he is hereby authorized and directed to take immediate possession of:

    —   abandoned estates

---

[10] The proclamation as made appears in Tarleton, *Campaigns*, 186-191, but is mistakenly dated 6th September. Its thrust is not markedly different, except that (a) the terms are extended to cover persons generally in the service or acting under the authority of Congress, (b) reference to France, Spain and the Colonies is omitted, and (c) certain provisions appearing in Cruden's commission (p 320) are incorporated in so far as they relate to the administration of his office.

- estates of officers of the Continental Army

- estates of persons notoriously disaffected not under capitulation[11]

- debts due or effects belonging to France, Spain, Congress, any of the Colonies or individuals in rebellion.

The accounts to be made up every six months and to be pass'd by the Commandant and Council.

A handsome salary to be allowed to the Commissioner either by a limited sum or so much per cent, to be fix'd when some judgement can be formed of the amount of the sequestered property.

Persons under capitulation not to dispose of houses, lands or Negroes, as it may give them an opportunity of defrauding their creditors in Great Britain or Ireland.

[CORNWALLIS]

Cruden to Cornwallis, 29th September 1780　　　　　　64(126): ALS

Charles Town
29th September 1780

The Rt Hon Lord Cornwallis etc etc etc

My Lord

I had the honor of delivering your Lordship's dispatches to Colonel Balfour, who, I beg leave to inform your Lordship, received me in the most kind and freindly manner, and he gave orders for the immediate publication of the proclamation.

From the letter and spirit of the proclamation and the idea I have of your Lordship's intentions I conceived that all property under the description pointed out was to be seized with all possible dispatch. In a conversation I had the honor to have this day with Colonel Balfour I understood from him that he imagined that your Lordship intended only to make a begining with a few of the principal estates. If the business is only to extend this farr, in the meantime I am persuaded a thousand devices will be practiced to remove or convey away such property as may be consider'd within the meaning of the proclamation; and where that is not effected, the Negroes on the estates that may be left will be destitute during the winter, which, if severe, may destroy many of them. Besides, there will be the appearance of injustice by seizing partially, which must be the case if the business is not taken up in a comprehensive light.

---

[11] Annotated: 'NB. This by order of the Commandant of Charlestown'.

I hope your Lordship will forgive me for being so explicit on this important subject. Colonel Balfour did me the honor to express his desire that I should communicate my ideas on the subject to your Lordship as he is anxious to be fully informed from your Lordship in what manner he is to proceed. I beg leave to assure your Lordship that it will afford me a very singular pleasure to be honor'd with your commands, and

I have the honor to be, my Lord, with the most perfect respect
Your Lordship's much obliged and most humble servant

JOHN CRUDEN

Queries from Cruden to Cornwallis about sequestration, undated   7(25): C

Sundry queries upon which Mr Cruden begs to have the opinion of the Rt Hon Earl Cornwallis

1st. Captains or field officers of the militia being often on duty and thereby prevented from attending to the taking of inventories of property seized, your Commissioner has for the present obtained the Commandant's consent to call in two creditable freeholders in the country to witness that business in the same manner as in town.

Is it his Lordship's pleasure to authorize this practice for the future when militia officers cannot attend?

[*Cornwallis*:]

> I agree to the calling in two creditable freeholders to witness the taking of inventories of property whenever proper militia officers cannot conveniently attend.
>
> CORNWALLIS

2nd. It has happened and is likely often to happen that returns of seized property by deputies and agents in remote parts of the country do and may not get to hand so as to be advertized within the limited time of twenty one days from the seizure.

It is requested that a longer time be allowed, perhaps forty days?

[*Cornwallis*:]

> Agreed.

3rd. Power is given your Commissioner 'to employ all slaves which shall come to his hands and are not attached or belonging to landed estates in any manner he shall judge best for the publick service'. The words 'and are not attached or belonging to landed estates' seem to imply a necessity for continuing all slaves found upon landed estates in the cultivation of such respective estates, whether profitable or not. As there are many plantations that have slaves upon them at present which are very unprofitable, either from the bad quality of the lands, the ruinous condition of the necessary buildings, banks, drains etc or from their *dangerous* and remote situations, the slaves belonging to which might be employed to much greater advantage in other places, it is requested that this article may be explained.

[*Cornwallis*:]

    Agreed, provided memorandums are taken of the estates to which the respective Negroes belong.

4th. Power seems to be given your Commissioner to sell and dispose ONLY the *produce of lands and slaves and all perishable articles of property*. PLATE and household furniture cannot be called perishable articles, and yet your Commissioner apprehends it is his Lordship's intention that all articles of this kind should be sold. An explanation of this is also requested?

[*No response*]

5th. One quarter of the nett produce is allowed for the support of the wives and children of delinquents whose estates are sequestered and one sixth part for the maintenance of the wife only, BUT no provision is made for the maintenance of *children only* where there is no wife.

[*Cornwallis*:]

    If there are not above two children, a sixth part, otherwise a fourth part.

6th. Several estates being very small and sometimes the families of the proprietors *large*, one quarter of such estates is far from being sufficient for the support of the wife and children.

Your Commissioner requests a discretional power may be given to allow on such occasions a larger proportion than one fourth, and in some cases perhaps to allow the whole produce or intirely to relinquish such estates even after seizure.

[*Cornwallis*:]

    I agree to give such a discretionary power to the Commissioner.

7th. Many estates are claimed in whole or in part by wives or trustees in virtue of marriage settlements or other contracts. Are such claims to be allowed? If allowed, will it not in a great measure defeat one of the great purposes of the commission by putting it in the power of the wife to enable her husband to carry his malicious and dangerous designs into execution? WHERE an estate is of considerable magnitude, one quarter part of the produce will generally be sufficient for the support of the wife and children, and where it is not, more may be allowed if the powers requested in the foregoing article are granted. Any decision now will not prevent the wife etc from getting possession of the whole property at the husband's death.

[*Cornwallis*:]

The claims mentioned in this article are not to be allowed.

8th. Various claims for debts due from the proprietors of sequestered estates have been made by British and other loyal subjects, particularly by brothers and sisters, who sometimes may have no other means of support than the interest of such debts. Several writs of attachment have also been served upon the Commissioner. Full instructions are requested upon this subject, which is of most material consequence.

[*Cornwallis*:]

No writs of attachment whatever are to be allowed to be served upon the Commissioner. If the loyal creditors chuse to lodge an account of their claims in the Secretary's Office, there can be no objection to it.

9th. Several colonels and commanding officers of the militia have omitted to make returns of the names of the delinquents in the districts in the country agreeable to orders sent them by Colonel Balfour, and this omission has occasioned considerable loss of property, the proprietors having made way with it; and it is impossible for your Commissioner to procure the necessary information if those persons whose duty it is to give it neglect so to do.

[*No response*]

10th. The necessity of having some line drawn becomes more and more necessary. The want of knowledge of characters must be supplied by placing dependance on the reports of those residents in the country who, tho' good men, yet, being warped by prejudice, passion or interest, often mislead instead of informing and thereby occasion in many cases the guilty to escape.

Your Commissioner most humbly begs leave to suggest the propriety of adopting some mode by which all appearance of partiality may be prevented. Every person now on parole has had sufficient time to determine whether they are with us or against us. Would not the most certain way to come at the knowledge of treasonable characters be to put the question to them? And those who still persist in their rebellious principles are undoubtedly fit objects for the operation of his Lordship's commission.

That this is a measure evidently necessary, every day furnishes proofs, those who consider themselves within the meaning of the proclamation disposing of their effects to prevent a seizure from affecting them, and the essential part of the produce of their estates (rice and indigo) they will be able to send to markett very speedily if some steps are not taken to prevent them.

[*Cornwallis*:]

The consideration of this article postponed.

11th. Is the Commissioner to take any cognizance of the estates and property of such persons as have died in rebellion?

[*Cornwallis:*]

> The Commissioner to take cognizance only of such estates as are pointed out to him by the commanding officer of the district or the Commandant of Charles Town.

12th. Your Commissioner, before he undertook this business, explained fully his motives and views and, conscious he has none that are mercenary, thinks it necessary and proper to state to your Lordship the following circumstances of his own situation: that he is already considerably in advance by the purchase of cloathing for the Negroes, plantation tools and necessaries; that when all the remaining slaves are cloathed and the plantations supplied with necessaries (many wanting provisions), which must be done, his advance will be greatly increased; that from the ruinous state of many of the estates, the elopement, sickness and idleness of both slaves and overseers during the planting season and all the summer, very bad crops have been made in general and upon many plantations scarcely anything, so that, when the families left upon them have been supplied with a bare subsistance, what is left will fall very short of the amount of your Commissioner's advances; and his commissions on the sales of the very inconsiderable produce of the present year will be far from sufficient to defray the charges of his deputies, agents, clerks etc etc, these charges falling very heavy by reason of the number of people he has been obliged to employ for the more speedy and effectual execution of his trust.

Very soon after your Commissioner entered upon this business, what he has now stated was obvious to him, but conscious that your Lordship did not mean to abide by the letter of the commission to his prejudice or in any manner to his detriment, he has in every instance to the utmost of his power taken such assistants in the principal districts as will enable him to do justice to the very important and extensive appointment which your Lordship has honoured him with. Emolument for himself is not now, nor ever was it, his first object. His humble wish is that your Lordship may secure him from embarrassment; but it would grieve him to the soul not to be able to do justice to those gentlemen who have favored him with their assistance.

[*No response*]

§ - §

3 - Correspondence with the Royal Militia

Fisher to [Haldane?], 25th August 1780 63(66): ALS

Orangeburgh
25th August 1780

Sir

I am honoured with yours of the 23rd[12] and I am happy to find that my conduct meets with my Lord Cornwallis's approbation. Assure his Lordship that the strictest attention will be paid to all his future commands.

You'l please to acquaint his Lordship that the lower companys of this regiment are before this time at Neilson's under the command of Major McMichael[13]. The upper companys that were collected at Congarees are on their march for Neilson's under the command of Captain Maxwell. They had got as far as Colonel Thomson's near McCord's Ferry on the 24th.

As the present service is not very urgent, I have posted a company of militia here. I was always of oppinion that this post would be useful, but since the arrival of the rebel prisoners it seems absolutely necessary. We are supplied with beef and flour in the neighbourhood but we have neither salt nor rum. If his Lordship intends to continue this post, I will send for a supply of these necessary articles from Charles Town.

I am glad to hear the rebel prisoners will soon be removed. They are far from being fit companions for the credulous country people. Besides, it would be imposing on the country people as they have nothing to pay them for their provisions, and I have reason to believe they will soon refuse to supply them.

Since the defeat of the rebel army on the 16th several suspicious people have been travelling to the southward, pretending that they were drove by the rebels. I have taken up some of them and sent them to Captain Maxwell at Congarees. If they cannot clear themselves, he will send them to Head Quarters. I wish some general rule was adopted to distinguish friends from foes.

---

[12] *yours of the 23rd*: no extant copy.

[13] One of three brothers who came to America from Scotland, George McMichael settled in Orangeburg District, South Carolina, in 1759, marrying Ursula, a sister of the Reverend John Giessendanner. Now major in John Fisher's Orangeburg Regiment of the royal militia, he has left no record of his military service and may have soon resigned his commission. When a federal census was taken in 1790, he was still residing in what was then Orangeburg County. (Daniel Culler, *Orangeburgh District, 1768-1868: History and Records* (Reprint Company, 1995), 322; information from Joanne B Stowe, 4th October 2002 and 22nd April 2004)

I have the honor to be, sir,
Your most obedient and most humble servant

JOHN FISHER
Colonel, Orangeburgh militia

Phillips to Cornwallis, 13th September 1780   64(54): ALS

Jackson's Creek
September 13th 1780

To Charles Earl Cornwallis
General and Commander in Chief of His Majesty's forces in South Carolina

May it please your Lordship

On the night of the ninth instant a party of rebels came into our settlement and caried off one John Hutchison[14] a prisoner with them. Their reasons for taking him, I believe, was that he had been very active with us in his duty since the surender of Charlestown and in consequence of your Lordship's orders had brought away a number of slaves, the property of the Kirklands[15] and Kennerleys[16], who are now with General Sumpter, notwithstanding they had surrendered to His Majesty's arms and taken paroles. As he is now in their power and the rebels whose property he took will do him every injury in their power, I am concerned for his life as they seem to make it a point of partly starving their prisoners; and as he has a large familly, who is now in the greatest distress, his wife now lying in a nerveous feaver and having several blisters upon her, and their children very small, I most humbly beg your Lordship to endeavour to have him restored to his family either by exchainge or such other manner as your Lordship in your wisdom shall think fit.[17] They were persued by several small parties but had got so far on their road they could not be overtaken, and I being down at Camden, it prevented me from being any way servisable in the persuit. They also caried off one Gardiner Williams, a young man who had done duty with us at Rockey Mount.

---

[14] A private in Captain James Millar's company of Phillips' Jackson Creek Regiment, John Hutchison would presumably be exchanged in accordance with the agreement soon to be reached between Cornwallis and Sumter. (Clark, *Loyalists in the Southern Campaign*, i, 161)

[15] Of the extended Kirkland family in South Carolina, Phillips is primarily referring to the brothers Joseph (*c.* 1733-1788) and William (1730-1806), both of whom had settled on Cedar Creek about 1755. They had already seen service in the war, Joseph as a lt colonel and William as a captain in the South Carolina revolutionary militia. In January 1782 they would sit in the revolutionary assembly at Jacksonborough. (DAR, Greenville County, SC; Kirkland and Kennedy, *Historic Camden,* i, 400-1)

[16] James and John Kennerly, who resided near Kennerly's Mill in the Dutch Fork, appear to have left no record of their military service, as evinced by their absence from Moss, *SC Patriots*. The Kennerly family was descended from Thomas and James, who about 1735 came to South Carolina from Culpeper County, Virginia. (Information from Dorothy Rushing, 22nd February 2001)

[17] For action taken by Cornwallis and Sumter's response, see pp 341-2.

I have the honour to be
Your Lordship's most obedient most humble servant

JN^O PHILLIPS[18]
Colonel

PS

The bearer, John Elison[19], will receive any instructions or orders your Lordship may have for me.

Since I wrote the above, I am creditably informed they swore the[y] would hang him as soon as they got to camp.

Floyd to Cornwallis, 2nd October 1780   3(168): ALS

2nd October 1780

To the Rt Hon Lord Charles Cornwallis
Charlotte
North Carolina

Honourable Sir

When I was in Charlotte, I neglected to perfectly inform myself whither your proclamation issued there[20] was to extend to those of my regiment that had made concession to Captain

---

[18] About 1770 John Phillips (c. 1730-1809) had migrated from County Antrim, Ireland, to the Back Country of South Carolina and taken up lands on Jackson's Creek north of the Broad River. A committed loyalist, he was confined in irons at Orangeburg jail in 1778 after vainly attempting to flee to St Augustine. He later spent four months in Camden jail for refusing to take the test oath. Now, in 1780, he had been commissioned Colonel of the Jackson's Creek Regiment of the royal militia, being, in the words of Cornwallis, 'one of the honestest and most zealous men in this province'. In February 1781 he was to be captured by Sumter but would be exchanged. When Camden was evacuated in May 1781, he abandoned his property and repaired to Charlestown with his wife and eight children, having lost two sons and a brother in the fighting. He then led part of his regiment in the relief of Ninety Six before becoming the Inspector of Refugees for Camden District. In 1783 he returned with his family to the north of Ireland and went on to present to the royal commission a compensation claim warmly supported by Nisbet Balfour. He was not included in the Banishment and Confiscation Act passed by the revolutionary assembly at Jacksonborough. (Lambert, *SC Loyalists*, 15, 119, 219, 229, 276, 278; *The Cornwallis Papers*; The SC Banishment and Confiscation Act 1782)

[19] John Ellison was a private in Phillips' regiment. (Clark, *Loyalists in the Southern Campaign*, i, 156)

[20] The proclamation was as follows:

'NORTH CAROLINA

By the Rt Hon Charles Earl Cornwallis
Lt General of His Majesty's Forces etc etc etc

Huck when here. Many of them, I learn, is inclinable to except of the terms offered in your proclamation; and where I am short is to know, if they be admitted to come in on the proclamation, what I must do in regard to the orders issued at Camden for redressing the loyal party that have suffered by being plundered by the rebels[21], it striking my understanding in this light, that, if the rebels comes in on the proclamation, that the Camden orders will be void. Your Honour will be pleased to favour me with further orders in regard to what I have brokenly exhibited to you above, and am, sir, with real esteem

Your most [obedient] and most humble servant

MATTHEW FLOYD

Cornwallis to Floyd, 3rd October 1780   81(14): C

Charlotte Town
3rd October 1780

Colonel Mathew Floyd

Sir

My proclamation of the 27th of last month was particularly intended for the province of North Carolina, where my letter to the commanding officers of militia dated the 25th of

---

A PROCLAMATION

WHEREAS the enemies of His Majesty's Government, continuing to practise every artifice and deceit to impose upon the minds of the people, have, as industriously as falsely, propagated a belief among the people of this country that the King's army indiscriminately makes war and commits ravages upon the peaceable inhabitants and those who are in arms and open rebellion against His Majesty's authority, I think it proper, in order to remove such false and injurious impressions and restore as much peace and quiet to the country as may be possible during the operations of war, hereby to assure the people at large that all those who come into the posts of His Majesty's army under my command and faithfully deliver up their arms and give a military parole to remain thenceforth peaceable at home, doing no offence against His Majesty's Government, will be protected in their persons and properties and be paid a just and fair price in gold or silver for whatever they may furnish for the use of the King's army, it being His Majesty's most gracious wish and intention rather to reclaim His deluded subjects to a sense of their duty, and obedience to the laws, by justice and mercy than by force and terror of His arms.

GIVEN under my hand and seal at Headquarters in Charlottetown, this twenty-seventh day of September one thousand seven hundred and eighty, and in the twentieth year of His Majesty's reign

CORNWALLIS

By his Lordship's command
J MONEY
Aid-de-camp

GOD SAVE THE KING'.

[21] *The Cornwallis Papers* contain no copy of the order of 25th August. Its main thrust may be deduced from Cornwallis's following letters to Floyd and Cary.

August 1780 had no effect. I am, however, well assured that His Majesty's good and loyal subjects of South Carolina wou'd not wish to protract the evils of this unhappy war by making any number of people desperate. It is therefore my intention to permit those who have fled from South Carolina to take the benefit of the proclamation in the following manner, which appears to me to be most just and equitable to all partys: that those who return and give their parole and bring in their arms faithfully shall be allowed to take possession of such part of their property as has not been already seized by the militia acting under His Majesty's Government for the use of the loyal sufferers; that, of such part of their property as may have been seized and not disposed of, one third shall be return'd to them for their support, and the two remaining thirds disposed of according to the order to the commanding officers of militia dated the 25th August 1780. If any shou'd return and comply with the terms of the proclamation whose whole property shall have been seized and disposed of, so that it shou'd be impossible to restore any part of it to them, I then direct the commanding officer of the militia of the district to make some provision for them, so as to give them a possibility of earning a livelyhood, out of the property not already applied of those who still continue obstinate in rebellion.

I am, sir,
Your most obedient humble servant

CORNWALLIS

Cornwallis to Cary, 3rd October 1780   81(13): C

Charlottetown
3rd October 1780

Colonel James Carey

Sir

As I have the highest opinion of your integrity, I have no doubt of your seeing strict justice done to all His Majesty's loyal subjects in the execution of my order of the 25th August, and that, wherever it may appear to you that the twelve persons appointed to judge may have been influenced by partiality or passion, that you will refer the final decision to me or the Commandant of Charlestown.

I do not mean to censure any judgement that may have been passed in the case relative to Mr Charles Ogilvie[22], but I think it may be proper to assure you that I look on Mr Ogilvie

---

[22] Perhaps Charles Ogilvie (?-c. 1787), who had migrated in 1751 from England to Charlestown and set himself up there as a merchant. He also became a plantation owner, possibly by his marriage ten years later to the heiress of James Mitchie, by whom he acquired considerable property. Now, in 1780, he would soon be appointed Deputy Commissioner for Sequestered Estates under John Cruden, an office which would lead to his banishment by the revolutionary assembly at Jacksonborough and confiscation of his property. In autumn 1782 he was one of two agents dispatched by the General Committee of Loyalists to make representations to Sir Guy Carleton, the Commander-in-Chief, in the light of the decision to evacuate Charlestown. Less than two years later he presented

to be a faithfull and loyal subject to His Majesty.

I am, sir,
Your most obedient humble servant

[CORNWALLIS]

Gibbs to Cornwallis, 12th October 1780 — 3(212): ALS

Camp at Colonel Williams's
October 12th 1780

Lord Cornwallis

My Lord

    In deep distress in many respects I write your Lordship to give an idea of our much distress'd frontiers. You were pleased to confer the command of the late Colonel Thomas's regiment upon me, pursuant to which Colonel Ferguson arriv'd in our back parts as Inspector General of Militia and call'd upon me. I accordingly rais'd the subjects and join'd him with sometimes upwards of three hundred, seldom less than two, and remain'd during the summer and cooperated with His Majesty's troops almost thro North Carolina. At last retreated back to the verge of South Carolina, where Colonel Ferguson met his unhappy defeat and death. I had near one hundred brave men kill'd and taken. I was at the same time sent into my regiment to raise my regiment to be ready to act with him when he shou'd fall back, which he never did to me. I am fallen back to Colonel Cruger and Colonel Cunningham, not having men to stand in my regiment. I never received part nor parcell of your Lordship's money sent the militia. My regiment in the front of the province has suffer'd much the most from rebel depredations than any other regiment. Having the Indian country and North Carolinians both to suffer from has caused me never to have it in my power to answer the full contents of your Lordship's order respecting the rebel confiscated property except by ordering each captain to give orders to each respective officer or private in their companys to hold in their possession any property taken from, forfeited by, or brought into the district of that species since I received your Lordship's orders for that purpose, as the summer has been little else but merching an countermerching, never two days' calm space to mind our farms or any domestick comforts. I had my dwelling houses burnt on two plantations[23], my property of every kind taken even to a spoon, which renders my case very extreme. Still, doubt not but I shall be on an equal footing with other back woods field officers. I hope your Lordship will consider the much distress'd backwood militia as naked and in every respect unfit for service. Major Plummer's regiment lost one hundred men or more with Colonel Ferguson kill'd and

---

a claim for loss of property to the royal commission in London. (Coldham, *Loyalist Claims*, 371; The SC Banishment and Confiscation Act 1782; Lambert, *SC Loyalists*, 251)

[23] One of Gibbs' plantations lay about four miles to the east of the Cowpens, another in the Fair Forest region (Draper, *King's Mountain*, 223 and 503).

taken, himself wounded and left in the field.[24] I think from every circumstance — and it the general opinion of the most experienc'd men — that the militia cannot hold the Back Country as long as Holstein's River, Nolachuckky and the Western Water people remain unconquer'd.

I am your Lordship's most obedient humble servant

ZACH⁰ GIBBS[25]
Major

PS

For the further particulars the barer can better inform your Lordship. If your Lordship is please present me a trifle, it will better enable me to remain with the militia, who were often promised by Colonel Ferguson but never received one penny.

ZG

§ - §

---

[24] Having migrated from Pennsylvania to the Back Country of South Carolina, Daniel Plummer settled between Fair Forest and Tyger. A staunch loyalist, he had been among those captured by Richard Richardson during the Snow Campaign in late 1775. Some four and a half years later he was commissioned a major in command of the Fair Forest Regiment of the royal militia and on 7th October took part in the Battle of King's Mountain. When all was lost, he attempted to break out with Ferguson but was shot down and left for dead on the battlefield. He would recover and resume command of the remains of his regiment, with whom he repaired to Charlestown when the Back Country was abandoned in the summer of 1781. Promoted soon after to colonel, he remained in Charlestown as a paid refugee until its evacuation in December 1782. Although he was not included in the Banishment and Confiscation Act passed by the revolutionary assembly at Jacksonborough, he felt it would be useless to return to his property and arranged to sell it to a relative before he moved on to East Florida. A man of pleasing personality, he is described as honest and open, kind and considerate to all. (Lambert, *SC Loyalists*, 111, 212, 265; Draper, op cit, 276, 483; Clark, *Loyalists in the Southern Campaign*, i, 323-7, 491 et seq; McCrady, *SC in the Rev 1780-1783*, 586; *The Cornwallis Papers*)

[25] Born in Virginia, Zacharias Gibbs (1741-?) migrated to South Carolina about 1763 and settled in the Back Country. Like Daniel Plummer a staunch loyalist, he took part as a captain in the action at Ninety Six in November 1775 and was among the band of loyalists defeated in the action at Kettle Creek in February 1779. Made prisoner, he was marched in irons to Ninety Six, where he was sentenced to death, reprieved, and imprisoned for fifteen months. Now, in 1780, he had been commissioned a major commanding the Spartan Regiment of the royal militia, whose catchment area lay towards the border with North Carolina. Having spent the summer and autumn in the manner which he graphically describes, he had been away on assignment when the Battle of King's Mountain took place. He nevertheless lost, as he says, near one hundred men in the engagement. When the Back Country was abandoned in the summer of 1781, he repaired with the remains of his regiment to Charlestown, where he received pay as a refugee militia officer until its evacuation. Included in the Banishment and Confiscation Act, he moved on to Nova Scotia and settled at Rawdon, but in 1791 he gave notice that he intended to sell his two farms and leave in the spring. His destination is unknown. Having obtained certificates of merit from Cornwallis, Balfour and Cruger, he was awarded £1,200 by the Crown for his losses in South Carolina. His wife, who also made a claim, was awarded £955 and a pension of £40. (E A Jones ed, 'Journal of Alexander Chesney: A South Carolina Loyalist in the Revolution and After', *Ohio State University Bulletin*, xxvi, number 4 (1921), 79-82; Lambert, op cit, 111, 145, 275; Clark, op cit, i, 277-284, 492 et seq; Draper, op cit, *passim*; The SC Banishment and Confiscation Act 1782)

4 - Correspondence with the enemy

Cornwallis to Nash, 17th August 1780   79(23): ADf

Camden
August 17th 1780

Sir

It has been reported to me that Lt Colonel Grey of the Cheraw militia and Mr Cassils and several other gentlemen of this province who were lately carried into North Carolina were put into a dungeon loaded with irons and treated in the most barbarous manner, and that the sick of the 71st Regiment have been neglected and left to perish. I take this opportunity of informing you, sir, that if I find these reports well founded, I will make a most severe retaliation on those now in my power and others whom I may seize when I march into your province, and of declaring to you that gibbetts and dungeons shall no longer be used with impunity as engines to enslave His Majesty's faithfull and loyal subjects in America.

I am, sir,
Your most obedient servant

[CORNWALLIS]

Nash to Cornwallis, 27th August 1780   63(70): LS

Hillsborough
August 27th 1780

By flag of truce

To the Rt Hon Lord Cornwallis at Cambden

Sir

Yesterday I had the honour to receive your Lordship's letter dated the 17th respecting Colonels Gray and Cassell and the sick of the 71st Regiment, prisoners of war with us, and am to acquaint you that a party of them under guard arrived here a few days ago; that two officers on their application, suggesting indisposition, were immediately paroled to a Minister's house in the neighbourhood, the rest sent on; that another part of them are now on their way to Virginia; and on the whole, as far as I can gain information, there is not the least foundation for the charge of neglect or ill treatment towards any of them. The charge indeed is so repugnant to our general method of treating prisoners that I am surprised to find it made the particular subject of a letter and have only to add that I shall be happy on all occasions to find our prisoners with you as well treated as those of yours are with us. With respect to

Colonels Cassell and Gray, have made particular inquiry but as yet can obtain no certain information respecting them and did not know, before I received yours, that they had been prisoners. If any particular ill treatment has been shewn them, I shall not fail to correct the abuse, and am with due respect

Your Lordship's most obedient servant

A NASH[26]

Gates to Cornwallis, August 1780

90(1): ALS

Head Quarters of the American Army
August 1780

Rt Hon Earl Cornwallis

My Lord

By this flag I take the liberty to request your Lordship will please to permit the bearer, Dr Johnson, physician and surgeon of the general hospital of this army, and Captain Drew[27] of Lt Colonel Porterfield's corps to visit and attend the sick and wounded officers and soldiers that were taken by your Lordship in the action of the 16th instant and afterwards from Colonel Sumpter.[28] Both these gentlemen are men of strict honor and probity and I can be answerable they will not in any the smallest instance forfeit the indulgence you are pleased to grant them. I must further entreat the favor that your Lordship will please to permit Lt

---

[26] Of Welsh descent, Abner Nash (c. 1740-1786) was born in Amelia (later Prince Edward) County, Virginia. After he migrated to North Carolina in 1762, he quickly rose to prominence in local politics and in the practice of law, serving terms in the Commons House of the colonial assembly and supporting Governor Tryon against the Regulators. A zealous and active revolutionary, he was a delegate to the Provincial Congress from 1774 to 1776 and a member of several of its prominent committees. Upon the adoption of a revolutionary constitution for North Carolina he became Speaker of the lower house, and then of the upper house, of the legislature. In the spring of 1780 he was elected Governor, but was to see his powers gradually usurped by actions of the General Assembly, first by its appointing Richard Caswell concurrently as major general in command of the militia, then by its setting up in the autumn a Board of War, and finally by its replacing the Board in the coming year with a Council Extraordinary. As a result he would decline to put his name forward for re-election in June 1781. In his personal life he is described as being genial, suave, luxurious in habit and taste, improvident, convivial, and gracious in hospitality. Publicly, when re-elected to the legislature after the war, he became a leader in opposing not only the restoration to loyalists of unsold confiscated property but also the repeal of all laws inconsistent with the Treaty of Paris. A delegate from North Carolina to Congress, he died in New York. (*DAB*)

[27] Thomas Haynes Drew of Caroline County, Virginia, had seen service in the Continental line from February 1777, almost entirely as a lieutenant in William Grayson's Additional Continental Regiment. He resigned his commission in July 1779 in order to accept another as captain in Charles Porterfield's Virginia State Regiment. (Heitman, *Historical Register*, 204; Revolutionary Pension Application of Bernard Reynolds, 7th August 1832, Law Order Book 9, 383)

[28] For Cornwallis's response, see Money's Journal, 8th September, p 361. The letter had been received on that date.

Colonel Dubison[29], aid de camp to the Baron de Kalb, to go to Philadelphia upon parole, as he has the Baron's dying directions with regard to his private family concerns as well in France as America. The baggage and papers belonging to the Baron are sent thither, where they are to remain until Colonel Dubison's arrival. I am to thank your Lordship for the attention and tenderness with which, Captain Hamilton[30] assures me, the wounded and prisoners have been treated at Camden. It has been an invariable rule with me to observe the like generous lenity to all that have fallen into my hands. Of this fact Dr Macnamara Hayes is a good evidence.

With sentiments of high respect and regard, I am, my Lord,
Your Lordship's most obedient humble servant

HORATIO GATES
Major General, Commander in Chief of the Southern Army

Williams to Cornwallis, 30th August 1780   3(37): ALS

Camp, American Army
30th August 1780

The Rt Hon Earl Cornwallis
Lt General and Commander in Chief of His Britanick Majesties forces in South Carolina

General Gates requests Lord Cornwallis will consent to the exchange of Mr Nellson and Mr Rutlidge[31], two volunteers of the Maryland line, for whom two soldiers of the 71st British Regiment shall be immediately sent to Campden. And Colonel Hall[32] will consider it as an indulgence if his Lordship will accept Alexander Monro of the 71st Regiment, a prisoner of war on parole, for William Pursell of the 4th Maryland Regiment.[33]

---

[29] Charles-François, Vicomte Dubuysson des Hayes (1752-1786) had trained in France to become an artillery officer but was discharged in 1776. Accompanying Lafayette to North America, he was commissioned a major in the Continental line on 4th October 1777 and taken on by Kalb as his aide-de-camp. Some four months later he was promoted to lt colonel. During the Battle of Camden he was seriously wounded in four places while vainly striving to save the life of Kalb. Admitted to parole, he would eventually return to France, where his wounds would lead to an untimely death. (Boatner, *Encyclopedia*, 337-8)

[30] George Hamilton (?-1798) had been commissioned a 1st lieutenant in the 5th Maryland Continental Regiment on 10th December 1776, being promoted to captain some thirteen months later. Taken prisoner at the Battle of Camden, he had towards the end of August been permitted to go on parole for one month to North Carolina, where he evidently took the opportunity of reporting to Gates on the condition of the revolutionary prisoners at Camden. He would return in conformity with his parole. (Heitman, *Historical Register*, 269-270; *The Cornwallis Papers*)

[31] According to Heitman (*Historical Register*, 411, 479), a Roger Nelson and a Joshua Rutledge of the Maryland line were taken prisoner at the Battle of Camden. The former, who was wounded, was a 1st lieutenant, and the latter a 2nd lieutenant, in the 5th and 4th Maryland Continental Regiments respectively. Both would be exchanged in December 1780 and Nelson would go on to be wounded again in the Battle of Guilford.

[32] Josias Carvil Hall (?-1814) was Colonel of the 4th Maryland Continental Regiment. (Heitman, op cit, 268)

[33] For the situation of the Continental prisoners, see the following report.

By order of the Commander in Chief

O H WILLIAMS[34]
Acting Adjutant General

[*Subscribed in Money's hand:*]

If Alexander Munroe is an *officer's servant*, Lord Cornwallis will admit of his being exchanged for William Pursell of the 4th Maryland Regiment.

JM

Booth to England, 10th September 1780
3(36): ALS

Camden, South Carolina
10th September 1780

To Richard England Esq
Major of Brigade etc

Sir

Pursuant to your directions I beg leave to report that the within named Mr Nellson is wounded and in this place upon parole and that Robert McCleod, a private prisoner of war of the 6th Maryland Regiment, attends him as his servant; that the within named Mr Rutledge is at Orangeburg within this province upon parole and that Barney Allen, a private prisoner of war of the 1st Maryland Regiment, attends him as his servant; and that the within named William Pursell is also at Orangeburg in the service of Lieutenant Isaac Hanson of the 4th Maryland Regiment at that place upon parole.

B BOOTH Boot[35]
Commissary of Prisoners

---

[34] A native of Maryland, Otho Holland Williams (1749-1794) was born to Welsh immigrants and from the age of thirteen until almost the beginning of the revolution was employed in the offices of the County Clerk in Frederick and Baltimore. Commissioned a 1st lieutenant in a Maryland revolutionary company in June 1775, he participated in the siege of Boston and was promoted to captain. When in 1776 a regiment was formed of rifle companies from Maryland and Virginia, he was appointed major. Wounded and captured at the fall of Fort Washington, he was at first placed upon parole but was later consigned to the provost on the ground of secretly communicating military information to Washington. Insufficient food and unsanitary quarters seriously impaired his health before he was exchanged in January 1778. In the meantime he had been appointed Colonel of the 6th Maryland Continental Regiment. Now acting as Adjutant General under Gates, he would be confirmed in the office by Greene and take a distinguished part in the race to the Dan and in the Battles of Guilford, Hobkirk's Hill, and Eutaw Springs. After the war he served as Collector of the port of Baltimore. Buried in Riverview Cemetery, Williamsport, the town which he founded in 1787, he has left a valuable narrative of the campaign of 1780. (*DAB*; Johnson, *Greene*, i, 485-510)

[35] *Boot*: a military prison camp.

Shubrick to Cornwallis, undated[36]   64(140): ALS

To the Rt Hon Earl Cornwallis
Lt General of His Majesty's forces etc etc etc

The subscriber begs leave to represent to your Lordship that General Lincoln obtained of his Excellency General Clinton for the gentlemen of his suite a parole of more local extent than what was granted to the other Continental officers, and particularly for the subscriber, who is one of his aids de camp, permission to remain on parole in St Thomas's Parish, notwithstanding which he has been ordered to Haddrell's Point by the Commandant, Colonel Balfour. As his residence from his family must be attended with many great inconveniencies and much and peculiar detriment, he applied to the Commandant for the continuance of the said permission according to the parole, which the Commandant (by your Lordship's orders) refused, assigning as a reason that your Lordship had been informed that the subscriber had forfeited that indulgence by his misbehaviour, particularly by spreading reports tending to render the minds of the people averse to His Majesty's Government, and was pleased to refer him to your Lordship.

The subscriber can positively assure your Lordship that every such charge against him is totally destitute of truth. His conduct has been strictly conformable to the nature and terms of his parole express or implied. His behaviour has been entirely consistent with his situation and such, in short, as to afford no just grounds for any dishonourable and disadvantageous imputation.

He makes no doubt that it will natura[lly] occur to your Lordship's reflection that in times and conjunctures like the present many will be exposed to unfounded suspicions and that false informations and vague charges may be easily and therefore will be too frequently made by malicious persons and private enemies more with a view of gratifying their own resentment or to serve their own purposes by a mischievous officiousness than to promote His Majesty's Service. From a consciousness of his own innocence he is apprehensive that motives of this sort have been too prevalent in his own particular case.

He therefore hopes your Lordship will be pleased to take into consideration what is premised and that you will be pleased to signify with all convenient speed your consent that the former parole may be restored to the subscriber, who is, my Lord, with all respect

Your Lordship's very humble servant

THO^S SHUBRICK[37]

---

[36] Probably written in late August 1780, when Balfour took action against those promoting the revolutionary cause in contravention of their paroles.

[37] Thomas Shubrick (1756-1810) had been commissioned a lieutenant in the 2nd South Carolina Continental Regiment in January 1777 and was promoted to captain one year later. Besides serving as an aide-de-camp to Lincoln, he had previously acted as a major of brigade under Howe. In December 1780 his estate would be sequestered. Exchanged under the cartel in June 1781, he would be taken on by Greene as an aide-de-camp and receive the thanks of Congress for his conduct at the Battle of Eutaw Springs. He would later act as a commissary of

Captain, 2nd South Carolina Continental Regiment
Aid de camp to the Hon Major General Lincoln

Money to an officer of the enemy, 15th September 1780   3(41): Df[38]

Camp
15th September 1780

Officer commanding at the advanced post of the enemy

Sir

Lord Cornwallis having received information that John Hutchison was taken from his plantation by a party of your militia in the night of the 9th instant, who threatned to hang him as soon as they got to their camp, I am directed by his Lordship to assure you that if the said John Hutchison should be put to death, he will instantly cause two of the most violent persons of your party who are now in our custody to be hanged; or should any other corporal punishment be inflicted on him, he will severely retaliate on two of your friends. If you should be inclined to exchange John Hutchison, Lord Cornwallis will release for him any man of nearly the same station of life.

[J MONEY]

Tate to an officer of Cornwallis, undated   4(442): ALS

To the officer commanding at the advance post of the enemy

Per Mrs How

Sir

General Sumter has received information that some gentlemen by Lord Cornwallis' direction have made proposals of exchainging any person, a prisoner to him, of near the same station of life for a certain Mr Hutchinson. I am directed by General Sumter to acquaint you that he will immediately release said Hutchinson upon promise that John How[39], a private

---

prisoners. After the war he was elected for several terms to the South Carolina House of Representatives and became the owner of several plantations, of which 'Belvidere' on Bull's Island was his main residence. Of his sixteen children, six sons served in the War of 1812, four of whom in the navy. At his death he owned 254 slaves. (Heitman, op cit, 496; McCrady, *SC in the Rev 1775-1780*, 729; *The Greene Papers*, ix, 271; Bailey and Cooper, *SC House of Representatives*, iii, 642-4; *DAB*)

[38] The draft is in Cornwallis's hand, but the letter as sent would have been signed by Money (see his Journal, p 363)

[39] John Howe would be released after 61 days' captivity, having no doubt been taken during the action at Fishing Creek. He was a commissary and would continue to be so in 1781. (Moss, *SC Patriots*, 466)

person now a prisoner to his Lordship, shall also be discharged from his confinement and permitted to return home in safety. A direct answer to this sent by the bearer, a lady, wife to said How, shall be properly attended to.

I am, sir, with due respect
Your most obedient humble servant

W^M TATE[40]
Brigade Major

Money to Sumter, 28th September 1780   3(87): ADfS

Head Quarters, Charlottetown
28th September 1780

Brigadier General Sumpter

Sir

   Lord Cornwallis, having received your consent to exchange John Hutchinson, a prisoner with you, for John How when on his march, had not an opportunity of giving his answer till this day. His Lordship desires me to acquaint you that the prisoner How is at Charlestown but he will by the first opportunity write to the Commandant and give directions for his immediate release and permission to return home, trusting you will observe the same rule with John Hutchinson.

I am, sir,
Your most obedient and most humble servant

J MONEY
Aid de camp

---

[40] William Tate had been commissioned a captain lieutenant in the 4th South Carolina Continental (Artillery) Regiment in October 1779. Taken prisoner in the capitulation of Charlestown, he had somehow managed to get himself exchanged and was now acting as Sumter's major of brigade. (Heitman, op cit, 533)

Hamilton to Cornwallis, 29th August 1780[41] *93(1): ALS*

29th August '80

The Rt Hon Earl Cornwallis
Lt General of His Majesties forces
South Carolina

Per flag

My Lord

I think my honour engag'd to inform your Lordship that the dragoon who was order'd to escort me without the lines parted with me and, contrary to my possitive orders to return back, deserted. I should have acquainted your Lordship of this affair sooner, but this is the first opportunity that has offer'd.

I am your Lordship's oblig'd and obedient humble servant

GEO HAMILTON
Captain on parole

§ - §

5 - From Carden

Carden to Cornwallis, 16th September 1780 *64(69): ALS*

Charles Town
September 16th 1780

My Lord

I am sorry that Colonel Bryan of the North Carolina militia has misrepresented an affair about a horse to your Lordship. The true state of the case is as follows (I am very unhappy to trouble your Lordship at a time your thoughts may be otherwise employ'd).

On the 10th of August an express came to me, informing me that Mr Sumpter and his men were crossing the river above Rocky Mount and that, with those that were collected on the

---

[41] According to an endorsement, England forwarded this letter to Haldane on 6th October. Hamilton (*c.* 1758-1798) was a captain in the 5th Maryland Continental Regiment and had been granted leave of absence in North Carolina, from where he returned to Camden on 23rd September. (Heitman, op cit, 269; Money, Journal, p 364)

Catawba River, he intended attacking Rocky Mount. Another soon after arrived, who confirm'd the intelligence, adding that Sumpter had two pieces of cannon with him. I immediately got my letters ready for Lord Rawdon, who then had the enemy in his front; and as I cou'd not get a horse any where else, I sent for Colonel Bryan, told him the necessity of immediately acquainting his Lordship with this intelligence, and, as he had a great many horses, begg'd he'd get me one – that I wou'd be answerable for the horse unless the enemy took him, which realy was the case, for I was ordered to march from the post in the mean time to Camden, which the express did not know. He returned almost the same way, but was oblig'd to dismount and take to a very thick swamp to effect his escape.

I assure your Lordship I never promis'd Colonel Bryan a single farthing for the horse, nor wou'd I give five guineas for him. He spoke to me at Camden about it. I told him he cou'd not expect I wou'd pay for the horse. He then said no, but he hoped Lord Rawdon wou'd do something. I told him I was going there and desired he wou'd spake to his Lordship about the matter.

I assure your Lordship I never took the smallest article from any person. I always endeavor'd to discourage every proceeding of the sort unless the exigency of the service required it. This, my Lord, is the truth of the matter.

I have the honor to be, my Lord,
Your Lordship's most obedient and most humble servant

JOHN CARDEN
Major, Prince of Wales's American Volunteers

§ - §

6 - Intelligence

List of certain disaffected persons, undated   *3(19): D*

Principal Insurgents in Colonel Mills's District of Militia[42]

Edward Jones

Trust Thomas[43]

---

[42] The Cheraw District of Colonel William Henry Mills. For information about the persons listed, see Gregg, *The Old Cheraws, passim.*

[43] Tristram Thomas.

―― Pledger ― has only one arm[44]

Nathanⁱ Saunders   }
                            } Seized Major Palmer
Dread Clarie[45]   }

Intelligence from de Treville, 23rd September 1780   *3(26): D*

At Hillisborough six brass field pieces, seven or eight hundred of the Maryland line, Colonel Blufort[46] from Virginia with 3 hundred Continentals, the whole entirly naked. Nelson[47], Washington and White have 250 mounted, their horses in great order.

A report prevailed at Hillisborough that General Morgan was upon his march and with a corps of a thousand rifle men. Farther report says that he was not to proceed out of Virginia unless it was absolutely necessary. A General Gregory[48] or Johnston[49] from Halifax will command at Mask's Ferry with a corp of seven hundred men. By a letter from the Board of War it is the intention of the enemy to keep a strong post at the above mentioned ferry. Johnston or Gregory has marched with a detachment of 3 or 4 hundred men to reinforce General Sumnor.

General Sumnor with 8 hundred men is eight miles to the north of Charlotte and is joined by General Davidson['s] militia, who are mostly mounted and consist of 4 hundred. Sumpter with 3 or 4 hundred militia, mostly mounted, luys upon the Cataber River close to the Indian settlement ― supposed to make a junction with a Colonel Davis[50], who is gone against

---

[44] Philip Pledger. In September 1771 he had been shot in the arm (which was amputated) when, as a captain of militia, he arrested Winsler Driggers, 'a notorious villain, who escaped out of Savannah Gaol'. (*South Carolina and American General Gazette*, 3rd October 1771)

[45] 'Dread' was no doubt a sobriquet of Ethelred Clary, who subscribed to the St David's Society in 1778 (Gregg, *The Old Cheraws*, 283; T W Lipscomb to the editor, 23rd August 2006)

[46] Lt Colonel Abraham Buford.

[47] When Greene assumed command in December 1780, one of his first decisions was to send Major John Nelson's corps of dragoons back to Virginia for refitting, 'as they were totally deranged and too naked for further service'. A Virginia state corps, they were not clothed until late May 1781 and even then they lacked saddles and bridles. After they were refitted, they remained in Virginia and by mid July some forty or so had joined Lafayette. (*The Greene Papers*, vi, 573-4, vii, 8, viii, 496, 498)

[48] Isaac Gregory had been taken prisoner at the Battle of Camden.

[49] Of the numerous Johnstons, Johnstones and Johnsons who served from North Carolina on the revolutionary side, none has been identified as the person to whom de Treville refers.

[50] *Davis*: William Richardson Davie.

Colonel Ferguson. Generals Sumnor and Davison are arawing[51] a light corps of rifle men consisting of 2 or 3 hundred men; those will be employed to flank our camp and harrass us as much as possible. The general plan is, in case of action, to allow their militia to fight in what manner they choose, which will be in the Indian method behind trees and bushes, and their army to support.

General Smallwood has been requested by the House of Assembly and the Governor of North Carolina to take the command of all the militia.

The private conversation I had with General Sumpter was as follows: he said he should retire upon Lord Cornwallis's advancing and attempt throwing himself into Camden or perhaps into the rear of the town. By a letter from the French Minister at Philadelphia it appears that the French fleet in the West Indies was sailed in hopes of reducing one of the British islands. Succeed or not, they were to shape their course for Charlestown.

Parker to Martin, undated[52]   3(22): DS

Stages and distance from Petersburg in Virginia to Hillsborough in North Carolina	
Stages	Miles
From Petersburg to Dinwiddy Court House	16
From Dinwiddy Court House to Edmundson's Ordinary on Notoway River	14
From Edmundson's to Edmund's Store in Brunswick County	20
From Edmund's Store to Pennington's Ford upon Maherrin River	15
From Pennington's Ford to Eaton's Ferry on Roanoke River in Bute County, North Carolina	15
From Eaton's Ferry to Callers Ordinary	21
From Callers to Harrisburg in Granville County, passing by Granville Old Court House and over two small but rapid creeks	30
From Harrisburg to Tar River Bridge and Ford	8
From Tar River to a ford on Flat River at a plantation formerly call'd Harris's but now Bennyhan's	14
From Flat River to Little River Ford opposite to Wm Johnston's plantation and store	2

---

[51] *arawing*: arraying.

[52] This document was prepared in readiness for progressing the war from North Carolina into Virginia. Whether it was written before the autumn or winter campaign is uncertain as James Parker (see below) was in South Carolina on two separate occasions between 1780 and early 1781. Only the final paragraph of the document is in Parker's hand.

From Johnston's to Hillsborough over very hilly ground	16
The distance from Petersburg to Hillsborough by the above stages	171

There are two other publick roads leading to Hillsborough from Petersburg, the one above and the other below the one here pointed out, viz: that above leads through Dinwiddy, the upper end of Brunswick and Mecklenburg Counties in Virginia and through Granville and Orange Counties in Carolina, the lower through Dinwiddy, or Prince George, Sussex, and the lower parts of Brunswick Counties in Virginia, and the upper part of North Hampton, lower of Bute, Granville and Orange Counties in North Carolina, tho' there is very little difference in the distance of either. All the above mention'd rivers have wooden bridges across them, excepting Roanoke, which is from 250 to 300 yards wide at the ferries of the different roads. The other rivers are from 50 to 60 and 70 yards wide. Flat River and Little River are alwise (excepting in time of great falls of rain) fordable.

The road for the distance of two miles on the south side of Eaton's Ferry on Roanoke is over a marshy, flat ground intersected with muddy creeks.

This I obtained from a very worthy man who lived long in Bute County, North Carolina - well acquainted in the country and may be depended on.

JAMES PARKER[53]

§ - §

---

[53] James Parker (1729-1815) migrated about 1747 from Scotland to Norfolk, Virginia, where he became a merchant carrying on an extensive trade in both Virginia and North Carolina. In November 1775 he was commissioned an engineer and master of works by Lord Dunmore with the rank of captain. On returning in 1776 from a mission to Boston, where he had gone to procure provisions, he was shipwrecked on the Eastern Shore of Virginia and taken prisoner, spending nine months in captivity before making his escape to New York. From there he went on to see action at the Battles of Brandywine, Germantown, and Monmouth and to take part in Mathew's and Collier's highly successful expedition to Virginia. Now, in 1780, he had been involved in the Charlestown campaign, returning afterwards to New York, and would soon accompany Leslie, first to Virginia, and then to Charlestown. Thought likely to be of use to Arnold in Virginia, he would have the misfortune to take passage in HMS *Romulus*, which struck to a French squadron off the Capes of Virginia in February 1781. He spent the rest of the war in captivity, latterly in France. On his release he repaired to London, where he carried on business for a time. He also presented a claim to the royal commission for the loss of his confiscated property in Virginia and North Carolina. (The Parker Family Papers (Liverpool Public Library); Coldham, *Loyalist Claims*, i, 379)

7 - Intercepted papers[54]

Regimental orders, Davie's corps, undated   2(405): DS

Regimental orders

Ordered:

— that the Tory property be immediately sold;

— that the men belonging to the corps have three weeks to pay up their proportions;

— that every other person purchasing pay ready money;

— that note or bond and security be given if the commissioners require it;

— that Captain Fleniken[55] is appointed commissioner with myself;

— that the commissioners will account as soon as possible.

W R DAVIE

Polk to Davie, 2nd August 1780   3(2): ALS

August 2nd 1780

Major William R Davie at camp

Lieutenant McCleary[56]

Dear Major

I receiv'd yours per Hagstead. Am very happy to hear of the spifligation etc. I have advertised the sale of Negroes etc according to yours and the Captain's request. I believe the will sell well.

---

[54] Whether the earlier papers came before Cornwallis prior to 24th August is uncertain. They are included here for completeness.

[55] David or John Flennikin was a captain in one of Davie's two troops of mounted riflemen. He led forty of them in the action at Hanging Rock. (Robinson, *Davie*, 49; Hay ed, *Soldiers from NC*, 496-7)

[56] A Samuel and a William McCleary served in the revolutionary militia of Salisbury District. (Hay ed, *Soldiers from NC*, 350, 359)

Captain Robinson[57] who was sent to Salisbury gaol has made his escape with a number of others, and all who are sent to that place will yet. It is a damned place of Tories of itself. A prisoner came to hand here last night. The guard heard of the escape before mentioned and, I belive, has killed the prisoner under a pretence of his making an escape.

You will be good enough to let me know every intelligence you can. Somthing has been whispered of the Rocky Mount affair but nothing certain. You and the captain will dine with me on Saturday. I thought of going to camp sooner untill I received yours.

I am living in clover here, you may be assured. As the song says,

> 'A bottle and kind landlady
> Cures all again.
> Come soon and enjoy Felicity.'

I am, sir,
Yours

W^M POLK[58]

PS

Uncle Spratt[59] is as well as can be. Compliments to Martin and Norris[60].

---

[57] Robinson has not been identified.

[58] The son of Thomas Polk (see p 115, note 115), William (1758-1834) was born near Charlotte and had been appointed to the majority in the 9th North Carolina Continental Regiment in November 1776. He went on to take part in the Battles of Brandywine and Germantown, in the latter of which he was severely wounded, and spent the winter at Valley Forge. When the nine North Carolina Continental regiments were consolidated into four, he was retired and returned to North Carolina, where he joined Richard Caswell's staff. He would soon be with him at the Battle of Camden. In 1781 he was present as a volunteer at the Battle of Guilford before being commissioned a lt colonel by Governor Rutledge and taking part in several engagements in South Carolina. After the war he remained in North Carolina, where he was widely popular, and became prominent in political, business, and social affairs. (*DAB*)

[59] William Polk's father, Thomas, had married Susan (Susannah) Spratt, whose family in 1753 had been the first to settle in what became the town of Charlotte. (Mary Polk Branch, *Memoir of a Southern Woman 'Within the Lines' and a Genealogicial Record* (Joseph G Branch Publishing Company, Chicago), 55-6)

[60] Martin was a captain commanding one of Davie's two troops of horse. Norris has not been identified. (Robinson, *Davie*, 43)

Rutherford to Davie, 5th August 1780

3(3): LS

Camp, Jennings Branch
27 miles from Cherraw Hill on way to Cambden
5th August 1780

Major William R Davie at his camp

Favour Mr Black

Dear Major

Your obliging letter of the 2nd instant came to hand an hour ago. I congratulate you on your various success. Am sorry for the loss of the amiable Colonel Neal and the precarious situation in which General Sumter is and has been some time past. It is not in my power to determine whether any or what number of aid may be sent you. General Caswell joined me at Cherraw Hill, and have marched to this place by order of General Gates, who will join us this afternoon with his whole force. What operations will then be carryed on is not with me to say. The enemy now commanded by Colonel Webster was yesterday evening 14 miles in our front, a mile beyond Lynches Creek Ford. Whether they may retreat or advance or stand to dispute the passage with us are uncertain. I am induced to think the former will be the case. Had General Gates been near enough or had we his permission last evening, perhaps a forced march would have been made, which I presume is now too late to effect any thing of consequence. The formidable appearance which we make in this quarter will no doubt divert the attention of the enemy in yours and General Sumter's and perhaps give you and he opertunities of advancing and cooperate in dislodging the enemy from every post on this side Charles Town and reinstating our suffering friends as well as punishing the traiterous.

With great esteem I am, sir,
Your most obedient humble servant

GRIFFITH RUTHERFORD

PS

Be so obliging as to forward the letter to General Sumter. General Stevens with the Virginia militia and General Butler[61] with the Hillsborough late drafts are a few days' march in the rear.

---

[61] John Butler (?-1786) had settled before May 1763 near Armstrong's Ford on the Haw River and by 1768 had become Sheriff of Orange County, North Carolina. In 1775 he was appointed to the Committee of Safety for Hillsborough District, and in 1776, having become a delegate from Orange County to the two Provincial Congresses of that year, he was appointed by the first as colonel of one of his county's two regiments of revolutionary militia. He would later serve in the North Carolina revolutionary legislature. Having been involved in the action at Stono Ferry in June 1779, he was by now the brigadier general of militia for Hillsborough District and would soon take part in the Battle of Camden, where his men occupied the centre of the North Carolina militia and promptly fled on the commencement of the action. In March 1781 he would again lead militia in the Battle of Guilford. (Powell ed, *Dictionary of NC Biography*, i, 290-1; Wheeler, *Historical Sketches*, i, 74, 78, 81, 85; Hay ed, *Soldiers from NC*, 495; McCrady, *SC in the Rev 1775-1780*, 677; *The Greene Papers*, vii, 434; *The Cornwallis Papers*)

Giles to Gates, 12th August 1780 3(5): ALS

Camp, Pee Dee
August 12th 1780

To his Excellency Major General Gates
Camp near Lynches Creek

Favour Captain Moore

Dear General

I received yours under date 6th instant and return you thanks for your instructions, but as I had before received intelligence from General Caswell to have all the corn I could collect ground up and prepared for the army, I had in a great measure complied with that part of your orders, had got three mills grinding for the troops; but, sir, I would be glad to know if you think you will have a call for such provisions shortly, as it is altogether corn meal and from the nature of the climate I assure you it will not keep fit for use over 4 or 5 weeks after being barrell'd up. Therefore with your permition I'll only have the corn carried to the mills and wait your farther orders at the same time to have a sufficientcy of barrels made to contain it. I have given orders to have a quanty of beef cattle collected in a secure place, and in a short time I am in hopes to have a great quantity collected in that place, which is the fork of Pee Dee and Lynches Creek, if it be agreeable to you, in which fork I have collected my regiment; and as there is another regiment between me and the enemy — and great part of them good men, which they have shewed lately — I think any stores of provisions lodged there will be very safe. As to the news, there is a body of Tories collected on the North Carolina line, which I am preparing as fast as possible to go against. I have only this day got intelligence of their imbodying, and has also got this day a sufficientcy of amunition to go against them; and you may rest yourself assured that the next time you hear from me I'll be able to give you a good account of them provided they keep themselves imbodied, which is a circumstance I much doubt. Colonel Brown[62] of Bladen County, North Carolina, is near the line incamped and will act in conjuction with me, and when those rabble are brought to a sence of their duty, which will be in a few days, I shall then attempt to retake George Town if I think I can carry it with my little force, which I shall be convinced of by my spies before I attack it, and then, sir, every thing necessary will be done in this quarter and I am in hopes it will so greatly augment the spirits of our dejected friends that I can with safety detach part of my regiment to join you. In consequence of your first letter I have issued a proclamation declaring that all who has not taken an active part against America that does not join me on or before the 16th instant shall be deemed as enemies and treated accordingly. There was a

---

[62] Thomas Brown (?-1815) had been appointed Lt Colonel of the Bladen County revolutionary militia in September 1775. Some three and a half years later he became a member for his county in the Commons House of the North Carolina revolutionary assembly. Now a colonel of militia, he had played a minor part in military affairs and would continue to do so, being mostly content with suppressing loyalism in and about his area. In later years he would become a general and own several plantations, the principal one perhaps being Ashwood (now Oakland) in Carver's Creek, which he built in 1781. Aspen Hall, a private residence about 37 miles from Raleigh along US highway 64, contains some rare antiques and portraits from his family. (Hay ed, *Soldiers from NC*, 503, 614; Robinson, *NC Guide*, 439).

party of Brittish and Tory horse march[ed] from next George Town and burned several houses on their way. I on the notice raised a party of men and pursued them but could not overtake them. Would be glad to hear from [you] as soon as convenient.

I am, sir,
Your most obedient humble servant

HUGH GILES

Caswell to Davie, 18th August 1780 — 3(8): ALS

Charlotte
18th August 1780

Major Davie

The bearer, Dr Williamson, is going into the enemy with a flag of truce in order to obtain a list of our dead and wounded as well as to assist, with medicine and his surgical opperations, the wounded. It is necessary two horse men should go with him; these I entreat you to furnish. I shall be greatly obliged to you to let them be sensible and clever that they may make the necessary observations and report to me on their return, as the doctor very probably may be allowed to stay. In that case his report will be sent by them, and I rely on you to give the persons you send with the doctor the necessary instructions.

I have ordered out the whole of the militia of Rowan, Mecklenberg and Lincoln; expect them to rendezvous at the old camping ground two miles from hence on Sunday next. In the mean time I request you will occupy some post on the rout the enemy will take if they should think proper to march this way, and endeavor by every means in your power to obtain intelligence of their movements and designs, which you will be pleased to communicate by express daily or oftener if occasion requires to Colonel Henry Dickson[63], whom I shall leave as commanding officer of the militia at this place until my return from Salisbury on Sunday next, as General Gates is gone on to that place. I wish to see him and am just seting out, but shall assuredly return on Sunday.

---

[63] Born in Dinwiddie County, Virginia, Henry 'Hal' Dixon Jr (1740-1782) migrated sometime after mid September 1763 to what became Caswell County, North Carolina. Tall and weighing almost sixteen stones, he had been commissioned a captain in the North Carolina Continental line before being promoted to major in October 1777 and to lt colonel in May 1778. By June 1779, when he was seriously wounded in the action at Stono Ferry, he had seen considerable active service, having been involved in the Battles of Brandywine, Germantown, and Monmouth. Now recovered, he had commanded a regiment of North Carolina revolutionary militia in the Battle of Camden. While the rest of the militia fled the field, his regiment held firm, leading Henry Lee to remark, 'By his precepts and example he infused his own spirit into the breasts of his troops, who, emulating the noble ardor of their leader, demonstrated the wisdom of selecting experienced officers to command raw soldiers.' Having made his escape when all was lost, he would go on to command militia at the Battle of Guilford in March 1781 before transferring to the 2nd North Carolina Continental Regiment in February 1782. While serving near Charlestown, he was mortally wounded and died at the Round O on 17th July. (William S Powell, *When the Past Refused to Die: The History of Caswell County 1777-1977* (Moore Publishing Company, Durham, 1977); Heitman, *Historical Register*, 198; Hugh F Rankin, *The North Carolina Continentals* (University of North Carolina Press, 1971); Lee, *Memoirs*, 187; Monument to Henry Dixon, Guilford Courthouse National Battlefield Park)

I am with very great respect and esteem, sir,
Your most obedient servant

R CASWELL
Major General

PS

Herewith is a letter for General Sumter, which I beg the favor of you to send immediately to him, as 'tis probable you may have received information where he is and have gentlemen with you well acquainted with the part of the country he is in.

RC

Lindsay to Peasley, 29th August 1780   3(13): ALS

August 29th 1780

To Colonel John Peasley[64] etc

Sir

The berar hereof, Pares Chipman[65], coms to you with an expectation (after he has made you aquented with the circomstance of his affairs) that he will obtain his horse which James Helar[y?][66] presed. The said Chipman to my ceartain knowledge has been much destresaed this while past by the publick. He had a verry likley mair presed in to sarvis last springe, which he has never had any account of since. Likley she was lost at Charlestown. Neither dos he know whither she was preaised[67] or not. Two of his horses was in the expedeition against the Tores this somer, and he allowes, if that horse is taken from him, he will be disfornished of creaturs to do any work on his plantation. There is numbers in the neabourhud who neaver had a horse in the sarvis as yet. I would be glad the old man would geet his hor[s]e again if you can posable geet a nough without him. The old man has taken the affermation to the State and behaves siveley and is verry sarvesable to the publick in his

---

[64] John Peasley had been appointed Lt Colonel of the Guilford County revolutionary militia in April 1776. On 14th October 1780 he would arrive with 300 of his men at the close of the action at Shallow Ford on the Yadkin, where a band of North Carolina loyalists was beaten and dispersed. Dated 27th October, a regimental return of his militia appears later in these Papers. In late February 1781 he would join Andrew Pickens with a few men and may have taken part in the Pyle affair and the Battle of Guilford. His plantation lay a little to the south of South Buffalo Creek about five miles north-east of Thom's Mill. (Wheeler, *Historical Sketches*, i, 81; *The Greene Papers*, vii, 355-8)

[65] Paris Chipman owned land in Guilford County, North Carolina. He was a Quaker. (Information from David E White, a descendant of Chipman, 31st October 1996)

[66] Not identified.

[67] *preaised*: appraised or priced?

station. He has suplied grait numbers of our solders with vituals verry freely, and him and all belonging to his sosiaty has taken wheet to Mors Mill for the use of the armey.[68]

These from your humble servant

ROB[T] LINDSAY[69]

IG to Davie, undated[70]   3(157): ALS

To Mag[r] William Davy in camp

Sir

After my compliments to you this is to enform you that, by the best discoverys that we can find out, that there is marched of the Tories to join the British about 2 thousand. We expetct about one hundred of the Tories' light horse about Saterday or Sunday. Holey[71] and fifty men was to be at Captain Foster's[72] last neight, which I sent woord as soon as I got the news, which I hope went to you emedietly as I could not com my self. I am a-going down this day amongst them my self to find out theire intents as much as posible I can. If you can send up some time to neight, for, if I com my self, the will draw a suspition of mee and the no dout but wood take my life the first opertunyty. Sir, I beg it to be cept privet from any

---

[68] Poor Chipman, his woes were not ended (3(12): ADS):

'February the 8th 1781

Received of Paris Chipman a blanket for the use of Major Campbell's corps of Verginia volunteers.

JA[S] MITCHELL JR
Quarter Master'.

[69] Robert Lindsay (1740-1801) was a Presbyterian who is thought to have settled on Deep River, North Carolina, about 1763. Becoming a man of influence and property, he operated an ordinary (tavern) and a grist mill. When in 1771 Guilford County was formed from parts of Orange and Rowan, the County Court was held at his home until a courthouse was built three years later. In 1777 he began to represent his county in the North Carolina revolutionary legislature. (Ethel Stephens Arnett, *Greensboro, North Carolina — The County Seat of Guilford* (University of North Carolina Press, 1955), 18; information from Ron Lindsay and from John Field Pankow, a descendant of Robert Lindsay, 25th May 2005; George Ward Shannon Jr in *The Palace* (Spring 2002))

[70] Being addressed to Davie when major, this letter was written before mid September 1780, by which time his promotion to colonel (on 5th September) had become generally known.

[71] James Holley was a loyalist in and around the Waxhaws who, like irregulars on the revolutionary side, had a reputation for plundering, or 'breaking up', his opponents' habitations and may not have been averse to murder. According to Colonel John Marshel of Sumter's Brigade, he was a 'notorious offender'. (*The Greene Papers*, vi, 606)

[72] The home of John Foster lay on Waxhaw Creek, North Carolina. In 1765 he had migrated there from Ireland and by the end of the war he would be a major in the revolutionary service. His grave lies near the site of his home. (Robinson, *NC Guide*, 504)

but them that comes formerly for the news, for my life depends on it being keept secret, but you may depend I will spare no trouble to find out what I can.

No more but remains your frend to serve

IG

Davidson to McCaule, 21st September 1780   3(40): LS

September 21st 1780

Mr Thomas H McCaull[73]
Center Church

Sir

I have the pleasu[re] to inform you that Colonel Davie with 40 dragoons and 80 light infantry compleatly surprised a party of Tories this morning at 8 o'clock 2 miles in the rear of the British camp, killed 12, wounded a considerable number, perhaps 30, and captured one. The party is intirely dispersed. Colonel Davie has made good his retreat with near fifty horses, as many saddles, and about forty guns, the whole effected without the loss of a man. One slightly wounded. General Sumner has joined us this evening. By the looks of his men I presume they are substitutes. One thousand good riffle men might make Lord Cornwallice's sittuation very disagreeable.

Adieu

W^M DAVIDSON

Hall to Davie, 15th October 1780   3(232): ALS

McKnit's
October 15th, 9 o'clock pm

Colonel Commandant Davie
Mr Peel's

Sir

I feel all in a puzzle on account of Captain Hart's letter. Oh that the news of Sumpter may be true and that we might secure his LORDSHIP in the trap! A hundred schemes have been in my head since the news came how to detain him.

---

[73] Born in Pennsylvania, the Reverend Thomas Harris McCaule (1744-1796) was not only pastor of Centre Church but also chaplain to the revolutionary forces in Mecklenburg County, North Carolina. When William Lee Davidson was killed at Cowan's Ford on 1st February 1781, McCaule was nearby. (Hunter, *Sketches of Western NC*, 229)

If you have any despatches from General Sumpter you will releave me much by letting me know.

The want of official accounts excite my fears that he is not nigh. If he is, I presume you see the propriety of letting General Sumner know as soon as possible. I would have conversed with you this evening on the subject had the intelligence been well authenticated. General Davidson has an extract of Hart's letter and Patterson's intelligence by this time.

Sir, your most obedient servant

JA᎐ HALL JUN[R74]

§ - §

8 - The Journal of Lieutenant John Money

3(89): AD

27th August 1780

Joined the army at Camden this day under the command of Earl Cornwallis, with whom I am to serve as aid de camp.

An express was sent this evening to Charlestown.

Lieutenant Campbell of the 63rd came express from Major Wemyss.

Received from his Excellency Governor Martin the key of the military chest, containing money, papers etc.

28th August

Lieutenant Campbell of the 63rd return'd with Colonel Mills of the militia to Major Wemyss.

Colonel Kirkman[75] gave in a memorial requesting payment for some waggons and horses

---

[74] The writer may well have been Lt Colonel James Hall of the North Carolina revolutionary militia, who had formerly served in the North Carolina Continental line. If so, he would be killed with William Davidson in the action at Cowan's Ford on 1st February 1781. (Heitman, *Historical Register*, 267-8)

[75] *Colonel Kirkman*: a reference to Moses Kirkland, who had arrived in Camden by the 27th (see Cornwallis to Cruger of that date, p 172).

from the Quarter Master General's Department. Gave him an order on Major Frazer[76] for 30 guineas on accompt.

Major Cooke[77] of Colonel Rugely's militia brought intelligence of a body of 200 rebels being at Hanging Rock and about 70 more on a branch of Lynch's Creek.

29th August

Mr Johnson, mate of the 63rd, came with a letter from Major Wemyss in answer to Lord Cornwallis's of the day before. I answer'd it at 12 o'clock. Lord Cornwallis wish'd Major Wemyss to begin his march as soon as he possibly could and gave him leave to draw on the Quarter Master General for such sums as he might have occasion for.

The party of rebels reported yesterday by Major Cooke found to be only a scouting or plundering party.

An express went off at ten at night with a serjeant of the Volunteers of Ireland, who had charge of Lord Cornwallis's duplicates of his dispatches to Lord George Germain and the Commander in Chief.

I inspected the waggons and horses of the Quarter Master General's Department. Reported the horses totally unfit for service. Waggons, 30, present fit for service only. 26 waggons with 4 horses each not yet inspected.

Received intelligence through Colonel Hamilton of Generals Gates and Caswell being at Charlotte, collecting the debris of the army; that a detachment of 800 men from Newbern, Edenton and Bute under the command of Colonels Sewell and Jarvis were to join Gates at Charlotte, from whence the whole were to march to Hilsborough to cover the Assembly at that place, who were sitting for the purpose of raising a new army; that not a man was on the Cheraw Hill, but a party was embodying on the Long Bluff.

---

[76] A major in the 1st Battalion, 71st (Highland) Regiment, Simon Fraser (1737/8-1813) was now acting on secondment as a deputy quartermaster general at Savannah, a post which he had occupied since December 1778. In earlier days he had served as a junior officer in North America during the Seven Years' War before entering the Portuguese service in 1765. There he remained for ten years until, on the outbreak of the revolutionary war, he returned to Scotland and on 23rd November 1775 was commissioned a captain in the 1st Battalion of the 71st. During the Danbury raid in April 1777 he was shot in the face and lost the sight of an eye but he recovered sufficiently to be present at the Battles of Brandywine, Germantown, and Monmouth. On 14th October 1778 he was promoted to his majority. After the war he rose steadily in the army, dying a lt general. (*ODNB*; *Army Lists*; *The Cornwallis Papers*)

[77] John Cook Sr was the major in Henry Rugeley's Camden Regiment of the royal militia, a regiment in which his son John Jr was serving as a captain. On 1st December he would be captured with Rugeley, who was his son-in-law, when the fortified post at Rugeley's Mills infamously surrendered without firing a shot. His will was made in 1782 and probated two years later. (Clark, *Loyalists in the Southern Campaign*, i, 147; *The Greene Papers*, vi, 600; information from M Bernard, 29th April 2001)

Major Brice[78] went this day on his parole to North Carolina for a month. He having offer'd his services in giving intelligence, I conferr'd with him on the subject and gave him directions to examine into the following circumstances and send a person with the information he got, giving him a parole, *Russia*, that he might be known by me: to find out if there were any reinforcements coming from the northward, if the French had landed troops in any part of America, or if the French fleet was on the coast and on what part; to inform of any movement of the rebel army or of any detachment of it that might be sent to intercept our convoys; to enquire into the strength of the rebel army, artillery, stores, magazines etc.

Lord Cornwallis sent orders to Colonel Cruger at Ninety Six for Innis's corps to march immediately to Camden at all events.

30th August

Issued a warrant for £1000 to Mr Charles Morris[79], Deputy Purveyor of the General Hospital.

Paid Captain Coates by order of Lord Cornwallis ten guineas.

Ditto Captain Ferguson[80] of Colonel Turner's militia 10 guineas as a reward for a detachment of militia under his command who had a skirmish with the rebels and took 3 prisoners.

Sent an order, to the officer commanding the New York Volunteers and Brown's company on their march from Ninety Six, to make a tour round Rocky Mount, intelligence having been received of some straggling partys of rebels being in that part of the country; after performing which service, he was to march to Camden, crossing the Wateree at Camden Ferry. He had orders to take a detachment of Colonel Phillips's militia with him.

Wrote to the colonels of militia to desire they would endeavour to procure conductors and drivers for the waggons, and, if there were any good waggon horses in their district, desired they might be sent to me at Head Quarters and I would give them an ample price for them

---

[78] Money may be referring to Captain Jacob Brice of the 3rd Maryland Continental Regiment, who may have been acting as a major of brigade. He had been wounded and taken prisoner in the Battle of Camden. If so, Brice would soon be exchanged, transfer to the 1st Maryland on 1st January 1781, and serve until April 1783. (Heitman, *Historical Register*, 120)

[79] As Deputy Purveyor at the General Hospital in North America, Charles Morris (?-1829) occupied one of the senior posts in the army medical service. He was now acting as commissariat officer to HM Hospital at Charlestown and had in his charge the purchase and distribution of food and medical comforts, together with all accounts dealing with those matters. A former pupil of Westminster School, he is said by a revolutionary opponent to have 'suffered not a difference of political opinion to destroy the recollection of early attachments', but to have extended to his suffering school fellows of the opposing party 'every gratifying attention and liberal assistance that could mitigate the severity of their sufferings'. In February 1784 he would be placed on the half-pay list but in 1793 would resume active service as Purveyor under the Earl of Moira (as Rawdon then was). He resigned some two years later. (Johnston, *Commissioned Officers in the Medical Service*, xxxiii and 61; Garden, *Anecdotes* (1st series), 265)

[80] Ferguson has not been identified.

in ready money. Dated the letters as to morrow.

Captain Coffin's company of light infantry of the New York Volunteers marched to take post at Colonel Carey's near Camden Ferry.

An express arrived from Charles Town — a letter from Captain Ross.

31st August

Sent an express to Colonel Cruger at Ninety Six to countermand the order for the march of Innis's corps, should Colonel Cruger apprehend any danger, but to be sent to Camden the moment the danger was over. Lord Cornwallis wrote to Colonel Balfour, expressing his approbation at his having apprehended the very violent and factious rebels in Charles Town and putting them on board ship to be sent to Augustine. General Rutherford and Colonel Isaacs, prisoners of war, were to accompany them.

A letter from Colonel Hamilton requesting a troop of dragoons from his Lordship to assist him in collecting cattle and horses for the army. *Refused.*

Colonel Cruger and Major Wemyss had each directions to endeavour to find out the propagators of the many infamous lies which have been of late so industriously circulated through the country and punish the offenders by publickly whipping them in the town they belong to.

In the evening an express arrived from Charlestown with a letter from Captain Ross informing his Lordship that Colonel Balfour had order'd the 7th Regiment and the battalions of militia of Ball and Wigfall to march under the command of Major Moncrieffe to George Town, that Captain Ross expected to embark for England the next day, Wednesday.

An express went off for Charlestown this night at ten. Lord Cornwallis wrote to Colonel Balfour to approve of the movement of the 7th etc and that the general plan would not be effected by it. This, and the letter in the morning inclosing a copy of Lord Cornwallis's instructions to Major Wemyss of the 28th instant, went by the express.

I wrote to Captain McKinnon, desiring an immediate supply of 30 or 40 set of waggon harness, 1,000 pairs of horse shoes and nails in proportion, ropes etc, and £500 or £600 in cash for the Department of the Quarter Master General.

Friday, September 1st

Wrote to Major Wemyss, in consequence of a report being made of his being ill, to desire he would inform Lord Cornwallis immediately whether he was able to take the command of the detachment order'd on the expedition that, in case he was not, another officer might be appointed in his room.

Received a letter from Colonel Hamilton at Ratcliff's Bridge informing that General Gates was at Hilsborough; Smallwood, Guess and Armand on the Yadkin River 7 miles to the northward of Salisbury; the militia embodying at Charlotte; that the rebels expected a reinforcement from Virginia.

Saturday, September 2nd

Sent an express to Colonel Rugely desiring he would immediately inform Lord Cornwallis whether he got the necessary information relative to forage at Waxsaw.

Wrote to Colonel Hamilton at Ratcliff's Bridge to acknowledge Lord Cornwallis's receipt of his letters and of my own. Acquainted him that a troop of dragoons could not be spared for the purpose he mention'd.

Sunday, September 3rd

An express from Charlestown this morning with a letter from Captain Ross to Lord Cornwallis. The sick of the 63rd from George Town were drove to Tybee. Paid Mr Bagnall in the Quarter Master General's Department 30 guineas on accompt by order of Lord Cornwallis.

Monday, September 4th

Received a letter from Major Wemyss inclosing a memorial to the Commander in Chief recommending Captain Lieutenant Roberts to succeed to a company in the room of Captain Croker, dead (28th August), and myself to the captain lieutenantcy; an hour after the receipt of which Lord Cornwallis received another from Major Wemyss requesting to stop the memorial till Captain Roberts's conduct could be enquired into, he having information of great negligence in him during his march with the prisoners of war and, the night his party was attacked, the whole lay without their coats or accoutrements. The memorial in consequence to lay over.

Sent an express to Colonel Cruger at Ninety Six with an answer to his letter to Lord Cornwallis of the day before. Lord Cornwallis made a requisition of twelve more waggons from that district.

Paid Mr Leacy[81] £4 7*s* 1*d* secret service money.

Tuesday, September 5th 1780

Ensign Lloyd[82] arrived express from Major Wemyss to acquaint his Lordship that he intended to move the next day on the expedition and that the remainder of the regiment under Captain Mallom would march the evening of the same day.

Colonel Hamilton's corps arrived at Camden this evening from Ratcliff's Bridge.

---

[81] Probably Edward Lacey Sr, a staunch loyalist. His son was Colonel Edward Lacey Jr, the noted revolutionary. (McCrady, *South Carolina 1775-1780*, 595-6)

[82] Owen Lloyd had been commissioned an ensign in the 63rd Regiment on 13th April 1778. (*Army Lists*)

Wednesday, September 6th 1780

An express went to Charlestown.

A commission of colonel of militia given to Colonel Gray. The 23rd, 33rd and Volunteers of Ireland with two 3 pounders received orders to march to morrow morning at day break. Paid Sergeant Whittle, Deputy Provost Marshall, twenty guineas on accompt of pay etc.

Gave a warrant to Lieutenant Forbes[83] of the 71st Regiment for [*blank*], being subsistence for himself as adjutant and Ensign Chisholme[84] as quarter master to the 3rd battalion of light infantry.

Thursday, September 7th 1780

The corps mentioned yesterday march'd this morning. The proviant train consisted of twenty waggons with a puncheon of rum in each and eighteen with flour and salt.

Lt Colonel Trumbull[85] of the New York Volunteers was left to command at Camden with the 71st Regiment, part of the 63rd, New York Volunteers, Hamilton's corps (a detachment of 100 men with Major Wemyss excepted), and Brian's militia.

The army marched to Rougely's Mill. Granted a pass from Colonel Rougely's for Mr Middleton McDaniel[86] to go to Georgia for a month. Wrote an order to Arthur Middleton Esq to repair immediately to Charlestown and to acquaint the Commandant of his arrival.

Friday, Hanging Rock, September 8th '80

The army marched from Rougely's.

Received a flag from General Gates with a letter to Lord Cornwallis requesting permission for Mr Johnson, a surgeon, to go to Camden to attend the wounded prisoners, which his Lordship granted.

Major Rutherford under sanction of the same flag requested permission to go to Camden with cash and necessarys for his father, General Rutherford, prisoner of war. Denied. If

---

[83] Arthur Forbes had entered the 2nd Battalion, 71st (Highland) Regiment, as a lieutenant on 29th December 1775. (*Army Lists*)

[84] Colin Chisholme had been commissioned an ensign in the 1st Battalion of the 71st on 3rd August 1778. (*Army Lists*)

[85] *Trumbull*: Turnbull.

[86] Middleton McDaniel was an inhabitant of Camden District, probably living in the vicinity of Rugeley's Mills. Requiring a pass, he may have been suspected of revolutionary sympathies, a supposition supported by his leaving no record of service in the royal militia. (Joan A Inabinet, 'Local Revolutionary Kin? Search a List from "Clermont" (Rugeley's)', *Newsletter of the Catawba-Watereee Genealogical Society* (Camden SC), January 2000)

Major Rutherford chose it, he might send in the money etc by Mr Johnson but could not be permitted to go into the town himself.

Colonel Porterfield, prisoner of war, applied for leave to go to Virginia to endeavour to effect an exchange for himself. Answer: Colonel Porterfield may have a parole to go to Virginia when his wound will permit him to move, but he cannot be exchanged.

Colonel Armand applied for his officers of the Legion to be exchanged or paroled. Denied, but his officers might have permission to examine the prisoners of war for the men of his corps, as he was uncertain who were prisoners with us. He also applied for some of his private papers to be returned to him, which were taken in the baggage, and his servant. Granted, if the papers could possibly be found and provided his servant was not a soldier.

Colonel Tarleton with the Legion marched this morning from Camden and crossed the Wateree.

Saturday, Berkely's House, Waxhaw, September 9th 1780

The army marched from Hanging Rock to this place. Wrote to England to desire him to send 3 or 4 expresses to remain with Lord Cornwallis. Expresses from Camden to be forwarded by the Rockey Mount Road. The pioneers at Camden to march with the 71st Regiment.

Sunday, Forster's House, Waxhaw, September 10th 1780

The army marched to this place. Brian's refugees, who join'd the army from Camden yesterday, march'd with the baggage.

Monday, Forster's House, Waxhaw, September 11th 1780

The army halted this day.

Tuesday, Crawford on Waxhaw Creek, September 12th 1780

The army took a position at this place and hutted. Two mills, one on the Catawba River at Blair's and another at Harper's, were employed in grinding wheat for the troops, which was collected from the plantations in the district.

Wednesday, Crawford's, 13th September 80

A mail arrived from England, brought by Captain King of the Volunteers of Ireland from Charlestown. Lord Cornwallis wrote to Colonel Trumbull, commanding at Camden, to order the 71st to march for this place on Monday, the 18th instant, and to send a large quantity of rum and salt by that opportunity.

Thursday, Crawford's, 14th September 1780

Received a letter from Colonel Tarleton dated Cross Roads, Fishing Creek. He proposed marching to morrow within about 20 miles of this post to White's Mill.

The commissary reported his having found a large quantity of flour on Broad River and that he intended 15 waggons should be sent to the army to morrow loaded with flour[87]. Lord Cornwallis wrote to Colonel Tarleton by the return of the express to request to see him.

Friday, Crawford's, 15th September 1780

Monsieur de Treville, a French officer in the rebel service, came from Beaufort, Port Royal. Paid him 15 guineas and 7,000 paper dollars secret service money. He went towards Virginia.

Lord Cornwallis received a letter[88] from General Gates requesting permission for Mr Drayton to go to Charlestown, which was granted, and inclosed some dispatches from the Congress to General Moultrie relative to the appointment of a commissary of prisoners in the room of Captain Turner[89].

Sent out a flag to the officer commanding at the nearest post of the enemy to acquaint him that, if John Hutchison, who was taken by a party of their militia on the 9th instant, was hanged as they threatned, Lord Cornwallis would instantly put to death two of the most violent of their friends in our custody, or, if they punish'd him, he would inflict the same punishment upon two of their friends. If they chose to exchange him, his Lordship would give them a man of nearly the same rank in life.

Colonel Tarleton came from White's Mill.

Saturday, Crawford's, 16th September 1780

Colonel Tarleton returned to the Legion, having received directions to take the earliest opportunity of attacking General Sumpter, who had taken post on McAlpine's Creek.

Sunday, Crawford's, 17th September

[*blank*]

Monday, Crawford's, 18th September

Received an account of Colonel Tarleton being dangerously ill of a fever. I was sent off

---

[87] See Knecht to Cornwallis, undated, p 286.

[88] *a letter..*: not extant.

[89] George Turner (1738-1804) had been commissioned a 2nd lieutenant in the 1st South Carolina Regiment when it was raised by the Provincial Congress in June 1775. Eleven months later he was promoted to 1st lieutenant. After the regiment was transferred to the Continental establishment he was promoted to captain with effect from 28th April 1777. Taken prisoner in the capitulation of Charlestown, he had been serving as an aide-de-camp and deputy commissary of prisoners. (Moss, *SC Patriots*, 942)

to him at White's Mill.

Sent a spy this evening to get certain intelligence of Sumpter's post, to pass the Catawbaw River and go on towards Charlotte, to return by the right of our post at Crawford's. Received accounts from Colonel Cruger of an insurrection in the Ceded Lands.

Tuesday, Colonel Tarleton's quarters at White's Mill on Fishing Creek, 19th September 1780

Colonel Tarleton being exceedingly ill, I staid at this post to day.

Wednesday, Crawford's, 20th September 80

Returned from Colonel Tarleton. The man I sent to find out Sumpter returned – reported him to have moved close to the Catawbaw River near Bigger's Ferry.

Surgeon Stuart of the 71st sent for from Hanging Rock to visit Tarleton.

Thursday, Crawford's, 21st September 1780

The 71st arrived within 2½ miles of Crawford's, where they took post. Lieutenant McLeod of the Royal Artillery came with the 71st and brought up the artillery stores etc.

Friday, Crawford's, 22nd September 80

Went to Tarleton to endeavour to remove him from the post at White's Mill, having received intelligence of Generals Davison and Sumner being between Charlotte and Sumpter's post with about 700 militia. Their intention was to endeavour to surprise the Legion if possible. Arrived at White's Mill about two o'clock pm. They had received intelligence of General Sumpter's intention and that he proposed crossing the Catawbaw that evening. Tarleton was so dangerously ill as to render his removal impossible with any degree of safety. The post was such that the cavalry in case of attack could not act. Those who had carbines were dismounted and took post in a wood to the right, and every other precaution taken to strengthen the post and prevent a surprise.

Saturday, 23rd September 80, Crawford's

Tarleton was so well as to be able to be removed from White's Mill to Blair's House across the Catawbaw.

The Legion marched at six in the morning and cross'd at Blair's Ford.

Mr Cruden went to Charlestown yesterday with the dispatches for England and New York. Captains *Treville* and Hamilton returned from their leave of absence in North Carolina to their parole, the former at Beaufort, the latter at Camden.

The intelligence brought by Monsieur de Treville was as follows...[90]

Sunday, Crawford's, 24th September 1780

The following corps marched this afternoon at four towards Charlotte, viz, 23rd, 33rd, Volunteers of Ireland, and Legion with 2 three and 1 six pounder.

Halted at Twelve Mile Creek till the moon rose and then proceeded towards Sugar Creek on the Charlotte Road. No certain intelligence being received of Sumpter's having pass'd the Catawbaw River, Lord Rawdon was detached with the Legion and flank companys of the Volunteers of Ireland to attack him. I attended his Lordship on this expedition. We marched to Bigger's Ferry, where we learned he had passed the evening before and that Sumner and Davison had retired from McAlpine's Creek.

Monday, Camp at Bigger's Ferry, 25th September 80

Took post at this place with the detachment under the command of Lord Rawdon, who moved as beforementioned. The army took post at Sugar Creek.

Tuesday, Charlottetown, 26th September 1780

The detachment under the command of Lord Rawdon marched this morning at day break and joined the main body under Lord Cornwallis at the cross roads within four miles of Charlottetown. The advanced guard fell in with a rebel party of cavalry near the town and pursued them, supported by the Legion, into the center of the town, when they received a fire from the houses, which obliged them to retire out of musket shot till the infantry came up, upon whose approach they abandoned the town and the cavalry pursued. They continued harrassing us for four miles, Lord Cornwallis having pushed forward in hopes of falling in with Sumner and Davison, but they had marched in the night. The cavalry pursued Major Davy's corps 8 miles from the town and cut up about 14 of them. This corps consisted of about 200 mounted militia riflemen and had taken post at Charlotte to cover the retreat of Sumner. Captain Campbell of the 71st light infantry was wounded in the pursuit, and Major Hanger and Captain McDonald of the Legion received slight contusions by the fire from the town. One horse kill'd and a man wounded. The army took post at this place, which has all the appearance of a healthy situation.

Lord Cornwallis received a letter from Major Wemyss...[91]

Wednesday, Charlottetown, 27th September 80

Lord Cornwallis publish'd a proclamation this day offering protection to all persons who

---

[90] Money paraphrases de Treville's report of 23rd September (p 345). He then summarises Cruger's letter of 15th and 16th September (p 187), which was received on the 22nd. He concludes by summarising Cruger's letter of the 19th (p 190), which was received in the evening of the 23rd.

[91] Money summarises Wemyss' letter of 20th September and Cornwallis's reply of the 26th (pp 214-6).

would deliver themselves and their arms to the commanding officer of His Majesty's forces at any post under his Lordship's command, giving their parole 'not to do or say or cause to be done or said any thing prejudicial to His Majesty's interest or Government'.[92]

Lord Cornwallis wrote to Colonel Balfour[93] and Lt Colonel Turnbull...[94]

Thursday, 28th September 1780, Charlottetown

I wrote to Brigadier General Sumter...

Lord Cornwallis wrote to Major Ferguson...[95]

Friday, Charlottetown, September 29th 1780

Lord Cornwallis wrote to Colonel Trumbull...[96]

§ - §

---

[92] See p 331, note 20.

[93] See p 99.

[94] Money goes on to summarise the letter to Turnbull (p 240).

[95] The letters to Sumter and Ferguson (pp 342 and 158) are summarised.

[96] Money partially summarises the letter (p 242).

Index[1]

Actions —
    at Augusta, 28, 39, 40, 46-7, 55, 88, 90, 94-6, 103, 110, 153-4, 156, 187-191, 236, 241, 305;
    at Black Mingo, 26, 113, 118;
    at Cane Creek, 27, 148-9;
    near Cedar Spring, 143;
    at Fishing Creek, 5, 14, 20, 72;
    at Hanging Rock, 10;
    near Lynches Creek, 235;
    at Musgrove's Mill, 5, 16-7, 144-5, 170;
    at Ramsour's Mill, 9;
    at Rocky Mount, 10;
    at Tarcote in the forks of Black River, 29, 128, 131, 263, 265;
    at Wahab's plantation, 88n, 355
Address of allegiance seeking freedom to trade, 95, 99, 107
Alexander, ——, 234
Allaire, Anthony (III, 460), 33
Allen, ——, 241
Allen, Barney, 339
Allen, Isaac (I, 259), 169, 174
Allston, Peter, 228n
Alman, Phillip, 307n
Amherst, Jeffrey, Lord, 21n, 298
Ancrum, George (I, 86), 70, 72, 246
Arbuthnot, Marriot (I, 7), 18, 47-9, 118-9, 318
Armand and his corps (I, 45), 230, 262
Augusta —
    garrison of, 30, 187;
    scouring of neighbourhood after Clark's attack, 103;
    relieved by abandonment of autumn campaign, 30;
    intention to erect better works at, 90
Autumn campaign —
    high risks of, 28-31;
    imprudence of, 32;
    the political imperative, 32;
    the march to Charlotte, progress of, 361-5;
    abandonment of, the reasons for, 30-1, 56, 58, 126-7;
    the lessons to be learnt from, 25-34

Back Country, The (*see also* 'Ninety Six') —
    split into tracts of loyalists and revolutionaries, 29;
    its possession indispensable for the security of the rest of SC, 56, 58;
    proposed post about the Enoree and Tyger Rivers, 82;
    small parties of the enemy on Pacolet River and Bullock Creek, 157;
    its situation at time of, and after, Clark's incursion into the Ceded Lands, 186, 198
Bacot, Samuel, 227n
Bagnall, ——, 360
Bain, James, 121-3n, 124-5
Balfour, Nisbet (I, 35-7), 16, 22, 34, 37-8, 43, 49, 62-139, 156, 172, 178, 181, 185, 187, 193, 201, 205, 207, 209, 219, 222-3, 239, 240, 246, 248-250, 252-3, 258-260, 271, 273, 276, 278-9, 302, 306, 312-3, 321-2, 324n-5, 328, 342, 359
Ball Sr, Elias (I, 51), 26, 64, 66-7, 70, 92, 209, 220, 244, 266, 359
Ballingall, Robert, 68, 75n, 92, 113, 132, 138
Barrington, William Wildman, Viscount Barrington, 52n
Battle of Camden, 3-5, 11-15, 19
Battle of King's Mountain, 31, 33, 55, 166-7
Bayard, William, 199n
Begbie, James and William, 316n
Berry, Edward, 125
Blucke, John, 27, 120n, 129, 132, 138
Board of Police, 316-8, 322
Booth, B——, 243n, 339
Bowie, John (I, 97), 134-5
Bradley, ——, 69n, 72
Brandon, Thomas (I, 295), 135
'Breaking up' of habitations: *see* 'Plundering'
Brevard, Hugh, 135n, 159, 163
Brice, Jacob, 358n
British strategy, 4, 16, 18, 25, 27-8, 32-3, 42, 46, 56-8, 82, 86, 100, 110, 126, 132, 172, 177, 187, 222, 240, 244, 246, 255, 273 —
    policy of severity partly pursued, 26-7
Brodrick, The Hon Henry (I, 22), 83
Bromfield, ——, 212n

---

[1] The letter 'n' after the number of a page indicates the presence there of biographical or identifying information in a footnote. Such information appearing in another volume is indicated in brackets immediately after a person's name.

Brown, ——, 177n
Brown, Malcom, 91, 104n
Brown, Thomas (I, 271), 28, 30, 34, 39, 40, 46-7, 55, 80, 88, 92, 94, 96, 100-1, 103, 136, 153-4, 156, 159, 183-4, 187-192, 197, 236, 241, 304-5, 314
Brown, Thomas, 351n
Browne, William, 309n
Bruce, Andrew, 87n
Bruen, Henry, 200n
Bryan, Samuel (I, 168), 9, 208, 343-4
Butler, John, 350n

Camden —
    Cornwallis's arrival there, 11;
    importance of post at, 69, 72;
    garrison of, 28-9, 247, 250, 257;
    prisoners at, 233-4, 239, 242-3, 259;
    sickliness of, 37, 80, 82, 86, 116, 120-1, 130, 139, 277, 279, 287-291;
    works at, 237, 257, 263, 265-6
Cameron, Donald, 283n
Camp, John, 145n
Campbell, ——, 130
Campbell, ——, 157n
Campbell, Archibald, 284n
Campbell, Archibald (I, 280), 294
Campbell, Charles (I, 227), 14
Campbell, David, 209n, 356
Campbell, John (I, 167), 54, 294, 314
Campbell, Patrick, 99n, 365
Campbell, Peter, 145n
Campbell, William, 33, 134n-5
Captured troops —
    enlistment of, 301-2;
    exchange of, 16, 49;
    paroling to Orangeburg of field officers captured at the Battle of Camden, 64, 238, 329;
    dispatching the rest to Charlestown, 67, 69, 72, 239, 242, 259, 289;
    liberation or escape of, 37, 172, 213, 226, 242-3;
    employing on defensive works at Charlestown, 85;
    putting on board prison ships at Charlestown, 43, 121, 130;
    mortality of, 133, 139;
    application to recruit for Spanish Main, 121-5
Carden, John (I, 183), 343-4
Cary, James (I, 245), 69-70, 72, 82, 85-6, 140, 236, 245-6, 333-4, 359
Cassells, James (I, 307), 26, 73, 83, 92, 98, 113, 121, 220, 240, 244, 266, 336-7
Caswell, The Hon Richard (I, 60), 4, 9, 229, 350-3

Cathey, ——, 154n
Cavalry or mounted infantry —
    need for by the British, 34, 105, 116, 121, 132, 193, 198, 201, 205, 263, 265-6;
    Tarleton's horses in wretched condition before the autumn campaign, 43-4;
    arrival of cavalry accoutrements at Savannah, 133
Ceded Lands —
    open revolt of, 28, 39, 40, 46-7, 55, 91, 153, 174, 186-191, 236, 273;
    scouring of after revolt, 30, 97, 100-1, 110, 158, 174-5, 192-7, 202;
    oath by persons not having broken their parole, 195;
    oath by persons having broken their parole, 195-6;
    bond entered into by persons having broken their parole, 196
Charlestown —
    defensive works at, 85-6, 93;
    laying in a magazine of provisions at, 85, 93;
    shortest route from there to Winnsborough, 128;
    Cornwallis ignorant of the state of, 255
Charlotte —
    occupation of by British, 26, 30, 99, 365;
    proposed post (aborted) there, 28, 30, 46, 82, 86, 222, 231, 273;
    British withdrawal from and reasons for, 30-2
Chew, William, 145n
Chewton, Viscount: see 'Waldegrave, George'
Chipman, Paris, 353n-4n
Chisholme, Colin, 361n
Civil affairs in SC, management of, 248, 319
Clark, Elijah (I, 257), 27-8, 30, 39, 91, 94, 103-4, 141, 148, 159, 162-4, 175, 186-194
Clarke, Alured (I, 330), 49, 73, 267, 292-308
Clary, Daniel (I, 264), 205
Clary, Ethelred, 345n
Clements, Josiah, 227n
Cleveland, Benjamin, 33, 135n, 157, 159, 160, 162-3
Cliffe, Walter, 294n, 303, 305
Climate, intense heat of, and sickly effect on troops, 15, 17-8, 25-6, 28-9, 37-8, 42, 44, 46, 79-80, 82, 84, 86, 90, 101, 114, 116, 118-121, 130, 133, 139, 153, 210, 233, 256, 258-9, 269, 273, 275, 277, 279, 282-3, 287, 289, 290, 294, 301, 304-5
Clinton, Sir Henry, KB, 15-17, 41-54, 57-61 —
    dispatches diversionary force under Leslie to the Chesapeake and places him under Cornwallis's orders, 49-50

368

Clinton, Thomas Pelham, Earl of Lincoln, 53n
Coats, William, 260n, 358(?)
Coffin, John, 94n-5, 246, 249, 359
Coker, John, 127
Commissaries, British, 66, 71, 243, 246, 248, 265, 269, 280, 283, 286-9, 309
Commissioners of the SC Navy, 318
Communication with Cornwallis, endangerment of the, etc, 30, 91-3, 102, 108, 117, 240, 248-9, 257
Contingent expenses at Ninety Six, 172
Convalescents, employment of, 26, 28-9, 42, 46, 65, 93, 101, 108, 113, 132, 174, 222, 239, 240, 243-5, 247, 251-2, 256-7, 271, 275, 277-8, 280, 283
Cook Sr, John, 357n
Cornwallis, Charles, Earl (*see also* 'Autumn campaign', 'British strategy', etc) —

    describes events leading up to the Battle of Camden, 7-12, 15-16;

    relates the Battle of Camden and the action at Fishing Creek, 12-14;

    directs, after the Battle of Camden, the NC loyalists to rise, but they fail to do so, 15, 36-7, 41, 58;

    on the action at Musgrove's Mill, 16-17;

    stresses the importance of a diversion in the Chesapeake but invites Leslie to come farther south, 16, 18, 42-3, 56-61, 127-8, 130-1, 137;

    lacks horses, gear and provisions at Camden before the autumn campaign, 66, 178;

    sanctions Ferguson's incursion into NC but fails to support him at a critical juncture, 31, 161, 164, 166, 172;

    on Tarleton's illness, 45-7, 88-9, 273;

    when leaving SC, devolves on Balfour the management of the posts there, 185;

    falls ill at Charlotte and does not fully recover till the beginning of November, 31, 34, 117;

    on the disaffection east of the Wateree and Santee, 26-7, 37, 41, 66, 208-9, 210, 212, 216;

    countermands Wemyss' orders for a second foray there, 252, 254;

    considers the perfect security of Ninety Six District to be of utmost importance, 173;

    proposes raising troops of dragoons for Camden, Ninety Six, and Georgetown Districts, 34, 105, 205;

    orders magazines of grain and forage to be laid up at Camden, the Congarees, and Ninety Six, 129, 201, 288;

    on dealing with persons who have revolted or who cannot be depended on, 19-20, 41, 174, 193, 208-9, 212, 216, 234;

    is of opinion that in a civil war there is no admitting of neutral characters, who must be disarmed, etc, 177, 185;

    his reasons for transporting certain principal revolutionaries to St Augustine, 38, 43;

    his reasons for issuing the sequestration proclamation, 38;

    on the naval weakness at Charlestown, 47;

    on the right of command in East Florida, 302;

    exhorts that care be taken in dispatches not to make Ministers too sanguine, 99

Cotton, Richard, 248n
Crabtree, ——, 274, 278
Crawford, Robert, 232n
Croker, John, 210n, 212-3
Crosier, ——, 132
Cruden, John (I, 219), 87, 105, 112, 268, 287, 320-8, 364
Cruger, John Harris (I, 152 and 258), 19, 20, 28-30, 34, 39, 40, 46-7, 55, 58, 71-3, 80, 86-8, 91-2, 94, 100-1, 103-5, 107, 109, 116, 118, 129-137, 145, 154, 156, 158, 162-3, 165, 168-207, 224-5, 231, 240-1, 243-4, 251, 254-5, 257, 273, 275, 302, 304, 334
Cuningham, Patrick, 176n
Cunningham. Robert (I, 117), 8, 39, 72-3, 105, 116, 131, 136, 171-2, 176, 178-180, 182, 186, 193, 199, 204-6, 334
Cusack, Adam, 215n

Dalling, John, 121-2n, 123-5, 314
Dalrymple, William, 54n
Davidson, John, 154n
Davidson, William Lee, 45n, 100-1, 345-6, 355-6, 364-5
Davie, William Richardson, 45n, 88, 99, 101, 156, 348-350, 355-6, 365
Dawson, George, 137n
Defectors, and the disaffected who revolt (*see also* 'Ceded Lands' and 'East of the Wateree and Santee') —

    punishment of generally and to the east of the Wateree and Santee, 19, 20, 26, 37, 41, 62, 98, 174, 208-9, 215, 234;

    ready to commence hostilities about the Enoree and Tyger Rivers, 82;

    in the Long Cane settlement, 104;

    offer of parole in Ninety Six District, 193;

    offer of pardon or parole to those east of the Wateree and Santee, 216-7, 244

De Lancey, John Peter, 114n, 118
De Peyster, Abraham (I, 249), 166-7, 173

De Peyster, Frederick (I, 104), 210-2, 213-4, 220-1, 249
De Rosset, The Hon Lewis Henry (I, 374), 73
Despard, John, 235n, 247
Disaffection —
    in Charlestown, 260;
    of the Congarees, 69-70, 72, 246;
    about the Enoree and Tyger Rivers, 82;
    in formerly revolutionary regiments of militia, 172-3, 175-8;
    in the Long Cane settlement, 39, 91, 100, 104, 172-3, 175-8, 186-8;
    of the Low Country, 9;
    on both sides of the upper Savannah River, 103, 190;
    widespread in SC, 55, 102
Disaffected not in arms —
    advantages to of their status, 183;
    contributions in kind from, 185;
    disarming of, 174, 177, 185, 193, 208, 211-2, 214, 285;
    dispatch of to Charlestown, 266
Diseases and illnesses prevalent, 247, 263, 272, 287, 289, 301
Diversion in the Chesapeake, 49-50, 111, 254
Dixon Jr, Henry ('Hal'), 352n
Dooly, John (I, 270), 192
Doyle, John (I, 185), 14, 133
Doyle, Wellbore Ellis, 119n, 126, 257-8, 260
Drayton, William, 84n, 363
Drew, Thomas Haynes, 337n
Dubuysson des Hayes, Charles-François, Vicomte, 338n
Dunlap, James (I, 74), 82, 88, 92, 107, 149, 153, 160-1, 187
Durnford, Andrew (I, 337), 294, 305

East Florida (*see also* 'St Augustine') —
    need for a permanent naval establishment there, 309-311;
    erection of blockhouse at the entrance of Mosquito (now Ponce de León) Inlet, 311
East of the Wateree and Santee —
    disaffection and open revolt there, 10, 11, 26-7, 29, 37, 55, 58, 99, 120, 138, 215, 217, 220, 229, 249, 257, 351;
    Moncrief's expedition, 26-7, 66-70, 74, 81, 93-4, 98, 266;
    Wemyss' expedition, 26-7, 99, 208-221, 226;
    cannot be kept by royal militia even if supported by small detachment of troops, 217;
    measures (aborted) to secure after the above expeditions, 219, 222, 240, 244-7, 249, 252;
    proposed ways to secure the territory, 218-220
Edwards, Arthur, 303n
Elliott, Andrew, 138n
Ellison, John, 331n
Enciphering, 65n, 82n, 89-90, 110, 130
England, Richard (I, 172), 14, 33, 63-4, 66, 75, 83, 88, 126, 138, 233-6, 242, 258, 260, 263, 265, 268-280, 362
English, ——, 157n
Estaing, Charles Hector Théodat, Comte d', 310

Fargie, John, 76
Ferguson, ——, 358
Ferguson, Patrick (I, 37-8), 10, 11, 14, 19, 20, 27-31, 33, 39, 42, 53-6, 58, 64-5, 82, 88, 101, 106-7, 109, 116-7, 126, 129, 135-6, 140-167, 169-173, 175, 188, 192, 198, 214, 224, 273, 282, 285-7, 334
Finch, George, Earl of Winchilsea and Earl of Nottingham, 119n
Fisher, John (I, 80), 136, 329
Fitzroy, ——, 83n
Flennikin, David or John, 348n
Flieger, H——, 270
Floyd, Matthew (I, 142), 165-6, 285, 331-3
Forbes, Arthur, 361n
Ford, ——, 217
Ford, James, 247n, 253
Fortescue, The Hon Matthew, 48n
Foster, John, 354n
Fraser, James (I, 25), 69, 73, 112
Fraser, James, 71n
Fraser, Simon, 357n
Fraser, Thomas (I, 243), 20, 106, 108, 132, 180, 216, 219, 240, 243-7, 249
French expeditionary forces, 47, 100, 102, 108, 260
Fuser, Lewis Valentine, 267n

Gage, Thomas, 293, 297-8
Garden, Alexander, 93
Gardner, ——, 78n, 85, 90, 102, 319
Garrett, Joshua, 227n
Gates, Horatio (I, 176), 3, 4, 9-11, 16-17, 21, 37, 48, 55, 58, 72, 80, 158, 169, 173-4, 229, 230, 260, 291, 304, 314, 337-8, 350-2, 361
Georgetown, its repossession, abandonment and reoccupation, 26-7, 55, 58, 113-5, 118, 120, 126, 129, 132, 138, 209, 249, 257
Georgia (*see also* 'Actions —— at Augusta', 'Augusta', 'Ceded Lands', and 'Savannah') —
    situation in, 95-7, 100;
    garrison at Augusta, 30, 187;
    The Disqualifying Act 1780, application of to parolees, 80, 183-5

Germain, Lord George, 7n-16, 36-40, 51-4, 87, 95, 99, 121, 310, 357
Gibb, Thomas, 239n
Gibbs, James, 202n-3, 205
Gibbs, Zacharias, 207, 334-5n
Gilbertown, 148n —
    Ferguson's declaration issued there 150-1
Giles, Hugh, 214n, 217, 220, 351-2
Gist, Mordecai (I, 230), 4, 230
Glasier, Beamsly (I, 355), 293, 302, 312-3
Goldesborough, Thomas, 111n, 114
Gordon, ——— (I, 166), 66
Gordon riots, 84, 153, 319
Graham, Colin (I, 81), 69
Graham, John (I, 164), 136
Graham, William (I, 303), 135, 141, 159, 163
Gratton, William (I, 175), 137
Gray, Robert (I, 135), 73, 106, 110, 132, 216-9, 240, 244, 248, 250, 253, 336-7, 361
Gregory, Isaac, 13n, 345n
Grierson, James, 190n

Habersham, John, 279n-280
Hagstead, ———, 348
Haldane, Henry, 14n, 64, 66, 263, 267, 272, 278-280, 290
Hall Jr, James, 356n
Hall, Josias Carvil, 338n
Hall, Thomas William Burly, 297
Hamilton, Andrew, 134n-5
Hamilton, George, 338n, 343n, 364
Hamilton, John (I, 55), 29, 37, 197, 208, 226-231, 240, 244, 251, 253, 255, 257, 265, 271, 274, 359, 360
Hampton, Andrew, 141n, 148-9, 154, 159
Hanger, The Hon George (I, 38-9), 34, 45, 49, 99, 365
Hanson, Isaac, 339
Harper, Daniel (I, 217), 242, 282n-3
Harrington, Henry William, 220n
Harris, Thomas, 264n
Harrison, John (I, 161), 8, 17, 39, 72, 99, 208-9, 216, 221, 226, 240, 244, 260, 263, 271
Harrison, John, 126n
Hart, ———, 355-6
Hay, ———, 69n
Hayes, John McNamara (I, 65), 17, 64, 66, 237-8, 276-7, 303, 338
Helar[y?], ———, 353
Henry, John (I, 59), 18, 22, 309
Hill, West (I, 204), 236, 269, 271, 273, 275-7n, 278
Holley, James, 354n
Hospitals or surgeons (including the enemy's) —
    at Camden, 17, 72, 177, 236-8, 252, 264, 269, 271-2, 275-7, 280, 289-290;
    at Charlestown, 130, 139;
    at Savannah, 303;
    regimental, 103, 136, 191, 239, 275, 303;
    senior surgeon during the autumn campaign, 276-7
Hovenden, Richard, 247n, 256, 258, 260-1, 278, 286
Howard, John, 195n
Howe, John, 341n-2
Howe, Tyringham, 138n
Huddleston, Richard, 277n
Hunt, Northington, 281
Husband, Vezey, 159n
Hutchison, John, 330n, 341-2
Huyn, Johann Christoph von, 53n

Incipient unrest, 9-10
Indian Department, 30, 54
Inman, Shadrack, 160n
Innes, Alexander (I, 17), 16-17, 62, 72, 140, 144-5, 168-171, 173-6, 179-182, 199-200, 241, 246, 272, 286, 304
Isaacks, Elijah, 64n-5

Jails and prison ships, filling of, 139, 202
Jarvis, Samuel, 228n
Jenkinson, Charles, 125n
Johnson, ———, 357
Johnston, ———, 345n
Johnston, Robert, 264n, 289, 290, 337, 361-2
Jones, Edward, 344
Justices of the Peace, appointment of, 248

Kalb, Johann (I, 163), 4, 5, 9, 13, 338
Kelly, ———, 203
Kemble, ———, 235n
Kennerly, James and John, 330n
Kilty, William, 289, 291n
King, James, 83n, 235, 362
King, Richard, 171n, 173
Kinloch, David (I, 114), 89, 239, 276
Kirkland, Joseph and William, 330n
Kirkland, Moses (I, 236), 137, 171-3, 193, 206, 356n-7
Knecht, Anthony (I, 212), 109, 248, 281, 286-8
Kolb (Culp), Abel, 221n
Kospoth, Heinrich Julius von, 53n

Leacy, ———, 360n
Lechmere, Nicholas, 84, 92n, 114, 132
Leland, John, 54n
Leslie, The Hon Alexander (III, 3-4), 32, 49, 50, 53, 119, 120, 254, 301 —
    invited to come south from Virginia, 55-61, 127-8, 130-1, 137

Lincoln, Earl of: *see* 'Clinton, Thomas Pelham'
Lindsay, Robert, 353-4n
Lloyd, Owen, 360n
Lord, Andrew (I, 86), 72, 246
Loughborough, Lord: *see* 'Wedderburn, Alexander'
Luckie Sr, William, 104n
Lutwidge, Skeffington (I, 180), 15

MacDonald, Charles, 99n, 365
MacLean, Francis, 199n
Macleod, John (I, 210), 12, 14, 68, 72, 268, 364
Mallom, John, 213n, 233, 360
Manley, John (I, 47), 14
Manson, William, 96n
Marion, Francis (III, 4-5), 26, 29, 37, 113, 118, 120, 172, 214-5, 217, 219, 220, 226, 249, 257
Marshall, Mathew, 126n
Marshall, William, 212n
Martin, ——, 349n
Martin, Josiah (I, 66), 8, 14, 48, 73, 180, 200, 278, 356
Mates, medicines, and hospital stores, 89, 273-8, 303, 357
Maxwell, Andrew (I, 252), 69, 81, 92, 129-130, 137, 257, 329
McArthur, Archibald (I, 87), 8-10, 27, 73, 109, 161, 164, 166, 180, 233-5, 242, 269, 271, 280-4
McCafferty, William, 31
McCarlie, ——, 260
McCaule, Thomas Harris, 355n
McCleary, Samuel and William, 348n
McCleod, Robert, 339
McCottry, William, 227n
McCulloch, John (or William), 127
McCulloch, Kenneth (I, 229), 10
McCulloh, Robert, 76n
McDaniel, Middleton, 361n
McDonald, ——, 235n, 287
McDowell, Charles, 27, 109n, 141, 148-9, 154, 160, 163, 166
McDowell Jr, Joseph, 135n
McGinnis, John, 135n, 167
McKenny (McKinney), Timothy (I, 264), 202
McKenzie, ——, 79n, 80
McKinnon, John (I, 127), 75, 78, 85, 93, 95, 233, 294, 302, 359
McLaurin, Euan (I, 252), 179, 182
McMichael, George, 329n
Mecan, Thomas (I, 190), 16, 49
Mecklenburg County, character of, 106, 126
Middleton, Arthur, 70n, 361
Militia, character of, 8, 65, 140-1, 142-3, 146, 155, 172
Militia, revolutionary —
    Georgia, 28, 39, 94, 96, 141, 148, 156, 159, 173, 175, 186;
    North Carolina, 3-4, 9, 33, 39, 45, 106, 109, 141, 157, 159, 160, 162-3, 166, 170, 173, 175, 197-8, 217, 220, 230, 249, 334, 345-6, 350, 352, 364-5;
    Overmountain, 33, 55, 109, 155, 157, 159, 160-3, 166, 170, 173, 197-8, 335;
    South Carolina, 9, 12, 14, 19, 20, 33, 45, 140, 146, 158, 166, 170, 172-3, 197-8, 213-5, 217, 219, 220, 226-7, 249, 257, 345;
    Virginia, 3-4, 12, 350;
    barbarous warfare waged by, 33-4
Militia, royal —
    admission of disaffected men, 146, 173, 249;
    arms, throwing away of etc by giving them to, 248;
    assembly of, measures to enforce, and to prevent the quitting of camp without leave, 142-4, 214;
    Bryan's corps: *see* 'North Carolina loyalists';
    Cheraw militia, importance of, but failure to raise, 26, 37, 215-8, 221, 240;
    defection, disaffection, or infidelity of, 5, 8-10, 37, 84, 146, 173, 214, 243, 249, 250;
    defectors, punishment of: *see* 'Defectors';
    demolition of in Back Country by Ferguson's defeat, 29-31, 33-4, 58, 129, 134, 202, 334-5;
    directions about property to colonels on frontier, 62-3, 170, 172, 174, 332-4;
    draft (aborted) of 500 young volunteers for frontier service, 129-132, 137, 205-6;
    formation, modelling or regulation of, 8, 38, 203-4, 210-2, 220, 246, 266;
    fragility of, 17, 26, 29, 37, 65, 72, 113, 145-6, 181, 219-220, 250, 263, 265;
    Gibbs' regiment, service undergone by, 334;
    irregularities and ignorance of, 163;
    Kirkland's and King's regiments, strength of, 171, 173;
    less active and warlike than the revolutionary militia, 146-7, 250;
    losses incurred by from doing duty, 155;
    Ninety Six District, strength there less considerable than expected, 173;
    Orangeburg regiment, employment of, 64, 329;
    order and discipline, lack of in part, 146;
    pay, gratuities or other rewards for, provision or lack of, 63, 73, 92-3, 101, 129, 155-6, 172, 182, 185, 203, 207, 219,

259, 334-5;
>provisions, supply of, payment or non-payment for, 102, 105;
>refusal or slowness to turn out, 58, 132, 134, 136, 188, 198, 202, 257;
>utility, or otherwise, of, 46, 90, 102, 132, 138, 147, 181, 250;
>when embodied, 16, 26-7, 30, 32, 37, 39, 42, 55, 62, 66-70, 72, 81-2, 92, 98, 102, 113-4, 132, 138, 140-167, 172-3, 175, 182, 185-6, 188, 192, 194, 197, 209, 227-9, 239, 240, 243, 245, 253, 257, 259, 287-8, 358-9

Millar, Thomas, 94n
Mills, Ambrose (I, 116), 82, 88, 135, 155
Mills, William Henry (I, 132), 62, 92, 110, 114, 209, 210, 212, 215-9, 240, 245, 247-250, 253, 356
Misrepresentations and falsehoods of the enemy, 63, 172, 174 —
>punishment of propagators of, 174-5, 210

Moncrief, James (I, 58), 26-7, 38, 53, 66-70, 73-4, 81, 85, 90, 93-4, 98, 101, 120, 132, 217, 219-220, 239, 240, 242-3, 245, 249, 260, 266-7, 278, 292-3, 302, 304-5, 308
Money, John, 45n, 64, 66, 81, 212-3, 234, 238, 276, 356-366
Monro, Alexander, 338-9
Moore, Andrew, 196n
Moore, Isham, 211n
Morgan, Daniel (III, 11-12), 258, 345
Morris, Charles, 358n
Motte, Jacob (I, 76), 237-8
Moultrie, William (I, 373), 78, 111-3, 130, 363
Mowbray, John, 73n, 293, 303, 309, 310

Nash, Abner, 336-7n
Native Americans, 30, 40, 46-7, 95-7, 304, 308 —
>employment of by the British, 33-4, 91, 100, 103, 118, 132, 136, 154, 156, 187, 189, 191-2

Neel, Andrew (I, 176), 350
Nelson, John, 345n
Nelson, Roger, 338n-9
Ninety Six (District) (*see also* 'Back Country, The')
— Cornwallis becomes ignorant of the state of, 126, 255-6, 258;
>proposed post (aborted) at Charlotte too remote to have any effect on, 198;
>reinforcement of regulars or British American troops needed between the Broad and Saluda Rivers, 29, 197, 204, 224-5, 231, 254, 260;
>its security of the utmost importance, 173, 201

Ninety Six (village) —
>fortification of, 131, 179, 202, 224-5, 257;
>garrison of, and its reduction to a bare defensive, 29-30, 198, 225, 257;
>intention to erect better works at, 90;
>safety of prior to and after Clark's incursion into the Ceded Lands, 175, 198;
>quantity of indian corn laid in at, 202;
>relieved by abandonment of autumn campaign, 30;
>reinforcement of garrison of, 204-5, 224-5, 231, 254, 260;
>large magazines of grain and forage to be collected at, 201, 204-5

Norris, ——, 349n
North Carolina loyalists —
>advise on stages and distances from Petersburg to Hillsborough, 346-7;
>Samuel Bryan's corps (NC refugees), 12, 25-6, 41, 127, 138, 208, 214, 216, 226, 229, 259, 280, 282-3, 362;
>disappoint British expectations, 55, 58;
>embody on the upper New River, 157;
>embody on the south-west frontier, 351;
>give strong assurances of support when the British shall have entered NC, 36-7, 41;
>instructed to take up arms etc after the Battle of Camden but fail to do so, 15-16, 36, 41;
>property of appropriated and sold by the revolutionaries, example of, 348;
>provide intelligence, 133, 228-230, 235, 260;
>repression and maltreatment of by the revolutionaries, 9-10, 37, 41, 90, 217, 223, 349;
>Scots Highlanders to join up or form a British American regiment, 73, 180, 200, 250;
>want of arms for, 46;
>Ferguson gives instructions to, provides captured arms for, and musters, in Tryon County, 151-4, 159;
>settlements of in Tryon County divided by tracts of the enemy, 154

Obman, Jacob Daniel (I, 276), 301
Ogilvie, Charles, 333n
Oldfield, John Nicholls, 75n, 183, 269, 271-2, 276
Oliphant, David, 112n-3
O'Neaill, Henry (I, 118), 201, 203-5
Overmountain settlers, 91, 94, 335

Palmer, ——, 345
Parker, James, 347n

Parker, Sir Peter, 54n, 314
Paroles —
> cautious restoration of parolees to the rights of citizens, 185;
> form of in Georgia, 184;
> offer of to the east of the Wateree and Santee, 216, 244;
> oath of allegiance, requirement for parolees to take, rejection of, 80;
> parolees employed to obtain intelligence, 345-6, 358, 363;
> subjecting the disaffected to, 285;
> substituting more restrictive, 340;
> violation of, and punishment for, east of the Wateree and Santee, 215;
> violation of in Georgia, 184, 193;
> violation of by ringleaders of rebellion and their transportation to St Augustine, 38, 43, 65, 67, 75, 77-8, 93, 312-3

Pasteur, ——, 228n
Paterson, James (I, 49), 53, 119, 120, 200, 301
Patterson, ——, 356
Pattinson, Thomas (I, 84), 95
Paymaster —
> at Charlestown, 49, 66, 322;
> for troops in the field, 49

Peacocke, George (I, 90), 126
Peasley, John, 353n
Person, Thomas, 230n
Phepoe, Thomas, 317n
Phillips, John, 82, 245, 262, 330-1n, 358
Phillips, William, 49, 118, 121
Pickens, Andrew (I, 79), 91, 100, 104, 118, 134-6, 141, 145, 148, 172-3, 175, 177
Pinckney, Charles Cotesworth, 111n
Pinckney, Thomas, 237-8n, 239, 272-3
Pledger, Philip, 345n
Plummer, Daniel, 334-5n
Plundering —
> by banditti, 102, 223, 285, 301;
> by loyalists and British or British American troops, 69-70, 72, 212, 216, 249;
> by revolutionaries, 33, 72, 205, 257, 263, 269, 271, 334

Polk, Thomas, 115n
Polk, William, 349n
Porter, James, 154n
Porterfield, Charles (I, 163), 9, 252, 280, 337, 362
Prescott, Richard, 306n
Prescott, Richard, 306
Prevost, Augustine (I, 64), 267, 301, 306-7, 319
Prevost, Jacques Marc, 301n
Prideaux, Edmund, 305n
Pritchard, Paul, 316n-8
Privateers, enemy, 85, 90, 102, 108, 111, 114, 121, 123, 133

Proclamations (*see also* 'Sequestration') —
> Gates's of 4th August, 38n;
> Cornwallis's of 27th September, 244, 331n-2;
> proposed for issue by Cruger, 105, 193

Propaganda, revolutionary, 34, 217, 230, 260
Property (not provisions), appropriation or destruction of enemy's, 26, 266, 278, 288, 315, 320-8
Protection (involving oath of allegiance), violation of, and punishment for (*see also* 'Defectors'), 174, 215, 234
Provisions (*see also* 'Stores and other supplies') —
> acquisition or supply of, 16, 25-6, 31, 44, 67, 73, 79, 82, 86-8, 126-7, 129, 130, 133, 138, 149, 171, 201, 235, 240, 250-1, 253, 256-7, 259-263n, 265, 269, 271, 274, 277, 280-3, 286-9, 329;
> lack of at Camden before the autumn campaign, 25, 66, 71, 178;
> payment, certificates or receipts for, 201, 243, 246, 262, 265, 288;
> acute shortage of flour in the Back Country, 182, 188, 198, 248, 251;
> magazines of grain and forage to be laid up at Camden, the Congarees, and Ninety Six, 129, 201, 204-5, 288

Public departments, lack of activity in, 78
Pursell, William, 338-9
Purvis, John, 104n

Quain, ——, 134
Quartermaster General's Department, 64, 66, 71, 75, 127, 210, 269-280, 357, 359, 360 —
> horses of in wretched condition at Camden after the battle there, 66, 357

Rawdon, Francis, Lord (I, 151-2), 9-12, 14, 21, 30-1, 49, 51-2, 55-61, 201, 203-6, 214, 245, 253-266, 275, 285-6, 344, 365
Recruitment of British American troops —
> by De Lancey's 1st Battalion, 171, 197

Regiments or corps, British —
> 7th (Royal Fusiliers), 26, 28, 38, 43, 55, 66-7, 69, 71, 74, 93, 98, 101, 126, 132, 233, 235, 240, 242-3, 245, 247, 252, 256, 258-9, 268-9, 272, 277, 282-3, 359;
> 16th, 72;
> 23rd (Royal Welch Fusiliers), 10, 12, 16, 25, 28, 37, 44, 46, 71, 235, 277;
> 33rd, 10, 12, 19, 25-6, 28, 37, 44, 46, 71, 271, 277;
> 60th (Royal American Regiment), 121-5, 293, 298-300;

63rd, 10, 12, 17, 26, 28-9, 37, 41, 64, 67, 69, 71, 74, 79-82, 113, 121, 126, 131, 134, 201, 204, 209-210, 213, 216, 221-2, 231-4, 240, 242, 252, 254-5, 257, 269, 272, 278, 360;
64th, 65, 67;
71st, 8-10, 12-13, 26, 28, 37, 41, 44, 46, 64, 71, 74, 80, 90, 180, 200, 229, 232-4, 240, 248, 268-9, 271-3, 277, 280-4, 291, 336, 338, 364;
Light infantry, 12, 140, 143, 361;
Pioneers, 26, 271, 362;
Royal Artillery, 12, 25-6, 242, 251, 268, 271, 278, 280, 364

Regiments or corps, British American, 5 —
American Volunteers (Ferguson's corps), 31, 39, 65, 114, 135-6, 172;
British Legion, 12-13, 37, 43-5, 69, 71, 88-9, 93-4, 99, 101, 105, 110, 116-7, 129, 159, 161, 163-6, 186, 240, 247, 256-7, 260, 268, 273, 278, 286, 362, 364-5;
De Lancey's 1st Battalion (Cruger's corps), 29, 168-207;
De Lancey's 2nd Battalion, 200;
Georgia Loyalists (Wright's corps), 200, 300-1;
Harrison's corps, 8, 26, 41, 208-9, 214, 216, 218-9, 221-2, 226, 240, 244-5, 247, 249, 251, 260, 263, 271, 274;
King's Rangers (Brown's corps), 30, 39, 40, 47, 154, 172, 175, 182, 294, 302, 304-5;
New Jersey Volunteers, 3rd Battalion (Allen's corps), 29, 30, 169, 174, 194, 196-7, 294;
New York Volunteers (Turnbull's corps), 10, 11, 28-9, 42, 64, 72, 93, 106, 170, 172-3, 177, 180, 200, 244, 250-1, 258-9;
Prince of Wales's American Regiment (Browne's corps), 12n, 37, 72, 81, 92, 95, 113, 118, 121, 132, 172, 200, 258;
Royal North Carolina Regiment (Hamilton's corps), 12, 26, 28-9, 37, 41, 71, 73, 93, 106, 200, 208-9, 214, 216, 223, 226, 229, 231, 240, 251-2, 259, 274, 360;
South Carolina Royalist Regiment (Innes's corps), 8, 16-17, 28-9, 42, 64, 72, 82, 90, 106, 132, 170, 172n, 174-5, 177, 179, 180-2, 200, 216, 232, 237, 240, 243-5, 247, 250, 269, 271-2;
Volunteers of Ireland (Rawdon's corps), 10, 12, 19, 25, 37, 44, 46, 51, 69, 71, 235, 275-6, 283, 357, 365;
failed attempts to raise new levies, 8, 17, 39, 72, 99, 176, 178, 180-2, 199, 204-5

Regiments or corps, Continental, 3, 4, 8, 12, 140, 262, 345
Regiments, Hessian, 130, 293, 305
Reid, James, 306n
Retaliation, threats of, 234, 336, 341
Returns —
of arrivals in Charlestown harbour, 75-6;
of captured troops sent to Charlestown, 71;
of disaffected persons transported to St Augustine, 77-8;
of losses sustained by the 3rd Battalion, New Jersey Volunteers, in the action at Augusta, 196-7;
of ordnance and ammunition in East Florida, 295-7
Risks run by the British —
of detaching beyond support, 31, 45, 89;
of losing control of much of SC and Georgia, 28-31
Roberts, Jonathan, 42n, 212-3
Robertson, Archibald, 54n
Robertson, James, 274n
Robinson, ——, 349
Rochambeau, Jean Baptiste Donatien de Vimeur, Comte de, 47n
Rodney, Sir George Brydges (I, 11), 49, 79
Rooke, Henry, 200n
Ross, Alexander (I, 73), 11, 14-16, 18, 21-2, 62-8, 71, 74, 83, 87, 117, 140, 180, 359, 360
Ross, George, 136n
Royal Navy, 54 —
Ships: *Daphne*, 119; *Charon*, 129, 138; *Galatea*, 121, 306; *Hound*, 76; *Hydra*, 76, 78, 81, 83-5, 87, 89, 90, 95, 102, 111, 311-2; *Iris*, 121, 133, 137; *Keppel*, 68, 74, 78, 80, 82, 90; *Loyalist*, 43, 68, 85, 102, 111, 114; *Mentor*, 76; *Port Royal*, 76; *Providence*, 11, 15, 18, 65; *Sandwich*, 43, 47, 83, 85, 90-1, 93, 111-2, 114, 117, 120, 126, 133; *Thames*, 117-8, 121, 128, 133, 138; *Triton*, 48, 90
Rugeley, Henry (I, 128), 82, 265, 281, 360
Rutherford, Griffith (I, 162), 9, 13, 41, 64-5, 264, 361
Rutherford, James (I, 162), 141, 361-2
Rutledge, The Hon John (I, 45), 70
Rutledge, Joshua, 338n-9

St Augustine (*see also* 'East Florida') —
fortification of, 267, 292-3;
garrison of, 292-3;
gun boats at, 73, 293;
Minorcans at, 293n;
ordnance and ammunition at, 73, 295-7;

St Augustine (*continued*)
    power of Civil Governor over the troops at, 293, 297-8, 302;
    supplies for the garrison of, 73, 294, 311, 313
Saunders, Nathaniel, 345
Savannah —
    fort at, 267, 305;
    works at Cockspur, 267
Scotch-Irish revolutionaries —
    flight from the Waxhaws, 25-6, 233;
    ferociously oppose the British occupation of Charlotte, 30, 166;
    threaten Cornwallis's communication with SC, 30, 86, 126, 257
Seawell Jr, Benjamin, 228n
Secret service, disbursement of money for, etc (*see also* 'Paroles'), 73, 241, 363-4
Sequestration —
    reasons for, 38, 46;
    proclamation on, 87, 89, 90, 116, 315, 323-4;
    Cruden's commission relating to, 87, 320-3;
    Cruden's queries about and Cornwallis's responses, 325-8;
    the case for proceeding comprehensively with, 324;
    funds from proposed to pay partly for militia provisions, 105
Shelby, Isaac, 109n, 135, 148, 155, 157, 159, 160, 166, 186
Shubrick, Thomas, 340n
Simcoe, John Graves (I, 10), 52, 54
Simpson, James (I, 95), 43, 87, 138-9, 315-320
Singleton family, 211n
Slaves, 26, 85, 87, 95, 98-9, 105, 173, 210, 215, 218-9, 260, 266, 269, 315, 318, 321-2, 324-6, 328, 330, 348
Smallwood, William, 56n, 230, 258, 262, 346
Smith, Edward, 284n
Smith, Jacob, 189n
South Carolina —
    loyalty of Germans in the Dutch Fork, 286;
    maltreatment, mutilation or murder of loyalists by the revolutionaries, 33-4, 162, 217-8, 263, 269, 271, 330;
    need for an intermediate post between Charlestown and Camden, 102, 132, 138;
    shortage of specie for carrying on the King's service, 139;
    timidity and supineness of the loyalists, 65;
    well affected inhabitants on the Little Pee Dee and the eastern frontier, 217, 223
Spratt, ——, 349n
Stapleton, Wynne (I, 207), 254
State troops of Virginia, 8-9
Stedman, Charles (I, 212), 31-2
Stevens, Edward, 3, 4, 62n, 350
Stewart, John, 284n, 364
Stirling, Thomas, 54n
Stores and other supplies —
    acquisition, shortage or sufficiency of drivers, conductors, horses, gear or waggons (including payment for), 71, 169, 170, 173, 175, 178, 182, 188, 207, 268, 272-6, 287, 358-9;
    conveyance of (including sea passage (aborted) to Wilmington), and difficulties or dangers, 10, 25-6, 64, 66, 68, 71, 73-5, 78-83, 85, 88, 90-1, 93, 95, 100-1, 105-6, 110, 114, 116-8, 120-1, 126-7, 129, 130-1, 133, 138, 200, 259, 268, 361;
    no magazines of for autumn campaign, 18
Sumner, Jethro, 100n-1, 106, 253, 258, 345-6, 356, 364-5
Sumter, Thomas (I, 149-150), 9-12, 17, 19, 20, 41, 45, 72, 88, 90, 100-1, 106-7, 109, 140-1, 144-6, 158, 163-4, 169, 173-4, 178, 241, 258, 280, 330, 337, 341-6, 350, 353, 355-6, 363-5
Symonds, Thomas, 129n

Tarleton, Banastre (I, 154-7), 14, 19-21, 26, 29, 37, 44-7, 49, 52-4, 66, 72, 81, 86, 88-9, 93, 98, 110, 117, 129, 140-1, 145, 153, 156, 164, 180, 273, 276, 280, 284-6, 362-4
Tate, William, 341-2n
Taylor, Nathaniel, 306n
Taylor, Thomas, 305-6n
Ternay, Charles Louis d'Arsac, Chevalier de, 47n, 86
Thomas Sr, John (I, 259), 169, 202
Thomas, Tristram, 344n
Thomson, William (I, 78), 329
Tonyn, Patrick (I, 24), 64-5, 93, 293, 302, 307-313
Townsend, Gregory (I, 294), 265, 287
Trail(e), Peter, 72n
Treville, Jean François de (I, 131), 81, 84, 89, 241, 345-6, 363-4
Turnbull, George (I, 138), 10, 11, 14, 19, 20, 28-9, 34, 72, 92, 106, 114, 126-7, 140, 145, 155, 180, 219-222, 231-266, 272-3, 278-9, 281, 288
Turner, George, 363n
Turner, William Vernon (I, 195), 82, 245, 248, 358
Tutt, Benjamin, 104n
Twiggs, John (I, 144), 175
Tynes, Samuel, 29, 92n, 114, 128, 131, 210-1, 213-4, 257, 263, 265

Wade, Thomas (I, 136), 249
Waldegrave, George, Viscount Chewton, 119n
Washington, George, 44
Washington, William (I, 46), 262
Waters, Thomas, 97n
Watson, John Watson Tadwell, 199n
Waxhaws, British encampment at —
    appropriating wheat for the supply of the troops, 232, 362;
    plantations mostly abandoned, 233;
    left as a staging post, 280-4;
    prisoners there, 281
Wayne, Anthony, 89
Webster, James (I, 9), 12-14, 17, 21, 49, 53, 350
Wedderburn, Alexander, Lord Loughborough, 319n
Weir, Daniel, 118n
Wemyss, James (I, 305), 10, 17, 26-9, 37, 41, 46, 62, 64-5, 73, 82, 90, 94, 99, 106, 116, 132, 201, 204-5, 207-217, 219-226, 229-231, 240-2, 244-5, 247-252, 255, 257, 260, 271-4, 278, 356-7, 359, 360
West Florida, 54, 76, 294, 314
West Indies, 76, 79
Westerhagen, Max von (I, 335), 67, 101, 130
White, Anthony Walton, 133n
Whitsen, ——, 159n
Whittle, —— (Deputy Provost Marshal at Camden), 361
Wickham, Benjamin, 293, 298-9n, 302
Wigfall, John, 26, 64n, 66-8, 70, 92, 209, 220, 244, 266, 359
Williams, Gardiner, 330
Williams, James (I, 295), 106-7, 158
Williams, Otho Holland, 3, 338-9n
Williamson, Andrew (I, 77), 65, 71, 91, 100, 104, 136, 171-2, 175-6, 178, 182, 186
Williamson, Hugh, 252n, 264, 280, 289-290, 352
Wilson, Robert, 135n
Winchilsea, Earl of: *see* 'Finch, George'
Windham, Amos, 221n
Winnsborough —
    its advantages for an encampment, 32, 201, 262;
    withdrawal to from Charlotte, 31-2;
    intention to remain there for considerable period, 203
Winstanley, Thomas, 317n
Woodford, William (I, 376), 93
Wormley, John, 197n
Wounded, conveyance of from Camden to Charlestown, 72, 85, 93, 95, 269, 271-2, 275-6, 278
Wright, Sir James, Bt (I, 345), 64, 94, 100-1, 110, 294, 305
Wright Jr, James (I, 238), 294, 300-2

Yonge Jr, Henry, 308n
Yonge, Philip (I, 342), 307
Youman(s), Levi, 243n

§ - §